GW01605749

Greedy Bastard's Business Manual

Small Business Wealth Building for the 1980's

Greedy Bastard's Business Manual

Small Business Wealth Building for the 1980's

Robert H. Morrison

MORRISON BUTTERFIELD & BOYLE PUBLISHING LTD.

3824 EAST INDIAN SCHOOL ROAD
PHOENIX, ARIZONA 85018
(602) 957-7932

Library of Congress Cataloging in Publication Data

Main entry under title:

Greedy Bastard's Business Manual
Small Business Wealth Building for the 1980's

ISBN 0-936062-02-9

DEDICATED TO

Thad Stevenson, my friend and business partner,
without whose contribution and
help this book would not exist.

CONTENTS

Strategy *Get a license to steal.*

Chapter 26 COMMERCIAL RESEARCH

PROLOGUE

The concept of this book is to show you how to make money from small business. It is not designed to show you how to run a business per se—but to show you how to maximize the personal income from small business ventures.

The first thing to get clear in your mind is what you want personally from a business venture, either one you own now—or one you propose to own. Too many small business owners don't have a clear concept of what they want from a business other than meat on the table and a roof over their heads.

The concept is to set some precise personal goals for your business operations and then go for it. I have always done that. It let's me know when I've been successful. I set my goals in terms of bank balances in my personal account and in material possessions I own free and clear. My businesses are simply a means to an end and not an end in themselves.

In order to be successful you must have a beginning and end to a journey. There is an old saying, "If you don't know where you are going any road will take you there." The business journey should not be a lifetime of meandering through the economic thicket; it should be a series of trips up the mountain—each goal set forth and reached before proceeding to the next one. You can set any terms you wish and any type of goal you wish—but have one. A clear and precise concept of just what you want to achieve and obtain each step of the way is important.

This book is going to give you many ideas on how to make money because you are in, or want to get in, a small business. It is my desire to show you how I made my money, not by putting all my eggs in one basket and watching the basket, but by keeping my eyes open for opportunity of any kind and then moving in on it as fast and profitably as I could.

I started out like most small business owners with a little business—with a lot of competition—fighting for nickels and dimes. I had no goal other than survival and food and shelter for my family. If those were my only goals they were reached in a few months—but I soon discovered that trying to do much better was next to impossible because of the competition.

I began looking in other directions, and I discovered a great truth—the one that has made me comfortable, with some wealth behind me. It was that the amount of competition for a dollar has a lot to do with how hard you have to work. The more competition—the harder the work. So, I decided to let others do the hard work. I would find the fields, front the plow, and provide the seed for them to plant, and they would share the crop with me. I became a professional entrepreneur!

Now, I know if you are working for a large corporation or are in some professional practice (as I was when I started out as an accountant) you will say the more you make, the harder you work. That's what I thought. But, it's just not true. It's not true if you know how to manage people. You can get them to work hard for you, following your directions. You can work an hour a day, and they will work fourteen. Get the picture?

So, if you are willing to work a lot less, and make a lot more—then this book is going to point you in the right direction. All you have to do is set some goals and find the concept for reaching those goals—and you will have the success you want. The right to live as you please, where you please, as long as you please. In other words—you have freedom and the income to support it.

PREFACE

This is a book for small business owners who intend to survive and prosper. It is not a book about serving your fellow man with selfless devotion—or whistling past the graveyard with phony optimism that the Lord will provide. It is a book about the real world of business—a rigged economic system created to benefit institutions and penalize individuals, a book for eagles who fly alone to make their living—and not for turkeys who run in flocks.

You won't find the simplistic concepts of business presented by professors who have never been in the game and who write and talk about serving the community and giving their time and treasure for the betterment of mankind, nor will you find a book written by the self-appointed experts who deal in hypocrisy and platitudes about self-motivation,that being a saint among sinners will bring you success and inner contentment.

It is a book written by a small businessman who is a winner—who recognizes the system for what it is and uses that knowledge to succeed—who doesn't buy the power structure bullshit—but who uses it to gain his own ends.

You have to look at the economic system with your eyes wide open. It is a system that is controlled by the Bigs—Big Government—Big Business—Big Labor—Big Professions and Big Do-Gooders Groups. All these Bigs are institutions.

Let's understand institutions first. What are they? They start out with a concept—and form an organization to sell the concept. It can be a product or service—or a political or religious philosophy. It begins by trying its best to be of genuine service to its customers or followers. But as it succeeds it becomes larger—extends its scope and reach, it builds in professional management and a bureaucracy to serve that management. The goals change from serving its customers or adherents to self-service. The institution makes all decisions from that point on, what is best for the institution not what is best for the people it supposedly serves.

We see big business in action every day using their clout to put the blocks to the public in general and small business in particular. Any small businessman who has a big business customer can tell you about them holding off payment of their accounts for 60 to 180 days so they can keep it in money market funds and make 17% interest on the small businessman's money they are holding. If the small business owner tries to press them they will simply change suppliers.

In the reverse case, we see big business dropping the hammer on small business customers who are late with extra charges—higher interest rates on unpaid balances—a demand that minimum orders be in unreasonable amounts—running service charge scams and kicking the small business customer in the ass in every way possible.

We see big business out gobbling up small businesses and using their leverage to try and dominate the competition. We see them jumping into all kinds of small business fields in their greed to expand and control more and more of the economy. We see supermarkets getting into selling flowers, clothing, tools, photo finishing, toys and games—you name it. We see giants like Sears going into income tax preparation, optometry, rug cleaning. Next you'll be offered brain surgery and call girls.

We see big labor forcing unrealistic minimum wage laws on small business through national legislation—not for the benefit of workers—but for the benefit of union fat cats. We see small business saddled with huge bills for unemployment compensation which is used as a racket by many employees to be paid for not working. We see a huge burden for Social Security payments shoved up the ass of small business by labor lobbies. We see labor allowed to burn, pillage and kill in the name of economic security—and it's all presented as a highly moral and reasonable philosophy by the institutions.

We see the growth of do-gooder, bleeding heart institutions who attack the free enterprise system with all manner of half-ass programs in the name of clean air and consumer protection. These are institutions that seek a police state—an end to free enterprise and control over every facet of our lives. They are aided and abetted by the mass media and political ass kissers hoping for votes.

We have the failure industry becoming institutionalized—the welfare institutions that seek to make poverty a permanent fact of life so they can enlarge their clientele. We see bankruptcy become big business for shyster lawyers who become trustees of bankrupt firms and bleed them for income for years. We see Medicare and Medicaid ripped off by the medical profession until its costs have exceeded reason. We see the mass media running like maggots to every social sore on the body politic and enlarging and inflaming it with sensationalized coverage creating greater problems and more sensation to build ratings and circulation. We see reporters and commentators, educated beyond their intelligence, becoming instant experts in every field of endeavor with so called exposes and investigative reporting. They write editorials of great profundity about what's wrong with America—a glance in the mirror could show them about half the problem.

As an example let's take our own government. It was organized to let people govern themselves—to be the servant of the people—to insure life, liberty and the pursuit of happiness for those who it served. Abraham Lincoln said "The government of the people, by the people and for the people." But, it became an institution and a self-serving bureaucracy. Jack Kennedy in his inauguration speech made a statement widely heralded as a glorious creed for the American people, "Don't ask what your country can do for you—ask what you can do for your country." In other words—serve the institution first—and don't ask the institution to serve you.

I have developed a slogan that summarizes the attitude and policy of institutions everywhere. It goes like this—**"For unguestion-**

ed compliance keep your objectives unlimited." In short, make them conform, and we will always increase our wealth and power. If you want to know what that means in terms of their service to you—take the first letter of each word in the slogan and make two short words out of it and you will have your answer.

The massive hypocrisy of the institutional mind is a major part of the problem. They set up a rigged game, then defend it with a moral fervor that calls in all the platitudes and slogans of a free society to defend it.

Let me give you a perfect example—The Stock Market. Here you have the place big business goes to dip into the public pocket for funds. They sell you a part ownership in their business at a price. As part owner, you are supposedly entitled to share in the profits. But, many corporations pay no dividends and most pay only token dividends. So, how are you supposed to make a return on your investment—you have to sell your stock to "A Greater Fool" willing to pay more than you did—who then must find a second "Greater Fool" to pay him more, etc. In other words, you are not sharing in the profits—you are a part of a swindle that has been institutionalized and is considered to be a bastion of the capitalistic system.

A small business owner who uses that same system to sell franchises is cited for fraud and tossed in the slammer. Such are the rules of the game as rigged by the Bigs.

Look at the banking system—controlled by the Federal Reserve—and operated in what is called Fractional Reserve Banking. You want to know where inflation comes from? Right there my friend—Fractional Reserve Banking. It works like this. The government needs money—and it wants to pump up the system to increase commerce. So, the U.S. Treasury sells a billion dollars worth of bonds to the Federal Reserve—the Fed issues Federal Reserve Notes and they are deposited in a bank or banks. The banks, operating on Fractional Reserves, can lend 80% of the billion dollar deposit out at once—so the one billion created by the treasury becomes $1.8 billion in new funds in the money supply—but that's just for openers. Those who borrow the money pay others with it—and it goes to other banks who can then lend 80% of those deposits—and in the second step you have $3.2 billion in the money supply. And the chain letter effect continues, expanding the money supply all from a billion dollars of counterfeit money—for which no production was involved to create—and you have several billion dollars more, in the money supply, chasing the same amount of goods or services. That is how the Fed waters the monetary soup, and inflation results from too much money chasing too few goods and services.

We have recently seen the American banking institution do a real number on the public. When the Fed jumped interest rates to control inflation (which is like rationing watered soup—you keep pouring in more water, but you make it appear to be more valuable because you make it harder to get)—the banks ripped off their credit card customers with huge increases in interest rates and fees and justified it by pointing to high interest rates which were making them richer as the reason. That, my friend is institutional morality.

We see elements of the legal profession opening up new avenues of income by creating malpractice suits calling for millions in damages (of which they collect a third to two thirds as fees and expenses)—creating phony product liability standards and ripping off manufacturers and sellers of goods for billions annually. And, what do we get from the Bar Associations—bullshit about justice and the protection of the innocent from rapacious businessmen. The concept that our legal system provides justice is as far fetched as the concept of the tooth fairy. Our legal system provides a transfer of wealth from producers to legal leeches who are sucking the economic lifeblood out of American commerce.

We have the great fallacy about exploited workers and business owners living off the sweat of their brows. What we have is a labor force that steals more from their employers than all the armed robbers, burglars, shoplifters and bad check cashers put together. This embezzlement can take various forms: the stealing of inventory, tools and equipment; under rings and pocketing the difference at the cash register; and, working just long enough to qualify for unemployment compensation, then forcing you to fire them so that they can collect their dole. And, they will tell you it's their right—a human right to lie, cheat and steal.

Then we have the Luddites—the back to caves group. The Luddites were a group of English workers that went around destroying machines at the beginning of the Industrial Revolution because they were replacing people. We have the anti-nuclear—anti-development of anything—anti-people modern day Luddites—who are opposed to any technological advancement except the manufacture and distribution of pot, coke and heroin. They are a collection of mush heads, given respectability by TV and mass media publications, whose editorial staffs agree with their goals. We see some freak pinching his pimples and expounding on nuclear energy given the status of an expert by some TV producer who longs to be back in the Haight-Ashbury smoking dope and getting venereal disease.

This then, is the game, and these are the players. The small business owner has them on his case and might as well understand that fact of life.

The Greedy Bastard's Business Manual, *Small Business Wealth Building for the 1980's,* is your guide to playing that game and winning it. It's using the rules as they are set forth to your advantage—to building your income through planning and perseverance so that you get what you want and need for you and yours—and you do it your way and to hell with the system that tries to prevent it.

So read on!

TACTICS

Always try to find a toll gate.

A toll gate is an automatic money machine—a kind of positional monopoly that collects a fee for everything that goes by. Always look for a possible toll gate position in any deal.

A toll gate is:

- A distributorship—if they want it—they must buy it from you. No other source in your area of control.
- A franchiser—where you share in the gross income of all franchisees.
- A patent or copyright—that receives a royalty off the top on every unit sold.
- A sole source—you make it—no one else does. You always get the first profit.

They can be by product type—by geographical area—by industry segment—by time of day, week, month or year—by government franchise.

If there is more than one toll gate in the marketing system, try to have the first one in the line up.

CHAPTER 1
FUNDAMENTALS

Anyone who likes money or sausage should never watch either one being made.

As I begin, I want to say something you should remember. The opportunity to be successful and build wealth from a small business' starting point is almost unlimited. The only thing you have to do is start running a business instead of just making a living.

I started out doing what 98 percent of all small business owners do—I created a job. As the business developed, I hired other people and all of us had jobs. I was so busy doing my job and helping them with their job that I really had no time to develop a business.

As I got further into running a business, I began to notice something that I considered important. That was, that I was dealing with two different kinds of business operations. The first, like mine, was run by one individual with some helpers who were all working together in a business that always seemed to be operating at about the same level. The second type of business I was dealing with was an organization. When I contacted these businesses I never talked to the owner, I was always talking to somebody in charge of something who knew what they were doing, and I realized that the people who were really making it were people who had developed organizations instead of just small business.

So I decided that if I was going to prosper the way I wanted to in small business, I was going to have to try my hand at creating an organization. To make plans and set policies and implement procedures that would meet goals that I set, I would become a member of an organization instead of a job holder.

And when I did this, I discovered I was playing in an entirely new league. A league where income can easily rise to six figures and opportunities are virtually limitless. If this book can convince you to start managing an organization, instead of just working the job that you have created for yourself; then I will have accomplished a goal, and you will open the doors to everything you have ever wanted.

Understanding The Economics Of Small Business

Now I want to touch on this business of economics. It is only recently that the so-called economists have convinced the politicians that theirs is a science. I will make a flat statement here — economics is not a science, it's a philosophy. It's filled with bafflegab, formulas and charts that are meant to impress other economists, but have little value in the real world. Economists try to create formulas or systems that stem from billions of random decisions made by business, the financial market, and consumers in regards to buying and selling. These decisions have no predictability because they are based on human nature and can stem from nothing more than a headache, a few shots of booze, or something someone dreamt last night. And anyone who tells you that they can predict the future based on decisions that are totally irrational is a con man. Now I'm going to give you some of the typical jargon that you hear from economists and read about in newspapers, books, magazines and so forth. Once I've told you about them, you can forget them because they have no importance to operating a business.

Positive Economics . . . these are the positive laws of economics that always remain the same. "Your wife will expand purchasing to the limit of her credit cards."

Nominative Economics . . . this is the opinion of economists as to the proper course to take. "You either burn your wife's credit card or start robbing banks on your lunch hour."

Micro Economics . . . the study of the decision making process of individual segments of the economy. "Dresses are on sale — so your wife buys two and saves you twice as much money."

Macro Economics . . . the study of the whole economy and its aggregate measures. "There were 100,000 bank robberies last week — (yours was number 62,469.)" Then we have economic assumptions!

The fallacy of composition . . . that what is true of the parts must be true of the whole. It's like the time the ayatollah stepped in a pile of horse manure and started to cry. One of his followers asked him why he was crying? He said, "I'm starting to melt."

The fallacy of the undistributed middle . . . is that one statement leads to a second conclusion that leads to a third that are not necessarily true. It's also called jumping to conclusions.

It reminds me of the story of the man and his wife standing before the judge. The man had two black eyes, a broken nose, and all his teeth knocked out. There wasn't a mark on the wife. The judge looked at the man and said, "What happened to you?"

The man replied, "My wife hit me."

The judge asked the wife, "Why did you hit him?"

The wife replied, "Because he called me a two-bit whore."

The judge looked at the man and asked, "What did she hit you with?"

The man replied, "A sack full of quarters."

Post Hoc Ergo Propter Hoc. . . this is the assumption that one thing always follows the other. That philosophy has put more stock speculators and horse players into bankruptcy than any other philosophy on earth. Every young man who has ever taken out a beautiful girl, given her an orchid, lavishly wined and dined her, and taken her back to her apartment, has found out about the fallacy of the proposition that when one thing happens, another thing always follows.

Now basically these are the economic propositions that you get from economists, people with horse racing systems, and people who know how to beat the stock market. The only thing you really have to know about economics is what you already know — make more than you spend, and you live well. Spend more than you make — poverty! All the rest is bullshit.

Scientific Management . . . is the art of winning track meets by hiring eight men who can jump one foot, instead of hiring one man who can jump eight feet.

Scientific management is probably the greatest load of B.S. ever dumped on the business world. Now I'm going to show you how they formulate their scientific management basis by giving you a few of the rules that are set down for scientific managers.

1. Formulate one or more testable hypothesis or tentative theory with appropriate assumption as to conditions.
2. Design an experiment so that each hypothesis may be used to direct the expected outcome of the experiment before it is conducted.
3. Conduct one or more experiment under adequately controlled conditions and measure the input factors and the output results.
4. Compare experimental evidence with prediction, and then either set aside as false, or accept as apparently true, each hypothesis under test.

Now, as close as I can figure it out, it means something like this:

1. Work up a couple of lines to pick up girls.
2. Try them out on your sister.
3. Test them at a singles' bar and see if you can get some input before you get output.
4. Use the one that works.

Scientific management is designed to get maximum efficiency out of a business organization. The problem is that the scientific manager, looking for maximum efficiency, is like the guy who got a pair of water skis and spent the rest of his life looking for a lake that runs down hill.

Do what you can, with what you have, where you are!
— Theodore Roosevelt

Small business is an art and not a science, and it is a talent that can be developed rather than one that must be inherited. The first thing to remember is that a child is not a small adult, and small business is not a miniature replica of big business.

Most of the stuff you read, get in seminars or from courses about running a business, is a trickle down system of giving you information on how big business is run. The professors, corporate consultants, accountants, banks, and lawyers assume that management is the most highly developed at the big business level, instead of understanding "The Peter Principle" which stipulates that in large organizations people rise to the level of their incompetence.

So, don't pay any attention to all of these complicated theories that are laid on you, because the small business, to be successful and eventually become big business and have everybody rise to the level of their incompetence, has to be run by someone who knows his trade and has the gut feeling of knowing what to do and when to do it. He needs a philosophy, an eye for the main chance and above all the guts to go for it.

Now the smart small business operator hires people who are better than he is for specific tasks. And he spends his time getting on with making a buck.

I'll give you an example, here is a problem—a man owns a beautiful horse that is lame some of the time and apparently normal at other times. The horse cost him one hundred dollars and he wants to know what to do.

Now you give that problem to the Harvard Business School and you would get a marginal utility analysis on the value of a lame horse — a demand elasticity study on lame horses — a research program determining why horses are lame, how they can be cured — and an endless flow of jargon, formulas, and statements with options on how to solve the problem.

Give the same problem to a smart old horse trainer and he'll tell you this — "The next time he appears normal — sell him."

The art of management is nothing more than applying common sense to a problem. All the formulas, studies, and research add nothing but confusion to the situation. If you know your business, know where you want to go, and simply apply common sense to problems as they arise, you're going to be a successful manager.

TACTICS

Pressure makes diamonds out of lumps of coal.

The successful small business operator loves the pressure situations. Welcomes them—thrives on them.

He loves the deal that *must* be made, the deadline that must be met. He's the pro quarterback, six points behind with two minutes to go, starting on his own ten yard line. Yet, he knows he's going to win, and thrives on the challenge.

He loves battle—the action—the challenge. He's out always running to daylight. Pressure is the thing that gets him moving.

He's an unreconstructed son-of-a-bitch, and he's proud of it.

In other words—get aggressive—if you want to make it big and enjoy the fight.

CHAPTER 2
ORGANIZATIONAL OUTLINE

A small business is both an economic and a social system.

The Organization

Question — Do you have an organization?

Or, do you have a group of people holding jobs?

There is a big difference.

An organization is a team — organized to reach goals. The coach (you) knows who should play each position, what the goals are to have a winning season, and has a game plan to make it happen.

The thing you have to decide is, are you and your employees just working for a living. Are you running your business one day at a time, concerned with the nuts and bolts of the operation without any real consideration as to where all this is heading? Most small businesses fall into this pattern. The result is that small businesses are largely a group of people holding jobs, and nothing more.

To change this situation so that there is upward mobility, and an opportunity for you to build real wealth from a business operation, it is necessary for you to develop an organization.

First, organize the boss.

Your job is to understand your personal goals — mesh them with your business goals — to create a structure for an organization that can be expanded to meet those goals.

The first step is to write a job description for your job. To put this into perspective so that you will understand what you actually have to do; write down the decisions that you have to make.

ORGANIZATIONAL OUTLINE 2—2

Here is a checklist to help you:

Hiring
Firing
Promoting
Sales
Purchasing
Advertising
Customer Relations
Credit Granting
Credit Collections
Taxes
Security
Maintenance
Insurance
Banking
Planning
Forecasting
Inventory
Keeping Records and Accounts
Business Location
Government Regulations
Civic Obligations
Dealing with the Competition

And any other decisions that you have to make on either a daily or time-to-time basis. Now analyze which decisions you absolutely must make and which decisions you may delegate to others to make on your behalf. And that is the beginning of your organization.

Once you have done that, write a brief job description for each employee. Determine what they are doing now, what they are capable of doing in an organized structure, and how you will delegate their responsibilities and their authority to carry them out.

Then you have to analyze your present employees and decide if they are capable of doing the kind of work that will have to be done in an organized structure. Establish a chain of command on who reports to whom. The problem with small business is that you are a general and all you have working for you are enlisted men. There aren't any managers between you and your working force to help you with the decision making process. And the first structure that you want to set up in your organization is giving other people responsibility for decision making to take some of the load off your shoulders so you have time to develop the organization to the level you want it to reach.

There is an old saying that's true of most small businesses, that if you don't know where you're going, you'll never get lost. And an organization has to know where it's going and it's necessary to set goals for each employee — including the boss! Now these goals should be developed:

1. To improve productivity.
2. To advance in the organization.
3. To stay within budgets.
4. To learn new skills.

Now You Have The Structure Of An Organization

Your job, pure and simple, is to make this organization work, grow and prosper. So the first step is to set a series of organization goals.

Set your goals:

1. Long range goals — two to three years.
2. Short range goals — six months to one year.
3. Daily performance goals.

You set your long range goals by:

1. Gross dollar volume.
2. Number of clients or customers acquired.
3. The market share.
4. Net worth of the firm.

You set your short range goals by:

1. Gross dollar volume.
2. Operating within budgets.

3. Increased net profit before taxes.

And set your daily goals by:

1. Volume of work done.
2. Reducing the friction in the organization.
3. Making a daily move to obtain new business.

When you've done this you have the structure of an organization in place; you know where you want to take it; and now it's simply a matter of implementing the program to get it done.

TACTICS

Always use problem transference when possible.

When you have a problem—look around for a pair of broad shoulders you can lay it on as your first move to solving it.

For example:

Henry was tossing and turning in bed. He couldn't sleep. It was 3 a.m. and his wife finally got exasperated.

"Henry," she snapped, "What's the matter with you?"

He sat up, "I owe George $10,000 and it's due tomorrow, and I can't pay him."

His wife picked up the phone and dialed George's number. "George," she said, "This is Henry's wife. He can't pay you that $10,000 he owes you tomorrow." She hung up and turned to Henry.

"Now it's his problem, go to sleep."

Any problem you have has a transfer point if you can think of it—if you need a certain product—let some salesman find it for you. If you go to the banker and he tells you he can't renew your note, look him in the eye and say, "That's too bad, I won't be able to pay it, maybe you can locate someone who would lend me the money"—like George, it's his problem now.

Look for a place to transfer problems and go on to the next one. There is a name for this—it's called managing.

CHAPTER 3
RELATIONSHIPS

Business relationships are an arrangement by which we undertake to exchange small favors for big ones.

Understanding Relationships

A relationship between an organization and other organizations, between people and organizations, and between people within an organization, are somewhat different than relationships between individuals.

There are five basic relationships that small business organizations have to deal with: employees, customers, suppliers, government agencies, and possibly stockholders. Each of these requires the development of systems and procedures that make it possible for the organization to act as a unit in these relationships rather than having each individual in the organization make his own separate relationships which ends up with the organization trying to tie knots in string with only one end.

Relationships With Employees — Internal Relationships

As you become the manager of an organization you will find that successful management is the art of getting things done by using people. Obviously the first thing that you must do is learn to manage yourself. When you set down the operational procedures for your organization you are going to have to follow them as well as the employees. Now the problem that afflicts most independent businessmen is the very fact of their independence. Involved in this is vanity, stubbornness, ignorance, greediness, vindictiveness, smartass attitudes and almost a childish desire to have things done the way they want them done at the time. All of these traits make it impossible to build and run an organization. The failure rate in small business is over fifty percent due to simple incompetence. This is the inability to comprehend what kind of business the individual is in; what it takes to make the busienss succesful, and the desire to do everything themselves.

All these attitudes are further reflected in the work of the employee. Unless they are motivated to do their work in the proper manner, nothing really happens. The attitudes of the boss are the primary reason for employees either being highly motivated and highly productive, or being a bunch of clutzes who could care less about what happens to the company because the boss has developed an advisory relationship with them. Now there are three things to consider in developing organizational relationships with employees. They are:

1. What are their goals?
2. What are their problems?
3. What will be their rewards?

The small business is in a unique position to develop a high degree of employee motivation because a small business is not only an economic organization, it is also a social group. It offers the employee a sense of belonging that is missing in larger groups; it develops a *esprit de corps* in the employees that want to make the organization successful. By arranging to do small favors for employees, you get results out of them.

You should understand their goals. First, job security; second, appreciation of their work effort; third, an opportunity for advancement both in terms of responsibility and income; fourth, pride in the product they sell or the service they render.

As to their problems, you have to remember that only twenty-three percent of their time is spent at work. The balance is spent away from work pursuing their personal goals, social activities, etc. So they have many problems that are not work related, in an effort to understand this and possibly help them with some of these problems when they arise, develop the loyalty and the productivity that you want and need from these people.

As to their reward, obviously income is important, but research has shown that even more important is visible appreciation for the work they do, and your willingness to give them responsibility and authority to carry it out. By giving people ego enhancement as well as monetary reward you will develop them into valuable employees.

Relationships With Customers

Obviously the customer is the key to your success or failure. In developing relationships with customers you want to keep these points in mind:

1. Make buying from you easy and pleasant.
2. Be sure that after sales service is maintained and the customer can use it with minimum expense and difficulty.
3. Maintain quality control of what you sell so the customer knows he will get his money's worth.
4. Thank them for their business on a consistent basis. (This is the point that 90 percent of all businesses overlook.)

Relationships With Suppliers

In many businesses the suppliers are essential to business success. Their willingness and ability to deliver what you need, at the right price and the right time can be vital. You must recognize your suppliers not as adversaries out to pick your pocket, but as business friends who can be developed into a valuable asset to your operation. Your organization's relationships with suppliers should:

1. Build a friendly relationship.
2. Show you how to handle problems when they arise.
3. Help you be a customer who does not chase prices.
4. Allow you to always use suppliers to your advantage.

Relationships With Governmental Agencies

As your organization grows, you're going to come more and more in contact with the various levels of government, and these can develop into serious problems if they are not handled properly. All relationships with government should be handled properly. All relationships with government should be handled on a need-to-know basis. Never volunteer anything. Never fill out a form that is submitted to you until the second or third request. Never admit anything to a government agent who calls up to determine whether you're in compliance with some rule or regulation. Whenever possible always deal with them through third parties—accountants, lawyers, etc.

It can be an important help to you to have political contacts in the government when you have an adversary relationship with some agency. Take some time to contribute to campaigns of politicians, and get to know some of the key bureaucrats in the various agencies in a social way. You can develop some power buttons that you can push if you have a problem with a government agency or some lower level bureaucrat that is out to get your scalp.

The smartest way to deal with government bureaucrats is to let someone in your organization handle the problem in the beginning. Don't let the bureaucrat get to you until some final decision has to be made. Many times the problem can be solved by an individual in your organization who will approach the problem with a somewhat less hostile attitude than you might, and develop a relationship with the bureaucrat that may serve you in good stead later on. Always try to keep bureaucrats and governmental agencies at arm's length by using the people in your organization as a shield whenever possible. The one exception to this is the I.R.S. Always deal with them through your accountant or your attorney if there is some question as to tax obligation.

The key to successful management is to pay close attention to relationships, and develop them by keeping in mind the bit of advice given at the beginning—exchange small favors for big one. In other words, always try to do something positive rather than something negative to make progress. If you do this, your organization will grow and prosper.

TACTICS

Become a "what" thinker.

Senator Hayakawa, a noted semanticist, once wrote—"If you see in any given situation only what everyone else can see, you can be said to be so much of a representative of your culture that you are a victim of it."

To be successful you have to open your mind—fight mental sets and welcome ideas.

Do "what" thinking—

What if we

What can we

Then add some whys—

Why can't we

Why don't we

Why should we

Try thinking beyond nuts and bolts—think in concepts about the business—look at what you are doing and ask yourself why do we do it that way. What if we did it this way?

Rudolph Flesch wrote—"Creative thinking may be simply the realization there is no particular virtue in doing things the way they've always been done."

Example—the concept of having boots and shoes differently for right and left feet is only a little over 100 years old. It took 10,000 years for someone to figure it out. Often the obvious idea is the one constantly overlooked.

CHAPTER 4
ESTABLISHING POLICIES

The successful manager thinks like Attila the Hun and acts like St. Francis of Assisi.

The key to making an organization operate properly is having policies in place that people can understand and can follow so there is a uniformity of action and reaction in running the business.

It is important that you understand the difference between objectives, policies, and procedures. Here is the example.

"She may get married some day when the right amount comes along." That is an objective.

"In God we trust — all others pay cash." Is a policy.

"Put the money on the dresser." Is a procedure.

It's important that you understand the difference between objectives, policies, and procedures. Now, in general terms you always set the objectives—these are your decisions alone to make. As you develop your organization you will probably also be making the policies, but as you increase the number of people working for you, you should make policies in connection with those who are going to have to carry them out. Get some input from the people who are implementing the procedures so that they will be more willing to carry them out than if they are simply handed down from above.

Now let's give an example of developing a policy — this is a policy about granting credit. Here are the things you have to consider in making our policy:

1. What is our per customer credit limit?

2. What do we have to know before granting credit?
3. What information indicates if we will grant credit?
4. What information indicates if we will not grant credit?
5. What information indicates the credit limit?
6. Who is authorized to grant credit?
7. How do we determine if we are granting too much or too little credit?

Now if you sit down and carefully answer those questions you have established policy about granting credit. Everyone who is involved, the salespeople, the order desk, sales clerks, people in accounting, etc., should understand the policy. And, based on that policy, you can recommend whether credit should or should not be granted. At some point in the organization you will have to delegate the responsibility for authorizing credit to whomever is in charge of that particular function.

By implementing the policy and allowing your subordinates to implement the policy, you do not have to make decisions about granting credit in every case. Only when a special case arises does the decision have to come from you. This is called management by exception. And by setting policies you are managing both by objective and by exception. Now as an example, one of the first policies that you will have to make for an organization is that of the hiring and managing of the employees. You'll find a little chart covering some of these points included below, and when you sit down to develop a policy, keep in mind that you can't write something that covers everything. Time, people and events vary too much for anyone to make a one hundred percent perfect policy. But, you want to make them as close to being perfect as possible so that there will be very few decisions that will have to be made outside of stated company policy.

The advantage of a policy is that everybody knows where they stand. If the policy is enforced, then there are few complaints about the operation of the policy, although there may be some complaints about the formulation. But the idea of the policy is simply to eliminate constant decisions at the management level about what the company will do under circumstances that repeat themselves day after day or week after week. It's a key management tool and one that the developer of an organization should sit down and develop for each area required.

Now here is a checklist of the general areas in which policies can be made, with the provision that making too many policies is probably worse than not having any. Policies should only be made when there is an evident need for them, and they should be short, concise and easy for everyone to understand.

CHART FOR EMPLOYEE POLICY

Hours: Number of hours of work per week, number of days of work, evening work, exceptions for Christmas and similar seasons, overtime needs, payment for overtime.

Vacations: Length, increases related to seniority, time of year scheduled, extra vacation time without pay.

Illness: Payment of salary, evidence of illness required, retention of employment rights during sick leave, provision of medical, surgical, and hospital benefits.

Holidays: New Year's Day, July 4th, Thanksgiving, and Christmas are standard. Further provision needed when these fall on Saturday or Sunday. Allowance made for voting on Election Day.

Personal leave: Emergency time off without salary deduction for such reasons as a death in an employee's immediate family.

Wages and salaries: Time and method of payment, bases for pay (may vary with department and responsibility of job), grading of jobs with wage scales for each job level, normal increases within the range of each job.

Fringe benefits: Discounts to employees, free life insurance, health insurance, educational opportunities such as tuition payment at schools and colleges.

Retirement: Retirement-age benefits, Social Security,

pension plan, annuity plan.

Accidents to employees: Workmen's compensation, other assistance.

Termination of employment: Layoffs, seniority rights, severance pay, conditions warranting summary discharge.

Promotion: From within, manpower development program to encourage promotion from within.

Personnel reviews: When conducted, who conducts, factors considered, relation of ratings to salary adjustments, merit increases.

Grievances: Procedure for handling, employee's right to demand review.

Organization Summary

The first thing the professional manager must have is information. He must apply that knowledge to the local market, learn the size and the make-up of the market—analyze the competition—and from that information develop his strategy.

The professional manager who has the knowledge of his industry and markets has a big advantage over most of his small business competition who do not. In any contest the participant who knows the right "game plan" goes in as a heavy favorite to win. Here is a check list of information the professional manager should find out about his industry:

1. What is the national annual sales volume for the industry?
2. How many firms are in the industry nationally?
3. How many firms locally?
4. What is the average gross volume per company?
5. What is the average number of employees per company?
6. What is the dollar volume per employee? (Divide number of employees into the average gross volume of

each business to get this figure.)

7. What percentage of national volume is controlled by large business?
8. What percentage of local volume is controlled by large business?
9. What is the annual average dollar volume gross of the industry nationally?
10. What is the annual growth of the market locally?
11. Is geographical location important to this industry? (The fishing industry has to be located close to a body of water, the timber industry must be located close to a forest, etc.)
12. If location is important, where is the best location?
13. What is the average capital investment for small business in the industry?
14. What is the average annual return on investment in this industry?
15. What is the average product turnover rate in the industry?
16. Where does most new technology come from in this industry?
17. What are the key sources of information in this industry? (Trade magazines, newsletters, government and industry reports, etc.)

Your Specific Markets

Then from the information you have gained on the national industry and the size of your local market, you want to develop specific information about that market. Here is a check list:

1. The demographics of a typical customer.
2. Population growth trend in the market—up or down.
3. Is business volume growing, static, or declining?

4. The average volume of each established business in the area.
5. The number of direct competitors established in the area.
6. The key competitors—and the reasons for successful operations.

Compiling this information will give you an overview of your market, and a look at the kind of business now being done and identify the most successful competitors and the reasons for their success.

Developing Specific Strategies And Objectives

When you have your marketing information you have set your course to develop your own specific strategies and objectives to capture a share of the market. Now I will give you a brief checklist for reference in preparing these strategies and objectives:

1. The segment of the market you intend to serve.
2. The products or services you will specialize in.
3. Your unique selling proposition.
4. Your dollar volume for the next twelve months.
5. What percentage of the total market that represents.
6. Your before tax net profit goal in dollars.
7. Your after tax return on investment goal.
8. Your personal income goals. (Salary and net profits.)

The segment of the market you will serve will depend on the concept of your business. For example, if you are a building contractor and you feel the most profitable segment of the market for you would be in commercial construction, that is the segment of the market which you intend to serve. If you are a retailer selling high fashion garments, the segment of the market you will serve will be upper middle income and wealthy people and the location of your store, its decore, and the type of merchandise you carry will reflect your attempt to sell to that segment of the market.

The products or services you specialize in are obviously dictated by the concept you have of what portion of the market you will serve. It will also help to analyze the key competition, those that are the most successful. In analyzing what they do, look for opportunities to render services or sell products that they are not properly promoting or you feel can be sold in direct competition with them using better merchandising or service methods.

Unique selling proposition is simply the major selling point that you intend to stress in inducing consumers to buy what you have to sell. In other words, you look over the products or services you offer and find something in them that is different, better, more appealing in some specific way and you key your advertising promotion around your unique selling proposition.

Your dollar volume goal in the next twelve months is your best estimate of how much business you can do with a well organized and functioning business attacking a specific segment of the market with a well developed plan.

You can determine what percentage of the market that represents by dividing the total market dollars spent in your particular industry and the amount of gross business you want, and the resulting figure will be your percentage of the market.

Your before tax net profit goal in dollars will simply represent your ability to manage your expenses on the one hand and create a volume of sales on the other hand to give you the target figure of net profit before taxes.

Your after tax return on investment goal is really the acid test of your manageability. A high return on investment bespeaks good management, and a low return on investment bespeaks average or poor management.

And finally set goals for your personal income both in terms of after tax profits and salary. Then go organize and develop the business to reach those goals.

TACTICS

"If it ain't broke don't fix it!"

If you have something working—making money—don't monkey with it. Too many people in business are constantly trying to fine tune a business doing well and end up busting it.

There's the story of the man who bought a machine that made the best donuts in town. It turned them out at a dozen every five minutes—and he could sell all he could make. So he decided to hire a mechanic to work on the machine and increase the speed so he could make more money. The mechanic came on a weekend, and the man told him the donut had two characteristics—it had a circle of dough and a hole. The mechanic went to work and the owner came in on Sunday morning to make his donuts—nothing happened. He called the mechanic and said, "You've ruined it; the machine won't work." "That's not true," the mechanic said, "I've got it making six dozen holes a minute, all I have to figure out now is how to add the circle of dough."

Remember—nothing will ever be perfect—so don't monkey with a good thing—look for other problems to solve.

CHAPTER 5
OUTLINING YOUR POLICIES

Writing A Policy

I want to give you some specific information on how you would write a policy for the various aspects of the business operations for which you feel a policy is necessary for proper operations. Keep in mind that a policy is developed so the organization has stability. It deals with specific functions in a specific way, and all the employees and managers understand the policy and implement it. This makes it possible to manage a diverse operation efficiently.

There are only three steps to writing a policy: 1) state the objective of the policy, 2) state the function, 3) state the policy in short and clear terminology.

I'm going to give you an example of how a policy is written. This is for the XYZ Company's policy on granting credit. Now the general policy statement goes like this, "Our object is to accomodate our customers by offering credit terms on sales based on their ability and willingness to pay when accounts are due."

1. Credit applications—all accounts must supply the information indicated on our credit applications before credit can be granted.

2. Credit limits—all new accounts shall be analyzed by our credit manager and limits set based on the information in the credit application.

3. Dun & Bradstreet ratings—all credit applicants with satisfactory D & B ratings need not give references other than their bank.

4. Credit granted—when credit is granted, an account

number is assigned to that customer and a ledger card is set-up and indicates the limits of credit.

5. Credit refused—when credit investigation reveals a credit applicant is not a good credit risk, the credit manager will notify the applicant of the decision and offer to supply products on C.O.D. basis.

6. Credit investigation—all our credit applicants will be checked through D & B ratings—through references given—and checked with other supply sources.

7. Credit limits—are based on the financial strength of the applicant—but under no circumstances can credit accounts be carried for more than $ 1,000.

8. Credit to new firms—credit to start-up firms will be checked out with the personal references of the owners. If it is a corporation—a note must be signed by the owner(s) assuming personal liability for the account—and the limit on new firms will be $500.

9. Out of area customers—credit applications from out of our trading area and service area will be declined. C.O.D. shipments can be made if the company requests them.

10. Requests for credit above the limit—this shall be passed on by management with the credit managers recommendations.

Once this credit policy is set-up it is given to the sales force, the credit manager, accounting, and any others who are concerned. It establishes a credit procedure that should cover about 95 percent of the cases for which credit is asked. In the other five percent of the cases, the credit manager will have to get a decision from higher up. This solves two problems; it uniformly applies a credit policy to all customers, and it eliminates the necessity for management decisions every time somebody applies for credit.

All policy statements can be prepared in the same way by simply following that outline and making short statements of policy after each function of policy as indicated. These then are easy for the employees and the managers to understand and will put the business on an organized operational basis.

The Policy Writing Checklist

The simplest way to determine which areas of your business require written policies is to mentally walk through your operation step by step and see what is being done and what needs to be done. This mental stroll through the business will enable you to draw the proper conclusions as to which areas of the business can be profitably managed with policy statements.

☐ Who opens business in the morning?
☐ When are first customers served or production started?
☐ Who opens, distributes, processes mail?

What happens when a sale is made?
☐ Who makes the sale?
☐ How is sale recorded?
☐ How is payment made?
☐ What type of record is prepared?
☐ How is product or service delivered?
☐ How is the inventory affected?
☐ What inventory records are prepared?
☐ Who does packing, shipping, etc.?
☐ Do papers have to be prepared for shipment?
☐ Who prepares them?
☐ What information does account get?
☐ Are there any checks against theft, fraud, or embezzlement in use of invoices, receipts, cash handling?
☐ How are back orders handled?
☐ If credit sale, is limit and approval checked before shipment?

What happens when purchases are made?
☐ Who makes or authorizes purchases?
☐ How are purchases to be received?
☐ What terms are used on purchases?
☐ Is more than one person always involved?
☐ Who checks receiving against purchase orders?

- ☐ Who authorizes payment of PO's?
- ☐ What happens if order arrives incomplete or incorrect?
- ☐ Who follows up to see purchases arrive on time?
- ☐ Who checks out vendors?
- ☐ Who compares prices, reviews bids, etc.?
- ☐ Who sets budgets?

Who answers phone?

- ☐ How are callers handled?
- ☐ How are phone uses checked?
- ☐ Who is authorized to call long distance?
- ☐ What equipment will best serve operation?
- ☐ What is budget for phones?

Office and Plant Maintenance

- ☐ Who opens and closes?
- ☐ Who cleans and maintains?
- ☐ Who is responsible for maintenance?
- ☐ What will budget be?
- ☐ What insurance will be needed?
- ☐ What security measures need to be taken?

Inventory

- ☐ Who is in charge ot it?
- ☐ Who keeps the records?
- ☐ Who inventories it?
- ☐ When are inventories taken?
- ☐ Who ships it?
- ☐ Who receives returned goods?
- ☐ What paperwork is required?
- ☐ What is the maintenance budget for inventory?

Equipment

- ☐ Who purchases it?
- ☐ Who installs it?

- ☐ Who uses it?
- ☐ Who supervises it?
- ☐ How will it be depreciated?
- ☐ Who will repair it?
- ☐ Budget for repair and maintenance.

Supplies

- ☐ Who buys them?
- ☐ What supplies will be needed?
- ☐ How will they be requisitioned?
- ☐ What is the budget?
- ☐ What are the sources?

Sales

- ☐ Who makes sales?
- ☐ Who confirms sales?
- ☐ Who routes sales to production or shipping?
- ☐ What commissions are paid?
- ☐ Who manages sales?
- ☐ Who plans sales programs?
- ☐ What is sales budget?

Advertising and Promotion

- ☐ Who plans advertising?
- ☐ Who places advertising?
- ☐ What will be advertised?
- ☐ Where will it be advertised?
- ☐ How will it be advertised?
- ☐ Who will handle public relations?
- ☐ What is advertising budget?

Credit and Collection

- ☐ Who grants credit?
- ☐ How is credit checked?

☐ What are credit limits?
☐ Can receivables be financed?
☐ At what cost?
☐ What will collections policy be?
☐ How will accounts be aged?
☐ How will collection efforts be made?
☐ When will accounts be written off?
☐ When will they be turned over for collection?
☐ What collection service will be used?
☐ What is average time for collection in industry?

Returns and Allowances

☐ What will be returnable?
☐ Who pays return shipping cost?
☐ How will credits be given?
☐ When are returns not acceptable?
☐ Will returns be resaleable?

Insurance

☐ What will be insured?
☐ Who will insure it?
☐ How much will it cost?

Prices

☐ Who sets the prices?
☐ How are prices set?
1. By cost of production and sales?
2. By the competitive situation?
3. By market demand?
4. By educated guesses?
5. By best profit margin?

☐ Are discounts allowed?
☐ How will prices be monitored?
☐ How will price increases be handled?

☐ Are price lists to be used?
☐ Will prices be advertised?

Wages & Salaries
☐ How much will you pay each position?
☐ How are salaries and wages arrived at?
☐ What is your policy about raises?
☐ Will bonuses be paid?
☐ To whom, and how much?
☐ What is the basis of bonus payments?
☐ How will vacation/sick leave pay be handled?
☐ How often will you pay?
☐ Who will prepare payroll & tax records?
☐ How will hourly wages be monitored?
☐ What about termination pay?

Employee Benefits
☐ Will you have a medical plan?
☐ How will it be paid for?
☐ What is your vacation policy?
☐ What is your days off policy?
☐ Will you have a retirement plan?
☐ Who pays for it?
☐ What happens when an employee leaves?
☐ What happens when an employee is fired?
☐ Will there be other benefits?
☐ How much will they cost/who pays?
☐ What is your promotion policy?

Employee Working Rules
☐ What days are you open for business?
☐ What days are holidays?
☐ What hours do employees work?
☐ What is your policy on being late for work?

- ☐ What is your policy on absenteeism?
- ☐ Are there production schedules to meet?
- ☐ Will there be quotas to meet?
- ☐ What are lunch/break rules?
- ☐ What rule infractions bring termination?
- ☐ What are pay docking rules?
- ☐ What are emergency days off rules?
- ☐ What are sick leave rules?
- ☐ What are maternity rules?
- ☐ Is a union involved?
- ☐ Who will negotiate with union?
- ☐ Who will handle grievances?
- ☐ What are temporary layoff rules?
- ☐ What are telephone use rules?
- ☐ Are there smoking/non-smoking rules?

Government Regulations

- ☐ Are you familiar with Fair Employment Practices regulations?
- ☐ Will you have to deal with Occupational Safety and Health Rules?
- ☐ What local and state occupational or other rules apply?
- ☐ Will you have hazardous substances?
- ☐ Will you have a waste disposal problem?
- ☐ Who will fill out government forms?
- ☐ How much will it cost?

Licenses

- ☐ What licenses will you require?
- ☐ How much will they cost?
- ☐ Are deposits required?
- ☐ Do you need special informaion ot get the licenses?
- ☐ Can a change in location eliminate expensive licenses?

Taxes

- ☐ What taxes will you be obligated to pay?

☐ When will they be due?
☐ Are their additional future taxes to consider?
☐ What tax planning needs to be done?

Utilities
☐ What power requirements will you have?
☐ Are hookups available?
☐ Will costs be a factor?

Areas Where Policy Making Is Useful

MANUFACTURING

- Inspection and Quality Control
- Purchasing Supplies and Materials
- Limits on Size and Cost of Inventories
- Maintenance and Replacement of Equipment
- Plant Maintenance, Safety and Security
- Handling of Waste Materials

RETAILING

- Store Hours and Days
- Handling Returns and Exchanges
- Cashing Checks
- Over and Under Register Counts
- Shoplifting Policy
- Credit Card Procedures
- Handling Customer Complaints
- Seeing Salesmen Who Call

OUTLINING YOUR POLICIES 5—10

MARKETING

- Channels of Distribution Used
- Operation of Territories
- Customer Relations
- Sales Commissions and Bonuses
- Types of Advertising Media Approved for Co-op
- Minimum Sales Quantities
- Sales Discount Schedules
- Handling Rush Orders
- Granting Credit

FINANCIAL

- Obtaining Long Term Capital
- Dividends — Stock, Cash, Distribution
- Insurance
- Budgets and Cost Control
- Short Term Financing
- Handling Surplus Cash

OTHER AREAS

- Salaries and Bonuses of Executives
- Retirement and Medical Plans
- Expansion Policies
- Merger and Aquisition Policies

REMEMBER

1. Policies should be clear — easily understood.
2. Input from those who are responsible for carrying them out is vital.

3. They are not carved in stone — but cover most contingencies.
4. They are stable — seldom changed.
5. They have a purpose other than some personal whim.
6. Policies do not dictate procedures — they indicate a desired result. Procedures are developed by those charged with implementing the policy.
7. There should be as few as possible.

TACTICS

Never try to deal with an institution on its terms.

George Santayana once wrote, "The workings of a great institution are mainly the result of a vast mass of routine, petty malice, self interest, carelessness and sheer mistake. Only a residual fraction is thought."

If you are selling something to an institution:

- Read all the fine print on purchase orders.
- State your terms and conditions clearly on the sales order—make sure it is signed by the proper person.
- Find out who okays the invoices for payment.
- Find out who writes the checks.
- Enforce the conditions of sale to the letter.

You have to remember—you are involved with a lot of petty bureaucrats who accept no responsibility—know nothing of what goes on beyond their desk—and are trained to follow instructions. They will take instructions from you if you make them believe it will make trouble for them if they don't.

If you are buying something

- Get terms and conditions in plain English signed by the salesperson.
- If it's a long term lease or sale—have your attorney examine the contract—and have him make up your counter-offer.
- Get your deal out of the hands of the system routine into decision maker's hands by making counter proposals. You are then

into negotiations and can often times get a better deal.

- When you will require after sale service—get the names of the key people who assign service work—contact them directly about service problems—don't deal with functionaries.

When you are dealing with a government institution:

- Never accept their first offer.
- Always file a counter-offer with the superior of the person responsible for your problem.
- Get your problem out of the routine system—make them respond to you on a different level.
- If the question is one of your not doing something properly—being in violation of something, etc.—always deny it—never admit anything—always throw some shit in the game by making counter-charges.
- When you get a demand from one person—always answer it by sending it to someone higher up. This throws their system out of whack—you force delay and regrouping on their part—always make an appeal for relief to an elected official who has some clout with the agency.
- This may not prevent you having to do what they want you to do—but there is always an outside chance they will give up the game as not being worth the candle.

CHAPTER 6
LAWYERS AND ACCOUNTANTS

"A lawyer starts life giving $100 worth of law for $5, and ends up giving $5 worth for $500."
— Benjamin H. Brewster

Outside Services

LAWYERS

Unfortunately, a professional business manager needs the services of a lawyer. He needs a lawyer who has some basic understanding of business and a willingness to represent the interest of his client whole-heartedly. A smart professional business manager gets the lawyer on his management team by offering the lawyer a piece of the action (in the form of stock or future stock options) once a favorable relationship has been established. This cutting the lawyer in for a piece of the action is the magic word in getting a lot of legal advice free at board of director's meetings, luncheons, etc.

They Are Negative Thinkers

It is important for the business manager to understand the kind of advice lawyers give. It is almost all negative. They tell you that this or that is either illegal, possibly illegal, or maybe later construed to be illegal. This is what they are paid to do, but it is important for you to remember that you do not have to take their advice. They can tell you what might happen if you take a specific course of action, and then you can decide whether the game is worth the candle.

Find A Real S.O.B.

If you don't have a lawyer, and you have to go out and find one, do so with one thought in mind. You want to find a mean son-of-a-bitch! It will probably work better if you don't like him personally. What you are looking for is a lawyer who operates by calling the opposition every kind of a son-of-a-bitch there is — and then lets them prove the kind that they're not. His primary advice to you will be on how to stay out of court or jail—and if problems ensue because of a specific course of action what he might do to defend you.

To find this S.O.B. you can ask around among other businessmen about the name of the dirtiest bastard they know that practices law — or you can send your wife to attend court sessions at the county courthouse for a week or so to see if she can locate one who acts like *Attila the Hun* in court — and wins.

Retain Control Of The First Interview

When you go to see lawyers about possibly representing you, it's important that you retain control of the interview. Remember, these are trained inquisitors. These people know how to ask questions, evaluate answers, and ask other questions to clarify answers in a systematic way. If you let them, in a half-hour they are going to know everything about you that you have to tell — and you are not going to know anything about them.

The purpose of your interview is to determine if this lawyer would be interested in representing your business organization. This representation will consist of legal advice, helping you with contracts, perhaps filing suit on your behalf on occasion, and possibly defending you against suits on other occasions. Your proposition is that if he is interested in this type of arrangement — you will pay his legitimate fees — and later on cut him in for a piece of the action in the company in the form of stock or stock options.

The key to selection is how he reacts to the offer to come in for a piece of the action. If he is not interested in that, stop the interview immediately and leave. You are looking for somebody who will get on your team and work with you as well as for you.

Get A Clarification Of Fees And Charges

If he is agreeable to those terms, you simply discuss his fees for doing the normal amount of legal work that you require. You discuss what he bases his charges on—whether he charges his full fee for work done by secretaries—and that you will expect the work that he does for you to be completed on an agreed date, and not have to be constantly chasing him to find out where your legal work is—and when you might get it.

Remember, you are hiring him — and we're dealing here with communications again. You want to be blunt, clear, concise as to what you expect him to do for you, and then let him decide whether he wants to accept the offer on that basis or not.

Next, discuss how fees are going to be paid. Some attorneys want to work for businesses on a yearly retainer fee.

This is generally an advance payment for advice and consultation—and any fees for filing papers, court work, etc. are over and above the retainer.

Don't Buy His Services In Advance

In hiring a new attorney, it is not wise to put him on an annual retainer of any kind. Let him bill you for the work he does, see how well he does it and then decide if there is any advantage to you in putting him on a retainer.

You might also discuss the lawyer's willingness to take cases on a contingency fee basis (where he takes a third of the settlement as his fee). Some lawyers are nothing more than legal entrepreneurs and want to work on contingency fee basis wherever possible. If your case is logical, and the amount is large enough, he may very well be eager to accept cases on that basis.

What You Should Get From Your Lawyer

Here is what you have a right to expect from a lawyer:

1. That he keeps all matters relating to your business confidential.
2. That he will fully disclose the exact status of any legal work he is doing for you at any time — in language that you can understand.
3. That he will accept your decisions on his recommendations — up or down — as the final word.
4. That he will stay on his agreed fee schedule—and perform the work as agreed, on time, in a responsible and professional manner.
5. That if he finds he cannot reasonably or competently do legal work for you that he will so inform you and recommend somebody who can.
6. That either of you have the right to terminate your association at any time by paying balances due or by completing work obligated for.

As your organization develops, you may want to have two lawyers representing you. You may want to employ the services of a large, respected legal firm to represent you in lawsuits, or file lawsuits where their prestige and obvious abilities tend to weigh in your favor. And, keep your mean son-of-a-bitch to attack other people, throw shit in the game, and generally make things miserable for people who are giving you a hard time but aren't worth suing. You can also keep the S.O.B. as your personal lawyer, to handle personal affairs for you. The large firms are too expensive for this type of work.

ACCOUNTANTS

When you are ready to install an accounting system keep one thing in mind. Try to make it as simple and as non-time consuming as possible. Accurate records are vital to your operation, but a small business doesn't necessarily need to spend thousands of wasted hours a year crunching numbers.

If you are new to business or going to get involved in restructuring your organization then you should look into outside accounting services to care for your records. These people keep your books balanced, make out and send in your tax forms, and give you monthly balance sheets and operating statements to show you how you are progressing.

CPAs—Good And Bad

The top of the profession are the Certified Public Accountants—CPAs. They are the most expensive, and supposedly most knowledgeable—which may or may not be true in cases of small business clients. A good many CPA offices are nothing more than a computerized bookkeeping service. They charge CPA rates, however the work is done by so-called junior members of the firm. They often even ask you to pick up and deliver your paperwork.

Bookkeeping Services

There is another way to go about this that can save you some money. There are a good many bookkeepers and bookkeeping services that the small business operation can use, and use profitably. These are often listed in the phone book as accountants or accounting services or bookkeeping services. These people have a deep understanding of the problems of the small business and know what needs to be done—and when to do it. They come to your place of business to work on your books, and deliver your reports—send in your taxes—sometimes handle your payroll and do all the other accounting chores required of a business or small corporation.

Use Both Types Of Service

You can use these people to do the number crunching in your books, and use a CPA firm to audit it periodically, as you can present audited CPA statements to banks and other lenders if you need to borrow money or raise capital.

It's important that the organization or person you employ for the bookkeeping service be reliable—and that they do not have more clients than they can handle. You want to remember these people are not creative thinkers or skilled in all forms of tax law and sophisticated corporate tax shelters. They are technicians who know how to do the job needed to be done and can help you in planning by showing you where you're springing profit leaks. You will have to keep certain daily records in your organization for their use and they come in and either pick them up or do the work in your office. It's a big help if the person you choose has had some experience in the same line of business you are entering or in one very much like it. It is wise to interview more than one, and find one who seems to have a little imagination and some initiative.

The Bookkeeping Systems

These are usually computer based systems like the systems you buy at the stationary store. You keep certain forms and records — send these to them for service and they return a computer print-out with the results. Operators of these services are almost always oversold in terms of personal service, so you won't get much personal advice or help from them as a rule. One important point is to stay away from the franchised small business consulting services. They will put anybody in the consulting business who's got the price of the franchise, and they generally sell their advice along with a bookkeeping service. The fact that they present themselves as consultants, enables them to charge more money for a package of services than they could get as a straight bookkeeping service. Few of them have any real help to offer, and it's far better to stick with people who are specialists in keeping accurate business records, and get your consulting advice elsewhere.

There's one proviso to choosing this accountant, and that is sooner or later you are going to have to use a CPA. But, if your business is small now, and CPAs are charging much higher rates than an accounting and bookkeeping service, you're just as well off with the bookkeeping service at the present stage of development. If you can find a CPA who has the computerized service at a reasonable price, then by all means use him as your bookkeeping service— because the additional advice you need will be available there at an extra charge when you need it.

Don't Pay For Prestige You Can't Use

There is one thing to keep in mind when you are hiring professional services. There's no real advantage to a small business in hiring a prestige name as his lawyer or his accountant. In the first place, you are going to be treated like kitchen help in these organizations because they can't make enough money from the services they render you to pay much attention to you. The second thing is that nobody is that impressed with who your lawyer or accountant is and the extra money you pay is largely wasted.

Concentrate on finding people who can do the job, at a reasonable price, and are reliable and have everything that you need at your present stage of development. As you grow you can change lawyers and accountants as needed. But don't spend money uselessly in trying to buy some prestige that won't do you much good.

TACTICS

Always buy—never be sold.

Very important! Never buy anything until you are fully informed and have totally checked it out.

Make all salesmen, selling anything with which you are not familiar, call back. Never buy on the first call. You are at a disadvantage information-wise—the salesman has the edge.

When you check them out with other people who have dealt with them—and you are still interested—call back and have the salesman return.

Always test the water—make a counter offer on:

- The price
- Terms of sale
- A better guarantee
- Who pays shipping costs?
- Can you add additional products, services, or capabilities for the same or lower price?

You will often be surprised at how soft the original offer was—you can negotiate much better terms by simply asking for them.

There's the old story about the man who asked the beautiful woman if she would go to bed with him for a million dollars—and she said "Sure." So, he asked her if she would do it for ten dollars and she snapped, "Hell no, what do you think I am?" He replied, "We've already established that—now let's find the right price."—that's how you should think about purchasing.

CHAPTER 7
CONSULTING

There are consultants available for every type of small business — and every function involved in a business. Consultants come in all sizes, costs and degrees of experience and expertise. Some are very good, most are mediocre, and a lot of them are absolutely worthless. This is not a situation that's limited to the field of consulting. It represents a cross-section of every field of professional advice in the country starting with lawyers and accountants, and ranging on down to people who give you tips on horse races.

At one point in my career, when I was sure I was the smartest and most capable business manager on earth, I thought using consultants was foolish. But like Mark Twain remarked on one of his lecture tours, "When I was 18 years old, I thought a father was the stupidest man on earth. When I was 25, I was amazed to find out how much the old man had learned in 7 years."

Consultants Can Help You

The fact is that consultants do have a place to help the professional business manager perfect the development of an organization. There is no one in any business who knows everything. Somewhere out there there is a consultant who knows what you need to know and can help you solve some problems.

They can help you design packages — design products — set up production lines — develop marketing programs — organize your paperwork — develop your telephone system — set up profit sharing and pension plans — help you train people and any other function of business that you have. You can find a consultant who can be a great deal of help to you.

Consultants Eliminate Payroll

The major reason I like to use consultants is that it gives me what I need to know without hiring employees. Many times a consultant, who I would pay a couple of thousand dollars, can show me how to do something for which some businesses would add another employee and pay them $18 to $20 thousand dollars a year to perform the job. As an example, a friend of mine hired a consultant to set up a production line for a product that he had been sending to job shops to manufacture for him. He decided to bring it in and do it himself. He paid this man $15,000 to set everything up and train the supervisor to handle it. To hire a production manager and engineer to do the same thing would've cost him $50,000. So consultants who know their business can be of great help to a small business manager.

Negotiating With A Consultant

When you have a problem you think a consultant can handle—identitfy it clearly. For example, you want to know the best way to market a new product. Your problem has several facets. You have a limited amount of capital to work with. Second, you have limited production facilities. Third, you have no one experienced in marketing in your company.

You set these down in terms of how much capital you have to invest in marketing—how many units you can produce each month—and what kind of manager is required to handle the program. Now you are ready to present the problem to the consultant. He knows what you can invest, what you can produce and what kind of help you need to carry out a marketing plan.

Then you decide on what kind of end result you want from this program in terms of gross sales, net profit, and the potential to increase production to meet expanding markets. This gives the consultant an idea of what you expect from the program.

Conducting The First Interview

You are ready to begin interviewing consultants concerning your problem. You give the consultant your outline of the problem — and get his impressions of your success potential — his concept for marketing it — his suggestions about how to proceed. You can interview as many as you like, looking for the one who seems most in tune with what you want and gives you logical concepts for getting the job done.

It is important to beware of Greeks bearing gifts. That is, don't be impressed by the consultant who tells you that you have a real winner and suggests that he can show you how to make pots of money from it at once. Pay more attention to the consultant who keeps asking questions and doesn't offer instant solutions.

Your Checklist For Consultant Evaluation

Here are the things you will want to know about a consultant:

1. His background and experience
2. Recent references
3. His timetable for completion
4. His perception of your situation. (Has he ever done anything like this before for a client in similar circumstances?) Beware of the consultant who has been soley engaged in work for large corporations and has had no experience with small business.
5. Remember the saying about consultants — "If you have failed at everything — become a consultant." There are a lot of those in the field who think negatively about everything.
6. The most important thing you are looking for is practical experience — a real veteran of the war and not a historian who has studied it and offers second hand advice. Stay away from professors.
7. Price and terms are relative; you can pay what it is worth to you. Don't try to hire cheap consulting. It's like hiring a cut rate brain

surgeon; you get what you pay for. Be careful in your selection. Don't let price be your criteria.

8. Be careful about large consulting firms, they have a lot of trainees who handle small businesses and who have never been in small business. You pay rates based on what the principals charge.

9. When you hire the consultant, let him do his thing. Don't try and tell him what to do, or try and force him to offer a result you want. He is there to tell you what you don't know, and it can be good news or bad news. Let him come to his own conclusions—it's the only way you get your money's worth.

10. One thing you do want is progress reports so you know that something is happening. It it is turning out the concept is not feasible, you can cut it off and go no further than needed to provide a clear result.

11. And finally, live with the result. You may not like it or agree with it—but if you are smart you will accept it unless you have other information to negate it.

Negotiating Payment

As to contract terms—you can negotiate it per diem, by the week—or on a contract calling for a specific sum on completion. I like the specified sum contract. I can't be sure how fast anyone works and paying $100 a day or more plus expenses is an open end deal. I would rather pay, more with a limit, because then we all know where we stand.

The Free Consultation

Your first consultation conversation is free—any consultant who wants to charge for the exploratory talks is going to be too expensive or too arrogant to deal with. I'll tell you a little secret about this first conversation. If you interview five or six consultants and control the direction of the conversations, you can often find the solution to the problem through these conversation. I did this by accident the first time. I was trying to get a consultant to help me market a business building program for beauty shops. The first one I talked to explained the marketing problems with beauty shops—the third one told me in general terms how it could be sold. The fourth one told me of a similar program—which I investigated and found out how to put the sales package together—and the fifth one told me about a contract that would cover everything I needed. The consultations had given me everything I needed—and it cost me nothing. The deal was a big success so, to be honest, I sent the four who had given me ideas a check for $100 each for the time they gave me. It would have cost me about $5,000 to get the same information from any one of them—I could have had it for nothing—but having done some consulting myself, I paid them for their time. That is one reason I want to talk to five or more consultants on any project—even if I finally hire one—I get a lot of free help from the others.

If you decide that the consultant might do the job for you, have him submit a basic plan and a price to you by letter. If you are satisfied with the proposal, you can authorize him to go ahead by letter.

To locate consultants, go to your library and look up the names of associations: American Management Association—The Association of Consultant Management Engineers—Association of Management Consultants—Society of Professional Management Consultants, etc. Write for lists of members in your area for contact.

The Consulting Panel

Here is a method I have used with success to get an in depth knowledge of problems and opportunities in various small businesses I was not familiar with. I ran an ad in the paper something like this:

CONSULTING 7—6

> WILL PAY $100 FOR FOUR HOURS OF YOUR TIME! WANT TO TALK TO YOU IF YOU HAVE OWNED OR MANAGED A (NAME OF BUSINESS). I AM RESEARCHING THIS BUSINESS AND NEED SOME EXPERT ADVICE. OUR SESSION WILL BE HELD SUNDAY AFTERNOON. CALL 234-5678.

I ran this in both help wanted and business opportunity classified and always got a good response. I would pick four people who had recent experience in the business either as owners or managers—and then I brought them to a motel conference room—set up a tape recorder and asked questions about the business ranging from licenses and permits needed to the most effective means of advertising. These were highly productive because the people were happy to discuss something they knew a lot about—and I had four hours of tapes which I would get transcribed into a reference manual on the business.

The Score Program

Using the Small Business Administration S.C.O.R.E. Program is of questionable value. They supply a retired business executive to consult with you. They seldom have one with any direct experience in your business—so they can usually only supply some help with basic business principles and bookkeeping information. The only cost is for their transportation—but I have never found the help useful in specific business subjects.

The University Programs

You can get some valuable help in research and number crunching from universities in your area. They have programs for small business that offer help in doing market research, analysing data, setting up operating budgets, etc. Again, the help is largely general and can take a long time to develop. But it is worth investigating.

Using A Writer As A Researcher

Another method I have used to find out what I wanted to know—particulary about competitors—was to hire a free lance writer to interview the owners or managers for an article the writer hoped to sell to a magazine. I could get an idea of their gross volume—their promotional plans and philosophy—have the writer interview some employees to get an idea of how well they related to their jobs and the firm they worked for, etc. I would pay the writer $200 or so for the job—and it always produced some valuable information I could use.

There are a lot of ways to get specific help by paying people, off the payroll, to do it. The use of consultants is often a valuable move, for a small business operator, in making plans for building the business and capturing new markets. I recommend it!

TACTICS

Don't try to do what you can't do well.

Doing stupid things once is human error—doing them repeatedly becomes an operating manual. There is a problem we all have—we think we can do things better than those whose profession it is to do them:

- Manage a baseball team
- Call the plays for the quarterback
- Run the government
- Run everyone elses business better than they do, etc.

But, when your money is on the line—recognize your limitations—and hire or get the right person for the right job.

Confidence is necessary—but smart assing is not. The greatest tactic for business success is to know what you don't know.

CHAPTER 8
OUTSIDE SERVICES THAT ELIMINATE PAYROLL

One of the first things to analyze in a small business operations is the payroll. This can be the largest expense and the biggest headache. It is not so much what you pay the employee, but the additional hidden payments in social security contribution, unemployment contribution, workman's compensation and such things as contributions to hospital insurance, vacation pay, absenteeism, etc.

First, look at the office work. Typing, filing, bookkeeping, etc. How much work is there? Should you use a bookkeeping service, a phone answering service (or device) when you are out? Could you use a typing service for letters, etc.?

I know of several cases where small businesses in an industrial park got together and put a couple of their office people in business. They rented them a space, leased them the machines, and the employees got a business license and started an office service company. They answered the phones — did the paperwork — and were free to take on other clients. The small businesses who organized this each cut 70% off their office payroll costs and got even better results than when they had their own staff.

In many cases, the small business has an office worker who really does not have enough work to do — but the owner feels he needs the prestige of having someone in the office. If there are days when someone should be there — use a termporary help agency — and let the agency handle the payroll.

Collating—Packaging—Assembling, Etc.

Many times the small business can make a better deal with one of the agencies who hire handicapped people to do such things as collating pages, packaging small products, putting a product together from components, etc., than trying to hire unskilled labor to do it. The handicapped agency will give you a flat price per unit—and they have an excellent track record for getting the work out on time and doing a better job than casual labor will do. This eliminates payroll costs—the cost of supervision—and reduces the amount of workspace you need to rent.

Shipping Your Products

Rather than maintaining a shipping department—you can hire a sharecropper shipping department. You can investigate the possiblity of hiring a responsible person who can store your products in his garage, basement, etc., and do your shipping work in his sparetime. If you have a modest amount of daily shipping to do—this is a plan that saves time and money. Your sharecropper is in his own business—you pay him a flat price per unit for his shipping services. He takes your orders—prepares the packages—and either hauls them to a shipping point—or arranges for the shipping company to pick them up. This eliminates payroll—supervision and storage costs. (If he lacks space he can rent a mini-warehouse unit for his storage). In fact, he can do all the work at the mini-warehouse in the evenings after work.

Co-op Buying Services

Many retail stores use co-op buying services for their inventory. It gives them one source to deal with—gives them some economy of scale by increasing purchasing power—and saves money. There are drawbacks in not dealing directly with suppliers as you lose a source of future help and advice—but in lines where such help and advice is of limited value—the co-op services should be considered.

Public Relations Services

This is an area almost every small business overlooks as beyond their means. Yet, a smart operator will use P/R techniques at every opportunity. There is an old saying. "In order to do something, first you have to be something." If you will take some time to develop a personality for your business—and then spend a little money to impress that personality on the public—you will quickly rise above the competition. A firm, and its owner, whose name appears in the news is perceived as being successful—so, a little planning and a modest investment (far less than you spend on advertising) can get you in the news. I will go into this in some detail in the section on marketing—but you can get P/R work done for you at a reasonable cost. The best way is to hire a working newsperson, with contacts in all the media to moonlight as you P/R rep. The advantage of this is you are the only client. If you use a P/R agency you are one of many—and not the most important one. There are many ways to bread into the news—and it's far more powerful than advertising, and far more beneficial.

Commercial Finance Companies and Factors

Commercial finance companies are middlemen who take risks that banks won't take. They borrow funds from banks and lend those funds back to business firms to finance their accounts receivable on a revolving basis, or they finance leases, sometimes finance property acquisition, make inventory loans, etc. They charge higher rates than banks and have somewhat more restrictive terms. But, often they are the only source of funds for small businesses.

The revolving fund to finance receivables is the most common service. The business takes full responsibility for their credit operations—check credit set limits, etc. They repay the finance company as the bills are paid, and are obligated for all bad debts, etc.

The commercial finance company will also purchase installment contracts depending on the collateral and the general credit worthiness of the payer.

Factoring is a different method of financing receivables. A factor purchases the accounts—just like he would purchase a product. Title reverts to the factor—and the factor assumes the risk of collection. If the account doesn't pay—the pure factoring service is stuck (some factors want buy-back clauses for bad debts). The factor will do the credit checking, bookkeeping and collecting. The factor will remit collectibles as they come in—or arrange for partial payments when purchased and balance on collection. Rates run according to risk. For normal businesses they are 1% to 3% a month.

The professional commercial financing firms can be of great help in developing capital and operating fund sources for the small business. They can help arrange funds from primary sources—then pick up the balance needed themselves.

Each May, The American Banker publishes a list of the commercial finance companies arranged by size and financial strength. You can get a look at it from your banker, or get the current address of The American Banker from your local librarian. Get the per issue cost—and send for the issue.

Credit Reporting Agencies

If you are going to be giving credit—then you will want to use the reporting services of the credit agencies. The biggest and best known for business credit is Dun and Bradstreet. They issue credit listings in books, which you can get from a banker in most cases—and for a fee they will send you the credit report they have on hand about the company you are checking on. You can contact the nearest office (check yellow pages in nearest city) for costs.

Local credit agencies also maintain commercial and business credit files, and they will report to you for a fee. You can look them up in the yellow pages under credit reporting agencies. Also check with your major suppliers, they often have credit information of value about firms in the industry you serve.

Equipment Leasing Companies

Leasing firms are middlemen—either operating independently—or some major sellers of equipment have their own leasing companies. Dealers who offer leases on equipment are offering the services of a separate leasing company, who buys the account from them, pays them for the equipment, and then collects the payments from you. It is smart business to check out terms and conditions offered by leasing companies because costs do vary. Never sign an equipment lease till you have figured out total costs to you and had your lawyer look over the contract. Check out the leasing companies financial situation—some of them are shoestring operations. You can get information on leasing companies from The Association of Equipment Lessors—check with your librarian for current address.

The sale-leaseback. Sometimes you can arrange to sell your fixtures and equipment back to a leasing company for cash—then sign a lease to payback over a period of years. This is a good ploy when you are taking over a business to get some operating capital or the money to complete the acquisition. Leasing companies are always interested in anything that offers them cash flow, so you can contact them directly when considering purchase of equipment and not have to go through the dealer's leasing program.

Custom Manufactures (Job Shops)

These are manufacturers who make products for marketers or other manufacturers who need more capacity but don't want to invest in the necessary equipment and labor. They offer various ranges of service, from simply stamping out parts to helping with planning, engineering and marketing of a product. If you have a product ready to go into production—you can get a lot of information about costs and production methods by contacting various job shops and talking to them. I have discovered that it's a good move to talk to job shops before I have a model made of the product. They can give you some production short cut ideas—suggest materials that are less expensive—and sometimes make you a good deal on making the model themselves—or giving you the name of a model maker who will do a good job cheap. On a couple of occasions I have gotten my model made by the job shop at no cost because they were really interested in getting the business. You will find them listed in the trade magazines of your industry—and you can find most of them listed in Thomas Registry under product titles.

Maintenance

Contract maintenance is not sweeping the floors and cleaning the toilets—it is hiring a contractor to maintain the equipment in your plant. They offer a range of services such as supplying skilled help when needed to meet sudden production needs—periodic maintenance of all equipment—supplying a continuing maintenance staff in your plant—and total maintenance management services. They research your maintenance needs and supply the necessary help on a contract basis. It eliminates payroll costs for you and finding good people to do the work. It is not primarily a service for small business, but if you have a growing plant and skilled help problems, it's worth looking into. You can get information on the service and who renders it from The American Society of Mechanical

Engineers. Get the address from local librarian.

Manufacturers Representatives

Manufacturers Representatives are independent sales reps that handle products in a specific territory. They represent many firms, and have people out making sales calls in the territory on a permanent schedule. They sell on straight commission ranging from 2% to 40% depending on the product. There are about 30% of the reps who do professional jobs for their clients—about 50% who run hot and cold —and 20% who are worthless. Small business has some problems in dealing with reps—and must choose with some care. If you engage four or five reps who cover the entire country—and they develop a strong product sale for you—you have taken in four of five partners. They can get together and start dictating policy, commission rates, production schedules, etc. The small business operation using reps should use a lot of them—small firms like themselves—and retain control of their operations. You won't get the best of all worlds this way, but you will avoid more serious problems caused by having all your eggs in a few baskets.

Most reps will cream their territory for you—and none of them—even the best will ever get 100% of the potential out of any territory. Most of them understand that the manufacturer with a hot product line is going to have his own sales people in the high volume territores sooner or later because of the potential volume. For that reason, they will not invest more than results warrant in developing it.

Reps are a good way to get initial market penetration, and regional distribution of a product with a minimum of marketing cost. Do not hire reps by letter or phone. Go to see them—get a feel for their operation—and try to get one who will be as professional as possible in handling your product. Stay away from any that are handling competing products even if yours is in a different price range. They are not going to upset buyers trying to place your products where competing products are used—and commissions already assured. Pay more attention to territory knowledge and sales experience than product lines when choosing a rep. Those that know the territory and know selling will do the best job because they can move faster on your line.

Always Use A 30 Day Cancellation Clause

Don't lock yourself into a contract that takes six months to cancel. Always use the 30 day notice clause. If you can't get rid of a rep for six months—you've lost action in the territory for that length of time—he won't open new accounts and will simply cash in on any repeat orders customers give him over the phone or by mail. And remember the law of unlimited choice. "You cannot tell which is the real top and bottom of a marble by looking at it." In choosing reps you have to guess at first, and then change as needed—there is no way to pick all winners.

Advertising Agencies

My best advice is not to pick an advertising agency for a small business. Pick free-lancers and moonlighters to develop advertising plans and materials. You will get the same brains without paying for the front the agency maintains to attract clients. You will have basic control without some instant expert, who has never been in your business, telling you he is the expert and not to argue with him about advertising decisions.

I must confess that I have a totally negative impression of advertising agencies. In all the businesses I have been in and all the advertising I have done—I have never gotten an original idea, a workable, creative thought, out of an ad agency. I admit, I was always in small business—and I assume those who serve small business are not the cream of the crop. But, after having watched the efforts of the best of them on TV, in magazines and newpapers, I have decided that good concepts are as rare in advertising as they are in politics. By the same token, I have had a lot of very good material come from free-lancers who had only my problems to think about, who took the time to learn something about my business and my markets.

My advice is to stay away from agencies. If you spot someone with good ideas—hire him or her as a moonlighter to work for you. Most of the people with the ideas are low level help in agencies. Those with contacts and a line of logical sounding bullshit are the chiefs—so the good people are always willing to moonlight for a reasonable amount of money.

Freight Forwarders

If you are shipping on a regular basis in less than carload lots—then you can use the services of a freight forwarder. They put less than carload lots together and make their profit on the difference between carload and less than carload charges. They pick up and deliver, they handle documentation, expediting, etc. As a rule they handle shipments between major shipping points and some are specialists in certain types of products. They are worth investigating and you can get information on them from the Freight Forwarders Institute. Check with your librarian for the address or look in your nearest city yellow pages under freight forwarders.

Public Warehouses

If you don't need or want to maintain your own warehouse to store inventory, parts, etc., then there are public warehouses to do it for you. They invest the capital for the warehouse and charge you only the operating costs for handling your goods. It gives you any amount of space you need, when you need it, and they charge by the piece, by hundredweight or other unit basis per month. So, you pay only for space used or goods actually stored. You get an accurate reflection of your inventory from their receipts and stock records—and they will even supply, for a fee, branch office services such as supplying office and display space—clerical and telephone service—pooled car and consolidated shipment handling and C.O.D. operations. You can get information on these services from American Warehouseman's Association. Get the address from your local librarian.

Employment Agencies

There are two types. The specialized agency handles a specific industry. This agency can find good people for specific jobs in the industry. The general agency is of little value. They are interested in generating fees—not adequately filling positions and they usually represent people who are too lazy or too stupid to find their own jobs. While they will tell you how carefully they screen applicants—they seldom check any of them out—and will send any employer practically their entire inventory of job seekers in the hope the employer will hire one of them and create a fee.

For the grunt jobs, the semi-skilled office and plant jobs, you do much better placing your own ads in the paper (that's where the agency gets their applicants) and screening them yourself. For management, skilled or judgement jobs you are better off looking around, getting others to look for you, to find a person who can fill the job without using an agency or an ad. The specialized agency can help here—and if you will pay the fee, can often find a good one for you.

The slickest deal I ever heard about in finding a top quality employee was used by a Los Angeles executive. He needed a top notch secretary and couldn't find one in normal channels. So he had his wife call up the twenty largest firms in his area and get the names of the executive secretaries. She used the pretext she was sending out invitations to a party to honor National Secretaries' Week. He then had twenty letters typed up listing the benfits of the job he was offering—which included a lot more than most jobs offered—and sent a covering note to each of the twenty stating he felt they might know of a secretary who would be interested in his job and that any inquiries about it would be strictly confidential. Four of the secretaries who got the letter applied for the job.

Employment agencies are a court of last resort in finding good employees. Use other methods first, and only turn to them if all else fails. You will find them listed in your yellow pages.

Executive Recruiting Agencies (Head Hunters)

These are agents that find executive and highly skilled technical people for business firms. They often raid other firms to find the people for you. These are not cost effective for small businesses—they cost too much and the results are too uncertain. As a rule they want 20% or more of the first year's salary—plus expenses, which can be horrendous. It is not cost effective to pay $7,000 to hire a $30,000 executive.

When I want talent, I raid the big corporations. I run ads in the Wall Street Journal stating what I am looking for and the benefits of the position—and I always include the offer to make the executive the president or chief executive officer. This gets responses from middle level corporate managers who have no future in their present position and look on a small business as a genuine opportunity. I usually make them a sharecropper deal where they take over the company and run it—while I do nothing but share in the profits. It works!

Temporary Help Agencies

These are very beneficial to small businesses. Instead of having a payroll for jobs that are not really full time, you hire through temporary agencies, use the people as needed, and then let them go. The temp agency handles the payroll and charges you a flat fee. Many times the fee they charge is going to be less than your payroll costs.

These work for semi-skilled jobs—but not decision making jobs. Many times a small business operator can sit down and figure out the amount of work an office employee is actually doing—and then cost out the hiring of a temporary worker for a few days a month. You will find yourself saving a lot of money. The one thing you have to do is gang up the work so they can have several consecutive days of work in a row—temp agencies are not too interested in sending someone out for a single day.

Store Planners

If you are going to open a retail store, or have acquired one, you might consider the use of a professional store planner in that field to develop your store layout and fixtures, and even help you choose a new location. These planners have the experience and contacts to get you started on the right foot. You can locate them through your trade association—or contact The Retail Merchants Association. Get the address from your local librarian.

Used Equipment And Fixture Brokers and Dealers

When you are thinking of purchasing equipment or fixtures, always contact the used market first. Find out what used equipment and fixtures cost—and check them out to see if they fit the bill. You can save 50% or more up-front costs using used instead of new—and sometimes the used is better than the new, because it has more quality in it. When you learn the prices in the used market—it also gives you a better fix on new prices quoted to you. You will find them listed in your local yellow pages.

Computer Programmers

If you need a computer program—you can find programmers in your phone book. And, if you have a simple program and a micro-computer, you can contact local hobby groups and find an inexpensive programmer through them who can do the job for you. Ask around at computer stores about the hobby groups—and about any programmers they know about.

There is really no need to pay IBM prices for computer programs—they are a function of logic and there are lots of moonlighters out there who can write programs for you that will work. The key to getting what you want at the best price is to get a flat quote on a program that will be paid when it is up and running and doing what you want it to do for you. You will have to allow for more lead time to get the program but you can save 80% of the cost.

The one thing to instruct all your program writers to do is to make the program totally self-promoting. That is, the computer tells the operator what to do—when to do it—corrects mistakes and offers advice. This makes it possible to quickly train people to use the program—and eliminates a lot of the GIGO (garbage in—garbage out) that plagues the computer field.

Art And Signs

This is another field where you can get mugged by the people rendering the service. Since artwork's value is in the eye of the beholder, it has no going market price. Some artists consider themselves Rembrandts—others, just sign painters. Skill often has nothing to do with their perception.

This is also a field where talented moonlighters are everywhere. An ad in the paper can get you a choice of 50 to 100 eager artists willing to work cheap. Rather than employing a professional who must pay all the overhead expenses of operating the business, you can employ a free-lancer who works in his/her spare time and get as good or better results.

The key to getting what you want is to know what you want. Get a clear picture in your mind of your sign, logo or other form of artwork—and make a rough sketch of it. Then let the artist do the rest. Where I have left the concept up to the artist—I have mostly been disappointed in the results. These people are not highly creative for the most part—and they have to have a definite outline to work from. Given that, you can get all the artwork you need for very reasonable costs from free-lancing moonlighters.

Always set the fee at a flat per-job rate. Never pay by the hour. Some of them can whip out what you want in five minutes and some will take five days. Since they are doing the work in their own homes or offices—you can't be sure about the hours they work—so let them quote a finished job price—and then everybody understands the deal.

Detective and Security Agencies

If you have a problem, a thief or embezeller you suspect but can't catch, then a detective or security agency probably can. There are degrees of competence in this field as in all others. Some private eyes are well versed in business and industrial investigation—some are not. It's going to cost money, so you want one that can do the job right. The best way to find out who is good and who is bad is to ask around. Ask other business firms that have used them—your lawyer can find out if he doesn't already know. And, try to make friends with a cop—he can give you the rundown on all of them.

When you go to the agency have your facts marshalled. Use your lawyer to help you get them organized, and take him with you. You are putting yourself at some risk doing this if you are going to name names of suspects. Let your lawyer be your guide here. Tell the agency what you know and if you decide they are your best bet, follow their advice. When they catch the thieves, be prepared to take the necessary action. File a complaint with the police and appear in court. If you are not prepared to do that, then simply let the suspected people go, and see if the problem continues.

If you are carrying a bond on the suspects, then you may have to notify the bonding company about your actions—your lawyer can help you on this. If they are not bonded, one way you can let them know you suspect them is to bond them. It won't cover any losses up to the date of bonding, but will either cause them to stop what they were doing, or quit their jobs.

If you want guards or detectives to prevent shoplifting, these agencies can provide them as well. It is better to use an agency to hire guards as they are responsible for their actions and their payroll. They will also provide a guard if the regular man is ill or can't get to work, which would not be the case if you hired your own.

Don't pass off the need for these sevices too lightly. The American employee, in aggregate, is the biggest uncaught thief on earth. They steal more from their employers than all the burglars, armed robbers and shoplifters put together.

Janitorial Services

This is a service most small businesses can use profitably. Rather than hiring a janitor, or sort of jack of all trades as a payroll employee, the use of a janitorial service makes more sense. The exception is in stores where they can easily steal inventory. But, in offices and plants where they can't easily steal, hiring a good service with bonded employees is an outside service that pays for itself. They come in at night and do the cleanup, so business is not interrupted. Just make sure you get a service with a good reputation. You will find them in the yellow pages — but check around in the business community to get recommendations.

Clipping Services

One service a small business operator often overlooks as a valuable outside service is the clipping service. This is a service that will clip articles and ads from periodicals and newspapers published anywhere in the country and send them to the client. A small business seldom would need this service all year around, but using it on a spot basis can be very valuable. For example, you can have them clip ads for firms in your business in other communities at times of the year when you need some advertising ideas. You can have them look for articles on products or services you are interested in — and by having them do it for two weeks to a month at times of the year they would most likely appear — you can build a valuable file of ideas and information to help in your marketing and other planning.

The key to using the services is giving them specific instructions — key words to look for in articles or ads so that you get only what you want and do not pay for a lot of useless information. If you are asking for articles from newspapers in various areas of your region or the nation, don't have wire service stories come from more than one paper. Wire services are AP, UPI, etc. These are stories that are written by wire service reporters or picked up from other papers and sent out on the wire to all subscribing papers. Thus, a hot story would appear in every paper in the country and if you were paying a clipping service, they would clip the stories from every paper, and they would all be exactly the same. You pay per clipping, so eliminate all wire stories except from one paper.

I have used clipping services profitably many times, and any business operator who wants to beat the competition can get lots of help through clippings.

To Sum Up

The use of outside services is a method of reducing payroll costs and increasing efficiency of operations. While up front costs may seem to be higher, when you figure in the intangible costs of employees — lack of motivation to do a day's work — the lack of interest in a job other than for a paycheck — the absenteeism — the potentials for fraud and theft — the hassles and arguments — the petty bitching and complaining — and the real cost in terms of wages paid and productivity delivered, the outside service is sometimes a real bargain. The coming of automation and use of electronic communications is going to reduce employment numbers and increase needed skills to hold jobs. The small business operators are going to be turning more and more to specialized outside services to perform many of the functions now performed by employees. It's the way of the future.

TACTICS

She's not here—she's in fine stores everywhere.

One of the most difficult tasks of wealth building is family management. Trying to make the spouse understand what is going on—why you can't be home on time—why you can't buy the new carpet or car because you need the money for new business equipment.

You can't fight a two front battle and keep your cool in either place. You have got to get support and understanding for the struggle if you are going to make it.

You have two ways to go—

- Either bring the spouse in as a partner and run the deal with him or her as an active participant —or keep them totally and completely out of it.
- Don't talk about it at home:leave your business problems at the office, and your home problems at home.

If you can see that the deal will not work on the home front then either drop the business or drop the spouse. If you don't, you'll lose both.

CHAPTER 9
DEALING WITH EMPLOYEES

Dealing With Employees As A Small Business Manager

Here is an area where you have to become an expert. You have to understand people — what motivates them and how to use that knowledge to build an efficient and profitable operation. The average small business owner hires on the spot, gets burned often and keeps on going by trial and error till he gets a group of people he's comfortable working with, whether they are really efficient and profitable to employ or not.

Rule 1 — Don't Be A Buddy To Employees

You can be friendly, interested in their welfare as far as the job goes without being a personal friend. If you try to be a friend to more than one person in an organization you are going to run into a situation, sooner or later, where you are going to have to decide something that will be good for one and bad for the other. Promoting one person to be a manager is an example. If you have three employees, and all are your friends, two of them will be upset at your choice, and you'll only have one friend and two hostile people. If you are a manager, then people who don't get a promotion may not like it, but won't look on it as being betrayed by a friend. There is a big difference. The second problem with a friend is that he is one you can goof off on—you can take advantage of from time to time. Your friend won't get upset, right? Familiarity may not breed contempt, but it does breed indifference. The employee who is a friend of the employer sees the friendship as a greater bond than the business relationship and will operate on that premise. The friend will assume you understand they owe their first duty to their family, and so they will operate on that premise. Time will be taken off to take care of personal matters because friends understand that. But employees also understand bosses don't give a damn about their family problems, and if they have to solve them they better do it on their own time, or else.

A small business operator comes in much closer contact with employees than professional managers of larger companies do, and they can't act like marine boot camp instructors and get away with it. But, they can keep a psychological distance from employees, and never let them forget the true nature of the relationship. As a manager you are after respect — you don't give a damn whether they like you or not. If you have respect, you can get the work done. If you don't — it will not get done, and it's that simple.

The Carrot and the Stick

The carrot and the stick theory of motivation has limited value. The idea of holding out a reward which the employee will chase works up to a point. Just like a mule, when they are not hungry a carrot is of no interest. Once an employee ceases to be hungry for more money and more advancement — they do not respond to offers of more — they have reached their rut, and are happy to stay there. If you try to apply the stick to get them out, you simply upset them and they either rise to the level of their incompetence and are unhappy, or they quit.

The point is that employees are like buckets, they can only be filled up so far, then they won't hold anymore. The idea is let them find their rut, and if they are happy and doing a good job, you won't need anymore inducements, or kicks in the ass — they will produce at the level they choose until they quit, retire or die. This is the natural order of things and the good manager recognizes it.

The POTB Instead Of KITA

I am a devotee to the POTB system of motivation. The Pat On The Butt instead of the Kick In The Ass. The POTB is nothing more than recognizing the employee's importance to the business and reminding them often of the nice job they are doing and how much you appreciate it. This is ego income and it goes a long way in replacing cash income in small business. Many small business operators think the paycheck is all the applause the employee deserves, and when they goof up, a kick in the ass is deserved as part of the package. This doesn't work.

Remember, they have pride, and a desire to be recognized as a worthwhile person. It doesn't cost you much to tell them you appreciate their effort, to remember their birthday with a card and a special check, to find out when their anniversary comes around and send some flowers and a note thanking both the employee and the spouse for the good work being done. When they have put out a special effort to get something done, a personal thank you is really appreciated. This makes the employee loyal, it makes them respect you for respecting them. And, I'll tell you something else, you can work the ass off of them on occasion or ask them to work at inconvenient times and they will do it because they know you appreciate it.

Don't Get Involved In Their Personal Affairs

If they come to you for advice on personal matters — you pass. You are not a parent or a priest, and if you stick your nose in, you can only get it bloodied. Keep all personal advice and commitment out of the relationship. The exception is when they might need an advance on their pay or arrangement for special funds for an emergency. You can treat this as a loan, and help them out — but only as a business proposition — no involvement in the affair itself. And make it very clear, that such advances or loans are a one time thing, not company policy—and the second time they ask, you say no.

The Chewing Out Process

You will have to chew someone out from time to time. This requires some different approaches. First, of all never do it when you are pissed off at them. Do it on reflection of what they did, and what you intend to do about it. You have to handle each person differently. First, do not humiliate anyone. Don't chew anyone out in the presence of other employees, and don't get involved in personal insults like—"that is the stupidest thing I've ever seen anyone do" or, "a four-year-old kid would have had more sense than that," etc. Bring them into the office or take them out for coffee away from the others and sit down and explain the cost of what they did. Next, suggest that they must have not been thinking clearly when it happened. And, finally tell them what your course of action is going to be regarding it. Do it all in a calm voice. If you can throw in a little acting, make it seem you were personally hurt by what they did, not by saying so, but by expression and tone of voice. This puts them in a position of wanting to make good or do better, and they will remember the incident longer because you treated them in an adult and responsible manner.

Your Emotional Stability

A second problem the small business owner has is his or her own range of emotions. Anyone who has ever operated a small business knows it's a roller coaster ride. On Monday, things are the pits. You are seriously thinking about shutting the damn thing down and getting a job. Nothing goes right and you are angry and perhaps frightened about the business prospects. On Wednesday, the big order came in, and you are in hog heaven. You can visualize the business becoming a giant—nothing will stop—everything is going you way, etc. These are your feelings, your emotions, and you have to keep them entirely to yourself. Do your screaming and your smiling in your office when you are alone. All the employees see is the same face, with the same voice, calm and collected, everyday, no matter how good or bad things are going. If you start yelling and screaming on Monday, telling everyone the whole damn thing is a bust, and are smiling and slapping everyone on the back on Wednesday and telling them how much money everyone is going to make, you are creating nervous and upset workers. They don't understand your problems — your ups and downs — and if they have to share them, they don't like it. You drive good people out and poor people crazy with your yo-yoing emotions.

The Fine Art of Firing

Some small business operators find it almost like cutting their own throats to fire someone. They hate the thought of it, and they delay it as long as possible. This usually stems from having been an employee and knowing the trauma of being fired themselves.

There are two approaches to firing — the coward's way and the professional manager's way. The coward's way, is one I used for a long time. I would start setting up the person I was going to fire for about two weeks. I would let them know that the business was in trouble, and that I was trying very hard to get a bank loan to tide it over. I would look gloomy and wonder what I would do if the business went under. The target would get the message that all was not well, and when I called him or her in to fire them, I blamed it all on my poor management and told them how sorry I was, but I didn't have any choice. This made it easier for them, they had been prepared to some extent, and they could go out and tell the world they were not fired because they were incompetent, but because the business was badly managed. It worked well, and I never had any serious problems with the people I let go.

The professional manager's method is to call them in, tell them the truth and fire them. This is a lot harder on the employee, but a lot easier on the manager. The manager simply states his case, and tells them to leave. This is the method I use now, because it's easier on me — I don't have to worry about setting them up and I've now reached the point where letting someone go is no different than hiring them —

it's a business decision that I have to make. I don't insult the people I dismiss, I simply explain that they have not worked out in the position and that it is necessary to find a replacement. If there is a discussion of what they did wrong, I tell them and if they want to argue about it, I tell them I don't have time to discuss it any further. In the long run it's better for the person who is fired to know why, than to con them. If they know why, they may do better on their next job. If they don't know why, they will repeat the same mistakes again. But, I no longer am interested in trying to justify it in my own mind. I just do it, and that's it. The sooner you reach that point, the better off you will be.

The Hiring Process

Professional hiring is a sequence — first you locate the person wanting the job — next, you get the person to submit a resume of their educational and job related experience — then, you interview them the first time—check out references and credit rating—you interview them again and make your decision.

I use resumes instead of job application forms. First, it's quicker. You get the resume from the applicant and have a look at how they present themselves. Secondly, it avoids this fair employment practices act crap about what you can or can't put on an employment application. No one can come back and sue you because the application asked something some bureaucrat considers sexist, racist or might possibly tell you if your applicant is a mass murderer. The resume tells me all I need to know to decide if I want to interview the person.

I interview at lunch or over coffee in a restaurant, never in my office. I want the person to be at ease, not on strange turf. I make some notes from the resume as a basis for the interview and talk to them about their past experience, their family situation, their ambitions and their reasons for wanting the job. It's all very friendly and easy going. This gives me an impression of the person, and their talents. It's purely subjective, but it works.

If I decide that I want to pursue the matter further, I check out their resume references, and always get a credit check — which tells more about their character than any reference will. I use a store I own a part interest in to get the credit reference so it can't be traced to me if it's illegal under fair employment practices. If the checks come out as showing the person is reasonably responsible, I invite them to come to my office for a second interview.

The second interview is used largely to determine if my first impression was correct. I take them on a tour of the premises, and then we talk about salary and the job. At this point I look for questions — questions about the job itself or my company. If all I hear is how much do I get, when do I get a vacation and what are the fringe benefits, I'm no longer interested. But, if they inquire about the job — or want to know more about the company, or are interested in something they saw on the tour, etc., then I'm interested in them. What I look for here is some initiative on their part about the job or company and its future prospects for them. This tells me I have a person who can be a good employee. Again, it's largely subjective judgment, but it does work. I don't get too many losers on the payroll.

If I decide to offer them the job, I do it then, and tell them to think it over — and call me back the next day with their decision. I insist they take the time to consider the offer, as it is the final test of their wanting the job — I have a tendency to sell people on things because I am a salesman, and I don't want people I've sold, I want people who sold themselves—so I give them time to consider it.

That's my hiring process, and it works out well. If you use it, you will find that you will eliminate 75% of the applicants on resume reading — 10% on first interview, and 10% on checking references and that leaves about 5% who will make it to the final interview.

The Art Of Reading A Resume

You can tell a lot about a person from their resume. the key is not so much what information it contains, but the order and method in which the information is presented. First, look for the place the most information was provided. This could be job experience, education, hobbies or outside interests, career objectives, etc. This is the motivation point, where the applicant has the most pride and interest. If it is about some outside interest—a hobby, a civic program, a church related activity—that seems to take up a good deal of time and interest, that's a warning signal. The job may be the hobby and the hobby the main interest in life, all consuming interest in something that makes everything else seem unimportant. A fanatic can also make a hell of a lot of trouble.

If the applicant stresses education—dwells on accomplishments in school—then you have another problem. You have the potential of an over-educated person who is always examining alternatives, always trying to see where the other person is coming from, and you seldom get decisive action. You can also wind up with a turkey educated beyond his or her intelligence who has answers to everything, including how you should reorganize your business.

If there is stress on jobs that are higher up the ladder than the one being applied for, you have two problems to consider. First, that the person is looking for a stop-gap income until an offer more in line with his or her abilities comes along. Or, you've got someone with some personal problems (booze—broads—debts—burn out) that will cause problems at once. Keep in mind you are not running a social rehabilitation agency, you are running a business to make a buck. Folks with problems usually don't carry their weight no matter how good they used to be.

If there is stress on career goals that go beyond the job you offer, then you've got a trainee who will move along at the first opportunity. If you have room for advancement in your company, then you might have a potential candidate for greater responsibility. The thing to keep in mind is that you are not interested in training people for better things.

Watch out for the guy who has included a bankrupt company in his resume to cover five or more years of work time. This time may have been spent in the slammer—or is meant to cover a string of jobs from which no good references would come. The best way to hit him on this one is get his home address during that time and have a credit check run on it—if you are considering hiring him.

The first thing to do with resumes is make three piles out of them. First, put together those with some direct experience in the type of job you must fill. Second, collate those with related experience, and, third, those with no experience. Go through the no experience first, and see if there is anyone there that might be hireable. Put those aside and the rest are nixies. Then, in pile two, related experience, go through the resumes and check ages, (they don't have to give them by law, but you can check from school graduation dates on the resumes and get the age within a year), family status, etc., and set aside those that may be considered, and toss the rest on the nixies pile. Then, go through the experienced people for prime prospects—almost prime—and little chance ratings. This should leave you with a half dozen to fifteen choices if you got a lot of resumes.

Begin to interview them in the order of your rating, best one first, etc. I would interview at least enough of them to have a second interview with three choices. Then you can decide among them.

The Problem With Women In Small Business

It may be sexist, but it's also true that there are some problems with hiring women. First of all there are the good looking ones and the ugly ones. The key to success here is to have them all the same—all good looking or all ugly. If there is a good looking one working with three or four uglies—then you've got problems with the uglies. The good looking one, through no fault of her own will attract attention—get treated better by customers, tradesmen and salesmen—and get the shaft from the uglies. It may not be right—it may be Chauvanist—but it happens. So, the advice is to group them in one or the other category.

The Racial Problem

This can also cause some bad news you don't need. There are two types of minority employees—very good and very bad. There seldom seems to be a middle ground. You either get a bright, hard working person who wants to make it, and is willing to put up with a certain amount of racial prejudice bullshit to do it without getting pushed out of shape—or you get the one with the chip on their shoulder, who defies everyone—and causes nothing but problems. If you use the interview technique I suggest you will spot the hardnosed type quickly. In my thirty years of hiring employees the two best and the two worst I ever had were all minority workers.

Dealing With Fringe Benefits

My concept is to pay cash—and let them buy their own benefits. The idea of having some medical or other benefit that is paid by me, is something I don't like. I have made deals on occasion where employees could buy their own on a group discount plan—but they paid for it, I didn't. I work for money—all I can get—and I pay my people all the money I can afford. They know this, and the subject of benefits does not come up.

Dealing With Unions

I have always run businesses too small to have a union problem. I have no real idea of how I would deal with them. Since I am never in love with any business, and can start or buy one anytime I want it, I suspect my reaction to a union organizing my workers would be to close the business and let the employees find other jobs. People who have had experience say that small business has very little chance to buck the unions—and the best course is to get employees involved in the business far enough so a union would not appeal to them. It would be like taking money out of their own pockets. There are some steps you can take if a union does show up. The first thing is don't talk to anyone saying he has bargaining rights. Don't allow union people in your office or plant. don't accept any sign up cards from employees calling for a union. And, hire a lawyer who knows how to deal with unions. He'll tell you how to fight and what you can and can't say to employees, and then go the course through an election or whatever.

Compensating Employees

I like a share the wealth plan. I get the wealth and they get the shares. I like the method of turning workers into sharecroppers, so they are tied to company profits and are motivated to increase them. I have used a program where I sold shares in the business to employees at a price below book value as the business progressed. I got an income from my shares and they gradually were getting control over the business. It was a legal salary kickback scheme which gave me the wealth and them the shares. This is called ESOP—more about it later.

As to salaries, I pay the going rate, and always tie bonuses to them based on achieving stated goals. This is the carrot that moves the mule. As I said before, I do not like fringe benefits other than an interest in the business. That will produce more bottom line profits. It has been my experience that small business employees are turned on by money, not benefits, and if they are getting enough money, and a chance to make more—they are happy. This kind of payroll arrangement also makes it easier to steal good workers from other businesses, not throw salary checks around like manhole covers.

TACTICS

The best things in life are free—while they last.

In business you have a powerful promotion program that does not cost you a dime—that will do you more good in the long run than all the advertising you ever do—and everyone benefits by using it. Here is what you can offer your customers:

- A friendly smile
- A friendly greeting
- A helpful attitude
- A thank you

This is small business' greatest weapon against big business—making the customer feel important—wanted and appreciated. It costs nothing, and puts tens of thousands of dollars on the bottom line, over the years, that would not otherwise be there. There is steady decline in common courtesy and a friendly attitude in business today. The entrepreneur who makes a real effort to put it in his business starts with a big competitive edge.

Sort of reminds me of the story of the young Indian who wanted to be chief. He went to the tribe wise man and asked what he must do. The wise man told him he must wrestle a grizzly bear—catch a cougar by the tail—walk through fire—swim the raging river and climb the great mountain. The young brave thought about that and said, "Whatever happened to good looks, a charming smile and a nice personality?"

CHAPTER 10
COMMUNICATIONS

Everyone lies — but it doesn't make any difference because no one listens!

The art of communication in an organization is perhaps the key to successful management. You have to remember that people do not hear what you say, but often hear what they think you say. There is a big difference, let me give you an example. The sales manager was sitting with a customer at his desk trying to work out a deal on a sale, and he got stumped on the discount. So he flipped the intercom to his secretary and said, "Miss Jones if I gave you eight thousand dollars with an eighteen percent discount, how much would you take off?" She replied quickly, "Everything but my lipstick." The problem with communications is that you have to give the person you are communicating with the entire picture before you can request a response, or expect them to understand what you mean.

We have the situation where people are talking to each other but each are thinking about different things, so a common subject means different things to different people.

For example, the bridegroom and his bride showed up at the desk of the Honeymooon Hotel. They registered, and the bridegroom asked the desk clerk how much it would cost. The desk clerk replied, "Five dollars apiece." The bridegroom thought for a minute, looked at the bride and handed the desk clerk fifty dollars. This was an example of two people thinking about two different things and one of them coming to the wrong conclusion.

Means And Content Are Communication Keys

So when you are thinking about communicating with employees or a manager in an organization you have to be careful about your means of communication and the content of the communication.

The most effective means of communication is one on one, the decision maker to the doer. The decision maker tells the doer what needs to be done, gets a response from the doer about the method, time, or other aspect of that decision. Make sure that the doer understands it.

The Meeting—A Poor Method Of Communicating

The least effective means of communicating is at the meeting where you have one on fifty or more in a group. Here you have fifty people and one speaker. There is no way that that speaker can get his message across in the same way with the same results to all fifty people in the meeting. Their minds simply are not on the subject and there is a tendency for people to begin to think of other things that are far more important to them than the subject of the meeting. Part of the problem is that our mind can handle speech at about 400 words a minute, while we can only speak at about 275 words a minute. Therefore, there is a gap between what is said and what is understood. People in an audience have thinking time for presumptions, or let their minds wander to other things. Many times they will begin to speculate on possible gain or loss to them on what is being said, rather than concentrating on the subject itself. Other people in the audience will be so busy writing down the facts and figures or other pertinent information that they have no real comprehension of how they fit together. Or, people can get hooked on one point and start tossing it around in their minds without really hearing anything else.

So there are many ways that an audience can avoid hearing what is being said and come out of the meeting more confused than when they went in.

The Key To Solving This

Make meetings on a single subject; break the communication down into specific points. After you have made a point, ask questions of members of the audience. If you ask for questions and no one asks you any, then ask somebody in the audience the questions and get the point you were trying to make firmly established in their minds. This tends to focus the listener's mind on the specific point, it solves any misconceptions that they might have about the point. If it's repeated two or three times, it seems to stick in their memory long enough for them to begin to implement it.

You have to remember that we all suffer from mental laziness. Something like the guy who bought the book "How to Conquer Laziness" and then had his wife read it to him. To be a successful communicator you simply have to accept the fact that this mental laziness exists, people do not listen to what you say and you have to do what is necessary to overcome that.

Obviously it is easier to do this in a one on one situation than it is in a group. But if group meetings are necessary because of time, then plan what you are going to say very carefully. Keep it as short as possible and make each point in some dramatic fashion. Then, take questions on it and repeat it several times so that it will be remembered.

Somebody who loves statistics once worked out the odds on communication with people and the kind of results that you would get. For example, you could tell four department heads at one meeting that you want a specific report at a given time period. You make this point very firmly with them and the odds on having all four of the reports on the time are scaled on a ratio of ten to one. That means it's ten to one that you will get one report on time, it's even money that you will get two reports on time, it's ten to one against you that you will get three reports on time, and it's one hundred to one that you will get four reports on time.

COMMUNICATIONS 10—4

Learn To Be Brief

It's important to remember that as the organizer and the manager, your job is not to make speeches, but to communicate instructions. And instructions can be communicated in very short sentences. So get into the habit of getting your point across in briet understandable terms and you will have a lot less difficulty with communication problems.

Written Communications

The memo is the life blood of the organization. The assumption is that the memo replaces personal contact and makes things work better. Written communications of this kind have value because they put the same words in front of each recipient. But, in most organizations they have a tendency to become greatly overdone. And the very fact that they begin to flood across the employee's desk reduces the value of each one proportionately. Memos should only be used where you have to reach a lot of people at the same time with a message, and it is not possible to get them together all at once or meet them one at a time.

The key to getting the point across in written communications is to make it short — concise — and issue it in the precise order it needs to be followed. Something like this.

Memo To: All Department Heads
Subject: Vacation Planning

1. List all employee vacation dates by person's name and job.
2. Note any jobs requiring temporary replacements.
3. If there are requests for exception to company vacation policies, attach a separate sheet with: 1) Name of Employee, 2) Job of Employee, 3) Nature of the Request, 4) Reason for the Request, 5) Your Decision on the Request.
4. All department vacation lists are to be completed and in the personnel office by April 1 — no exceptions!

5. Call personnel office and confirm you have received this memo, understand it and carry it out by the end of business on March 29.

That memo does two things—gives instruction—and requests two-way communication. The recipient must confirm that it has been received, understood and will be implemented.

Meetings

Meetings should be held for specific purposes, be short, and above all be productive. To have a productive meeting here are the points to consider:

1. Fix the purpose.
2. Determine the agenda.
3. Fix a start and stop time.
4. One person will control it.
5. If it is important, record it.
6. Transcribe important points and get them back to the participants.
7. Have a follow-up system to determine the action taken.

If your company has daily or weekly meetings of sales, production or other personnel, these points should be stressed to those persons in the meetings and a constant monitoring should be done to see whether the meetings are actually serving any useful purpose, or simply wasting people's time. It is essential for managers to meet on some kind of regular basis so that everybody understands what everybody else is doing and thinking. But, too often, the meetings are held simply because they are scheduled, and nothing really productive comes out of them. The smart manager will have meetings when they are needed, and eliminate them when they are not.

Open Your Lines Of Communication

Communication is a two-way street in an organization. You have the option of communicating with your managers and employees in any way you choose, and you should implement a policy where they have the option to communicate with you when they need to. You can set up specific appointments for employees to come in and talk to you one on one; you can have them in groups in regular sessions from time to time to discuss grievances or other problems; or you can use a suggestion box.

It is important that you set up a method whereby employees can freely communicate with you regarding their jobs, their problems at their work, or any other subject concerning business.

Communicating is vital to small business because you have both an economic unit and a social unit. People feel like they're a member of the family and when they've got something on their chest they like to get it off. By allowing them to do so in a friendly and informal manner, you will solve a lot of problems with the level of productivity you get out of your managers and employees. Give some attention to the art of communicating and pay particular attention to the problem of over communicating. Don't tell them more than they need or want to know, and only communicate with them when there is a specific and valid reason to do so regarding company operations or policies.

Remember the key to successful communication in an organization is to make sure that there is ample opportunity to get communications from the bottom up rather than always from the top down. It encourages communications between managers and employees as well as from managers to you or employees to you. One of the smartest businessmen I knew always gave employees memo pads with their names printed on them so that they could issue memos to other employees about problems that they were having with the operations of their particular job. He made it a rule that every such memo issued by any employee to a manager or to himself had to be answered. This gave the employees the feeling that they had some power and authority over their own welfare in the organization. Surprisingly, memos were used sparingly, and got good results when they were used.

Listening!

The art of communication is a two-way street. When you speak you expect to be understood, and when you listen the other person expects you to understand them. The unfortunate part of communication is that very few people listen to what the other person is saying. They hear words, and accept meanings to those words without focusing their full attention on what is being said. When somebody is speaking to you and you want to be sure that you hear precisely what they are saying, then you have to focus your full attention not only on the words that they say but the tone of voice that they use. Try to read between the lines as to the real meaning of what is being said. One of the best ways to keep your attention focused is to use the systems that attorneys use. As the individual speaks you make notes of the important points that they are making, and if you do not fully understand the point they have made, then ask questions. The way to be sure that the communication is received and understood is to get points clarified so that you are sure that you understand completely what the individual is trying to tell you. This also gives you a reference point if you need to recall a conversation and make a later decision.

To give you an example, let's assume that the sales manager is in your office to explain why sales were off twenty percent in the past month. At the top of your pad you put Dick Johnson, sales manager then underneath, the subject of communication—why sales fell twenty percent last month. As the sales manager launches into his explanation, the first point he makes is that a large account was going into receivership and all business from that source was lost. The second point that he made was that two salesmen were out on vacation. The third point that he made was that the new territory just opened didn't produce as planned. Next, sales were up fifteen percent the previous month because of a sales contest which reduced the number of sales the following month. And, finally he stated that the economy is slowing down.

As you listen to his explanation and perhaps ask a question or two for clarification you can then determine whether he is making a valid explanation or he is simply making excuses. For example you can determine what percentage of total business a large account that went into receivership represented; learn why two salesmen out of a staff of five would be allowed to be on vacation at the same time. Determine exactly what the problem is in the new territory. Ask the sales manager to explain why you pay sales bonuses in one month forcing the salesmen to press the companies for business in order to make bonuses, and the result is that there is a drastic fall in the second month's sales. What is the point of holding a contest? And, if the economy is slowing down, shouldn't there be some additional sales push developed to make-up for lost business?

By listening carefully to the sales manager, making notes of what he said, you can come to some definite conclusions about his performance.

Use The System With All Important Communications

Every time that you have such a conversation with someone in person, or over the telephone, if you will use this technique of focusing your full attention on what they are saying by taking notes — and asking questions to clarify a point — you then have the benefit of proper communication.

This is very effective in dealing with problems in an organization. A customer calls with a complaint, and you note carefully the extent of the complaint, what the customer wants to have done to rectify the problem, who the customer considers responsible for the problem and any other information that is pertinent. Then you call the individual responsible in the organization and get their side of the story regarding the problem—taking notes of the points they make. And by comparing the two note sheets you have made, you quickly make a decision as to the nature of the problem and the probable solution to it.

Get The Whole Story

The one thing to train yourself to do is to not make any decision, or come to conclusions about what is being said, until you have heard the full story. By simply keeping an open mind and making sure that you understand what they are telling you, you will be able to make a proper decision when you have all the information and are sure that you properly understand it.

This art is extremely important in managing an organization. Since proper decisions can only be made on the basis of having all the available facts at hand, this method assures you of having those facts and being able to make the proper decision.

I think the best comment I ever heard about conversation, and speaking without thinking, comes from an old Vermont proverb that goes, "Never speak unless you can improve the silence."

The Telephone

The telephone is largely replacing the letter as the traditional means of business communication. Letters are one way communications that take days or weeks to complete a circuit. A letter is now very expensive for a business to produce, and has the added disadvantage in times of fast moving technology, high inflation, of commiting the business to a position in writing which may be necessary to change before the letter even arrives.

When you call a supplier, customer, or other business contact on the telephone you are in a position of being able to inject your own personality through the inflection in your voice, and to sound them out in advance of making or accepting offers. It enables you to overcome obstacles by answering questions, to change your attack if you discover your present approach is not working, and insures you of being able to discuss any differences with the individual on the spot. With the cost of postage, secretarial time, making copies, etc. It is probably cheaper now to make a telephone call than it is to produce a letter.

So more and more companies are beginning to rely on the telephone as their primary means of communication—because it is a two-way communication.

Telephone Hardware

It is important for the professional manager to understand what is available in the way of telephone communication — in other means of moving communication over the telephone lines — in order to manage most effectively. There is a constant development of new technology in the field of telephone communication, and the professional manager would be wise to stay abreast of it.

One of the first steps you can take to discover just what is available, is to contact your local telephone business office and have them send you the information on their various systems — PBX systems, internal phone systems, external phone services, etc. We are in fast moving technology; new services and hardware are being added almost every month.

You can have an internal telephone system with the phones on the desks of your employees. One or more of the buttons on the phone are for intercom use and not for outside calling. This system enables an employee to put a caller on hold and contact another employee or department to get some information and get back to the customer on the phone with the information at once.

External communications are developing at a rapid pace. The so-called tie-lines, which are networks put together to enable businesses to make long distance calls at a considerably reduced rate over what they pay the bell system, are becoming much more popular as long distance rates increase.

WATS Lines

The WATS (Wide Area Telephone Service) line is a service provided by the bell system that enables a business to call out anywhere in the country for a specified hourly fee (considerably less than normal long distance charges) — or have customers call them on incoming WATS lines at the same reduced costs. This enables a business operating anywhere in the country to contact any other business in the country by telephone for fees probably less than it would cost them to call one hundred miles from their own office at a long distance rate.

There are new devices called WATS Extenders that enable WATS subscribers to tie into WATS lines from outside phones. Thus, a businessman might use such a device to enable him to call from his own home on his own company's WATS lines.

Call Diverters And Answering Machines

There are also call diverters that combine telephone answering and automatic dialing to forward your calls from a business phone to a home phone after hours. And call diverters can also tie in with a paging system so the person can be reached any place in a metropolitan area to be notified of the call. Telephone answering machines replace telephone answering services in some small businesses. There have been many improvements in these units since they first came out. You can break in to hear who is calling before you have to answer the phone — you can change the prerecorded message any time you wish — you can call from an outside phone and using a electronic coding device get the recorded calls released to you — and commercial units can have virtually open-ended recorded times for callers' messages so they can operate as a device not only to answer day-to-day business calls, but also they could have a tape recorded message and take orders.

Other Communication Devices

There are units called call sequencers which deliver calls to live answerers in the order in which the calls come in. You've run into these when you've called an airline for reservations and have been put on hold until someone is available.

Automatic dialing machines are now being offered in many varieties—some even by the phone company itself—which enable you to punch one button and get a phone number that you call often. These are great time-savers and avoid calling wrong numbers.

Elapsed time counters alert those answering phones to the length a caller has been on hold. These are primarily for order desks where you don't want to keep someone waiting too long.

Then we have telephone management systems that monitor telephone usage and that provide information on service levels, take incoming calls and so forth. These systems are especially useful for situations in which there are large volumes of incoming calls — telephone order desks as an example. There are even units that provide management with printout summaries of the telephone usage.

You have the data phone system that can be used for data transmission between offices and plants of material on computers — to place orders — or transmit high-speed electronic information in many forms.

The telephone is becoming the key communications instrument in business, and every professional manager should be up-to-date and fully aware of the various options available to him through telephone technology.

Telephone Manners

One of the key training programs that all professional managers should institute is teaching telephone manners to employees. Nothing is more frustrating, irritating and conducive to losing business than ill-mannered or untrained people taking telephone calls from customers, suppliers and others interested in talking to somebody in the firm.

Perhaps the most irritating answer to a telephone caller is the response—"This is the XYZ Company, will you hold please." If this is happening on any kind of a regular basis in your company, you need more people.

A second problem that I often see occurs in retail establishments. A customer is standing at the counter, goods in hand, ready to pay, the telephone rings and the sales clerk turns around and holds a five or ten minute discussion with somebody on the telephone while the paying customers are stacked up behind the counter waiting. Any retailer who wants to retain customers should instruct all clerks that the waiting is being done by the person on the telephone, and never by the people standing by the counter waiting to buy merchandise.

The Bell System has some good booklets and information on proper telephone procedures and techniques that every professional manager should have and study carefully.

And every professional manager should call his own company from time-to-time, and make some difficult or unreasonable request and find out how his company is responding to them. This is one of the quickest ways to detect employee indolence, arrogance, and potential problems in the company.

TACTICS

Before you burn your bridges—stash a raft.

Anytime you are considering a decision that involves a degree of risk—and you are moving into territory you are not familiar with—think about some loopholes—something you can crawl back through if things go badly.

Use a loophole specialist—a lawyer who can put them in where they might not be obvious to the other party.

If it's an investment—get a time option—a clause that will let you out for a set price—a non-responsibility clause for worst case eventualities.

If it's goods or inventory—look for a fall back source who will take them off your hands if you can't move them, or, a time clause that allows returns of unsold goods.

If it's a marriage—use a pre-nuptials contract to retain your assets if it goes sour.

Always try to have a back door in every deal—you will need it sooner or later. A little foresight can be a hell of a lot better than a lot of hindsight.

STRATEGY

Know what you want from a business!

Precisely!

In terms of:

- Income
- Total Assets
- How Soon

There is an old saying—"If you don't know where you are going any road will take you there."

Set your goals first!

Choose your first road—the business you are in or going in.

Take the first step—goal setting.

Make a list of what you want in:

- Personal possessions in the order of acquisition. House—cars—furnishings—amenities—toys (the airplane—boat—hobby equipment)—travel —and the prices you are willing to pay.
- Financial holdings in dollar amounts. Cash in personal accounts—stock portfolio—real estate—life insurance—annuities, etc. Now begin!

CHAPTER 11
PHILOSOPHY

The Philosophy Of A Business Organization

If you can develop an understanding of what being in business means, your ability to develop an organization that will become a profitable enterprise is greatly enhanced.

There are only two functions that a business performs. It produces and it sells. That's all! It is not an institution that is serving the public — creating jobs — making magnificent products — paying taxes — supporting charities or civic organizations, etc. All those are supplementary to the business purpose of producing and selling. So if you keep in mind, when developing your organization, that the keys are production and selling, nothing else, you have the key to successful development.

Evaluating the Jobs in the Organization

As you are developing your organizational plans, it is going to help you a great deal to evaluate the jobs in your organization, not by what the employees do, but by the results they get. For example:

1. Salesmen do not sell—they fill needs.
2. Accountants don't keep books—they keep score.
3. Machine operators don't make parts—they produce inventory.
4. Purchasing agents don't buy products—they solve problems.
5. Quality control people don't create quality—they remove defects.
6. You don't run a business—you manage capital and labor.

If you will judge each job by the results they get, not by the function they perform, they become more important. If you talk to your employees in terms of results and not in terms of function, they will have more motivation to do good jobs.

So the objective goals of the manager of any organization is to develop maximum production, maximum sales, which equal maximum profits. All other functions merely support the attainment of those two objectives.

Summary

An organization puts you in a position to go from a small business that makes a living, to a growing enterprise that builds wealth.

Organizations are developed and operated by professionals. The concept is to develop professional management so you are free to do other things. Rather than be involved in the day-to-day nuts and bolts operations of a business, you can either develop plans for bigger and better things for that business, or turn your attention toward building personal wealth through investment or acquiring other businesses.

If you go through the process of putting an organization together on paper, setting goals, and developing an organizational philosophy for dealing with employees, customers, and others, you will have a much better understanding of the business and a clearer look at its ultimate potential.

Take the time to write policies for your organization. Remember, a policy is the organization's stability—they provide guides for people with diverse personalities and backgrounds to handle uniform organizational response. It also relieves management from making decisions that are not necessary. And finally, by developing organizations and learning how to manage them you have developed a skill that is transferrable. You will notice that the chief executive will go from the management of a broadcasting company to the management of an appliance manufacturing company. The reason this is possible is that he is a professional manager, keeping in mind that the two goals of business organizations are production and sales, the abilities to organize and develop the functions that produce maximum production and maximum sales can be applied to any business organization.

So developing yourself as a professional manager opens up the doors of opportunity to you in virtually every line of business in this country. You will have developed a skill that pays the highest dollar per hour in the business world.

In these dealings you have a hodge-podge of relationships both good and bad being developed that are beyond the control of management. So it is necessary for you to develop an organizational relationship philosophy that presents a unified face to each segment of those the organization will have to deal with.

There is no need to write down long tedious reports or develop specific policies on the subject of relationships. All that is important is that you develop the philosophy you want your organization to use in its relationships, and you pass that philosophy along to your managers and your employees. In each case the philosophy should represent the best interest of the organization in terms of long term relationships with those you have to deal with. In general terms this means "quid pro quo" (something for something) relationships. Keep in mind the original statement that an organization is developed to do small favors in order to obtain big favors. By doing something extra for those who you deal with in small things, you will find that they will return the favor by doing big things for the organization.

Just get those concepts of how you want the organization to be presented to other people firmly in your mind, and then you will not have any difficulty in developing that philosophy among those who work for you.

TACTICS

Always try to have two "GOTCHAS" when competing.

The successful competitor makes things happen. He does not wait for them to happen and then react. He keeps the competition worried about what he will do next instead of the other way around.

There is the story of the hacker who was offered a golf game by a professional golf hustler. The bet was to be $500 and the hacker could name his own handicap within reason. The hacker said he wouldn't take any strokes, just two gotchas. The pro asked what a gotcha was, and the hacker said he would show him on the course. The pro took the bet, and they began play.

The pro reached the first green in two strokes, and it took the hacker five to get there. The pro putted first, and just as he pulled the putter back, the hacker reached between his legs and grabbed his family jewels and yelled, "Gotcha." The pro drove his putt a hundred yards off the green.

The hacker said, "That's the first gotcha, I've got one more coming. He stood behind the pro on every shot and won the game by 12 strokes and never had to use the second gotcha.

Look for the gotchas that will keep the competition nervous, and you have a big edge in the battle.

CHAPTER 12
LONG GREEN MACHINE

The corporation is the primary business wealth builder. It offers so many creative ways to accumulate wealth, and at the same time avoid and defer taxes, that every entrepreneur should understand it — use the options it offers and pyramid holdings to whatever point is desired.

Perhaps the greatest story of a small business wealth builder who understood how corporations could be manipulated is that of Jimmy Ling. He started as an electrical contractor down in Texas. He discovered corporations and their potential — sold his first stock issue out of a booth in the Texas State Fair — and went on pyramiding corporate holdings into Ling-Tempco-Vought, the seventh largest business in America at one point. To be sure he lost it all when his pyramid toppled, but it proves the opportunities are out there and can be exploited.

What Do You Want to Get From Your Corporate Activities

Here is a check list to show you how to think about what corporation wheeling and dealing can do — and what you want it to do for you.

- ☐ Protection from taxes on income.
- ☐ Paying the most income (salary and dividends) for least tax obligation.
- ☐ Building and retaining future value for the family.
- ☐ Providing for payment of estate taxes.
- ☐ Tax free — or minimum tax insurance on you.
- ☐ Tax free — or minimum tax medical plans.
- ☐ Tax free — or minimum tax disability income insurance.
- ☐ A profit sharing retirement plan with maximum dollars.
- ☐ Will it absorb most or all travel and entertainment costs?
- ☐ Can you protect excess corporate income through property depreciation or sale leasebacks with option to reacquire them?
- ☐ Will it provide the necessary capital base to pyramid your holdings?
- ☐ Will it attract capital and loans?
- ☐ Will it attract good management talent?
- ☐ What steps can be taken to create a market for the stock?
- ☐ Look into special benefits for doing business in foreign countries.
- ☐ Have you planned to start a corporate stock portfolio to take advantage of the 85% tax free dividends?
- ☐ How will you retain control of the corporation — voting trusts — non-voting stock issues, etc.?
- ☐ Have you looked into the opportunities to transfer wealth to the family through living gifts, corporate employment and profit sharing plans, etc.?
- ☐ Have you made plans to have stock sold and transferred to estate in case of death to pay estate taxes and administration expenses?

In other words have personal goals that you want to achieve in income distribution when you form corporations, and they will be included in the pre-incorporation agreement so no later case can be made that such plans were the result of a tax evasion scheme.

The Pre-incorporation Agreement

The formation of a corporation requires a pre-incorporation agreement. Promoters who are putting a deal together want their rights, shares and other benefits spelled out in the pre-inc. agreement, or they can be changed at will by the Board of Directors. Profit sharing plans — insurance — medical benefits, etc. should all be included so the IRS can not make a case for tax evasion in setting these up later to avoid taxes.

A lawyer familiar with corporate law should draft the agreement — setting forth all the goals and plans for distributing income — setting up reserves, etc. You only pay for these once, because you can use it for any other corporations you set up later.

The Pre-incorporation Agreement Checklist

- ☐ Corporate name — is it available?
- ☐ In what state will the corporation be formed?
- ☐ Is publication of intent to incorporate required?
- ☐ Who is responsible for filing papers, etc.?
- ☐ What classes of stock will be issued?
- ☐ What bonds or notes will be issued?
- ☐ What dividends will be paid — how and who decides?
- ☐ How will voting rights be allocated?
- ☐ What securities will pre-inc. agreement parties get?
- ☐ Will stock be issued to others?
- ☐ What will all parties give for the stock?
- ☐ How many directors — will they be named in pre-inc.?
- ☐ Are the housekeeping rules to be put in pre-inc. (when meetings will be held — what is quorum, etc.?)
- ☐ Are by-laws part of pre-inc. agreement?
- ☐ Are officers designated in pre-inc.?
- ☐ Are salaries fixed in pre-inc.?
- ☐ Must employment contracts or agreements be included?

- ☐ What goods, services, securities, patents, copyrights, leases, property or assets, other than money, are to be turned over to corporation by incorporators or investors?
- ☐ How are they to be valued; what will be given in exchange?
- ☐ What liabilities will the corporation assume from the incorporators or stockholders?
- ☐ What does the corporation get to offset such liabilities?
- ☐ Any commitments to lend money to the corporation?
- ☐ How much and how to be repaid?
- ☐ Are any options to be granted?
- ☐ For what — what time limit — what to be received?
- ☐ What insurance will the corporation buy?
- ☐ Life — casualty — disability — etc. for whom and how much?
- ☐ Will corporate charter and by-laws be prepared—okayed by incorporators and approved to pre-inc. agreement?
- ☐ Will Rule 1244 be used and printed on stock certificates?
- ☐ Will Sub-Chapter S be used?
- ☐ Will accounting methods and services be part of pre-inc.?

Tax Considerations In Pre-inc. Agreements

One thing to consider in incorporating an existing business is to incorporate only one part — and let the other part run as before. You can incorporate the part that can shelter the greatest amount of income — leaving the other with minimum income to get greatest tax advantages.

Consider the advantages of tax free incorporation. The incorporators can transfer property tax free if they wind up owning 80% of the voting stock in the new corporation.

Transferring encumbered property will not set aside the tax free transfer. The incorporators can then use corporate income (with appropriate deductions for interest and depreciation, etc.) to pay off the debt.

Would it be preferable from a tax standpoint to lease property to the corporation rather than making an outright transfer? It makes for two deductions on the same property. The owner who is leasing takes depreciation — the corporation takes the lease cost as a business deduction.

Promoters should transfer patents, copyrights, plans and models to the corporation for their stock to avoid having it taxed to them as income. The earlier the promoters receive their stock — the safer they are from tax obligations. Consider setting up a cheap class of stock to issue promoters early.

In setting up the capital structure of the corporation the following tax considerations should be reviewed.

1. Interest on loans is deductible — dividends on stock are not.
2. Debt reduces possibility of taxing surplus accumulating.
3. Tax liability on debt retirement is less than that on stock redemption.
4. Debt imposes fixed obligations — possible need for sinking fund from cash flow — and default may cause loss of control.
5. No par stock gives wider latitude in fixing dividends.

Avoid the tax liability of a thin incorporation. This is where investors buy debt equity rather than stock. If the ration of debt to equity rises to 2 to 1—the IRS starts looking into calling the debt instruments capital contributions and taxes accordingly. One key is not to have all stockholders have the same amount of debt instruments. If they do—then it's capital investment.

If initial capital paid in is to include debenture bonds, then be careful. If the IRS decides the bond investments were designed to get the corporation a "good credit rating" by having a large cash in the bank fund, it may call the debentures stock and tax accordingly.

If you want to create a preference in earnings or equity for one or a group of stockholders—do it by creating a preferred stock issued at the time of incorporation. If you try to create this preference stock later — the IRS could call it a #306 stock — and any gain on its sale would be considered ordinary income — not capital gains.

All stock you issue should be 1244 stock. Rule 1244 allows the investor to write off up to $50,000 in each tax year (joint filing — $25,000 single filing)for losses incurred in sale of the stock.

Beware Of The Personal Holding Company

Keep a close eye on planning to avoid being classified as a personal holding company and paying 70% tax on income. A corporation in which five or fewer individuals own more than half the stock may be declared a personal holding company by the IRS if 60% or more of the income comes from dividends, rents, royalties, and interest. Rents equal to at least 50% of the adjusted ordinary gross income do not create a personal holding company if royalties, dividends and interest do not exceed 10% of adjusted gross income.

Accumulating surplus — you can accumulate surplus funds in your corporation up to $100,000 before a tax penalty is imposed on accumulated earnings. It ranges from 27½% on the first $150,000 and 38½% on the balance — on what the IRS terms unreasonable accumulations. Your pre-inc. plan should include plans to replace equipment, expand the business—move to larger quarters, sale-lease back of assets to reduce surplus, etc. or have definitive business plans for new projects in place when sufficient funds are accumulated. This will prevent you from having your corporate pocket picked because you are successful.

Another point the IRS is constantly challenging is what they term unreasonable salaries to avoid payment of dividends. Salaries are deductible business expenses and dividends are not, and dividends get taxed twice. Figure on a fixed salary to start — then once break even is passed, a percentage of gross sales added as the inducement to take the job. The key to big salary building is not to key the salary to the amount of investment—but job performance. This tends to reduce the IRS' argument to one of it being too much money. But if there was a period when there was too little money for the job, then you have a chance in tax court.

Restricting Resale Of Founder Stock

In most small corporations there must be restrictions on the sale of stock to outsiders. If there are not you can fall into a registration trap with the SEC—and difficulties with state authorities as well. The best way is to make the corporation the first buyer—when there is a market for the stock—then, make the corporation have the first option to buy. This keeps control in the hands of the founders. Important note—sale restrictions must be printed on the stock certificates.

Testamentary purchase options—these agreements should be in the pre-inc. agreement where the corporation buys out the holdings of a deceased founder from the estate under a pre-arranged formula. (This is usually covered by life insurance on the founder.) This prevents control from going out of surviving founders' hands.

Take care not to get caught in a collapsible corporation declaration by the IRS. This is a ruling that a corporation was formed as a tax dodge, then put out of business to transfer assets to founders. This converts the capital gains payable on corporate stock or assets into ordinary income and the much higher tax rates. The usual judgment is that a corporation in business less than three years which is discontinued with profitable assets to distribute is a collapsible corporation.

Sub-Chapter S declaration—this is a corporation with ten or less stockholders who may vote each tax year to be treated as a partnership and all profits or losses passed through to them as personal income or personal losses which they may use in declaring their personal income. This is a form used when losses are expected in the first few years and allows investors to use them to reduce tax obligations.

Plan to use Section 303 — this allows the estate of a deceased stockholder to redeem enough stock from the estate to pay off all estate taxes and administration costs tax free.

Plan to use Code 248 — which allows the organization costs of the corporation to be deducted as "deferred expenses" over a period of time — not less than 60 months from the date the corporation began business.

The Business Plan For The Corporation

The business plan should be made part of the pre-inc. agreement by attaching it to the other papers. The concept of the business, an organization chart at the start and covering periods of growth, brief job descriptions of key position, listing all assets, patents, copyrights, royalty agreements, and a note where each document is filed, list of all contracts, list of any suits or pending legal matters, notes on your outside services, attorney, accountant, banker, etc., should be included.

Also include your marketing plan — the products and services you intend selling — where they will be sold — how and by whom. Indicate your advertising and promotion plans — and the advantages over the competition you expect to enjoy.

If production is involved, include a summary of methods, list of equipment, raw materials and sources, estimate of labor required, plan on how production will be scheduled, etc.

Definite purchasing — accounting — inventory management procedures—and who is responsible for the decisions in each area should be included.

The financial facts — pro-forma balance sheets and operating statements for first two years — cash flow projections — market growth projections — market share projections — credit and collection policies, etc., should also be listed.

This gives you a pre-incorporation agreement that everyone understands — and it can be referred back to when disputes arise as to corporate purpose or policy. It also gives you protection against arbitrary rulings by the IRS as to company intentions when tax avoidance moves are made.

Checklist for Articles of Incorporation

- ☐ The corporate name.
- ☐ The purpose for which corporation was formed (as broad a definition as possible).
- ☐ Principal place of business — office address.
- ☐ Length of time for which it is incorporated.
- ☐ Powers — usually defined by state law.
- ☐ Designation of agent to accept legal documents for corporation (usually the Secretary of the corporation).
- ☐ Capitalization — covers:
  1. Number and classification of shares issued.
  2. Other securities (bonds — notes, etc.).
  3. Par or no par value of stock.
  4. Rights and limitations of each class of stock.
  5. Voting methods.
  6. Priority of securities issued if liquidation occurs.
- ☐ Minimum capital — if required by state.
- ☐ Preemptive rights.
- ☐ Shareholder liability for corporate debt (in a few states shareholders are liable for wages).
- ☐ Names and addresses of incorporators.
- ☐ List of directors at formation.
- ☐ Transfer restrictions on stock issued.
- ☐ Voting requirement to amend, adopt or rescind by-laws.
- ☐ Fixing value of no par stock (as a rule Board of Directors decides this).
- ☐ Voting and quorum requirements for directors — state law in some cases regulates this — attorney should check.
- ☐ Whether or not to have cumulative voting.
- ☐ Whether to have executive or other committees.

- ☐ Election of officers — check state law for any statue requirements.
- ☐ Removal of directors by other directors—or protect directors by cumulative voting.
- ☐ Classification of directors—state law varies. Check it.
- ☐ Fixing the record date — state law may restrict this.
- ☐ Natural resources operations—where natural resources extractive operations are involved (oil, mining, etc.). Provisions can be made to pay dividends out of depletion reserves.
- ☐ Indemnification of officers and directors — check state law for proper use.

TACTICS

When it's hot—you're not.

When the economy is booming—business is great and the profits are rolling in—don't get caught. Sooner or later the economic dice turn cold—and business is bad—things are bleak and the fat fall. The key is this—if you are in a strong cash position in bad times—cash is king—it can command twice or more the goods and services it could in good times. Bargains are available everywhere.

You can buy things for peanuts—you can build your personal assets for half of what it would have cost you in the prosperous times. The old adage—buy low and sell high is here.

The economy will turn—things will get better and what you bought low—you can now sell high and get ready to repeat the cycle.

It's called Contrarian Thinking—and it builds fortunes.

CHAPTER 13
FACTS ABOUT CORPORATIONS

Definitions

The legal fiction of a separate corporate personality—distinct from the real people involved—gives the corporation one of its greatest advantages as a form of business organization. "Limited liability" of the owners is the big thing; it is *the single most significant*—overriding—reason for most people to incorporate. In order to fully understand the concept of a separate legal "entity," it is essential for you to know the real nature of the "corporation."

The classification definition of a corporation given by Chief Justice Marshall in the famous Dartmouth College case is:

> "A corporation is an artificial being, invisible, and existing only in contemplation of law. Being the mere creature of law, it possesses only those properties which the charter of its creation confers upon it, either expressly or as incidental to its very existence. These are such as are supposed best calculated to effect the object for which it was created. Among the most important are immortality, and if the expression may be allowed, individuality, properties by which a perpetual succession of many persons are considered as the same, and may act as a single individual. They enable a corporation to manage its own affairs, and to hold property without the perplexing intricacies, the

> hazardous and endless necessity of perpetual conveyances for the purpose of transmitting it from hand to hand. It is chiefly for the purpose of clothing bodies of men in succession with these qualities and capacities that corporations were invented, and are in use. By these means, a perpetual succession of individuals are capable of acting for the promotion of the particular object, like one immortal thing." 4 Wheat (US) 518, 4 L ed 629.

The corporation exists only by virtue of law. And, as a legal personality it is capable of acting in many ways like a natural person, but it can act only through its directors, officers and agents who direct its affairs. With this kind of set-up, the first question most people ask is: "Does the corporation offer an opportunity to unscrupulous persons to hide behind the cloak of the legal entity?" Yes and No! Yes, they try, but, no, they don't generally get away with it! Courts have disregarded the separate entity when recognition of it would sanction a fraud, promote an injustice, or when it is used as a device to frustrate or evade the law. Even though "limited liability" of the owners is the major factor in the separate entity of corporations, courts and legislatures tend to protect the general public against abuses of the legal entity concept by making those who are responsible for the conduct of the corporate affairs personally liable for illegal acts with which the corporation has been charged. More about this later. On the other hand, state legislatures also want to encourage the organization of corporations under their laws. More business is good for the state—it results in more jobs and taxes; legislators want to encourage business and economic activity in their states. Most state laws are favorable to corporation, but the judges (who are generally not elective officers) try to close the barn door on crooked people who try to hide behind the "corporate veil." Piercing the corporate veil is discussed in detail later.

Two Types Of Law Involved

All business, regardless of the form of its organization, is subject to two types of law: (1) common law rules, and (2) statutory law. The common law is a body of rules laid down by judges in court decisions; it is based on the customs and prevailing attitudes of the times. It may change with the winds of the times. Each state has its own common law which has its origin in the English common law. The common law rules in the United States are basically the same because of the influence of the English laws. Statutory law means the acts of state legislatures or of Congress. Statutory law may add to the common law, codify it, change it, supersede it, or repeal it. *It is extremely important today for you to keep abreast of the rapidly changing laws, rules and regulations because non-compliance could put you out of business*—**or in jail!** Other definitions of legal terms which will help you understand the language of the "corporate" world are included in the text.

Corporate Existence: What Is Meant By The Terms "Creation" And "Organization" Of A Corporation?

As we have seen, the owners of stock of a corporation are not personally liable on corporate transactions entered into after the corporation comes into existence. Moreover, a corporation—after it is formed—may, in some states, relieve promoters or incorporators of liability on contracts entered into on its behalf. But here's the catch: If the corporation does not come into existence the stockholders, active and inactive, as well as promoters and incorporators may be personally liable to creditors. This rule of law is similar to the "piercing the corporate veil" discussed later; the law frowns on "hanky-panky" from any angle! Whether a corporation has come into existence is therefore important in determining who may be liable when contracts with the "corporation" are not performed. It is a long story—*but damn important*—so hang on. You can get stuck "before" your corporation is completed, and you can get stuck—if a judge pierces your corporate shell.

A few of the states are still operating under the older statutes, therefore, the following discussion is related to the application of the old statutes.

Under the old statutes the term "organization" of a corporation had no precise, universally accepted meaning. This is part of the reason we make so much of it here. There is a subtle difference between "creation" and "organization" of a corporation—as these terms are applied to the older statutes.

The term "organization" is sometimes used to designate the doing only of those things necessary to bring the corporation into legal existence. It can also go beyond that and mean doing those things after incorporation which are necessary before the corporation can enter into business transaction. This latter meaning is the one we use here. The term "creation" of a corporation is used to designate the formal filing of incorporation papers with the state official and the issuance of a formal certificate.

Some courts have held shareholders and organizers personally liable for obligations of a corporation that had not yet been organized, even though it was an existing *de jure* corporation. These cases are more like cases of "piercing the corporate veil" or "alter ego" cases, discussed later. On the other hand, some courts, once the statutory act bringing the corporation into existence has been complied with, will not hold organizers or stockholders liable even though the corporate "organization" has not been completed. Because of this uncertainty in the court cases and the statutes it is recommended that you take the easy course—organize it! Don't drop any stitches.

Some states require the organizers or the corporation to perform certain acts before the corporation can commence business, although it has come into existence. These acts may include paying in a minimum capital, filing an affidavit that it has been paid in, and perhaps holding the organization meeting or election of directors.

De Jure Corporations and De Facto Corporations

Under the older type statutes stockholders and promoters were often held personally liable for the debts of a corporation which was defectively incorporated. The legal theory was that limited liability of stockholders was offered only to those who strictly followed the incorporation statutes. Harsh consequences resulted from the strict application of this rule. In an effort to avoid these inequitable consequences, the courts developed the doctrine of *de jure* and *de facto* corporations. The rule was that if substantially all incorporating steps were taken, the corporation was *de jure* and entitled to all the incidents of incorporation including limited liability of stockholders. If some substantial step was omitted, the corporation would be *de facto* that is a corporation in fact. This rule was that if (1) the law existed under which the corporation could have been formed, (2) a good faith attempt was made to form it, and (3) the corporation exercised its powers, the courts would consider it a *de facto* corporation which conferred limited liability on the persons who organized it. The *de facto* doctrine has been called an example of legal conceptualism at its worst. It's a now-you-see-it—now-you-don't proposition. It didn't work very well in practice, and the results depended entirely on what the particular judge in any specific case decided. The difficulties encountered by the courts in applying the doctrine resulted in the adoption of modern statutes by most states making recourse to it unnecessary in most cases. Incorporating procedures in most states (but not all) have been so simplified that the corporation is either *de jure* or not a corporation at all. If it is not a corporation, aggrieved parties can pursue their normal remedies against the individuals involved. Although a corporation has *de jure* status, stockholders may still, in some circumstances, be held personally liable for corporate debts under the "piercing the corporate veil" or "alter ego" theory. More about this later. You will recognize the importance of knowing the basic law of your state on these important items.

A *de jure* corporation exists upon substantial compliance with all statutory conditions precedent to incorporation, and its corporate entity is generally immune from both direct and collateral attack on the basis of alleged incorporation defects.

Under the *de facto* doctrine, a corporation which is not *de jure* because of its failure to comply substantially with all statutory requirements may still be recognized as a corporation for most purposes, except in a direct attack on its existence by the state. The traditional elements of the *de facto* doctrine are (a) existence of a statute under which the corporation might have been validly incorporated; (b) colorable attempt in good faith to comply with such statute; and (c) activity as a corporation. Where the required elements are found, the application of the doctrine also depends on the nature of the case and the fairness to the parties under the circumstances. You can see how this rule would be very hard for a judge to apply. The doctrine has also been applied to corporations whose charters have expired or been terminated and then revived or reinstated with respect to activities during the interim period.

De Facto Doctrine—A Fiction On A Fiction—Is Illuminated By The New Statutes

The application of the *de facto* doctrine was to stack a fiction on a fiction—it was difficult to apply and created as many problems as it solved. In response to the confusion brought about by the cases that applied the doctrine, most of the states have recently adopted specific statutory provisions regulating the point as to when a corporation comes into existence. Most of the new statutes are based on the Model Business Corporation Act which provides:

> "Section 56. Effect of Issuance of Certificate of Incorporation: Upon the issuance of the certificate of incorporation, the corporate existence shall begin, and such certificate of incorporation, shall be conclusive evidence that all condition precedent required to be performed by the incorporators have been complied with and that the corporation has been incorporated under this Act, except as against the State in a proceeding to cancel or revoke the certificate of incorporation or for involuntary dissolution of the corporation.

Most of the new statutes also make special provision for what happens if persons operate as a corporation without the "issuance of the certificate of incorporation." Generally the statutes expressly make the incorporators—or persons—liable personally for all debts and liabilities created. In addition, these new statutes also tend to eliminate dual filings (local county, for example), minimum capital requirements, and other requirements— under the older statutes—before legal commencement of business.

A recent case which illustrates the application of these new statutes is Timberline Equipment Company, Inc. v. Davenport, 514 P 2d 1109 (Ore 1973). The question presented in the case was whether the corporation had come into existence. The court held:

> "We hold the principle of *de facto* corporation no longer exists in Oregon."

The holding was based on ORS 57.321 of the Oregon Business Corporation Act which provided:

> "Upon the issuance of the certificate of incorporation, the corporate existence shall begin, and such certifcate of incorporation shall be conclusive evidence that all conditions precedent required to be performed by the incorporators have been complied with and that the corporation has been incorporated under the Oregon Business Corporation Act, except as against this state in a proceeding to cancel or revoke the certificate of incorporation or for involuntary dissolution of the corporation."

In other words, the answer to the question was whether the "certificate of incorporation" had been issued. If so, there was a corporation; if not, no. Now, what happens if the certificate is not issued?

The court went on to point out that the Oregon Business Corporation Act, ORS 57.793 provided:

> "All persons who assume to act as a corporation without the authority of a certificate of incorporation issued by the Corporation Commissioner, shall be jointly and severally liable for all debts and liabilities incurred or arising as a result thereof."
>
> The courts said:
>
> "We are of the opinion that the phrase, 'persons who assume to act as a corporation' should be interpreted to include those persons who have an interest in the organization and who actively participate in the policy and operational decisions of the organization. Liability should not necessarily be restricted to the person who personally incurred the obligation," id 1114.

The effect of the statute is to create personal liability where persons "assume to act as a corporation" without the issuance of a certificate. This eliminates the old struggle with the application of the *de facto* doctrine. The statutes discussed in this case—based on the Model Business Corporation Act—have not been enacted in all states, but it is anticipated that practically all states will have made these changes within a few years.

Incorporators

How many people does it take to form a corporation? Can a corporation incorporate another corporation? How about a partnership? A Trust? Others?

Only a few years ago most all state statutes required "three or more natural persons to form a corporation." Usually the age requirement was 21. Frequently there were also residency and citizenship requirements for incorporators. Some statutes provided that incorporators must be subscribers to stock in the corporation.

Today practically all states have modernized their corporation statutes—most patterned after the Model Corporation Act of the

Committee of Corporate Laws of the Section of Corporation, Banking and Business Law of the American Bar Association. The modern statutes permit incorporation by one person, a corporation — domestic or foreign — a partnership, association, trust or other legal entity. Age requirements for natural persons is usually 18.

Only a few statutes still have residency or citizenship requirements, and only a few require incorporators to subscribe to stock. The Model Act proposal is as follows:

> One or more persons, or a domestic or foreign corporation, may act as incorporator or incorporators of a corporation by signing and delivering in duplicate to the Secretary of State articles of incorporation for such corporation.

The statutory provisions of all 50 states (and DC) are contained in the book *"Summary of the Corporation Statutes of the 50 states"*.

A corporation may be incorporated under the laws of more than one state. It then becomes a citizen of, and domiciled in, the several states wherein it is incorporated. This is a "multiple" corporation arrangement and may result from a consolidation of several companies incorporated in different states.

Organization After Existence Begins (Under The Older Statutes):

After a corporation comes into existence its organization must be completed before it can commence business. The procedural requirements vary with the different states, but typically a board of directors is elected, officers are appointed and other steps taken to carry on the business for which it was incorporated. A few states still require specified amounts of paid-in capital before the corporation can commence business—usually $1,000 or less. Some of the older statutes required meetings to be held within the state; most modern statutes do not. Most new statutes expressly provide that meetings may be held anywhere. It is easy to get a copy of your state statutes to check on all these matters.

Manner of Completing Corporate Organization

Within a reasonable time after the beginning of corporate existence, a meeting of the incorporators or of the board of directors named in the "certificate of incorporation," is held to complete corporate organization. Irrespective of whether your state has the "old" type statute requiring these meetings, or the new statutes, you should complete the "organizational" meeting procedures. As mentioned, under the "old" statutes the incorporators who do not complete the organization of the corporation may be personally liable for liabilities of the corporation. This is called "protecting the corporate back side," and these steps ought to be completed whether required by statute or not.

The First Meeting

The meeting is conducted in the same manner as other stockholders or directors meetings. The business transacted at this meeting depends largely on whether it is a meeting of incorporators, of stockholders or of directors named in the articles of incorporation. In most small business operations the incorporators, directors, stockholders and officers are the same persons.

Generally, at the first meeting, a temporary chairman and secretary are selected, notice of meeting or waiver of notice is presented, and a report of the filing of the articles of incorporation is received and the certificate is ordered into the record of the meeting. The bylaws—usually prepared before the meeting—are adopted. If the meeting is composed of the incorporators, they generally elect directors. Stock subscription books, if any, are opened, a report of subscription to capital stock, if any, is received and the subscriptions are made a part of the record of the meeting. Generally the board of directors will authorize the issuance of stock and fix the terms and conditions for the issuance of preferred stock where the statute requires or permits this to be done. The board of directors elect or appoint officers, adopt a corporate seal, and take any other procedure steps that may properly come before the meeting. The secretary is authorized to purchase corporate record books, and the filing and recording of required reports, if any, are ordered. A principal office is designated and, if a resident agent is required by statute, one is appointed. The officers are authorized to open a bank account and pay the organization expenses, and to proceed with the business for which the corporation was formed.

Finally, the adoption of the Section 1244 Plan should be approved, and a decision on whether the corporation shall elect to be taxed under Subchapter S of the Internal Revenue Code should be made.

A few of the older statutes still require a minimum amount of capital to be paid in before commencement of business. Typically this is $500 to $1,000. One or two statutes state the amount as a percentage of the authorized capital stock of the corporation. A few states require an affidavit to be filed to the effect that the minimum capital has been paid in. Apart from the statute, a few courts require the corporation to be adequately capitalized before it commences business. Undercapitalization is one of the factors considered by the courts in the "piercing the corporate veil" cases, infra.

The consequences of failure to pay in required capital differ as to the corporation and its officers,directors or stockholders.Even though the minimum statutory capital has not been paid in, the corporation can generally enforce its contract. Only the state can question corporate existence for failure to pay in minimum capital. One state, by statute, provides that corporate acts are not void even though the prescribed minimum capital has not been paid in. Although most states do not require a minimum paid in capital, some courts refuse to enforce a corporate contract when the capital paid in is insignificant compared to the scope of the enterprise. In essence there is generally no specific penalty for failure to have the required paid in capital, but it is strongly advised that you follow your statutes in this regard.

In some states the directors, stockholders, or officers, or all of them are made expressly liable by statute for corporate acts done before the prescribed statutory minimum capital has been paid in. This is *vitally important* to you personally: *be sure you comply with the statute in those states where the individuals become personally liable.*

Steps In Creating And Organizing A Corporation:

1. Select the state of incorporation:

Where to incorporate: Many years ago it was considered stylish and advantageous to incorporate in some other state that had liberal laws for easy incorporation. This was called "corporate forum shopping." This practice is *no longer advisable* and has distinct disadvantages rather than having any real advantages. Now, it is almost universally accepted that the state of principal business activity is the state favored for incorporation. This is true for large corporations as well as small corporations that are not, or will not be, actively engaged in business activities in other states. In the case of a local business operation, it is especially important to incorporate in your state. And now that most all states have simplified incorporation statutes you will find it is very easy to form a corporation in your own state. It can be done easily with or without an attorney. You can save a bundle by doing it yourself.

Under current conditions, incorporation in another state will usually add to organizational and recurring operational costs, including tax costs. A further disadvantage may include the possibility of a suit against the corporation in what will likely be an inconvenient and hostile forum (court). Moreover, your company will be considered a foreign corporation in the courts of your home state. This could subject you to attachment proceedings (seizure of property by legal authority) and other procedural disadvantages. Also, if you incorporate in another state, you will be required to register in your state as a foreign corporation before you can legitimately carry on a local business in your state. Usually, the expenses to register a foreign corporation to do business in your state are much greater than the costs of forming your corporation in your state—just an example of how foreign forums are hostile to outsiders. It therefore follows that the outdated advice to go forum shopping to incorporate could be a mistake and costly to you. For example, in some states the filing fee to register a foreign corporation to do business with the state is over $400.00. The new California Corporation Code, effective January 1, 1977, hits the high mark of around $550.00

Today there is much greater uniformity in the corporate laws of all states. However, if you wish to go shopping for a foreign forum, it is strongly recommended that you get good legal advice before making a final decision.

2. Name:

When you decide where to incorporate, you then must determine the availability of the name you wish to use as a corporate name. As the writers say, "you can't use General Motors or IBM—they are already taken." And many other names are already taken by other corporations. Simply call or write to the Secretary of State to see if the name is available. Most states will give this information on the telephone, but some require a letter. If it is desirable, you can reserve a name by paying a nominal fee, but this is usually a waste of time, money, and effort unless you have some extensive delays in filing or someone else is jockying to get the name before you. Besides—you can incorporate in about 15 minutes time. The name must not conflict with any other name used by any other business organization in the state. Some state statutes require the use of certain words in the name (like Corp., Inc., Company, etc.) and others prohibit the use of certain words (like trust, bank, insurance, etc.). Once you determine that the name is available, you simply fill out the papers, file them and pay the filing fees.

3. Purpose:

It is common for the general corporation laws of each state to provide for the formation of a corporation for any lawful business purpose or purposes—with certain specific exceptions, like insurance and banking. Naturally, one may not legally form a corporation and use it for the purpose of conducting illegal activities or other purposes contrary to the laws. Moreover, a corporation may be organized for the specific purpose and intent of escaping or limiting personal liability of the individual. This is, of course, one of the primary reasons for forming many private corporations. The law is clear: incorporation for the purpose of achieving limited liability is recognized under all state statutes on the theory that limited liability is one of the principal objectives of incorporation. Limited liability is enjoyed even by a controlling shareholder where corporate formalities are observed, initial financing is reasonably adequate, and the corporation is not formed to evade an existing obligation or a statute, or to cheat or to defraud. See discussions of "Piercing the Corporate Veil."

The term "purpose" refers to the objectives of a corporation, what it is formed to do. The term "powers" refers to the means by which the objectives are achieved—the acts taken to do what the corporation was formed to do. It is easy to get these terms confused, but for filing your articles of incorporation you need only state the purposes in terms of what general business the corporation will carry on.

Corporations may engage in any lawful business, but these purposes must be specified in the articles of incorporation in most states. A few states permit incorporators to state in the articles that the corporation can engage in any lawful activity, without further specification except as limited by the incorporators themselves. This is the modern view—and the definite trend of the new statutes. In those states that require specific statements of purposes you need only state the purposes in terms broad enough to include everything essential and incidental to corporate activity. It is a good practice to end the statement of purposes with the phrase "and all other acts authorized by law."

The Model Business Corporation Act, Sec 3 provides:

Corporations may be organized under this Act for any lawful

purpose or purposes, except for the purpose of banking or insurance.

Most of the modern statutes use this—or similar—language.

4. Duration:

Most statutes permit corporations to be organized with perpetual existence. Some older statutes have limitations, but they are usually very liberal in permitting renewals.

5. Capital Stock:

You should determine whether in your state (1) there is any minimum for total authorized capital stock, or for the par value of a share; and whether (2) par or no-par shares are to be used. Taxing authorities frequently place an arbitrarily high value on no-par shares for initial, annual, and stamp tax purposes.

You should decide whether you desire any restrictions on cumulative voting, and decide whether you want stockholders to have pre-emptive rights to new shares when issued or to treasury shares and whether you must make provision for granting or denying these in the articles of incorporation.

6. Paid In Capital:

You should determine whether your state statutes require a specified amount of capital to be subscribed for and/or paid in before commencement of business. Most states do not require this.

There is a difference between capital and capital stock. The capital stock of a corporation is the amount of money, property, or other means authorized by its articles of incorporation and contributed, or agreed to be contributed, by the shareholder as the financial basis for the operation of the business. These contributions are usually received from the capital investment of the shareholders or through the declaration of stock dividends. Capital is sometimes used broadly to indicate the entire assets of the corporation, or more narrowly, that portion of the assets of a corporation, regardless of their course, which is utilized for the conduct of the corporate business and for the purpose of making gains and profits. It is said that capital belongs to the corporation, and capital stock, when issued, belongs to the stockholders. Capital may be *either* real or personal property. The terms are frequently used interchangeably, *but it is important to note the difference.*

A share of stock is a unit of interest in a corporation. Even though ownership of stock does not confer title to any of the property of the corporation, it entitles the shareholder to an equivalent part of the property, or its proceeds, when distributed according to law. Each share represents a distinct and undivided share or interest in the common property of the corporation. Shares of stock constitute property distinct from the capital or tangible property of the corporation and belong to different owners. The capital is the property of the corporation. The shares of stock are the property of the several shareholders. *You should not* treat corporate property and assets as yours even though you may own all, or substantially all, of the stock of the corporation.

7. Prepare incorporation paper:

The next step is to fill out and file the incorporation papers. The statutes of each state prescribe what incorporation papers must be prepared—generally a one page document (or form) entitled Articles of Incorporation in which you fill in the blanks. In most states the law requires that the forms provided by the state must be used.

The articles of incorporation are sometimes referred to as a contract with the stockholders, and should be specific enough to advise the stockholders of their rights, obligations and liabilities. *Before the* articles are filed with the Secretary of State (or other official) they should be *carefully checked* to make sure all of the information required by statute is included.

Generally, the articles contain the following items:

A. Name of corporation
B. Purpose or nature of business
C. Place of business; registered office
D. Amount of capital stock and number of shares into which it

is divided and if more than one class is created, a description of the different classes with terms on which respective classes are created

E. Duration

F. Name and address of incorporator or incorporators

G. Statement indicating what officers are to conduct the corporate affairs

H. Number of directors and names and addresses of directors selected for first year

Completion of the form is a relatively simple matter, but there are several items you should consider. The following suggestions include the practice of most people who form their own corporation. The duration is usually filled in as "perpetual." Describe the basic purposes as specifically as you can by describing the things the corporation will do and then end the description with the phrase "and all their acts authorized by law." In some states the filing fee is determined by the aggregate number of shares the corporation is authorized to issue. In these states you should authorize the minimum number on the sliding scale to keep the filing fee to a minimum. It is important to distinguish **authorized** shares (those you may or may not wish to issue) from **issued** shares (those actually issued by the corporation). In a small corporation you may wish to issue only a few shares in the beginning—perhaps no more than 10 or 100 shares among 10,000 to 50,000 authorized shares. The idea is to have additional authorized shares that can be issued later as other capital is needed in the corporation. It is recommended that you indicate cumulative voting of shares of stock as authorized, and that there shall be no provisions limiting or denying to shareholders the preemptive right to acquire additional or treasury shares of the corporation. The name of the initial registered agent should be one of the persons most actively engaged in, and responsible for, the creation and operation of the corporate business.

8. *Take care to properly execute the forms:* Most states require

that the articles be acknowledged or verified—signed under oath. Doing it right the first time can save a lot of time and possibly some embarrassment.

9. File corporation papers and pay filing fees.

10. Prepare the bylaws:

The bylaws of a corporation are the rules or laws for its internal government. They prescribe the rights and duties of the members with reference to the internal government of the corporation, establish the procedures, practices, and policies of the business operation, approve the rules for the management of the corporate affairs, and establish the rights and duties existing among the members. Bylaws are self-imposed rules to regulate the manner in which the corporation will function. They include all self-made regulations of a corporation, but generally do not bind or affect the rights of third persons. Until repealed, the bylaws are continuing rules for the government of the corporation and its officers, their function being to regulate the transaction of the incidental business of the corporation. Bylaws differ from corporate resolutions in that a resolution applies to a single act of the corporation while the bylaws are continuing rules to be used only with reference to the rules which the directors and officers may pass for their government. Bylaws are valid if they are reasonable and calculated to carry into effect the objects of the corporation and are not in conflict with the general policy of the state and federal laws. Generally, whether done by a lawyer—or by you—the trick is to *buy a corporation kit* which has form bylaws that can be adapted to your situation.

11. Hold first formal meetings of incorporators, shareholders or directors:

The next step is to prepare for and hold the first formal meeting of incorporators (where required), shareholders and directors, at which corporate organization is completed. Just what meetings must be held and what papers must be drawn in connection with such meetings will be determined by the laws of the state of incorporation. See previous discussions about "creation" and "organization" of corporations.

12. Prepare minutes of first meetings:

As a general rule there are no specific statutory requirements as to precisely what minutes, proceedings or resolutions must be recorded in the minutes of corporate meetings. Nevertheless, it is important to keep complete and accurate records of all meetings and proceedings—**especially the first meeting.**

Form: Minutes of Organizational Meeting of ____________ Corporation

The organization meeting of the incorporators (and/or stockholders and/or the members of the board of directors) of (corporation) was held at (address) on (date) at (time). The following were present: (list names) being all the incorporators (and/or the stockholders and/or the members of the board of directors) of the corporation.

John Doe was appointed chairman of the meeting and Jane Doe was appointed secretary.

The secretary then presented and read to the meeting the waiver of notice of the meeting, subscribed by all the persons named in the Articles of Incorporation, and it was ordered that it be appended to the minutes of the meeting.

The secretary then presented and read to the meeting a copy of the Articles of Incorporation and reported that on (date) the original thereof was filed in the office of the Secretary of State of this state. The copy of the Articles of Incorporation was ordered appended to the minutes of the meeting.

The chairman then stated that nominations were in order for election of directors of the corporation to hold office until the first annual meeting of stockholders and until their successors shall be elected and shall qualify.

The following persons were nominated: (names)

No further nominations being made, nominations were closed and a vote was taken. After the vote had been counted, the chairman declared that the foregoing named nominees were elected directors of the corporation.

The secretary then presented to the meeting a proposed form of bylaws which were read to the meeting, considered, and upon motion duly made, seconded and carried, were adopted as and for the bylaws of the corporation and ordered appended to the minutes of the meeting.

Upon motion duly made, seconded, and unanimously carried, it was:

Further Resolved, that the specimen stock certificate presented to the meeting be, and hereby is, adopted as the form of certificate of stock to be issued to represent shares in the corporation;

Further Resolved, that the corporate record book, including the stock transfer ledger, be, and hereby is, adopted as the record book, stock transfer book, and ledger of the corporation;

Further Resolved, that the board of directors be, and hereby is, authorized to issue the unsubscribed capital stock of the corporation at such time and in such amounts as it shall determine, and to accept the payment thereof, in cash or services or such other property as the board may deem necessary for the business of the corporation;

Further Resolved, that the corporation be, and hereby is, authorized and directed to accept the payment of capital required for the commencement of business, and that the same be properly reflected upon the books and records of the corporation;

Further Resolved, that the principal office of the corporation be and hereby is designated as (address) and the board of directors is hereby authorized to change said designation as it deems proper, and it may designate branch offices from time to time as it shall, in its judgment, determine to be necessary and proper;

Further Resolved, that a plan for the issuance of common stock of the corporation to qualify under the provisions of Section 1244 of the Internal Revenue Code, which plan was read to the meeting, be and the same is hereby adopted, approved, and confirmed by the corporation, and the officers and directors of the corporation are hereby authorized and directed to take all steps, procedures, and action necessary to implement the plan;

Further Resolved, that all other actions, notifications, publications, filings, and any other procedural requirements for the full authorization of this corporation to commence the business for which it was created be completed by the secretary, and that a record thereof be filed in the corporate records of the corporation.

Upon motion duly made, seconded and carried, it was:

Resolved, that the signing of these minutes shall constitute full ratification thereof and waiver of notice of the meeting by the signatories.

There being no further business before the meeting, on motion duly made, seconded, and carried, the meeting adjourned.

Date: (date) Signed: (chairman) Signed: (secretary)

A true copy of each of the following papers referred to in the foregoing minutes is appended hereto:

Waiver of Notice of Meeting; Articles of Incorporation; Stock Certificate; Bylaws; Section 1244 Plan.

13. Establish corporate records and corporate books:

Generally speaking the records of a corporation include its articles and bylaws, the minutes of its meetings, the stock books, the books containing the accounts of its official activities, and the written evidence of its contracts and business transactions. They are the property of the corporation, and not of the officers or employees. Most state statutes require the keeping of such books and records. The statutes also require that corporations make periodic statements or reports to the state agency regulating corporations.

Stockholders have a right to inspect the books and records of a corporation, subject to reasonable regulations. Inconvenience to the company from an inspection of its books **is no ground** for a denial of the stockholder's right to examine the records. A stockholder's right *cannot be defeated* by a corporation's offer to purchase his shares of stock. Moreover, an offer to furnish extracts or copies from the books or to furnish annual reports will not satisfy a demand for inspection of the original records. It is easy to see that a stockholder's lawsuit or other demands of shareholders for examination of corporate books and records could result in considerable expense, inconvenience, and disruption of the business operations of a corporation. In an attempt to resolve or improve this problem, the courts, while recognizing the fundamental right of the stockholder to examine the books and records, have placed certain restrictions upon the exercise of those rights. One of the most important of these qualifications is that before the right of inspection will be granted over the corporation's objection, an inquiry will be made into the applicant's motives.

14. Arrange for purchase of a corporate kit:

You can get these at most large stationery stores, or order them from various companies that specialize in furnishing the kits. Many of these companies advertise in most all of the legal journals. Two of them are:

Excelsior Legal Stationery Co., Inc.
62 White Street
New York, NY 10013
(212) 431-7000

Corpex Banknote Company, Inc.
21 Hudson Street
New York, NY 10013
(212) 964-7454

Management During Organization

General corporation laws do not, as a rule, deal with management during the period of organization. When they do cover this point, they usually provide that the management shall be by the incorporators or the board of directors named in the articles of incorporation. In the absence of statutory provision, the corporation is managed during the period of organization by the promoters or the incorporators, who effect the organization and retain charge of corporate affairs until permanent directors, officers and agents are selected. And, as pointed out earlier, some of the modern statutes create liability on the individual persons who assume to act as a corporation before it comes into existence.

Managing A Corporation

By corporate management we mean the regulation of the company's affairs—its internal government. The nature of this management and how it functions can be understood only by referring to the defined powers, rights, duties and liabilities of the corporation, its directors, officers and shareholders.

Traditionally the business of a corporation is considered as being managed and directed by a board of directors. Technically this may still apply in many instances, however, the recent changes in the statutory laws and the changes in the business practices has brought about some dramatic changes. The trend—especially in small businesses—is for the board of directors to have infrequent meetings and delegate most of the operations of the business to the officers. Frequently the board—officers—and stockholders are the same persons—or the same person. The delegated authority, in many instances, is not limited merely to ministerial functions, but includes matters which previously were exclusively confined to the entire board and not delegable. State legislatures are beginning to recognize that the closed corporation, as a business entity, should not be governed by the same rules as a publicly held corporation. In some states, for example, statutes permit stockholders to manage closed corporations directly, without the need for a board of directors. This is the modern trend and more states will adopt these changes in the laws. Indicative of the trend in the statutes was the enactment by the state of Wyoming of the Wyoming Limited Liability Company Act (Chapter 158, Laws of 1977, effective June 30, 1977). In all events all the state laws are bending *in the direction* of giving the small business owner more flexibility in the use of the corporation form of business.

Laws Concerning Directors

Most states have no statutory qualification for directors, but under common law a director must be *sui juris* (legally competent to contract). An infant, for example, would not be competent as a director. Some states require one or more directors to be residents of the state of incorporation. Most statutes do not.

Under the older statutes the usual number of directors was three or more, but most modern statutes permit one or more, and this is the trend that probably will be passed in all states within a few years. Generally, directors are elected by the shareholders at a regularly scheduled meeting. The term of office for directors and the filling of vacancies, is usually prescribed in the bylaws.

Unless the right to resign is limited by statute, or by a provision in the articles, a bylaw, or in a contract with the corporation (they are usually not) a director may resign at any time. A provision in the statute or articles or bylaws that a director shall hold office until his successor is elected does not limit the right of a director to resign.

Although the rules and laws are liberal in permitting directors to delegate many of the day-to-day operations of a corporate business to the officers, agents and employees, the directors are not necessarily absolved from the responsibility to see that the business functions are legal and lawful. A corporation's trustee in bankruptcy can hold its former directors liable for negligence or mismanagement if he can show they (1) failed to devote sufficient time to the corporation, (2) abdicated the management of the business to the officers, (3) permitted loans to be made to financially unsound companies controlled by officers of the corporation, or (4) failed to keep informed of corporate affairs that result in losses to the company. In other words a director can let somebody else do it, but he better be **sure it is done right!**

Directors who do not know about secret commission payments being made by the corporation to other directors, may be personally liable for the payments. The courts reason that if the directors had properly participated in the management of the corporation and assumed the responsibility of the office to which they were elected, they could have discovered these secret arrangements. Directors must render to the corporation a conscientious consideration of every question involving the interests of the corporation including the prevention and redress of wrongdoing by fellow directors or officers. They have a duty to use diligence in selecting officers and agents who should be competent and responsible.

Good Faith And Reasonable Care

They must act in good faith and with reasonable care. Directors occupy a position of trust and confidence and are considered in the law as standing in a fiduciary relation to the stockholders and as trustees for them. This "fiduciary duty" imposes *enough responsibility* on directors to keep them wide awake. Many lawyers—famous personalities—and well known political figures are now reluctant to be a "director" of corporations where they do not have sufficient time, interest and authority to "know" what is going on in the corporate closets. Directors *may be personally liable* for withholding taxes not paid by the corporation to the Internal Revenue Service; they may also be personally liable for other penalties or fines because of failure to pay taxes!

In Summary

The first meeting may be the *most important meeting you will ever have* especially if you should ever have any legal questions about the legality—or sufficiency of the legalities—of your corporation. The rule of law is well settled that a corporation is for most purposes an entity distinct from its individual members or stockholders, who, as natural persons, are emerged in the corporate identity, and remains unchanged and unaffected in its identity by changes in the individual membership.

By the very nature of a corporation, its property is vested in the corporation itself, and not in the stockholders. The stockholders, as such, do not have the power to represent the corporation or act for it in relation to its ordinary business, nor are they ordinarily personally liable for the acts and obligations of the corporation. In no legal sense can the business of the corporation be said to be that of its individual stockholders or officers. The courts have repeatedly held that a closed corporation—a one man corporation—or one family corporation—is recognized by the law so long as they are *not used for illegitimate purpose,* if (a) the business is conducted on a corporate and not on a personal basis, and (b) the enterprise was established on an adequate financial basis. The trick is for you to do (a) and (b) right.

It is equally settled as a matter of law that a subsidiary corporation or other affiliated corporations are generally given the legal green light as a separate legal entity so long as they are not used for illegitimate purposes, where (a) their respective business transaction, accounts, and records are not intermingled; (b) the formalities of separate corporate procedures for each corporation are observed; (c) each corporation is adequately finanaced as a separate unit in the light of its normal obligations forseeable in a business of its size and character; and (d) the respective enterprises are held out to the public as separate enterprises. If you comply with these requirements you should have no legal technicalities to trip over in terms of organizing your corporation in accordance with the laws of your state. But it's easier said than done.

Internal Revenue Code Section 1244 Stock Plan:

When you organize a corporation, it is always wise to qualify the stock under Section 1244 of the Code. This section provides that, in the case of an individual, a loss on Section 1244 stock issued to such individual or to a partnership which would (but for this section) be treated as a loss from the sale or exchange of a capital asset shall, to the extent provided in this section, be treated as a loss from the sale or exchange of an asset which is not a capital asset. Section 1244 (a), for any taxable year the aggregate amount treated as a loss under this section shall not exceed $25,000 for an individual return or $50,000 for joint returns. In other than section 1244 stock, the owner can only offset his losses as capital losses against capital gains for 6 years, and can reduce his ordinary income by no more than a specified amount ($3,000 for 1978) per year for those six years. **This can make a significant impact on your personal tax picture.**

What is Section 1244 Stock? It is common stock—voting or non-voting, but not convertible—of a domestic (U.S.) corporation. To qualify under the Code it must meet these standards:

a. When the plan is adopted the corporation must be a small business corporation, and no part of a prior stock offering must then be outstanding. Outstanding stock rights or options are considered prior offerings and can disqualify.
b. The stock must be issued for money or property (other than stock or securities and not for services).
c. If another offering of stock is made after the plan is adopted, stock issued thereafter under the plan will not qualify.

A "small business corporation" is one which, at the time of adoption of the plan to issue Section 1244 Stock has no more than $1,000,000 equity capital, and has capital paid in after June 1958, not in excess of $500,000.

The adoption of such a plan is a relatively simple procedure—but important. It is not necessary to file anything with the Internal Revenue Service. All you need do is to comply with the requirements of the Code which are:

1. The corporation must be a domestic corporation, it must be a

small business corporation, and the stock issued must be common stock.

2. The corporation must adopt a written plan to offer stock for a period specified in the plan not ending later than two years after the date the plan is adopted.

3. The stock must be issued for money or other property (other than stock, securities, or services), and the plan must be adopted by the corporation before money or other property is paid into the corporation.

4. At the time a loss on such stock is sustained, the corporation must have derived more than fifty percent of its aggregate gross receipts from sources other than royalties, rents, dividends, interest, annuities, and sales or exchanges of stock or securities, as defined in subparagraph (c) (E) of the Code.

5. There must not be a prior outstanding offering of stock made by the corporation.

6. At the time the plan is adopted, the sum of the aggregate amount which may be offered under the plan, plus the aggregate amount of money and other property received by the corporation for shares of common stock as a contribution to capital and as paid in surplus, shall not exceed $500,000.

7. At the time the plan is adopted, the sum of the aggregate amount which may be offered under the plan, plus the equity capital of the corporation shall not exceed $1,000,000.

8. The written plan pursuant to which the stock is issued should specifically refer to Section 1244.

The following form can be used to assist you in preparing your written plan. You should be careful to have the plan prepared before the first organizational meeting so it can be adopted before the payment of money or property, as specified in the Code. All stockholders should be advised of the plan, and complete records should be maintained so that adequate proof of compliance with the Code can be shown if it should become necessary.

Here is a suggested form of a written plan:

Section 1244 Plan for Issuance of Common Stock of __________ ____ Inc.

The board of directors of (name), Inc. deem it advisable and in the best interest of the corporation to offer for sale and issue shares of common stock to shareholders under and pursuant to the provisions of Section 1244 of the Internal Revenue Code of 1954, as amended, in such a manner as to qualify all shares held by qualified stockholders so that said shares shall receive the benefits of the Code.

1. The corporation is a domestic corporation and is a "small business corporation" as defined in Section 1244 of the Code. The stock to be issued pursuant to this plan is common stock.

2. This offer to sell and issue shares of common stock shall terminate no later than two years from the date this plan is approved and adopted by the board of directors of the corporation. The corporation shall not make any subsequent offering of shares of common stock or securities convertible into common stock prior to the expiration date specified herein.

3. Stock issued hereunder shall be in exchange for money or other property except for stock, securities, or services. Stock issued hereunder shall not be in return for services rendered or to be rendered to, or for the benefit of, the corporation.

4. No stock shall be issued under this plan prior to the adoption of this plan.

5. There is not now outstanding any prior offering of the corporation to sell or issue any of its stock.

6. The sum of the aggregate amount which may be offered under this plan, plus the aggregate amount of money and other property received by the corporation for shares of common stock as a contribution to capital and as paid-in surplus, does not exceed $500,000.

7. The sum of the aggregate amount which may be offered

under this plan, plus the equity capital of the corporation, does not exceed $1,000,000.

8. No stock offered hereunder shall be issued on the exercise of a stock right, stock warrant, or stock option, unless such right, warrant, or option is applicable solely to unissued stock offered under the plan and is exercised during the period of the plan.

9. The date of adoption of this plan is (date).

The officers of the corporation are hereby authorized and directed to offer, sell, and issue as many shares of common stock and at such prices, payable in cash or other property, other than stock, securities, or services, as they shall deem to be in the interest of the corporation.

It is the purpose and intent of the corporation to comply with the provisions of Section 1244 of the Internal Revenue Code, as amended, and this plan shall be interpreted and construed in a manner as shall enable the corporation to qualify as a plan meeting the requirements of the Code and as will enable the shares of common stock issued thereunder to qualify as "Section 1244 Stock," as defined in the Code.

Dated: (date) Signed: (Chairman) Attest: (secretary)

Approved and adopted by the board of directors on the ____________________ day of ________________________ 19__.

Sub-Chapter S Election

If you have no more than 10 shareholders, you will certainly wish to consider whether to adopt an option under the tax code to have profits of the corporation flow through to stockholders to be taxed individually rather than at corporate tax rates. This provision of the tax code gives a business owner the advantages of incorporating a business without a double tax payment — by the corporation — and the individual. A corporation that wants to take the advantage of this tax break does not have to comply with any special statutory requirements. If the corporation meets the requirements of the tax code, it pays no corporate income taxes, but all the income is passed on to the stockholders who pay taxes at their own individual level.

To qualify the corporation must meet the following code requirements:

1. A domestic corporation must have no more than 10 stockholders for the first 5 years of its existence as a Sub-Chapter S corporation. After that it may have as many as 15 stockholders (Tax Reform Act of 1976).

2. Stockholders must be individuals or estates: no stock can be owned by another corporation. Certain trusts, in limited circumstances, may be stockholders.

3. No stockholder may be a nonresident alien.

4. Not more than 20% of the corporation's gross receipts may be from royalties, rents, dividends, interest, annuities and gains on sales or exchanges of stock or securities.

5. Not more than 80% of the gross receipts may be derived from sources outside the U.S.

6. It may have only one class of stock.

7. Corporation may not be affiliated with any other corporation; there are some limited exceptions.

How the Election is Made

To qualify, the corporation files IRS Form 2553. The consent of all corporation stockholders must be filed with it. If there is a change in stock ownership, the election continues unless the new stockholder affirmatively acts to terminate it. If the Subchapter S corporation has a maximum number of stockholders and one of them sells some of the stock to another person, the corporation automatically loses the Subchapter S status and becomes taxable like any other corporation.

The notice and consent must be filed during the first month of the company's taxable year, or during the month immediately preceding. The notice remains effective from year to year until revoked or unless the corporation disqualifies itself. The company has a right to revoke or cancel its election for any year after its first election; but if it does so, it cannot make another election to come under Subchapter S until the fifth tax year beginning after the year of cancellation, unless the Commissioner agrees.

Effect of Election

When the election is made the corporation does not pay corporate income tax, personal holding company tax, or tax on improper accumulation of surplus. The income is "passed through" and taxed directly to the stockholders at their individual tax level. Each stockholder in a Subchapter S corporation must pay a federal income tax on his share of the taxable income. Corporate long-term capital gains are passed through to the individual stockholders as are any net operating losses.

Piercing The Corporate Veil

(Breaking Up Your Corporate Shell; Penetrating Your Corporate Shield; Disregarding the Corporate Entity; Alter Ego; Formality; Fraud on the Law; Nominal Identity; Subterfuge; ... etc. ...)

Introduction

Now that we have told you (1) how to create, organize and manage your corporation, (2) how your corporation may be defective — not a corporation at all — or a *de facto* corporation, as the case may be — unless you comply with the statutory requirements, and (3) how you may be exposed to personal liability (a) as an incorporator, (b) as a stockholder, (c) as a director, and (d) as a natural person, we will now tell you how the courts — after you get it all set up — *can tear it all down!*

The general rule of law, subject to exceptions, is that corporate entity, with attendant corporate attributes, will be recognized and not disregarded. However, there is an equally well settled rule that corporate entity will not be recognized to produce unjust or undesirable consequences inconsistent with the purpose of the concept.

I'm sure you have heard the terms or expressions, "Piercing the Corporate Veil," and all the other terms that indicate the web of the corporate entity may be brushed aside by the courts. Your first reaction may be, "Why bother with all this 'don't drop any stitches' bit if a judge can rip it all apart?" Well, right on! That's a good question, but there are some good answers. And you need to know them so you can avoid having to face the problems.

The basic proposition — the rule of law of piercing the corporate veil—may sound somewhat absurd, outrageous, perplexing, and puzzling — but you better understand it and look out for your own hide — *Number One* — because nobody else will. This so-called "quagmire," this complex and precarious rule of law, all the double-talk, the high sounding phrases and the apparent inconsistency, is really a result of the courts being faced with a very tough legal problem: How to create—by a legal fiction—a separate entity of a corporation—and at the same time prevent persons from using the device to do wrong.

There's only one way you can beat this rap — make sure you know the law — follow it — and don't go to sleep at the switch. **Not before — during — after — incorporation**.

Discussion Of The Rule

Rule of the Corporate Entity:

The doctrine that a corporation is a legal entity existing separate and apart from the persons comprising it is a legal theory introduced for the purposes of convenience and to subserve the ends of justice. The entity theory — that the corporation is a separate entity, distinct from its shareholders — provides the traditional basis for the concept of limited liability, as well as the corporation's capacity to hold property, to contract not only with outsiders but also with its own shareholders, to sue and be sued, and to enjoy continued existence notwithstanding changes in its membership. The concept cannot, however, be extended to a point beyond its reason and policy, and when invoked, in support of an end subversive of this policy, will be disregarded by the courts.

Rule Of Piercing The Corporate Veil Or Disregarding The Corporate Entity (Or Exception To The General Rule)

Disregard of the corporate entity in various cases of technically correct incorporation is the converse of the recognition of corporate entity in instances of defective incorporation (*de facto* doctrine). The following discussions will cover the extent to which courts have gone in upholding the corporate entity and, conversely, in what situations they have seen fit to disregard corporate entity or to "pierce the corporate veil."

Legal History And Development Of The Rule

How the Rule Got Started:

As early as 1809, it was perceived by the courts that in many cases the literal application of the notion that a corporation is only a legal entity, and nothing more, would work injustice. The Supreme Court of the United States, from its beginning, had taken over the language of the old English year books, and proclaiming its allegiance, had agreed with the early English writers that "a corporation aggregate of many is invisible, immortal, and rests only in intendment and consideration of the law." Now, if a corporation is merely a legal entity, if it is clothed only with invisibility and intangibility, it could not, of course, be a citizen of a state. The Federal Constitution, however, limits the jurisdiction of the federal courts "to controversies between citizens of different states." In 1809 Chief Justice Marshall, in order to preserve the jurisdiction of the federal courts over corporations, was compelled to look beyond the entity "to the character of the individuals who compose the corporation." The court proclaimed that "substantially and essentially" the parties to the suit are the stockholders, and that their several citizenships would be recognized for purposes of federal court jurisdiction.

Later cases and statutes evolved the rule, recognizing the corporate entity, that a corporation is deemed a citizen of its state of incorporation and state of its principal place of business. See 28 U.S.C.A. Sec. 1332.

However, even at this early date, the U.S. Supreme Court did not regard it as reasonable that the operation of the separate corporate concept should oust the federal courts of their important and far-reaching jurisdiction over corporations, a result which any overzealous adherence to the theory of corporate entity would inevitably require. From that time on the courts have "drawn aside the veil and looked at the character of the individual corporators," in certain cases.

Defrauding Creditors

An important and most illuminating line of cases where courts refuse to be tied down by the entity story is seen in the numerous instances of judicial impatience with all attempts to hamper, delay or defraud creditors by means of "dummy" corporations. In all such instances courts do not hesitate to penetrate the veil and to look beyond the corporate entity at the actual and substantial beneficiaries. One of the early leading cases was *Booth v. Bunce, 33 N.Y. 139 (1865)*.

Leading Cases:

In the Booth case the members of a financially embarrassed partnership united in forming a manufacturing corporation under the general incorporation laws of New York. They then transferred to it the property of the partnership. "A" was a bona fide creditor of the partnership; "B" of the corporation. You guessed it: the issue was a contest between them to secure their respective claims out of the property in question. The court held that the property might be taken by "A" since the evidence showed that the corporation was formed in bad faith and with the intent to defraud creditors.

The trial court gave a charge to the jury that:

"They had to determine but one question, and that was that if this corporation was fairly organized, and the sale of the property to it by Montgomery and Lund (the partners) was also fair and done without fraudulent intent, the defendants (B) were entitled to recover; if, on the contrary, the company was organized to defraud the creditors of Montgomery and Lund, and the property was transferred to them by Montgomery and Lund in furtherance of that fraudulent purpose, the plaintiff (A) was entitled to recover ..." id156.

This jury charge, on appeal to the New York court of last resort, was upheld. The defendants, of course, invoked the sacred doctrine of corporate entity. They insisted that the court had no right to ignore the holy concept. The court, however, recognized that there was no magic in incorporation and declared that the vice of fraud contaminated anything — even the device of incorporation — and held the entity, for all practical purposes, a nullity. The scheme was clever, but it did not meet with success. The court, again, lifted the veil.

The court, in its opinion, said:

"Deeds, obligations, contracts, judgments, and even corporate bodies may be the instruments through which parties may obtain the most unrighteous advantages. All such devices and instruments have been resorted to, to cover up fraud, but whenever the law is invoked all such instruments are declared nullities; they are a perfect dead letter; the law looks upon them,

as if they had never been executed." id157.

In other words, courts do not tolerate any attempt to hinder, delay, or defraud creditors by means of a resort to "the veil of corporate entity." The ingenuity of the rogue, with his arsenal of scholastic sophistry, was met and overwhelmed by the sane and stern refusal of the court to be bound by the entity theory.

These earlier cases laid the ground work for one of the classic statements of the modern rule made by Judge Sandborn in United States v. Milwaukee Refrigerator Transit Co., *142 F. 247, 255 (C.C.E.D. Wis 1905)*, that:

"If any general rule can be laid down, in the present state of authority, it is that a corporation will be looked upon as a legal entity as a general rule, and until sufficient reason to the contrary appears; but, when the notion of legal entity is used to defeat public convenience, justify wrong, protect fraud, or defend crime, the law will regard the corporation as an association of persons ..."

The general rule, with its exceptions, has been applied as a form of judicial regulation of corporations, both large and small, notwithstanding their full compliance with statutory incorporation requirements. The test is simply whether or not recognition of the corporate entity would produce unjust or undesirable consequences inconsistent with the purposes of the concept.

The concept will be sustained only so long as it is invoked and employed for legitimate purposes. Perversion of the concept to improper uses and dishonest ends (for example, to perpetuate fraud, to evade the law, to escape obligations, etc.) will not be permitted by the courts. There are a great variety of cases and situations (discussed in detail later) in which courts will disregard the corporate entity to achieve a just result.

While the same principles for disregarding the corporate entity apply whether the corporation has one shareholder or many shareholders, the facts necessary for the application of such principles are most frequently encountered in cases of one-man, one-family, and other closed corporations, and subsidiary or other affiliated corporations.

The doctrine of disregarding the corporate entity is difficult to apply, and has been described as a problem that is still "enveloped in the mists of metaphor."

Is It A Rule Of Law Or An Exception To A Rule

Both. Few legal subjects have had so much trouble with semantics when it comes to the courts trying to give a lucid, clear statement of a principle of law. Many courts have referred to the concept of "piercing" the veil as a "rule" of law, a basic "principle" of law, "legal theory," and others. Other courts and writers point out that it is a "basic, fundamental principle" of law that the separate corporate entity is recognized by the law, and the opposite — disregarding it — is an exception to the rule. Either way, most modern courts and writers now refer to it as a rule of law; we will hereafter continue to do so.

Modern Statement of the Rule

An all inclusive statement of the modern rule as applied by the courts is:

> *"When the concept of the corporate entity is employed to defraud creditors, to evade an existing obligation, to circumvent a statute, to achieve or perpetuate monopoly, or to protect knavery or crime, the courts will draw aside the web of the corporate entity, and will regard the corporation as a sham, subterfuge or a fraud on the law, and will deal with the parties as individuals and will do justice between real persons."*

The principle of piercing the fiction of the corporate entity is, however, *to be applied with great caution*, and not with reckless abandon. While corporate entities may be disregarded where they are made the implement for avoiding a clear legislative purpose, they will not be disregarded where those in control have deliberately adopted the corporate form in order to secure its advantages and where no violence to the legislative purpose is done by treating the corporate entity as a separate legal person. This is your goal. If you comply with the laws and avoid wrongdoing you will be home free.

This Rule Is A Common Law Doctrine (Made By Judges) And Not Legislative

The legal doctrine that a court may disregard the corporate entity in specified cases is a common law rule developed by the judges only. There are no statutes that directly control the application of the rule; this is another reason that makes it so difficult to apply. Court decisions depend largely on the particular facts in each case — and the attitudes and experiences of the particular judge or jury. Essentially most cases are "fact finding" contests. That is why it is *important for you to know what "facts"* are important — and remember you make most of the significant, controlling, facts.

Particular Applications Of Principle Of Disregarding Corporate Entity

Each case involving disregard of the corporate entity must rest upon its special facts, however, the courts have developed broad general categories of cases — with infinite variations — as general rules, guides, or guidelines — for the application of the doctrine. There are six genral categories of cases in which the courts will disregard the corporate entity — pierce the corporate veil. They are:

1. Where the fiction is used to promote a fraud
2. Where the corporate fiction is resorted to as a means of

evading an existing legal obligation

3. Where the corporate fiction is employed to achieve or promote a monopoly

4. Where the corporate fiction is used to circumvent a statute

5. Where the corporate fiction is relied upon as a protection of crime or to justify wrong

6. Where a corporation is organized and operated as a mere tool or business conduit of another corporation.

The Court Used Guidelines To Determine Status

Insofar as you are personally concerned there are certain telling signs that courts look for in assisting them to determine the status of any particular case. These are:

1. Where the stockholders ignore the formalities of a running corporation (for example, failure to hold meetings, failure to record minutes of organizational meetings, etc.)

2. Where the stockholders ignore the existence of the corporation, for example, by mixing personal and corporate funds or by dealing with the corporation's customers as if they were the stockholder's customers; or treating the corporate debts and income as your own

3. Where the corporation is inadequately financed, for example, where the stockholders do not contribute enough capital so that there is a reasonable likelihood that the corporation can pay its debts

The mechanical application of some legal formula in determining whether or not the corporate veil should be pierced is inherently dangerous, and, as a practical matter, there is no general formula to fit all cases because of the ingenuity and imagination of the American business owner.

One court has made this observation about the rule:

"The general rules of law with respect to the piercing of the corporate veil and disregarding the corporate entity are well established, but they offer very little aid when it comes to the

decision of a particular case. The decisions are framed in broad principles and there are various theories used to justify the piercing." National Bond Finance Co. v. General Motors Corp. (1964, DC Mo) 238 F S 248, affirmed 341 F 2d 1022.

The courts are faced with the same problem as the Congress in its attempts to close tax loop holes. As soon as one tax loop hole is closed the American taxpayers think up two new ones. Under these circumstances the courts frequently say that each situation must be considered by the courts on its own merits. That's a wide range of booby traps!

Summary

A variety of metaphorical language has been used by the courts when they find it desirable to hold the real owners and operators of the corporation when the corporate form has been used for a purpose not permitted by the legislative privilege of carrying on a business in this form. Much of this language has appeared in parent-subsidiary cases though it is quite as applicable to the natural-person-solely-owned corporation or to one operated by unanimous consent of the shareholders where the corporation has more than one shareholder. Where the corporation has been used as an "instrumentality" or "adjunct" of the parent, or is merely an "alias" or "dummy" or "agency" or "alter ego" of the parent, the corporate veil will be pierced and the persons behind it exposed to the bright light of liability. They, not the corporation, were the real actors on a stage already set by themselves. If all this colorful language means is that the corporation is an agent of the shareholders who are the principals, there can be no quarrel with it though it does have a tendency to confuse. The corporation may, like a natural person, be an agent of natural or artificial persons. But the language has not been confined thus narrowly. It has been used to explain results which have a legitimate and realistic basis of explanation in the doctrine which limits the use of the corporate privilege to decent and fair objectives. Where the privilege is used in a manner not contemplated as a proper use of the corporate device it will be struck down and its shareholders held because of their misuse of the privilege.

Application Of The Rule

Cases in Point:

Even though the rule is stated in all inclusive language and we have carefully listed six general categories of cases, you must remember that cases come in all colors, shapes, forms, and varied factual situations; the courts simply put all the facts in a pot, stir it a bit and come up with a magic legal "decision." In order to give you a better picture of the rules we will discuss some of the general categories of cases and give selected, leading cases to illustrate the actions taken by the courts.

STRATEGY

Never deal with middlemen in investment deals.

Always deal with prime sources.

Never give a middleman an offer.

Never give him a financial statement.

Never give him references or personal information.

Always have your bullshit filter fine tuned when listening to a middleman—remember this about them—they have nothing to lose by telling you what you want to hear. They deal in icebergs—they show you the top, and let you find out what is under the surface later.

Negotiate only with prime sources.

Make your offers directly to the source—not through the middleman.

If the source won't deal directly with you—pass.

Finally, never—I repeat never give a middleman any kind of offer—written, oral or hand signal on any deal anywhere.

Middlemen in investment deals are brokers—bankers—accountants—lawyers—finders—relatives or anyone else who has no vested interest other than making the deal.

STRATEGY

Never fall in love with a product, service or business.

Treat them like mistresses not wives—wham, bam, thank you mam.

All products and services have limited lives—as they ripen you either have to plant new seeds to replace or improve them, or they will rot and become worthless.

The one certain thing is change—always be looking for the better way—the improvement—the future, not the past. If you need proof, look at the American automobile industry—the steel industry.

When is the last time you saw:

- An American made TV set
- An adding machine
- A fountain pen
- A wooden produce box
- A corner hamburger stand
- A laundry list
- A lot of men wearing hats
- A lot of women wearing hats
- A shaving brush
- A shoeshine stand on every corner
- A cigarette case

One third of the products and services we use today did not exist 20 years ago. One third of the products and serivces we use now will not exist 20 years from now.

Always be ready to move on!

CHAPTER 14
MAKING BUSINESS TAKEOVER OFFERS

The one reason it is simple to set up your wealth building program in the areas of these small retail and service business areas is the way you can make offers. You don't have to do an in depth financial study of the business financial records—you know from observation what they will show. All you do is make one standard offer. You will pay 80% (or less if investigation confirms) of the cost of the inventory-—and whatever price the fixtures and equipment would bring in the used market. That's it. The seller assumes all his current obligations —you take over the lease on the property—the lease or rental payments on any equipment needed in the operation—and you own the business. The seller pays all his obligations up to date of transfer—you assume no accounts payable—and he must have clear title to all fixtures and equipment he is selling to you.

This system makes it easy to submit offers. You pay nothing for so called good will—nothing for improvements made to property, etc. Remember, you are taking over a problem—not buying a business, and your offer reflects that. The seller will lose money on the sale—he expects that—he is willing to pay that to be rid of the problems.

You Can Do It All On OPM

You can take over these businesses with a line of credit at the bank. It may not work on the first one, but, the second one on: if fully financeable on a bank loan. Your sharecropper will assume the loan, so you have nothing invested yourself.

You arrange with the bank to borrow against the inventory and the assessed value of the fixtures (get an offer from a used equipment dealer to verify fixture value) and acquire the business. You can take over as many as you like with this kind of credit behind you—so size or number means nothing.

Preparing Your Plan

Once you have the business—you can prepare your business plan to turn it around and build it into a profit machine. You decide on the concept of the business—the possibility of name change—and then prepare a management plan—writing the necessary policies to implement it. This will come in four sections:

1. The Operations Plan
2. The Marketing Plan
3. The Financial Plan
4. The Expansion Plan

When this is finished you are ready to go after your sharecropper.

How to Close a Deal

If your offer is accepted, you will want to close the deal so all bases are covered and there are no surprises after you take over. Be sure:

1. All suppliers are notified that you will be taking over on the chosen date—and that you are not responsible for any debts prior to that date.
2. All taxes, federal, state and local are current to the date of take-over, and any not paid will be deducted from the seller's money in escrow and turned back to you.
3. Any leases that you are taking over have been cleared with the lessor so you take over without prejudice.
4. All business licenses have been transferred to you.

5. All wages have been paid to date of take-over—schedule take-over date on a Monday after payroll checks were issued to cover previous period.
6. All utilities have been transferred and all bills paid to date of transfer by seller.
7. All inventory you are buying is paid for.
8. All fixtures and equipment have clear titles.
9. Any contracts or maintenance agreements will either be cancelled at date of take-over, or assumed by you from take-over date—with clear understanding of those issuing the contracts you are not liable for any payments prior to take-over date.
10. All insurance has been transferred or cancelled as of take-over date.
11. All assets or other items belonging to the former owner have been removed from the premises prior to take-over date, and if not removed, sign and date an understanding you are in no way liable for them.
12. Your new set of books is set up and ready to open.
13. Your bank accounts are established and opened.
14. If there are accounts receivable—they go to seller with checks—you are not responsible for them in any way.
15. Publicity release has been prepared and given to local media.
16. New signs, stationery, etc., are on order—but not to be delivered until sharecropper takes over.
17. Pre-incorporation agreement is ready for sharecropper.
18. Your business plan is ready—with a 30 day transition plan in place to use until sharecropper takes over.
19. You have employee briefing on day of sale.
20. You have changed locks and security system.

If you follow the checklist you will make closing day a lot less hectic, and you will avoid bad surprises after the seller has taken the money and run.

As soon as you close, and the business is yours, you implement your sharecropper recruiting plan. You prepare an ad to run in the local paper—not a classified, but a display ad to be run on the business page—offering ownership of a retail corporation that will be expanding into a chain operation. You quote nominal salary and profit figures—state the experience required—and quote your investment price—stress that the applicant will be in complete charge, president of the corporation. Something like this:

RUN YOUR OWN COMPANY

HERE IS AN OPPORTUNITY FOR AN EXPERIENCED MANAGER WITH A GOOD TRACK RECORD TO TAKE OVER AS CHIEF EXECUTIVE OFFICER OF A RETAIL (KIND OF BUSINESS) OPERATION. YOU WILL RUN THE COMPANY — OWN A MAJORITY OF THE STOCK AS YOU DEVELOP IT — AND YOU START WITH $18,000 SALARY AND SUBSTANTIAL SHARE OF PROFITS (MINIMUM INCOME $30,000 FIRST YEAR) — NOMINAL INVESTMENT OF $12,000. SEND RESUME AND ANY PERTINENT INFORMATION TO — (BOX NUMBER)

An ad along that line will get the kind of response you are looking for—and you will be able to choose the person you want. That ad is a dream filler—every middle management executive in a large company dreams of being the CEO of his own firm—calling the shots and building the business. The ad will pull.

Interviewing the Sharecroppers Applicants

Best to have lunch with them. Give them a general outline of what you are doing—what part they will play in it—and then ask them about their background, interests, etc. The first meeting is to feel each other out—get the measure of the person and decide if any further discussion would be useful.

The second meeting should be at the store, after hours. You show the applicant the business plan—the financial projections, your timetable—and discuss the pre-incorporation agreement. You then ask for a commitment. You want a specific answer, within a time limit. Show him your stack of resumes, and tell him that you have to move on this. This sets the stage for his making the decision—you have applied legitimate pressure—and it's fish or cut bait.

You will have little trouble getting your man or woman with this program. In many cases they will be getting more money than they are making now, and the idea of owning a chain of successful stores, and the prestige of being the owner and president will do the job. This is the easiest part of the whole operation.

What You Want From the Deal

You have to decide clearly what you want from this deal in the way of income and building of assets for future conversion at capital gains tax rates. This will be included in the pre-incorporation agreement.

As a minimum I would want this:

1. A consulting fee income based on 2% of the gross volume of the business.
2. Stock that would be re-purchased by the corporation for at least five times earnings as projected in the business plan. The re-purchase plan can be two, five or even ten years in the future—a sinking fund to be set up and put in a trust fund against re-purchase.
3. An insurance policy paid for by the corporation to cover your investment—starting with $50,000 the first year and increasing as value of your holdings increase.
4. A trigger mechanism for you to regain control of the corpora-

tion if the sharecropper fails to meet certain minimum targets —with the right to buy him out at book value of this stock—less any wages, dividends or bonuses paid.

5. The right to borrow against the sinking fund, with a nominal interest rate—(this creates a bank for you to tap anytime you need funds).
6. Membership on the board of directors along with your lawyer and CPA—always have three members of the five man board. the sharecropper is one, and he chooses the other.
7. A policy in the by-laws on dividend payments that can create or defer income as needed.

You can add any goals you might have. In addition, have your attorney and CPA work these up in the pre-inc. agreement so they will stand up in operation.

The Sharecropper Agrees

When the sharecropper agrees, you file the corporation papers—and he pays in the money to cover costs on incorporation, opening of new books, and miscellaneous fees. Plus, I would always add $5,000 in cash for myself to cover my costs of setting up the deal. The sharecropper is getting in on a shoestring—he couldn't buy a hot dog stand for what he invests, and he is now in charge.

You can meet with him for lunch once a week to earn your consulting fees—and help him with ideas in implementing the plans. You have him under contract to your CPA for the bookkeeping, you are always in touch with the profit and loss situation. After he gets it going, you can leave him alone—let him do his thing—and you go on to the next deal.

Some Specific Examples of How This Works

Some years back one of my first deals was a small supermarket in an outlying area. The banker lent me the money to take it over. It was the only market in the area, but was not doing anywhere near the business it should. It had great turnaround potential. I did a market survey using Census Bureau Statistics and found that the average family was spending over $300 a month for groceries, and were driving a ten mile round trip past my store to get them. I got some incidental business — beer, bread, cigarettes from most people, but no big dollar grocery sales. I also discovered that nearly seventy percent of the people I interviewed on the phone had never heard of my store. I began asking customers what they thought about the store and the one major complaint was no fresh meat.

So, I leased some meat equipment (the store already had a locker we could use), and got a butcher to come in on a percentage deal. Then I set up some kids in the circular distribution business to cover the area. Then I got my sharecropper to come in and operate it. The business tripled in a few months, and I made a real killing.

Another deal was a motel that was barely breaking even. I got it on my terms because the owners didn't need cash, and they didn't want the headache. I put in a movie system, a swimming pool (with money borrowed from my banker), and the place was full every night — sometimes several times a night — because my movie system was both first run movies or X-rated movies. I sharecroppered it, and I had less than $2,000 of my own money invested and got all that back the first month. From then on it was gravy.

The point is that you don't have to do big things, just spot the marketing method that will turn the business around. Small business can be turned around in a few months, and grow steadily from that point when professional management techniques are applied. The hardest job you have in this is getting the right takeover deal — the rest is really very simple.

TACTICS

Cost is secondary in purchasing income producers.

Price is not the primary consideration when you are buying things or services to make money. Getting it cheap is often the most expensive.

That is true of:

- People you hire
- Equipment you buy
- Services you use

The primary consideration is contribution to business success—to the bottom line. This does not mean that most expensive is necessarily the best—it means that you do not make a decision based purely on cost.

The young man went with the old farmer to the cattle show. The farmer looked at two animals—one an old cow that cost $100 and the other a fine young bull that cost $50. The farmer bought the cow—the young man asked him why he paid twice as much for an old cow rather than pay half as much for the young bull. The farmer replied, "I would have to feed either one—the cow will eat my grass and provide me with milk, butter and cheese. The bull would eat my grass and all I would get is bullshit."

CHAPTER 15
MARKETING SURVEYS OF TAKEOVER PROSPECTS

The key to getting the right takeover deal is to identify a market that has turnaround potential, one with enough purchasing power to support a higher volume of business and where the competition is weak or non-existent. The best way to do this is to use the location survey techniques that professionals use to choose a new store location.

The basic source of information on defining a marketing area is the standard metropolitan statistical area tracts put out by the Census Bureau. There are 241 of the SMSA's published to cover the United States. They cover about 70% of the total population. The reports cover metropolitan areas in one mode — counties, cities and census tracts in others. These are published once every ten years — and can be outdated quickly — buy, updates are printed every year in July by Sales and Marketing Management magazine, and the tracts can be kept fairly accurate by adjusting dollar figures for inflation — and population figures from growth or decline statistics available from local government agencies or Chambers of Commerce.

First, identify your area by census tract number. Then you can go to specific information.

Use census tract data pages 4-5-6-7-8.

You can update this from average growth/decline rates in the community and adjust dollars for inflation/deflation since date of census.

The Census of Retail Trade

This is called the Economic Census by the Bureau — they are taken every five years and come in area reports, giving number of stores, gross sales per year, size of payrolls, etc. There are merchandise lines reports that give the number of establishments carrying various lines of merchandise — such as cosmetics, drugs, cleaners, dresses, footwear, etc., giving gross sales, and percentage of gross sales each line produced for those store carrying it. There are tracts of major retail centers — gross retail trade in counties, cities, etc. and much more. These tracts tell you how business is doing in your line in your area, how many stores are in the business, and the numbers of their employees, payroll, etc.

Using the SMSA's and the Economic Census materials, here is the kind of information you can come up with. We'll use curtain and drapery sales as an example.

METHODS OF ESTIMATING POTENTIAL DRAPERY SALES IN A SPECIFIC TRADING AREA

Method #1

Data

(1) Total 1970 SMSA drapery sales = $4,544,000.

(2) Total owner-occupied homes 1970 SMSA = 58,032.

(3) Divided #1 by #2; the average expenditure per household for curtains in 1970 was $78.30 in the specific SMSA.

(4) Adjustment for changes in cost of living = 173.5% from 1969 to 1978.

(5) Multiply #3 by #4; the average estimated expenditure per household for draperies in 1978 is $135.85 in the specific SMSA.

(6) 82% of the households in census tract 205.03 are owner-occupied.

(7) Multiply #6 by 2,577 households (projections in Table 1); an estimated 2,113 households in census tract 205.03 are

owner-occupied.

(8) Multiply #7 by #5; estimated drapery sales in census tract 205.03 are $287,051 by Method #1.

Method #2

Data

(1) 1970 SMSA drapery sales = $4,544,000.

(2) Total 1970 income of SMSA = $841,239,000.

(3) Divide #1 by #2; .005% of total income in SMSA was spent on curtain item.

(4) Multiply average 1977 household income (Table 1) by #3; an average of $127.78 per household for curtain items in 1977.

(5) Multiply the number of owner-occupied households in the census tract by #4; estimated drapery sales in census tract 205.03 are $269,999 by Method #2.

So, you can use this information to make an intelligent estimate of your market potential — and base your marketing plans on that information.

Summary

Using Census Data In Small Plant Marketing

The statistics published by the Bureau of the Census concern the economic lives of people. These facts and figures are valuable marketing information for the owner-manager of a small plant. While you will not find ready-made answers in the Census data, the owner-manager can find clues which will be useful in working out solutions to your particular problems — whether marketing consumer or industrial products.

This aid stresses consumer products. However, the procedure for using Census data — breaking the marketing problem down into questions — is similar for industrial products. The aid offers examples of how small manufacturers use Census statistics.

"I know I need it, but I can't afford it," is the way many owner-managers of manufacturing companies feel about marketing research.

They are right, in a way. Often their companies cannot afford complex studies to gather a wide range of information about markets, potential markets, their products, and new products.

Yet, small companies are the ones that often need marketing information in order to compete effectively. When the money you can spend for product development and marketing is limited, you have to make every dollar count. For example, you cannot afford to spend a thousand dollars on advertising that goes to the wrong people — ones who are only marginal prospects for your products.

In using every marketing dollar to the best advantage, you may be overlooking a useful source of information. It is the United States Bureau of the Census. The statistics which this agency gathers are a valuable resource. In fact, the information concerns your greatest resource for marketing — the people of the United States and their economic activities.

By knowing and applying the appropriate statistics to your problems, you can market your products to better advantage. For example, you might use Census information to stretch your advertising dollars, to reduce the risk of new product introduction, or to improve the accuracy of marketing decisions.

Kinds of Data

The kinds of Census data used depend on your products and the types of markets you serve. If you sell an industrial product, valves, for example, you would need information about manufacturers. On the other hand, if you make a consumer product, such as neckties, you would need information about people — especially about men.

The various kinds of Census statistics are listed in the section,

"Getting Census Reports."

Whether the data is about manufacturing, mining, population, or housing, the pattern is the same for using the information in marketing research. In this **Aid**, the Census of Population and the Census of Housing are used as examples.

Population and Housing. The Census of Population and the Census of Housing provide information about: sex, race, number of persons in household; number and types of rooms; water availability; method of house heating; availability of telephones; presence of clothes washer, dryer, television, radio, air conditioner; and number of automobiles, and other items. The Bureau gathers this information every 10 years and updates it with periodic estimates. The 1980 Census statistics were available in the spring of 1981. Some preliminary statistics were available between July and November 1980. The next Census will be in 1990.

The reports are issued by area and subject and are sold by the Superintendent of Documents, Washington, D.C. 20402. For example, the population report for the State of Missouri consists of 1,071 pages and is entitled **Census of Population: 1970, Volume 1, Characteristics of the Population, Part 27, Missouri**.

The summary report on the Nation's population is titled **1970 Census of Population, Volume 1, Characteristics of the Population, Part A, Number of Inhabitants** (Section 1 and Section 2). These 2 books are sold as a set and include chapters of tables for each of the 50 States, the District of Columbia, Puerto Rico, Guam, the Virgin Islands, American Samoa, and the Canal Zone.

The housing report for Missouri is titled **U.S. Bureau of Census, Census of Housing: 1970, Vol. 1, Housing Characteristics for States, Cities and Counties, Part 27, Missouri.**

Business. The Bureau also provides information on retail, wholesale, and selected services in its **Census of Business**. These reports present data, such as sales size of establishment, employment size of establishment, and sales by merchandise lines. For additional information, see the **Bureau of Census Catalog**.

In addition, the Bureau of the Census, for a fee, will tabulate special data to meet a company's individual needs. The policy on such services is described in the **Bureau of Census Catalog**.

Interpretation Starts With Questions

In applying Census statistics to your market planning, you should keep in mind that the Bureau of the Census compiles descriptive data. You have to do the interpreting.

Interpretation starts with questions. The pieces of Census information you use depend on the questions to which you need answers. Suppose that you want to set up several new sales territories. Your question is: what geographical areas contain the best products? In working out an answer to this type of question, data extracted directly from the Census tables can be immediately useful. You can use information such as income, family size, and occupation, for example. This type of information is reported for areas as small as "census tracts" in 267 metropolitan regions. A census tract consists of about 4,000 —5,000 persons.

A limited amount of information is provided for each block in cities of 50,000 or more inhabitants. This information includes the population count, condition of housing unit, plumbing facilities available, tenure, value of owner-occupied units, rent of rented units, color of occupants, and units with 1.01 or more persons per room.

A sales territory may be set up by using multiples of these basic units, such as city blocks. This arrangement is particularly valuable for a door-to-door sales force.

Once you have determined where to establish your territories, the sales manager can use Census data as an aid to setting equitable sales quotas. A study of detailed Census reports of employment levels, income, and population density for each unit of a sales territory can show the potential or lack of it for each unit.

If your type of product is actually covered in the Census, you can use the information without translating it. For example, the Census of Housing carries statistics on home appliances, such as, washing machines and freezers. However, when there are no Census figures on your type of product, you have to use related data. By assuming that areas with heavy concentrations of a certain product are also good prospects for a similar type of product, you often make valid inferences about your market potential.

Examples of Use

The experience of a small manufacturer of automobile dashboard accessories provides an example of using Census figures as an aid in adding new sales territories. "Where are the high concentrations of automobiles?" was the first question.

With the answer, the accessory maker then looked to see which of the geographical areas under consideration had concentrations of auto supply stores and variety stores — the kinds of retail outlets that did the best job with these products. This information was in the **Census of Business**.

Another example of relating Census data to an individual company's problem is the market research done by a manufacturer of paneling and room accessories. This company had franchise arrangements with local contractors who used the materials to convert basements into finished rooms.

In this case, to widen your market, you first have to find an answer to: What areas will be best for franchises. The Census statistics on housing helps you to learn: (1) the type of homes that predominated in a particular area, and (2) whether they were built on concrete slabs or with a full basement. You can quickly rule out the areas where the houses have no basements.

Your next question is: Can people in the particular area afford to finish off their basement. You examine data on family income and the number of children. Then you examine the statistics on car ownership. You look for families that owned more than one car — an indication that they had discretionary income which might be spent for home improvement. As a result of your study of Census data, you are able to grant franchises in areas which had a good market potential. Census data can be useful also for keeping a company in step with its customers. One apparel manufacturer, for example, studied Census statistics for possible trends that might affect his business. When the figures showed that the population in the areas where he was selling had a high concentration of teenagers and young adults, he added new styles directed at these groups.

Advertising

You can also use Census data to help control your advertising budget. The fact that the sales of many small plants are regional rather than national makes the advertising and promotional job easier.

Even if you sell in the national market, the analysis of individual regions can be useful in planning advertising. Looking at the regions that make up the national market should indicate whether you need to design different sales strategies and advertising campaigns for each area.

Some national magazines operate on production schedules that allow advertising content to vary by type of market. In addition, spot radio and television commercials can be changed to pinpoint specific areas with tailor-made sales messages.

Thus stretching your advertising dollars becomes a matter of answering two questions: (1) In what areas should I advertise, and (2) Which medium reaches the right audience — the one that contains my customers and potential customers. The answer to either question depends on the audience composition in each area.

The Census data can detail an audience profile in terms of buying power, education level, occupation, and other factors bearing on the selection and tailoring of a marketing approach. The information is available from the Government at low cost. With these facts, you can more accurately select media and relate advertising potential to cost. An example is seen in the experience of a cosmetics company which markets its products in serveral sections of the country. Its owner-manager uses Census data to keep track of the age groupings of the female population. From the Census figures, the manager learns what groups are prospects for certain products and where these groups are located and then places advertising in media which are used by members of the groups. The manager also sees that sales outlets are stocked with the advertised products.

New Product Introduction

When developing and introducing new products, the owner-manager can also use Census data in two ways. First, new products may be suggested because the statistics reflect the living patterns of consumers. Second, the statistics may be used in connection with marketing testing. The Census supplies demographic characteristics, such as age, sex, color, and marital status, which can be helpful in selecting test market cities.

The experience of a small meat packing plant provides an example of using Census data in new product development. You learn that the statistics for your sales area showed an impressive number of home freezers. In these, you see a new market — cuts of meat sold in bulk lots for storage in home freezers.

There is no "typical" test city in which a new product can be put on sale to measure consumer reaction. The problem is to select a city or area that will yield the information you need for deciding whether to go ahead with the product or to drop it.

Because they indicate the characteristics of a city's population, Census reports can be used to help pick a test city or cities. Along with this data, you use information which you have about your product distribution and information about the available advertising media.

Update When Possible

In using the Bureau of Census reports, it is important to regard them as basic guides and update them with other information whenever possible. The vital thing in marketing is using current information or as current as possible. To make sure that you have it, you should consult sources of marketing information. In some cases, you can update Census information by conducting your own survey. For example, one builder of houses believes that most people buy homes valued at approximately 2½ times their annual salary. Before the builder decides on the type of houses to build in a particular area, the builder updates the Census data by making a survey of the income level and the prices of homes in that area.

Getting Census Reports

The Bureau of the Census issues many publications of information that is gathered in the following censuses:

Population and **Housing** Censuses taken every 10th year ending in "0", example 1970.

Government Census—taken every 5th year ending in "2" and "7", example 1967, 1972. (This Census provides data on the characteristics and functions of state and local government.)

Business, Manufacturers, and **Mineral Industries** Censuses — taken every 5th year, beginning in 1967, in years ending in "2" and "7".

Agriculture Census—taken every 5th year ending in "4" and "9", example 1969, 1974.

In addition, the Bureau makes a monthly report of business conditions in a publication called **Business Conditions Digest.**

The publications are listed under the following headings in the Bureau's catalog: General, Agriculture, Construction and Housing, Distribution and Services, Foreign Trade, Geography, Governments,

Manufacturing and Mineral Industries, Population, and Transportation. The catalog indexes the reports by subjects. A special section describes the Census data files and unpublished materials which can be used for special tabulations. These are offered on an annual subscription basis.

The catalog is issued quarterly, with monthly supplements, available from the Superintendent of Documents, Washington, D.C. 20402. Ask for **Bureau of the Census Catalog.**

If you will follow the outline for the business plan I give you, you can put together a plan that will get the results you want.

TACTICS

Always chase prices on expense items.

Look for the bargains in expense items—such products as:

- Common office and plant supplies
- Maintenance supplies
- Non-critical devices and machines
- Common services
- Fuel and utility costs

Look into:

- Discounts for bulk purchases
- Used equipment
- Auction buys
- Closeout deals
- Special discounts offered trade, etc.

Remember—at 5% (the nation average net profit), every dollar you can save on expense items equals $20 in gross business.

STRATEGY

Multiply yourself and get lucky.

Use people as assets in building your business and personal wealth.

Let them find opportunities for you—bring good ideas to you—increase your potential.

Turn the people you know into a network of contacts and finders—who will help you find new sources of business—tell you about new opportunities. All you have to do is tell them what you want—ask their advice on how to get it.

This will result in a thousand pair of eyes and ears out there finding things that will help you succeed.

Luck is defined as being in the right place at the right time when something of benefit happens. The more you multiply yourself through others—building a network of relatives, friends and people you buy and sell to—the more good luck you are going to have.

It's like having a no cost bet on every horse in the race—you can't' lose.

CHAPTER 16
BUILDING WEALTH WITH SHARECROPPERS

I'm going to show you how you can use professional management planning, corporations and people who want to own their own businesses to make your fortune. One hundred years ago, four out of five people in this country were entrepreneurs. They made their money as farmers, merchants, professionals, ranchers, builders, etc. Today, four out of five are living on paychecks. But, the yen to be independent, to have a shot at economic security and the personal freedom it brings is one that runs deep in the American spirit. It can be harnessed to build a fortune.

There is an area of opportunity in this country that few people are aware of, that small retail and service businesses can produce very sizeable incomes when they are properly managed and developed. Unfortunately, very few of the people now in these businesses understand that, and most of the businesses are only marginally successful. They are paycheck providers for the owners who have few real skills beyond their ability to serve customers or render a service of some type.

To give you an example, a research team tracked 80 small business firms from their inception. Just two of the eighty made substantial successes. Six, made above average livings for their founders. And the rest either failed or provided only marginal incomes for the owners. The national statistics of small business income bears this out, and presents the individual willing to apply professional management skills to the operations, and some imagination and sustained effort to the marketing, an opportunity to make 200% to 500% return on investment in a year—and a possible fortune after that from just one venture.

The Art Of Becoming A Professional Entrepreneur

There are thousands of marginally profitable small businesses out there, and the easieist ones with which to start your sharecropper program of wealth building are the small, retail businesses that have a lot of potential for turning around, in their present locations, and making a lot of money doing it.

Over half the small businesses in operation right now have this potential. They are run by people who are making a modest living, little, if any return on investment and will never get any better under the present ownership. All of these are for sale—and many of them can be had for little or no investment on your part. They are problems for the present owners, who have no more idea of how to sell their businesses than they do of how to sell their products or services. They want to get something out of the business in the way of cash—but the main goal is to have someone take the problem off their hands.

These situations are easy to spot. The place of business will reflect the problem with an eyeball survey. The key spot is the backroom—if it's dirty—in disorder—inventory carelessly stacked and scattered—parts and pieces of things laying around, etc.,—you've got a loser. You can verify this by talking to the owner.

Comments like "You can't get good help anymore," "The customers are stealing me blind," "Advertising never works for me," "My competitors are crazy for selling at those prices," "Training employees is a waste of time because they won't stay anyway," "Taxes are killing me," "I never depend on hired help or borrowed money," are what you hear from losers who want out.

It doesn't take any intensive search to find these businesses—just walk through any business district or shopping center and you'll find them. You'll find business opportunity brokers with hundreds of them listed. You'll find some owners advertising them in the papers. No problem finding them—just sort out the wheat from the chaff. Many of them cannot be saved or turned around because of existing competition—poor location—lack of market—or simply it's been run down too long to make the effort worthwhile. But, others are diamonds in the ruff, simply needing faceting and polishing to turn them into gems.

I'm going to give you a list of some of the best local opportunities in terms of return on investment. These businesses, when turned around, can produce a substantial return on investment. (This is not important to you as you will have little or no investment—but it will be to your sharecropper who will have an investment).

NAME OF BUSINESS	INVESTMENT	ROI
Building Materials & Hardware	$ 90,000	80%
Retail Bakeries	30,000	100%
Candy and Nut Store	30,000	100%
Candy Making Store	30,000	100%
Convenience Foods	45,000	100%
Delicatessen	45,000	100%
Donut Shop	40,000	80%
Health Foods	50,000	90%
Liquor Store	90,000	125%
Retail Meat Market	25,000	250%
Specialty Foods	40,000	130%
Fast Foods	50,000	100%
Restaurant and Bar	100,000	90%
Pizza	60,000	150%
Bridal Shop	50,000	130%
Curtain & Draperies	85,000	90%
Furniture Store	250,000	90%

Camera Store	85,000	80%
Drug Store	250,000	80%
Florist Shop	50,000	150%
Hobby Shop	35,000	100%
Lawn & Garden Supply	50,000	100%
Sporting Goods	75,000	100%
Beauty Shop	50,000	100%
Coin Op Laundromat	50,000	80%
Dry Cleaners	60,000	70%
Key Shop	12,000	130%
Travel Agency	30,000	150%
Auto Specialty Store	50,000	100%
Luggage and Leather Goods	125,000	100%

This gives you an idea of the potentials for managing a small business to its greatest potential. The return on investment means—that after reasonable salaries are paid to the owner—manager and the help and all expenses paid, the yearly net profit is 70% or more of the total investment.

Some Information On Preparing Your Plan

Your plan will implement good management—the proper mix and amounts of inventory for the area—and the sales program to sell the goods or services. In addition you will show pro-forma financial projections of income and profits based on marketing results—then a plan to expand the operation into either a larger store or branch stores.

These projections will be made to indicate the following results:

1. High sales per employee.
2. High return on investment or net worth.
3. Efficient return on total assets employed.
4. Efficient sales to inventory ratio.
5. A 20% or more annual growth rate in sales and profits.

Here is a look at how successful firms operate in these areas.

Sales per employee	$35,000–$55,000
Return on net worth	12% to 20%
Return on total assets	6% to 15%
Inventory/sales ratio	15% to 25%
Annual sales growth	12% to 40%
Annual profit growth	15% to 35%

These are your target figures in developing your business plan for the venture.

The retail trade looks at dollars per square foot as the key to profitability. Here are some figures from major shopping centers as indicators of how many stores operate on various $ per sq. ft. ratios.

Sales Per Sq. Ft.	% of Stores
68 to 76	14.0
77 to 85	25.6
86 to 94	27.9
95 to 103	24.4
104 and over	8.1

These vary from center to center in similar businesses, but it gives you an overview of dollars per square foot selling in the most efficient retail market.

Another angle is to estimate the number of retail people needed to handle business per square foot. (This excludes labor intensive businesses like restaurants—beauty shops, etc.—these are for retail stores.)

Size of Store	Full Time	Part Time
1,000 or less	1	0
1,500–2,500	1	1
3,000–4,500	2	1
5,000–7,000	3	1
8,000–7,000	4	1
10,000	5	0

This will give you a horseback estimate of the number of employees needed to run a store you take over.

One important fact you need to know is the estimate of sales required to break even for various businesses. You can use per sq. ft. sales to make this estimate. First, you need to determine your fixed costs per square foot. Then you need to establish a percentage of variable cost rates. You take the cost of goods sold (what is paid for inventory), add in freight, shrinkage (theft, breakage, etc.), markdowns, bags, string, etc. This cost is expressed in percentages of gross dollars taken in. The chart below will show you a quick estimate of sales per square foot needed to break even using a dollar fixed cost—and a percentage variable cost.

FINDING BREAKEVEN SQUARE FOOT SALES

Fixed Expense (dollars/ sq. ft.)	Variable Cost Rate 0.60	0.65	0.70	0.75	0.80	0.85	0.90
10	25	28.57	33.33	40	50	66.67	100
12	30	34.28	40.00	48	60	80.00	120
14	35	40.00	46.67	56	70	93.33	140
16	40	45.71	53.33	64	80	106.67	160
18	45	51.43	60.00	72	90	120.00	180
20	50	57.14	66.67	80	100	133.33	200
22	55	62.85	73.33	88	110	146.67	220
24	60	68.57	80.00	96	120	160.00	240
26	65	74.28	86.67	104	130	173.33	260
28	70	80.00	93.33	112	140	186.67	280
30	75	85.71	100.00	120	150	200.00	300

The Axioms Of Profit Building

Here is a chart that will put the deal in perspective for you. By looking at the sales per square foot, and noting the way profits increase as volume increases — you will find these things to be true.

THE FIGURES OF FORTUNE BUILDING

	Sales per Square Foot		
	$50 ($1000)	$100 ($1000)	$200 ($1000)
1000 square foot store			
Total sales	50.00	100.00	200.00
Variable expense	37.5	75.0	150.0
Fixed expense	12.5	12.5	12.5
Total expense	50.0	87.5	162.5
NET PROFIT	–0–	12.5	37.5
2000 square foot store			
Total sales	100.00	200.00	400.00
Variable expense	75.0	150.0	300.0
Fixed expense	25.0	25.0	25.0
Total expense	100.0	175.0	325.0
NET PROFIT	–0–	25.0	75.0
4000 square foot store			
Total sales	200.00	400.00	800.00
Variable expense	150.0	300.0	600.0
Fixed expense	50.0	50.0	50.0
Total expense	200.0	350.0	650.0
NET PROFIT	–0–	50.0	150.0

When you double the size of a store losing money — you double the losses.

If you double volume in the same size store you triple profits.

If you expand without increasing sales — you reduce profits.

The goal then, is to double the volume of the stores, without increasing the size. Write your business plan to that goal and you will get your sharecropper to implement it with no trouble.

An Example Of How It Might Work

I will hypothesize a situation where you have found a curtain and drapery shop for sale. The owner is asking $75,000 for the store. It has been in business three years in a good location, and is grossing $210,600 in a 2800 square foot store.

You talk to the owner on the phone and he tells you that he is selling the business because his wife is in poor health and he must move to a warmer climate. He tells you business is good and growing and that he wants all cash.

You arrange to meet with him at the business, and he takes you on a tour of the place. You find the merchandise is not well displayed, piled up and a certain amount of clutter. There is one woman employee serving customers in a rather disinterested way. The back room is a mess, the owner explains he hasn't had time to put things in stock, and his part-time helper who handles it has been out of town for a week. His office looks like an unmade bed, and you are interrupted by several phone calls in which he is angrily talking to suppliers about late shipments, and another to a dissatisfied customer who he treats rather brusquely.

The man is nervous and obviously under pressure, and you can assume that he is not a good manager and is suffering daily problems because of it. You begin to see the reason for the attempted sale and it has nothing to do with his wife's health.

You get a financial statement from him; it has been prepared by an accountant — so you can assume it is not too far off the mark. The first thing you want to find out is what the value of this store would be to you. You find this on the statement.

Inventory Value	$25,000
Fixtures and Equipment	8,500
Prepaid Cash Deposits	2,000
TOTAL VALUE OF THESE THREE ITEMS	$35,000

Now, assuming that you would be interested in this business — you have all the figures you need to prepare an offer. You have no interest in his quoted price, and are only interested in the assets he has to offer. You pay no attention to goodwill (after listening to him on the phone you know there is very little of that) or to other assets listed on the financial statement. On the basis of the information your offer would look like this:

Inventory Less Markdowns	$20,000
Equipment & Fixtures at Today's Market	3,500

Prepaid Cash Deposits	2,000
TOTAL OFFERING PRICE	$25,500

So your offering price is roughly $50,000 less than his asking price. It is important to remember in this program the asking price is meaningless. So, why would the seller even consider such an offer? Let's look at the financial statement to determine the real reason for selling the business.

The store is 2800 sq. ft., and annual gross sales amount to $72 a square foot.

Annual Gross Sales	$210,600
Cost of Goods Sold	110,800
Gross Operating Profit	90,720
FIXED COSTS	
Rent and Utilities	24,192
Payroll (Includes $15,000 for Owner)	22,176
Other Fixed Costs	6,048
VARIABLE COSTS	
Payroll (Part-time Help and Overtime)	22,176
Other Variable Expenses	10,080
Total Variable Expenses	32,656
Total Operating Costs	84,672
NET PROFIT	6,048

By looking at these figures we can begin to see the light. Here is an owner — working his tail off — probably 80 or more hours a week and he has a $15,000 draw and $6,000 and change in profit — a $21,000 a year income. If we break that income down to hourly pay — he's earning just over five bucks an hour before taxes. He can do better than that pushing a broom.

So, we have discovered the real reason for selling. He is not selling a business he's trying to unload a problem. This is why, if he can't find a sucker willing to pay him the $75,000 — he will consider this offer. It represents more than a full year's salary he won't have to sweat for, and he'll have some losses to write off his taxes so he can keep most of the money.

What Can You Do With This Business

You investigate the industry and find that it is hot and growing. People are not buying new homes they are fixing up the old ones. So, you have a growing market and a good location with a three year old business already established and operating at a profit.

You decide that professional management applied to the business can be put together with a solid marketing plan and the gross sales easily doubled with the present payroll and store size. You can put in a sharecropper, and make a bundle. Here is what the same business would look like with $150 per sq. ft. of sales.

Gross Sales	$420,000
Cost of Goods Sold	231,000
Gross Operating Profit	189,000
FIXED EXPENSES	
Rent and Utilities	25,200
Fixed Payroll Costs	23,100
Other Fixed Costs	6,300
Total Fixed Costs	54,600
VARIABLE COSTS	
Variable Payroll	23,100
Other Costs	21,000
Total Operating Costs	98,700
NET PROFIT	90,300

By doubling the volume, you can increase net profits 15 times what the seller is making. You can sell a sharecropper on that business plan easily.

You Turn The Deal On The Banker's Money

You can swing this deal with a bank loan. You show the banker your plan and projections — you arrange to borrow the $25,500 from him, if the seller accepts your offer. You show him that his bank will get the corporation business — it will assume the loan — and there will be more business in inventory loans as it grows. If the banker knows you, he'll like this deal because it builds a fat account for him.

Writing The Business And Marketing Plan

The key to your success with these deals is your ability to write a logical, proveable business and marketing plan to turn these marginal small businesses into highly profitable operations. The Business Plan Writer (Chapter 29) you will find further along in the book will make it simple for you to do this. It takes you step-by-step through the business plan writing sequence so you finish up with a logical and useable plan to reach a stated goal.

The plan should cover the professional management aspects of the business, an organization plan, writing the policy statements and careful selection and training of employees. The key to any business turnaround is the people working in the business. In most cases you will find that you will have to replace the present staff with people that you hire. The staff that has been working for a marginal business operation is not receptive to changing its ways and working a lot harder.

The plan is what you are going to use to get your sharecropper into the business and run it for you. So, it has to show him or her that there is more to come than just running a small store. All plans should have specific expansion timetables in them so the sharecropper will be president of a profitable corporation — not a store manager.

The Looking And Offering Process

The first thing to consider is how to frame an offer on a business. You know, at first look, your offer is going to be insulting to the owner. In fact, some of these hardheads will close the business down, and lose it all rather than sell out to someone who makes what they consider an insulting offer. But, remember this — you are not interested in how the seller feels, all you want from him is a yes or no. You have no real interest in anything but taking over the business on the terms and conditions you outline — and you never have to have any one deal. There are always more of them out there — and one or two deals a year are going to make you a multi-millionaire.

You never offer more than the value of the assets if they have to be sold at the market prices at the time of the offer. This is vital — don't get excited about any deal and don't push to get it by raising the ante. This gets you in trouble, and eliminates the true leverage you have in this program.

After you see the owner's place of business and have the financial information — then frame your offer and make it to the owner in writing. Tell him frankly that it is all you can offer at this time, and if he is interested in accepting it to notify you within 30 days — otherwise the offer expires. This puts the ball in his court and he will either take it or leave it.

The thing I like about these small business offers is that there is no negotiating. The offer is cut and dried, and it's accepted or rejected. When you get into deals where you are trying to buy manufacturing plants, or processing businesses there are many facets to them, and it takes a lot of analyzing of financial statements — audits of the books and other investigations to get a deal. Small retail businesses are just what they appear to be, and you can make an offer based on inventory and assets.

Getting The True Financial Statement

Many small businesses have no real summary account records — no accurate balance sheet or income statement. The buyer is supposed to audit the books to find out what he needs to know — at his expense. Forget that! Here's all you have to do if the seller has no statements prepared by a responsible accountant. Have the owner write the IRS and have copies of his last three years Schedule C of the 1040 Tax Form sent to you. This is the form used to report business income for tax purposes; it gives you the information you need to make an offer. The gross business, the net profit and the depreciable assets are listed. You don't need any other financial information — and you can assume the figures are probably close to correct because of the threat of audit. Don't accept copies of the Schedule C unless you get them from a tax preparer, the owner can make up his own to show you. Either have them come from the IRS or from the files of the person who prepares his taxes.

If he uses an accountant have the accountant give you the financial statements, then get the Schedule C's to see how they compare.

If the owner refuses to give the C schedules, then you pass on the deal. You don't have time, or the need, to play hide and seek with sellers or brokers. Either they are ready to deal — or they are running a scam. You will not talk any further until you have the C's — and that's final.

On Dealing With Business Opportunity Brokers

The seller has to pay the broker — that makes him the seller's problem. If you are asked to sign a release, or waiver form by a broker before you see a business he has to sell — pass on it. That means he does not have the seller locked up — and wants to lock you up. If you check the form it will cover the obligation for you to pay the broker's fee if the buyer refuses — and not just on one deal but on any deal you make where he might have a listing. Sign nothing with brokers, and make no oral agreements with them about anything. If they can't handle the seller, that's their problem.

Some brokers will try to get you to make an offer on a business before you can see the financial statements or audit the books. Forget that too! You make no offers, sign no papers and make no promises about anything. The best move to make is to tell the broker that your offer is that you won't kick him in the ass this time, but if he ever tries it on you again, you will.

There are different types of brokers. Some specialize in certain fields where the suckers gather. Those who sell taverns, liquor stores, cafes, etc., sell to virgins who have never been in business before. They sell business garbage, and this is where you get them to make an offer, sign a paper pitch.

There are some brokers who are realistic, and do as good a job as can be done in this field. You've got to remember this is a poker game — everyone is lying to everyone else — the only truth you hear is "money talks and bullshit walks," to quote one of the ABSCAM Congressmen. This broker will give you listings, introduce you to the owners, and act as a middleman in the deal. Just keep one fact in mind about brokers — the only interest they have in you is the commission they can earn. You are meat on the table, and that's all. So, whatever they tell you is to get you to buy. These people don't have much repeat business, so anything goes in making a sale.

Always give your offer to the owner — by mail — to his business or home address. Never submit it through a broker as he will probably tear it up. He would rather wait for the sucker to come along, and pay the asking price, than get the seller off the hook. The buyer can react as he chooses, but he does get your offer. And, remember this about your offer — you have some powerful psychology working for you even though the offer is nowhere near the asking price. The day the owner decided to sell was the day he really started losing interest in the business. He no longer considers the business as his — he is only a caretaker till the buyer shows up. His daily tasks become a lot of hard work — and he is thinking about greener fields, and a better life. As the days roll by, your offer is in the back of his mind, and as the petty problems pile up, and the things he hates to do keep rolling around, the better your offer begins to look. At some point, when he's really had a day where everything went wrong, he says "to hell with this," and calls you up and takes the offer.

Let me remind you — your offer is not negotiable. If the owner calls up and makes a counter offer — you turn it down. You have made the only offer you intend to make, and it's yes or no. Put a 30-day time limit on it — so he knows where he stands. If he brings in a lawyer who wants to discuss it — put your lawyer in touch with his lawyer. Never negotiate with anyone.

If you follow that rule, you won't have to put up with a lot of BS from the seller — the broker — or lawyers. If you ever give in on a single point, then you are back at the starting point, and have to negotiate all over again. Don't do it — there are too many other deals around to get involved with anyone beyond an offer.

How To Find The Deals And Make The Offers

You can find deals through brokers, through ads in the newspaper, and, if you like to do a little hustling, by going around to good shopping areas and visiting places of business. When you spot one that you can see is poorly managed, and because of location has a good turnaround potential, ask to see the owner an tell him or her you are looking for a small business to buy. And ask if they would like to sell. You'll be surprised at how many would.

It is important to keep in mind that this is a program where one or two acquisitions a year are all you are interested in — and you can run the operation like a hobby. Look over businesses in your sparetime — and build a file of them. A guy who won't sell this month, might be in the market two months later. And this is important. Always have a half a dozen under consideration at any one time. By under consideration, I mean, six you haven't made an offer on, but are considering.

You've got lots of time to make offers in this field — as businesses are not sold like hamburgers. The average business for sale will be on the market six months or more before it's sold, folded or withdrawn from the market.

The reason for having six or more to think about is that you want the best potential turnaround deal you can find. As you discard one, pick up another — and don't be too hasty about making offers. You can take some time to research them — decide on the potential — and compare results in order to pick the right property.

Investigating Turnaround Potentials

The turnaround potential of a small business is not too hard to determine. It relates to two things — the size of the market in both population and dollars — and the degree of competence of the competition. If you have a solid market from the business location (most small businesses have a two to three mile radius around the store as the primary market) — and the competition is average — you've got a possibility. But, if there are already too many competitors in business, and one of them is doing a good job, it's a no go.

In our chapter on starting a research service you will find detailed information on doing market research — and you can use that to identify the market and do some telephone surveys of the area to determine what the customers like and dislike about the present stores. You will also find market identification explained in the business plan writer.

You need time to do this, and you must do it before you make an offer. One of the major problems all small business operators have is they literally know nothing about their market and assume that a given number of people living in an area provides the business they need. They have no real idea of how much an average household spends per year for what they sell, no concept of the age, income level, family status of the average person living in their area, and no idea of the size of the market in dollars, and no information about whether the market, for what they sell, is growing or declining. Part of the art of professional management is to get this information and make intelligent business decisions based on it.

When you have the markets identified and analyzed, you have some choices. Which of the businesses offers the best potential? You are looking for a business where you can at least double the gross dollar sales in the same size store, at the same location with a reasonable payroll and overhead. By checking the net profit results on doubling the sale, you can see which will produce the most dramatic returns, and those are the ones you make offers on.

If you are willing to do your research and write your business plan, you will not be gambling on these deals. You are betting on sure things, because you know what you are doing. The opportunities are almost limitless. It takes so little effort to turn a small business around that it's like having a license to steal. There are no trade secrets, no formulas for it. Just apply common sense, and a willingness to be of service to the customers, and you get the job done quickly. Many times you can have it done in 60 to 90 days after you take over and install your sharecropper.

STRATEGY

Aquire assets, not income, to build real wealth.

Dollars are taxable as they come in—assets only as they are converted to dollars.

If you take in $100,000 you can pay $50,000 or more in tax.

If you have a million dollar asset that appreciated 10% in a year—you have made $100,000 tax free.

Assets can be depreciated—dollars can't.

You can use depreciation dollars to acquire more assets tax free.

You can exchange assets tax free.

You can convert assets to income at the time of lowest tax obligation.

Mark Twain wrote, "It's better to have old second hand diamonds than none at all."

Build an asset base—the income will follow as needed.

CHAPTER 17
AN EXAMPLE OF A SHARECROPPER DEAL

Here is an example of how you might put a sharecropper deal together on the curtain and drapery store. You begin by putting an ad in the local area paper and the Wall Street Journal. It could read something like this:

EXPERIENCED RETAIL MANAGER
WHO WANTS TO OWN
HIS OR HER OWN COMPANY. A RETAIL CURTAIN AND DRAPERY FIRM READY TO EXPAND INTO A MULTI-MILLION DOLLAR CHAIN IS LOOKING FOR AN EXPERIENCED MANAGER WHO WANTS TO OWN AND OPERATE HIS OWN COMPANY. ALL PLANS IN PLACE — PILOT STORE IN OPERATION — WILL GROSS OVER 400K THIS YEAR WITH HIGH NET. SMALL INVESTMENT — UNDER $18,000 REQUIRED — SALARY AND PROFIT SHARING OVER $40,000 FIRST YEAR — THE MAJOR INVESTMENT IS YOUR SKILL, ENTHUSIASM AND DESIRE TO OWN YOUR OWN COMPANY. SEND RESUME — WITH COVER LETTER GIVING DATE YOU WILL BE AVAILABLE TO TAKE OVER — BOX 1234.

That ad will get all the responses you need to find your sharecropper. When you get the resumes, interview the likely looking prospects by phone. Tell them the general plan — but don't discuss specifics. Explain that you own the store and are too tied up in other things to run it, you want someone to take it over and buy it from you out of earnings. If the response is positive — then make a lunch date with them. Or, if they must come from out of town make a weekend date.

Have first interview over a meal or drinks. Talk in general terms, and get them talking about their hopes and ambitions. Get the feel of their personality, how they think and what kind of manager they will make. You are looking for someone who is a leader, not a mooch who is over eager and says yes to everything. Always interview three or four people at first interviews — then if you think they have potential — take them to the store and give them an idea of your plans — no specifics yet — but an indication of how your concept for this store can be built into a chain. Then, kiss them off and make them get back to you. Tell them to think it over, and if they are interested in the program, to call you back and you'll get into specific details with them.

When they call you back — you want to take the best prospects first — take them to the store, and show them the plans. Explain the procedures you have set up — tell them they can make any necessary changes — show them the marketing plan — and the projected financial statement for the first three years.

If they are interested then show them your pre-incorporation agreement which can go something like this:

1. The Corporation Name, etc.

2. The sharecropper becomes the President and Manager of the company.

3. You are a consultant, paid 2% of the gross income for your services.

4. You will issue 2500 shares of stock — you will get 1250 shares for the company at the time of issue — the sharecropper will get 200 shares for his investment — and then each quarter that goals are met — the sharecropper gets options on 200 shares at a stated value. He can redeem these options at any time at a fixed price. So, if the goals are met he has options on 1000 shares and owns 200 outright.

5. You will put in a buy back agreement on your shares whereby the corporation buys them out at a stated price, or you have the option of holding them in case the company goes public or is taken

over.

6. The corporation agrees to buy a Life Insurance Policy on your life for $50,000 the first year (tax deductible to the corporation and tax-free to you), and increase it each year to cover the value of your holdings. So in case of death your estate could sell your stock back to the corporation for stated or book value whichever is greater.

7. The Board of Directors will be you, your accountant and the sharecropper.

8. The salary and bonus arrangements for the sharecropper (over and above the stock bonus) will be fixed on the incorporation by-laws.

9. The stock will be 1244 issue — so that if the company fails you can declare your losses on the stock on your income tax.

10. An arbitration clause is included in the agreement so that all disputes will be settled by arbitration — not legal action.

In general those terms are what you want in the agreement. (See details Chapter 14.) In the case of the curtain and drapery store, I would set the minimum stock value at $300,000 — that is the minimum the corporation would have to pay if they bought you out by your consent. If book value for your stock were greater — then they would pay the larger amount.

The sharecropper would invest $18,000 — this would pay the incorporation costs — new licenses and fees for the corporation — a $5000 payment to you for the business you are putting up (which will cover some of your expenses in closing the deal for the business and miscellaneous expenses, plus cash to open business).

What have you, now? You have the following:

1. $5000 in cash from the sharecropper.
2. 1250 shares of stock in the corporation.
3. A consulting fee of $5000 to $8000 the first year.
4. A guaranteed future interest of at least $300,000.
5. No risk and no responsibility for the operation.
6. In case the business fails a possible $300,000 write off on your 1244 stock against other income.

7. A stated policy on declaring dividends so some dividend income is generated each year.

And it costs you virtually nothing but some of your time.

Swing a couple of deals a year like this and you will be in the chips in a hurry. When you have four deals on the books in two or three years — you've got something in the area of $50,000 a year in consulting fees — well over a million in stock holdings — with dividends coming in — and you only have to talk to your sharecroppers once a month or so at lunch to earn your consulting fees.

Use Your CPA And Lawyer For Each Pre-Inc. Agreement

Tax laws are changing everyday, it seems. New IRS rulings on sheltering income change the game, constantly. It is vital that you use your CPA and lawyer to set up the stock buy back arrangements so that you pay the least taxes and can shelter the most income through capital gains, or tax-free exchanges, etc. Remember this — you are letting the sharecropper in virtually free — you don't have to worry about the tax obligations of his corporation — you want full protection on your income and dividends.

The Kick-out System

One important point is to have an agreement in the Pre-Inc. papers about the sharecropper wanting out or having to get out because he isn't cutting the mustard. If he is not meeting goals and the business is being poorly managed he's got to go. You have yourself and your accountant on the Board of Directors as a majority — and you own the majority of the stock. So, he can be removed at any time you wish. That is the reason for only giving him options to buy shares — he will only own 200 shares when he is booted out and you can put a clause in the contract that pays him off at X dollars a share when he leaves — he must give up his stock — his options become invalid when he fails to meet goals. Get your lawyer and CPA to work carefully on this one, as it will happen — and you want it to be automatic with no lawsuits or problems.

Incorporating Your Wealth Building Business

It is important for the wealth builder to understand the uses of corporations, to provide the means of piling up surplus cash without taxes, of building a Pre-tax Retirement Plan out of corporate income (up to 25% of salary paid each year), and pre-tax insurance premiums paid by the corporation — a medical payments plan — and with proper care in incorporating and managing, a shield against loss of personal assets should the business fail.

As your wealth building progresses, you will find keeping cash from the tax collector your major concern. To give you an idea of how the ability to split your taxable income between corporate rates and personal rates can save tax dollars, here is a comparison of an income split into two types of salaries and retaining surplus after tax cash in the corporation for tax-free investment. Plus, a look at what a sole proprietor would pay — and retain.

	THE CORPORATION		SOLE PROP
Net Corporate Income	$80,000	$80,000	$80,000
Salary Income	30,000	50,000	- 0 -
Corp Taxable Income	50,000	30,000	- 0 -
First 25,000 at 17%	4,250	4,250	NA
Second 25,000 at 20%	5,000	1,000	NA
Total Corp. Taxes	9,250	5,250	NA
Net Retained Income	40,750	24,750	80,000
25% of Salary in Retirement Fund for Corporation Salaries and Maximum of $7,500 for Sole Prop. in Keough Plan.			
Retirement Fund	7,500	12,500	7,500
Income From Fund at 10% Yr.	750	1,250	750
Total Fund Value 1st Year	8,250	13,750	8,250

AN EXAMPLE OF A SHARECROPPER DEAL 17—6

Corporation Can Retain Balances Up to $150,000 With No Tax to Pay Until Dividends are Declared.			
Corporate Surplus	33,250	12,250	- 0 -
Invested at 10%	3,250	1,225	- 0 -
Total Surplus Value	36,500	13,475	- 0 -

Personal Income Tax Obligations Corporate Salaries and Net Income From Sole Proprietor Less His Keogh Deduction.			
Salaries or Income	30,000	50,000	72,500
Personal Deductions	12,500	16,000	21,000
Taxable Income	17,500	34,000	51,500
Approx. Tax to be Paid	3,000	9,700	25,750
Net Spendable Income	14,500	24,300	25,750

Total Assets Retained Either Tax-Free or Tax-Deferred.			
Retirement Fund Value	8,250	13,750	8,250
Cash Surplus Retained	36,500	13,475	- 0 -
Net Personal Incomes	14,500	24,300	25,750
Total Assets Held	59,250	51,525	34,000

As you can see from the figures those with corporations are able to retain assets and while future taxes are due on the cash surpluses and retirement funds, as dividends or payouts, they can be at much lower rates than the sole proprietor must pay. This gives a corporation owner a lot more manuevering room — a better balance sheet to borrow money and a faster track in building wealth.

It is not my purpose to go into corporate formation for controlling your income in detail — there are new laws coming that could offer better results than these figures do. Your lawyer and CPA can set you up. You can form a one person corporation, if you like, and own it all yourself. But, it's smarter to get a few friends and family members to invest in it, to have a member of the Board of Directors outside the family in order to establish a corporate shield in case of business failures or lawsuits. A one-man corporation has little standing in court as a corporate shield. The courts hold that it is simply a device to avoid high taxes and the sole owner is fully liable for corporate debt. But, if there are stockholders with interests in getting increase in value in their stock and receiving dividends and they have a member on your board, the court looks at it differently than a corporation who has kept accurate records, kept minutes of all meetings and held all meetings according to law, the corporate shield should stand except in cases of fraud.

There is a very fine book out titled "Inc. Yourself," by Judith H. McQwown, published in paperback by Warner Books that goes into some detail on forming a corporation and the benefits it offers. You can see the various means available to you for shielding income from taxes and building substantial assets in a corporation format.

Tax Planning Is Vital

As your income develops and it comes in the forms of dividends, rents and interests, you are getting into a position of a personal holding company. I suggest when you set up sharecropper deals you arrange for long term consulting contracts that bring you earned income as a consultant to offset passive income. If your passive income gets to be over 60% of corporate income, you can be declared a holding company. If part of your corporate income is from dividends in stocks you have purchased in other corporations — sell some of that stock and invest the funds in tax-free municipal bonds — the income from these bonds does not count toward passive income.

When you have reached the $150,000 surplus cash point in your corporation, you can no longer retain cash without a stiff tax penalty — you will have to start issuing it as dividends. If this is going to be a big tax problem, and if you plan for it a year in advance, you can purchase some real estate income property with your surplus cash — drain the rest of the cash from the corporation so that all is left in assets is the real estate, then collapse the corporation in 30 days, and transfer the real estate to your personal control tax-free. Your tax obligation will come when you sell the property. Then you can start a new corporation and build up another $150,000 in cash surplus before you have to start paying dividends and paying the double tax rate.

Another angle is when your sharecropper issues dividends from their corporations — and you want to arrange their income so they will have to issue dividends in order to get their needed annual income — you can shelter 85% of the dividends paid against taxes. That is, only 15% of the dividends paid to corporations are taxable income at the going corporation rate. So, this is another way to build wealth by deferring taxes at income rates and arranging to get them out at capital gains rates.

There is still another angle that you have available when you have your own corporation — your Board of Directors can vote to issue new stock, and you can use that stock to take over other businesses or real estate. In effect, you have the right to print your own money — and pay for it out of future dividends.

The corporation also can pay your estate taxes — you can borrow money at any rate of interest you set — you can lease it your assets — lease assets from it — raise capital by selling bonds — notes — commercial paper — and all interest you pay is deducted from income.

So, when you start your wealth building program — start with your own corporation and use all the advantages it offers to shelter income and increase your assets. Get good advice from your CPA and lawyer and you will become as wealthy as you wish.

Writing The Business Plan For Your Sharecropper

The key to getting your sharecropping people to take on your deals is your business plan. It must be credible and proveable. In order to make it so, you must understand the difference between strategy and tactics. Too many people get them mixed up, and create problems for themselves.

A strategy is a method of reaching a long range goal. A tactic is the method of implementing the strategy. For example, let's make a comparison with strategy and tactics in football. The coach decides that his strategy will be ball control. The tactic he will develop to implement the strategy will be to work out plays that will gain 5 more yards on first downs. This will give his quarterback pass or run options on second down keeping the defense loose. Or, another coach will decide his strategy will be to go for quick strike scores from any position on the field. His tactics will be to isolate his wide receivers deep in the defensive secondary.

In making a business plan your strategy will be to design a product that will sell one million units the first year, a product that will fill a perceived need. Your tactics will be to either sell it on a market-by-market basis with TV advertising directly to the consumers through telephone and mail orders—or you will run the TV advertising and put stock in local stores who will prominently display the products.

Your secondary strategy will be to introduce additional products which you will either sell direct or through stores using the same tactics.

In writing your business plan to get a sharecropper, you will want to develop the strategy by having the first product ready for production, and suggestions for additional products to be introduced later. Then, you will give the sharecropper a choice of tactics to implement the strategy. You will not go into great detail on the tactics other than suggesting various markets—or further sources of information on how to use them.

This makes your plan writing a simple task—and leaves the options of management to your sharecropper. So if mistakes are made they are his not yours.

One rather dramatic display you can put in your business plan is a series of probability trees—what can happen using various tactical methods. This is purely judgmental, but helps in decision making.

The Probability Tree

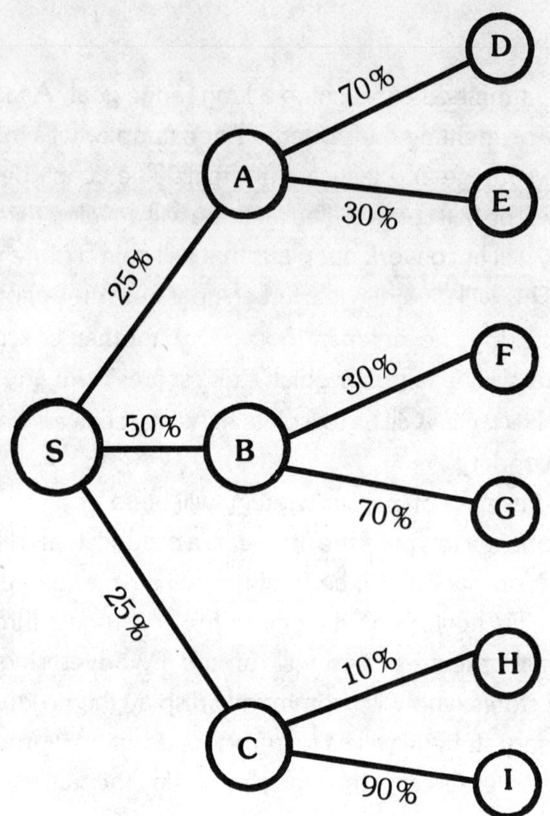

The Success Percentages

D = bonanza = 18%
E = well above average = .075%
F = above average & growing = 15%
G = average or slightly below = 35%
H = below average but growing = .025%
I = total failure = 22.5%

The Probability Tree gives you both percentages of success or failure and a time factor. You will note there are three rows of circles. The first has one circle, the starting point. The second has three circles, the first time period. And the third has six circles, the second time period.

As an example, let's use the two six-month periods for our deal. In the first six-month period, there are three possible results. First, great success; second, average success; and third, loss of some or all of your investment.

Now, we assign probabilities to each result. In the chart above, we will say there is a 25% chance of great success, a 50% chance of average success, and a 25% chance we will lose some or all of our investment.

We draw three lines—from S to A, B, and C. We mark our percentages along the proper lines.

Going to the second period, we'll say there are six possible results. We will gain or lose from the results in the first period. In the case of A, we draw lines to D and E, and assign percentages to each possibility. We will estimate there is a 70% chance that our great success will remain the same or improve. We will assign a 30% chance that we will drop off some in results in the second period. Now we multiply our 70% line (A-D) by 25% (the first period result) and come up with 18%. This is our estimate of great success in one year. On line A-E, we multiply .30 times 25% to get .075% as a probability for slightly less than great success after one year.

We do the same things for the other two results. Line B-F indicates the business will start getting better-than-average after one year, and B-G that it will drop below average. Line C-H indicates the business will start to recover after initial losses, and C-I that it will fail completely. The results of each computation are in the table above.

If you want to carry it on to the next period, you will have ten possible results (line C-I is eliminated, as it is total failure).

This is not infallible, by any means. Your judgment as to the percentages of each possible result are the keys to accuracy; but it does give you a look at Murphy's Law in action—the more time involved, the more chance for loss.

When you have assembled all the information, go over it once, then put it away for a day or two to cool off. Then when you have some free time, with no distractions, get it out and go over it again.

This time you will be better able to separate the signal from the noise and make a better decision. Don't think scared, but don't bet unless you are odds on.

You can juggle the percentages according to your own estimates and present them as you wish—if you have a small computer you can write a simple program for the probability tree and get a whole range of answers in a few seconds.

One key thing you are going to have to do is present a solid base of marketing information in your plan. This is not difficult because the Federal Government has most of what you need. In a later chapter you will learn how to organize a commercial research service—use a sharecropper to run it—and get more detailed information on making these plans.

TACTICS

Remember Murphy's Law in tactical planning!

Whatever can happen —will happen

Be ready for it. Don't be caught with your pants down.

Think about best case/worst case situations and how you might deal with them.

You have to work from action/counter-action bases.

Example—the business burns down. You make plans like this:

1. Loss expected/covered by insurance.
2. Personal income loss/business interruption insurance.
3. Customer files/duplicate set in another place.
4. Notifying customers of fire/use home phone.
5. Inventory replacement/store in mini-warehouse.
6. Replacing equipment/rent office machines.
7. Workspace/rent temporary quarters.
8. Delivery equipment/rent trucks.
9. Relocation/contact realtors at once.
10. Employees/keep on payroll till new facilities are ready.

And so forth—setting up lists of what will happen, and what to do when it does—you are preparing for Murphy, and also remember Mrs. Murphy's Law—it will always happen when it is least convenient.

CHAPTER 18
TURNAROUND MARKETING PROGRAM

Once you know the market is there, you are in business. All you need from that point is the plan to double the volume of the business, and produce a high net profit. One thing that few people understand about small retail businesses is the ease and speed with which the business can be turned around. You are dealing with a small market, and in most cases, satisfied competition who have about all the business they want—and are not doing much to increase it—and the big chain stores to whom the business is only one department with a low paid manager to run it. This is an ideal situation for the professional entrepreneur to step in and grab a larger share of the market before anyone else really knows what is happening.

Getting To Know The Customers

The people in the market area are someone's customers. You know about how much a year they spend on what you are selling, you know about how many there are, and your next step is to survey them. Find out what they like and dislike about the places they do business in now, what they would like to see a store put in stock, what kind of service or help they would like they are not getting, and anything else that relates to making it easier and more pleasant to buy what you sell. You can find out how to organize a telephone or personal research program to get this information in our chapter on commercial research. (Chapter 26)

The results of this survey will give you some definite ideas on how to develop a marketing plan for your store—one that will fill needs and create new business. You will know more about the market and what the customers want than anyone in the area—and that knowledge will pay off big dividends at the cash register.

The Competition

Your next step is to build a file on your competitors, the local stores and the chains. Shop them—have your spouse, your friends and relatives shop them. Pump the sales help for ideas (and also keep your eye open for a sharp one you can steal for your payroll). Get the mail order catalogs—Sears, Wards, Penneys, Aldens and specialty mail order catalogs, and see what they offer in your line, they are competitors, too. Then run a credit check on the small businesses you will be competing with to get an idea of how they are doing. With this information you can decide on points of attack—and strategies that will get a larger share of the business—take it away from them.

Most small business owners are satisfied to hate their competitors and let it go at that. The professional is constantly studying and watching them—shopping their stores—watching their ads—checking their progress. The old military axiom—"Never underestimate your enemy" is the name of the game. You can learn from them—you learn to anticipate them and beat them to the punch—and in a small market you can put them away.

The Next Step Is To Analyze Your Own Store

What is going on there? You need to start with some statistical information so you can make intelligent marketing plans. The first thing you should know is how many people are coming into your store everyday. Put an electronic counter on the door or doors—if you have only one door to go in and out then divide results by two.

You can adjust the daily count by estimating how many times your own employees go in and out the doors—how many deliveries you get through the doors each day—and a small percentage for people who go in and out twice for one reason or another. The resulting figure is your walk-in count. The number of prospects who came in the store.

The next step is to count the number of sales made each day to different people. This will tell you how well you are doing in converting prospects who walk through the door into customers.

The final step is to count your gross receipts for the day and you have the basic figures you need to work up your marketing plan to increase business.

Your First Goal

Using these figures you can find out these things:

1. What the average dollar value of each sale is. You divide the number of customers into the gross dollar volume for the day. The first goal will be to increase this sale by 20%.

You can do this by changing your inventory mix to reflect a higher quality of goods. This gives you larger unit sales.

You can do it by developing creative selling in the store. This involves dealing with identifying the customer's needs—and providing options to fill them. The staff has to be trained to serve customers—not write up sales. They have to become a friend of that customer,one even willing to help them solve the problem, in some cases by sending them to another store to find exactly what they need. They have to learn to smile—to be pleasant—suggest additional items each time a purchase is made—and to make the customer remember the store and the service. This increases unit sales dramatically. A furniture store in Cleveland selling knocked down furniture does $1.3 million gross in a 4,000 sq. ft. store by training his salespeople to ask the customer what they need furniture for in order to start solving problems and filling needs. To give you an idea of how this increases profits—the average store in the field expects to do $400,000 gross a year in a 4,000 sq. ft. store. He does three times as much. That is the power of selling instead of order taking.

The next thing you will want to do is to work on converting 10% more of the walk-ins into sales. This will require better staff service—perhaps another person hired to work the sales floor. To have enough staff to contact the walk-in quickly and be of help.

The second way is to have bargain tables, and signs in the store for specials This keeps the walk-in occupied for a few minutes till a salesperson can get to them.

By working at the problem of conversion steadily, you can easily add a ten percent increase in this area.

The third step, and the most important is to increase the foot traffic in the store. To create a larger number of daily walk-ins and holding a higher conversion rate, you will do a lot more business.

This is done with well thought out advertising and promotions, getting attention and delivering a message that will bring them in the store.

It is also done by constant, positive contact with customers to bring them in more often. This can be done in a variety of ways we'll get into a little farther along.

You should also pay close attention to window signs and displays that can be seen by those passing by. Good signs and displays pull them in off the street—and these walk-ins are the least expensive of all prospects in your store.

Concentrate on those three goals

1. Increase average unit of sale 20%
2. Convert 10% more of the walk-in trade into sales
3. Increase store traffic by 50%

You will then have what you need to at least double gross volume of business. You will find our chart below showing how a business grossing $210,000 can double its income using the three goal technique.

How To Double Volume Of Store Doing $210,000 Gross Revenue Based On 300 Days Per Year

Average Daily Sales Are 700.00
Average Number of Daily Sales Made 50
Number of Walk-Ins Daily Is 100
Average Amount of Each Sale Made 14.00
Average Value of Walk-Ins Is 7.00

The first goal is to increase average amount of each sale by 20%
1. By changing inventory mix
2. By creative selling in store
3. By improving display and signs inside store

Average Amount of Each Sale Made Now 16.80

Second goal is to convert 10% more walk-ins into sales
1. By better staff service
2. By bargain tables—unique displays

Average Number of New Sales Is 10

Third goal is to increase number of walk-ins by 50%
1. With advertising and promotion
2. By constant contact with regular customers
3. By better window signs and displays

Number of Daily Walk-Ins Increased To 188
Annual Increase From Increasing Average $ Sale $42,000.00
Annual Increase From Customer Conversion Is $50,400.00
Annual Increase From New Customers Gained $117,600.00

Total Increase In Business From Three Goals $210,000.00

High Gain—Low Profile Marketing

I'm going to give you a system for allocating your advertising budget into building business from your customer base—using your customers as sales people for your store—and staying out of the regular media so your competiton has no real idea of what you are doing. This system makes the store more like a friendly club with members instead of customers, and creates tremendous loyalty in your customer base—and they return your favors by spreading the word far and wide about your store and build your business steadily.

The Customer Base Building Contest Instead Of A Grand Opening

To start yourself off with a broad base of potential customers when you begin your operations—send out a sales letter-flyer with coupon specials, making one coupon a chance to win a valuable prize—something really nice that would appeal to the average profile of your customer. They fill out the coupon and return it to the store, no need to buy anything. This will pull in a good return—4% to 15% depending on the prize. Thus a 10,000 mailing in your trade area would pull 400 to 1,500 entries. These names go on your mailing list.

The Profit Sharing Plan

You can allocate a portion of your ad budget, to a customer profit sharing plan. Each time a customer buys something—you get their name and address on a sales slip and a duplicate goes in the profit sharing box. Each month names are drawn and profit sharing checks are sent to 25 or more people. Lots of little checks $1.00 to $3.00 are sent—with a little note thanking them for the business. This is a word of mouth advertising promotion. They will tell their friends. Did they ever get a profit sharing check from K-Mart—Sears—any big store? Everyone who makes a purchase during the month has a chance, and arrange it so that no one gets more than one check in any three month period. This spreads the action around and keeps new people spreading the word.

Appoint A Board Of Directors Each Three Months

They meet with you once a month for a luncheon at a nice restaurant. You get their ideas and opinions about how to improve service—what kinds of merchandise they like best. Get them to shop your competition and tell you how they compare your store with theirs. Each member gets a nice Certificate of Appreciation for service as members of the board. This will bring you more word of mouth promotion and create new customers who hear about it.

A Newsletter For Your Customers

You can publish a newsletter six times a year for your customers. Include news and information they can use. Take a picture of your current board of directors luncheon and include that—announce any news about your customers such as birthdays—anniversaries—promotions—travels, etc., just like a club. Hire a free lancer to write it and handle the news for it. Offer prizes to the customers for sending in poems, jokes, funny sayings, household hints, etc., to build interest and readership. Include discount coupons, notices of sales and specials you have coming up—new lines you are offering, etc. This is a powerful business builder if you spend enough money to make it professional and interesting.

The Free Lending Library

Build a lending library of books, pamphlets, magazines with how-to-do-it information about your products. Any customer can borrow them for a couple of weeks at no charge. Have them racked in the store—and it works on a "We Trust You" policy. They sign a slip, and take them out. The slips are dated and filed in a 1-30 file—they are checked each 15 days to see who is late, and a telephone reminder is made—if others are waiting for the book. The call gives the store a chance to pitch the person on some non-advertised special offer they will want to look over when they return the book.

The Mail and Phone Order Catalog

You can gradually build your newsletter into a mail and phone order catalog. Customers can use their bank charge cards to order—you ship UPS. As you develop your customer base—you can spread your selling efforts farther out with the catalog technique. You can build a sizeable mail and phone order volume—20% to 50% additional gross dollars.

No Media Advertising Used

This program puts all your advertising dollars into building a solid and loyal customer base—rather than relying on sales and promotional ads in the media that pull price buyers, but have varying rates of results and are becoming very expensive for small businesses. You are creating your own media through your newsletter—you can get help in paying for it by using cooperative advertising allowances to publish ads in it. This high gain—low profile system builds the business the right way—with very high percentage customer retention and repeat business. And, it's easy to keep within the budget because you are not committed to outside media who can raise rates suddenly pushing your budgets out of shape.

TACTICS

Never try to tiptoe across a chasm.

In every business there is a time to go for it. You have a new promotional program—or are planning a sale—or opening new territory—launching a product, etc. You are making a serious move.

At this point many small business operators start to hedge the bet—they want to nickle and dime their way into the deal—stick their toe in the water first. Bad policy! You can't tiptoe across a chasm—you've got to make the jump all at once. Go for it with all you've got. This is what makes small businesses successful—the willingness to back a play all the way.

There is the story of the three soldiers, two officers and a sergeant lined up to receive medals in France during the first world war. They were being presented by the beautiful daughter of a French politician.

She came to the first officer and said, "With which hand did you kill the Boche?"

"My right hand," he replied, and she grabbed his right hand and kissed ferverently.

The second officer said his left hand and got his kiss.

She came to the sergeant, and he thought for a minute and said, "Mam, I bit him to death."

Take a chance when you have to—and don't get cold feet.

STRATEGY

Never buy what you can't sell.

Never be sold on a product, service or idea until you are able to sell it to others. If they won't buy—you don't buy.

More money is lost by enthusiastic entrepreneurs who take products and services to market and discover either there is no market—or they are too early or too late. They are soon broke.

Point!

1. It takes an average of 17 years for a new, marketable innovation to be successful in the marketplace from the time it is patented or offered for sale to a producer. It took 24 years for Xerox to be marketed after the first patent. The first TV set was invented in the 1930's—it became a household product in the 1950's. The first computer was invented in the 1940's—it became a houshold product in the 1970's.

2. If your banker, your peers and your tested potential customers won't buy—then you don't buy.

3. Never high dive into a body of water till you have tested the depth.

CHAPTER 19
PRODUCT & SERVICE CONCEPT

How To Make Money From Product And Service Concepts

The first thing you have to do with any concept is reduce it to practice. This means making a working model of it. You will have to do that in order to get a patent in most cases. The lineage of a new product goes something like this in inventor terminology:

1. **The Breadboard Model.** This is the rough working model that proves it will work but is usually much larger or smaller than the final product. It's often made up of spare parts and homemade devices of varying materials.

2. **The Brassboard Model.** This is a smoothed out version using standard parts, machine tooled parts if needed, and the types of materials that will be used in the production models. This usually does not have the outer case, but is primarily for working parts inside.

3. **The Prototype.** This is the expertly made model that will have all the parts used in final production including the outer case design.

4. **The Production Model.** This is the model the manufacturer will put on the assembly line. All costs are figured and industrial design and production engineering have been done.

When you have a brassboard model you can do some market research with it by getting a consumer jury together, showing them the final designs, and showing them the brassboard model in use. You can find out what they say about it — what they might be willing to pay to get it — get ideas for improving it — and check out the appeal of various names for it—colors for the case—design of the product, etc.

This information can be evaluated before you go to the prototype — and will be used as market research to prove the sellability of the product.

You can test it on various consumer juries to be sure you have solid information. It's easy to get a jury together. Go to a group with average consumers, anything from a church to a bowling league, and offer to donate money to the group for letting you choose a jury from their members. Develop a set of specific questions you want answered—and it might be wise to use an experienced market researcher to run the program. You can find lots of these people willing to moonlight for a reasonable fee by running an ad in the paper.

Once you have the prototype, you are ready to get into business with your concept. You could try to sell it to a manufacturer, but if your time is worth over 10 cents an hour, don't bother. It's a very hard and very long game that idea people seldom win. You might try an investor looking for a new product — but again, it's tough — and if the investor sees your prototype, reads your marketing material — what does he need you for after that. He can duplicate your product and be in the market before you.

The one way you can be sure to make money is to use what I call the sharecropper technique. You prepare a pre-incorporation agreement first. Do-it-yourself (Refer to Chapter 13)—then get your marketing and production figures together—project sales and profits for five years—and run an ad for someone who wants to manage a new venture. You will note I said manage—not buy or invest. There are hundreds of people working for large companies who dream of owning their own company—being president of their own corporation and becoming financially independent. There are at least 100 of these people for every person ready to start a small business.

Your ad offers these people a part-time management position — one they can handle without leaving their present employment — in a new company that will do a million dollars worth of business in the next 12 to 15 months. They are in full control—they run it—and they will wind up owning it outright — lock, stock and barrel.

Here's the kind of ad I mean:

NEW CORPORATION WITH MILLION DOLLAR PRODUCT NEEDS EXPERIENCED CEO. CAN START PART-TIME HELPING ORGANIZE MARKETING AND PRODUCTION. FULL CHARGE OF ALL OPERATIONS—STRONG STOCK POSITION IMMEDIATEDLY—MINIMUM SIX FIGURE INCOME FIRST YEAR. INVESTMENT OPTIONAL. EXPERIENCE AND ENTHUSIASM NOT OPTIONAL. WRITE BOX 1234— ALL INQUIRIES ANSWERED.

That will get response at once from all sorts of people. You will have little trouble getting your sharecropper from among them.

The system works like this. You interview prospects who answer your ad. You show them your product, your business plan, your market research and your projections. The idea is to sell him/her on taking on the management of this enterprise — with full decision making powers of ownership. You will form a corporation — the prospect will have 51% of the stock and be the president. You will receive a royalty for every unit sold. You will have the corporation buy a $50,000 life insurance policy on you (tax free to you) — and you will have an agreement that the corporation will arrange to go public, or to buy out the remainder of your stock at a fair market price within a given time limit.

You will make the corporation a Sub-Chapter S, and use rule 1244 so that the corporation can elect to pass losses through to you in the formative years. You can deduct them from your personal income tax. You put all these conditions in the incorporation agreement so that it cannot be changed later without your permission.

Your prospect agrees to pay in whatever sum you feel is needed to start marketing the product. The concept, the business plan and the prototype are your investments. This includes copyrights and patents.

Now, what have you done? You have hired a sharecropper who puts up capital and labor to market your concept and who will pay you for every unit sold, plus buy out your interest at some future time for cash. You have only the start-up costs invested (and you can even recover those by a separate agreement with the prospect whereby he pays you a consulting fee for the first year).

You use an attorney to set up the pre-incorporation agreement so that you get all the benefits and assume none of the liabilities. The investor-owner is totally responsible for the operation — you are not on the Board of Directors and have no say in the operation of the company. If there are problems, there is no way for you to be involved for corporate misdeeds.

Now, why would a prospect go for this deal? Because within every corporate manager lies the dream of being the chief executive officer of his own corporation. This is a driving ambition. Here is an opportunity to get something going in his spare time, without giving up his paycheck. He can pull in friends and associates to be his team and put up more capital. He can, he is sure, build the business into a solid corporate enterprise. All you have to do is convince him the market is there — and this product will get the business off the ground to a flying start. It's not hard because he wants to believe you — and he has never seen an opportunity structured like this before. Your story as to why you are offering this to him is simple—you don't have the management experience to run a business of this kind. You need someone who can—and are willing to give him the lion's share of the profits in order to get this fantastic product to market. And, it's ready to go. That will do it — and you have a monthly royalty income — a free $50,000 insurance policy — and a plan to get capital gains income from your stock should the business succeed, plus you can take losses off your own income tax through election of partnership taxing as a Sub-Chapter S Corporation. Plus, you now have an asset to put on your personal balance sheet — your shares of stock — your royalty agreement (which can generate personal tax deductions).

This can all be run out of your home or a small office. Remember, you are a manufacturer in name only. All the manufacturing work is done by others — you have no investment in machinery or equipment — no payroll — no overhead to speak of. When the investor takes over he can do as he will — start his own plant — move to a suite of offices — hire a staff, etc.

All this comes from your idea — your concept put together in a package. Now, you might say you don't know anything about designing products or assembling them. You don't have to — all you need to do is hire some moonlighter who knows how to put a machine together—tell him what you want—get a price (you can sometimes get it done for promise of stock in the company)—then send around the specifications for bids on making it. For example, on the knife sharpener—you need a grinding wheel system that moves up and down the blade, a timer that starts and stops it automatically, and a couple of lights to show when it's working and when it's finished. It's not really very complicated and any competent mechanical engineer could design it for you in a day or two. So, don't worry about getting the product designed and made — just figure out whether it fills a recognized need and how it can be marketed. Obviously you could have fifty of these corporations set up using this system — and if only three of them succeeded, you would be a multi-millionaire.

Now, I'm going to give you some shoestring marketing plans that will get you started marketing a product by creating immediate cash flows so you can build your business from sales rather than from investment. These plans are easily organized and implemented, and have built many small start-ups into large and profitable companies.

The first one is marketing through trade shows to get initial orders, then building a network of manufacturer's representatives to sell the product to retailers, wholesalers or end users depending on the type of product it is. The second is for consumer products and uses TV to get orders directly from consumers. And, the final system is to sell your product initially to independent agents who pay cash for it, and re-sell it using a marketing plan you give them.

The advantage of these three systems is immediate cash flow. There is no long term marketing program that involves a large inventory investment spread across a huge market to create a cash flow.

CHAPTER 20
PROTECTING IDEAS

Protecting Your Ideas — Ways And Means

When you develop an idea that you can take to market you have to consider protection for it. There are four basic types: first, a patent; second, a copyright; third, a design patent; and fourth, the registered trademark. A patent is expensive and time consuming — but it has a value in starting a business. This is not because it will protect your idea in the marketplace all that well, but because it gives your concept status in the eyes of people who are going to provide the financing and do the work for you.

A patent for a product by an inventor or small business that has a huge market potential is no real protection. Big business will knock it off and let you try and sue them. The legal expenses of trying to protect the patent will eat up all your profits and then some. It can take 10 years to get a decision — and then you only have a marginal chance to win. Courts are very reluctant to uphold patents — most inventors lose their cases.

I would suggest this, if you have simply an innovation, such as the knife sharpener we discussed, get a trademark on the name Compusharp, copyright all the collateral material, packaging, ads, instruction guides and all illustrations, and get a design patent on the outer case. This won't give you any serious protection—but some knock off artists are so stupid they will copy some of your designs, packaging or advertising. Then you can easily put the blocks to them for copyright infringement. This is a cut and dried deal — and many lawyers will take the case on consignment and split the profits with you.

If you want a patent—then I would execute my own patent application while I went into production and put patent pending on the product to scare off some knock off artists. You can do this rather inexpensively, and with a little time, effort and energy, can get a patent for the product. If you hire a patent attorney to get it, it can cost big bucks and still not provide you with anything more than a pretty certificate to hang on your wall.

Getting A Copyright

A copyright is really your strongest protection. It only costs a few dollars, and it lasts for your lifetime plus 50 years. All you do is write the copyright office, Library of Congress, Washington, D.C. 20504 — (703) 557-8700. And ask for free information about applying for a copyright.

You will want to obtain a copyright on each separate printed item you use — and on all illustrations, designs in your literature and advertising. Each individual piece of literature, an ad, a box, an instruction manual, a catalog sheet, sales letter, audio-visual material, etc., requires a separate application (present fee is $6.00 per application) to get complete coverage.

You can now get a copyright on material before it is printed or published. You can get it from submitting manuscripts and drawings — so you can be sure to nail down your copyright before your material appears.

The Trademark

You may want to get a trademark for your name and logo. This comes from the patent office — and is filed with them only after your product is being sold in inter-state commerce. You file your trademark as it is being used if there is artwork involved. It's simply a name put in block letters with no punctuation or hyphen. You may be asked to submit proof of your product or service if it is being sold in interstate commerce in order to have the trademark granted. The application fee as of this writing is $35. You will get a receipt that it was received and in due course (a matter of some months) you will get an acceptance or denial. If it is accepted it is published so anyone who wishes to contest the use may do so — if no one does — you are granted trademark protection and can use the symbol ® with a circle around it — which tells the knock off artists they have to use something else or it's court time.

The Design Patent

This is similar to the trademark. It's not very involved and it offers virtually no protection. Anyone can change or modify any design and avoid patent infringement. But, if you are selling the idea, a patent of any kind gives it prestige and helps put a deal across. You get these from the patent office as well. Write the U.S. Department of Commerce, Patent and Trademark Office, Washington, D.C. 20231 — (703) 557-3158, for application forms and lists on instruction manuals available.

What's the Point of Patents and Copyrights?

For a small business operation it's purely psychology. There are some birds that defend their nests by puffing up and making their feathers stick out so they look twice as big as they are — this is the same principle. The knock off artist is not sure what you will do — and if there is some doubt about how much they can make before you hit them, they will look for something else.

The second point is that in putting a deal together, to go to market with, the patent, copyright or trademark is an asset. You can actually take depreciation on a patent as a tax loophole. If you spent a minimum amount of money to get it—you can get it all back with a huge profit by having it. That is the point—not the protection.

TACTICS

Reduce every complex problem to the sum of its parts.

Things that are complex in the whole can become simple when reduced to their components.

A computer is nothing more than a collection of thousands of simple circuits (like your doorbell circuit) that are either open or closed—push the doorbell and close the circuit—leave it alone and it stays open. Everything is based on that premise—add the ability to remember which are open and which are closed and you have your computer.

Any business proposition can be broken down to its components, and a clear picture developed from them. Break down your complex propositions like this:

1. Who is involved now?
2. Who will, or might, be involved later?
3. What does it cost now?
4. What can it cost later?
5. What is at risk now?
6. What can be at risk later?
7. Who will guarantee what?
8. Who gets what now?
9. Who gets what later?
10. Worst case/What's the most I can lose?

11. Best case/What's the most I can gain?
12. How much time do I have to decide?
13. Where can I find out what I need to know?
14. What kind of help am I going to need?
15. Where can I get this help?

Once you have those answers—you know what is involved and can intelligently decide on a course of action.

CHAPTER 21
TRADESHOW PROMOTION

The Trade Show And Manufacturers Representative Program

This is a standard start-up method for new product marketers. The program is simple. You pick a trade show that will have the potential retailers, wholesalers and reps attending that sell your products — and you show them what you have. You take orders at the show, and develop prospect lists for others who show interest. You use the results of your trade show sales and interest leads to get reps to take on your product.

The key to success here is to do well at the trade show. There is more to it than just setting up a booth and waiting for the orders to roll in. If you will prepare for the show — get an organized plan together and do the necessary work — you can get the results you want.

Step one is to pick the right show — a little investigation into the industry and some conversation with the firms who sell what you will be making will reveal the most attended shows. Some are national — some are regional. You can find out who the promoters of the trade show are from the trade magazines in the industry. Write to the show management and get a list of registration breakdown—who is going to attend. See if the type of people are coming that will be interested in your product. In most cases you will find there is one major show that pulls the most interest in the trade and possibly some regional shows that would do well for you. If you have time — attend these trade shows — check out the booths and presentations — see where the crowds gather — where the action is and make notes — take a tape recorder with you and make them verbally as you walk. Pick up literature — pose as a buyer and see how products are pitched. Get the feel of the show and what would work best for you.

The purpose for you is to make sales. When you make them to recognized firms with D&B ratings or good credit references — you can factor the purchase orders for cash with a bank or commercial finance company creating an immediate cash flow.

If you will follow the check list I give you — you will be able to put together a complete and productive trade show package. If you want to know how to blitz a trade show and make everyone aware of your product booth, then read "How I Made a Million in Mail Order," by Joe Cossman. The chapter on how he worked a trade show will give you a free course in how to get the action you need.

When you finish with the trade show, then start making contact with reps — show them the orders you got — have your program of commissions ready, along with catalog sheets, order forms and other necessary materials.

Your first contacts may come at the trade show itself. You can put up a sign in your booth — we want to talk to reps about representing our product. Next, you should check in the trade magazines of the industry and contact those who advertise there. They know the trade and have the territory organized. Third, talk to buyers who buy the kind of products you sell — get names of rep organizations they feel do a good job and contact them. Always try to get the reps who have the experience and territory knowledge. If you can't interest them — don't go to second line reps — look for the newcomers who want lines and will hustle to prove their worth. People who know the rep industry say about one-third are good and two-thirds are not. If you can't get the top people — then don't settle for the creamers — those who will only work the big end of the territory and will put on any product offered them just in case it takes off and they will get credit for orders from their territory even though they did nothing to make the sale. It's a lot better to take a chance on a new rep who might turn out to be a go-getter than on those second line reps who will really do nothing for you.

If you prove your product at a trade show you won't have any trouble lining up reps to start working their territory. It would be a smart idea to find a moonlighting sales manager who has had experience dealing with reps to set up your rep network. Just give him a percentage of gross sales instead of a salary and you can get a good job done at no up front cost. Lots of them will answer an ad offering a deal like this.

You can arrange to factor your purchase orders from reps as well until you are able to carry your own accounts. This system is simple, brings you to market a step at a time and an area at a time, and builds your cash flow and order base on a steady, upward climb that you can handle.

You can actually go to a trade show with your prototype — take orders and later notify the firms that ordered there has been a delay in production, and use those orders to prove the market to a potential sharecropper. Gives you a much stronger presentation.

Trade Show Checklist

Here is a checklist of points that must be covered when planning to exhibit at a trade show. The use of this list will assure you the maximum return from your trade show investment, and give you the assurance you have touched all the bases in making your plan.

1. Evaluate opportunities

A. Procure complete list of scheduled national, international and regional trade shows and conventions.

B. Itemize those pertaining to your markets and product applications.

   1. List by name, date, location, show management.

C. Send for latest available registration breakdown for each.

D. Compare registration lists carefully against the names of your own customers and prospects; evaluate objectivity.

E. Coordinate all information needed to simplify management's show decision, including:
   1. Selection of equipment to be displayed.
   2. Display development or adaptation required.

F. Arrange joint meeting of all decision makers.

G. Establish specific "closing dates" for each function.

H. Establish an effective follow-up system to cover all parties with assigned responsibilities. Put assignments in writing and maintain files for instant reference.

I. Execute and mail all show contracts promptly.

2. Arrange hotel/motel accommodations

A. Obtain authorized list of personnel assigned to the show.
   1. Verify with copy to management.

B. Forward official reservations to convention bureau or designated authority. (It is usually best to use standard convention forms and procedure.)

C. Establish a checking date for receipt of reservations.
   1. Follow through on any failure to obtain these within a reasonable time lapse (dependent upon lead time involved).

D. Advise all personnel involved of their participation and responsibility in writing. Ask for suggestions from each regarding ways and means for increasing the efficiency of the particular show.

3. Make hospitality arrangements

A. Secure early management decision and authorization.

B. Discuss the project thoroughly with the sales manager.

C. Place reservation with the hotel/motel, providing specific instructions in writing.

D. Upon arrival check assigned rooms for accessibility, condition, and fulfillment of your specifications.
E. Weigh advisability of securing beverage and food supplies from a more economical outside source.
   1. Make arrangements for delivery and financial source.
F. Arrange with hotel/motel service for advance delivery of needed glassware.
   1. Ask for periodic housekeeping chores on a specific schedule.

4. Establish show objectives

A. Define the exact purpose of your exhibit.
B. List, in order of importance, the specific results to be achieved.
   1. Avoid generalities — exactly pinpoint the jobs to be done.
   2. Communicate this motive to all concerned.

5. Analyze means for accomplishment

A. Consider the use of operating models as a prime sales tool.
   1. Stripped down or "cut-away" displays.
   2. Live product demonstrations.
   3. "Do-it-yourself" audience participation.
   4. Motion pictures.
   5. Automated slide projection.
   6. Toy replicas.
   7. Give-away items.
   8. Other methods for telling the complete product story.

6. Select space

A. Obtain equipment weights and measurements for all products to be displayed.
B. Estimate space required for sales and relaxation areas.
C. Determine realistic space loss from obstructions — posts, pillars, pipes, boxes, conduits.

D. Evaluate traffic flow patterns; proximity to entrance and exit.
E. Evaluate space lost to display projections.
F. Allow for orderly parking of coats, hats, parcels.
G. Determine literature storage needs; the advisability of locked storage space.
H. Check ceiling height.
I. Check lighting requirements.
J. Check area for maximum visibility.
K. Check proximity to needed power, water, air lines, drains, etc.
L. Check for weight load limitations.
M. Check for product size and shape conformation affecting effective placement of equipment for most effective display.

7. Plan the exhibit

A. Conceive overall design based on function.
B. Research the customer and prospect on the basic information they would need before purchasing your type of product.
C. Plot exact scale floor plan.
   1. Spot your display, equipment, tables, chairs, stands.
   2. Re-evaluate adequacy of available floor space and allowance for audience inspection and discussion ... for relaxation. Avoid cramping.
D. Plan for complete communication of the sales story — in action — or in terms best understood by the audience.
E. Strive for originality and showmanship.
   1. Conceive show applications for your products, ways to demonstrate and dramatize specific product usefulness.
F. Don't overlook audience and sales personnel comfort (rubber tile flooring, good seating, refreshments).
G. Utilize light, motion and personality where possible to attract attention; you are in competition with your neighbors.
H. Merchandise your operating models, etc. Use effective display boards to solidify benefits.

1. Display prominently.
2. Provide for maximum operation usefulness.
3. Use showmanship with every display function. Put it all to work!

I. Evaluate potential expenditures of exhibit.
   1. Through planning and replanning strive for maximum utilization of the available dollars.

J. Determine advisability of building shipping crates. Include in your estimates costs for repairs of those crates when determining shipment method.

K. Design exhibit for simple assembly and disassembly.

L. Always keep in mind the factor of potential shipping damage.

8. Place accessory orders

Order electrical service, floor covering rental, exhibitor invitations, badges, floral services, furniture, photographer, telephone, water cooler, etc. in advance. Keep in mind that these contracts are cancellable at the show if not required.

9. Arrange for product availability

A. Recognize product availability delays as your number one enemy.

B. Obtain top management support in establishing priorities for the development of new products on schedule.

C. Make it a point to check research, engineering and production periodically to determine progress.
   1. Report any apparent and uncorrected delays to management ... in writing.

10. Plan product appearance

A. Evaluate the attention value of the product's standard color(s).

1. Could they be strengthened by application of a special "show color?"
2. Seek management approval for the change, if necessary.
3. Supervise obtaining replacement paint if not standard stock.
4. Test for final results early.

11. Organize publicity

A. Preplan and develop maximum publicity for exhibited products, their application potentials and uses.
   1. List potential newsworthy subjects such as new product designs, special demonstrations, prominent people, flash items, and cheesecake.

B. Establish specific media and release dates.
   1. Look for corollary markets in addition to those previously used.

C. Capitalize on available convention press services.
   1. Know their extent before the show.
   2. Follow instructions to the letter — and submit on or before time.

D. Utilize toy model replicas for human interest photos and as a source for additional publicity.
   1. Plan news creating "give-away" presentations.
   2. Tie in local newspaper coverage at show by slanting story civically.
   3. Tie in trade paper coverage.

12. Preplan literature needs

A. Decide on distribution method.
   1. Choose among free circulation, controlled distribution, personal distribution by hired models, the card request system.

B. Evaluate advantages and disadvantages of currently available literature in line with show objectives.

C. Plan and execute the printing of new literature well in advance of show date.
   1. Determine quantities needed.
D. Consider possible need for special packaging.
E. Plan for literature storage at exhibit.
F. Plan for orderly replenishment of depleted stock.
G. Plan for effective display at all times as an added sales effort.
H. Plan for post-show disposition of remaining supplies (distributors, dealers).

13. Establish firm show authority

A. Vest responsibility for "show operation" in single individual and see that he has necessary authority to command cooperation.
   1. Assign him responsibility for coordinating all efforts.
   2. Responsibility to include: erecting display, supervising manpower, schedules, organizing sales methods, controlling exhibit expenditures, maintaining the booth and following through on show results.

14. Coordinate field sales

A. Plan proper utilization of district representatives, distributors, dealers, agents and salesmen to maximum sales advantage.
B. Advise on all show plans beforehand.
C. Promote their attendance.
D. Formally assign specific duties and responsibilities to each.
E. Provide information, materials and instructions to all pertinent personnel in advance — for the maximum sales effort.

15. Make shipping arrangements

A. Compare relative merits of display and product shipment by REA, truck, van, Air Freight, etc.
   1. Prior to ordering shipping crates.

B. Schedule early arrival.
   1. Allow safety factor for tracking down "lost" articles.
C. Note and follow show instructions implicitly — they are for your benefit.
   1. Avoid extra handling charges.
D. Arrange for adequate insurance coverage.
   1. On both products and display.
E. Plan the inclusion of necessary exhibit tools — hammer, pliers, screw driver, touch up paints and brushes in the exhibit shipment.
F. Pre-arrange post-show shipment to predetermined destinations.
G. Provide for anticipated emergency replacement parts for repairs to operating equipment.

16. Establish customer-prospect communication

A. Promote show early.
B. Develop preferred list of contacts.
   1. Extend invitations to your booth by personal letter.
   2. Provide pre-registration cards (furnished by the show management).
   3. Assist prime customers and prospects with hotel reservations.
C. Consider an "open house" tie in with local shows.
   1. Capitalize on the advantages offered by "live product demonstrations" at your plant.
D. Plan and organize effective contact between users and prospects — your most effective sales tool!

17. Erect and maintain exhibit

A. Avoid use of overtime labor wherever possible.
B. Carefully spot products and displays for optimum visibility to major traffic flow.

C. Evaluate need for more effective floodlighting (usually needed).

D. Present immaculate appearance in all respects.

   1. "Touch up" all paint defects daily.

E. Check all electrical connections.

F. Check and operate all working mechanisms.

G. Make arrangements for "early-bird" housekeeping maintenance.

H. Carefully identify all crates before storing.

18. Use booth personnel effectively

A. Establish a sound work schedule for top sales team efficiency and morale.

   1. Be considerate and fair to each ... for maximum cooperation and spirit.
   2. Provide for skilled sales coverage at all times; do not leave booth unattended.
   3. Avoid "overwhelming" representation at any time.
   4. Assign a "team captain" for each shift.

B. Coordinate team on procedure: objectives, method of prospect contact, literature distribution, handling of inquiries, model operation, maintaining records.

C. Control activities of distributor and dealer salesmen.

   1. Insist upon conformance with overall show regulations and objectives.

D. Pretrain hired models.

   1. Provide written instructions on duties.

19. Remove the exhibit

A. Read show instructions carefully.

B. Verify all shipping arrangements with the moving contractors one or two days prior to terminal date of show.

C. Pre-locate storage crates and packaging materials in the convention hall for quick access at close.

D. Make all drayage contracts as soon as office is open for contact before closing.
E. Arrange for delivery of equipment, etc. to customers or distributors at earliest possible time.

20. Evaluate show results

A. Consider evaluation a prime objective.
B. Procure daily registration lists for subsequent analysis of show potentials.
C. Contact all salesmen daily for personal, objective reaction.
   1. Obtain their suggestions for future changes or improvements.
D. Contact other exhibitors for their reactions.
E. Personally compare your exhibit location with competing displays.
   1. Note particulars of other impressively successful exhibits.
   2. Make a list of more desirable locations.
F. Register all complaints with the show management immediately.
   1. Follow through in writing.

21. Handle inquiries wisely

A. Initially encourage prospects to register name, address and area of interest.
   1. Establish simple, effective registration procedures, using printed forms.
   2. Enforce salesmen's vigilance in their acquisition.
B. Arrange facilities for prompt replies during or immediately following the show. Never neglect this vital contact!
C. Maintain careful records of all leads.
D. Plan effective field follow-through.
   1. Control field performance.
E. Establish sales results obtained from show.
   1. Seek all available proof of show effectiveness.

22. Pursue trade show improvement as a permanent quest

A. Make it your business to continuously study the existing techniques of skilled trade showmanship — and to keep abreast of new techniques and uses.

CHAPTER 22
PROMOTING PRODUCTS ON TV

Direct Marketing With TV

A second way to get action at once is to market a consumer product by using television advertising as the method of selling the product to consumers. Showing orders from this program is dynamite — the profit margins are huge as the orders go from manufacturer to consumer with no middle man. If you can produce orders at a profit in this media — you have two ways to go. Take it national one market at a time on TV — or cream it on TV as a direct sales deal — then pass it along to reps to put in stores after you've reached the point of no return on TV.

Sell It On TV

TV is the most powerful ad media ever offered if it is used properly. Not all products are suitable for TV sales, but if your product has certain characteristics, direct marketing on TV can be a real fortune maker.

Because of the nature of TV, and the short length of time you can make your sales pitch, products must be useful to large numbers of people. TV is not profitable for reaching highly selective groups. Mass merchandising is TV's game.

Your product must be known and understood by most of the people watching. It must have a unique benefit that can't be found in similar products the consumer has access to. The benefit can be real or it can be perceived, but it must be shown. The benefits can be as varied as a different use or package; more quanitity for less money; a unique appearance; a special use others cannot offer; a stronger guarantee; in short, you need a unique selling proposition.

The second most important factor in a successful TV pitch is that the product must be demonstrated. The viewer has to see it, and what it does, to gain the attention and impact you need. If you watch ads that are selling products directly to the consumer you'll find demonstration of the products is the most powerful part of the pitch.

When K-Tel sells records they play parts of each album while listing the titles. When Popiel sells the pocket fisherman, they show it in use. When Time or Newsweek pitch their magazines they show their stories, pictures and features. The demonstration gives credence to the unique selling proposition. Successful demonstration turns TV into a money machine.

One Market At A Time

The smart way to shoestring your way into national distribution is to attack it one market at a time.

Your first choice is not of vital importance, the best market is the one closest to you. But, don't try to capture New York, Los Angeles, Houston or Chicago first. Stick to Peoria, Pueblo, Tucson, Sacramento, Spokane, Rochester, Orlando or other areas of similar sizes. This gives you a chance to test your pitch and adjust it if necessary before you run out of money. TV time costs less, there is more available time and your volume of orders will not overwhelm you if you've got a bonanza on your hands.

The time element in each market is important. TV ads burn out quickly. Seven to fourteen days is about the maximum anyone uses TV selling direct to the consumer. This makes it possible for you to move rapidly from market to market, building cash flow as you go.

The First Step

Your first step is to find your test market and prepare a TV commercial for it.

There is one book that will give access to all the information and talent you need to do this. It is the **Broadcasting Yearbook,** published by Broadcasting Publications, Inc., 1735 DeSales St. NW, Washington, DC 20036.

As you will note below you get marketing maps and information on all areas of the country. Listed are names and addresses of all TV and radio stations, names and addresses of ad agencies, those who produce commercials and other services. Write Broadcasting Publications for latest price.

There's a specific technique to preparing a commercial for direct selling on TV. In terms of length of the commercial most direct marketers like the 120 second (2 minute) commercial because it gives them the needed time to do proper demonstrations and make a powerful closing pitch. Others use 60 second times when they have a product that has one function that can be shown quickly and effectively. The big users of time are about evenly split on useage of one or two minutes, depending on what they are selling.

The Grabber

The grabber or hook is the most vital part of your commercial. You've got to stop them from heading for the kitchen or bathroom. If you are a TV watcher you will note that this is now commonly used by the networks to hold people on their station for the next show. They come in with flashes of action of the upcoming show to intrique the viewer before they can change channels.

The grabber is like the headline in a printed ad. It must catch the viewers attention and pique their interest at once—a second or two. You lead with your aces stating the unique selling proposition in dramatic terms.

Let's take an example. Our product is a collection of costume jewelry displayed in a case (necklace, bracelet, ear rings, ring and brooch). We have styled it to resemble that worn by beautiful and powerful women of history. Cleopatra, Catherine the Great, Catherine de Medici, etc. On our TV commercial we are aiming at the Disco market. The young swingers who are dolling up to go disco dancing. So, our grabber might start out something like this: now you can own the jewels that brought mighty Caesar to his knees before the dazzling beauty of Cleopatra. You can have this fabulous collection of jewels of mystery, free. The visual would show Caesar kneeling by a couch holding Cleo's hand, then cut to a close up of the jewels in a box. The voice over would go on to describe the magnificent scarab necklace, the symbol of love and power in ancient Egypt. The rest of the items are described similarly. Then the visual goes to the items being offered for sale, similar descriptions are made—then the pitch stating prices for the items, getting the Cleopatra collection free, then showing a jewel box, and a pitch that fast action also gets the jewel box as a free premium, then back to the price and how to order. This is repeated several times and the commercial ends.

The structure here was to introduce a free premium, and sell it. Then show the products for sale—sell them and quote price. Then kick in with another free premium for fast action (call the toll free number now), then show all of the offer together, quote price again, then, close by telling them how to order. Then repreat price and order instructions again—be sure and have addresses, phone number overlayed on the screen as the ordering instructions are given.

The key to successful selling of any kind is to establish value before you quote price. Keep that elementary fact of selling life in mind as you develop your commercial concept.

Making The Commercial

Your best bet is to have a pro make your commercial. It costs money, and you have to be careful who you deal with. Many of these commercial makers throw money around faster than Washington bureaucrats. Your best bet is come up with a figure you can afford and see who will do what for you based on that amount.

Your second option is to have the TV station you will use first make the commercial. This will cost you far less, and in some cases may be a better deal.

But, one thing is vital—you decide how to sell the product. The sequence in which the offer will be made, and the general outline of what will be said and shown on the screen. You are making a pitch to sell a product, not an arty little show that will amuse people. Too many TV advertising people are hung up on jokes and gags as the basis for a commercial. This may work for frozen pizza and coffee, but it isn't worth a damn when you are trying to sell something and get the money now.

When you get a copy of the Broadcasting Yearbook, you will find listings of books in the back. There will be some listed there on making TV commercials. You would do well to get one or two of them and study them carefully so you can understand what is possible and what isn't.

Next, watch late night TV on independent stations. If you have a video tape machine, record the direct selling commercials you see. Then go back and break them down into time segments and visual and copy blocks. See how they opened the commercial, how long they took establishing value, demonstrating the product, how many different advantages they showed, how they handled a premium offer, how they quoted price, and how they closed by asking for the order.

If you don't have a recorder, then make notes with a stopwatch. You may have to watch several nights to get all the data, but try to do it. This is a free education in what works. If the ad is repeated, you know it's pulling money, so you are learning from success.

As you do this, you will discover a pattern, similar to that I mentioned to you. If you use that pattern and follow the timing you will have a good pitch worked out. Whether it pulls the orders or not depends on how the audience reacts. If your product is good, and there is a need or desire out there to have it, you will score; if not, you won't. But, if you don't, you know it is the product and not the pitch that is at fault.

Buying The Time

TV time is expensive, and direct selling propositions will not work at certain times.

First, you will be dealing with independent stations or network stations in late night time segments. The best response usually comes from after primetime viewing on independent stations that show movies. Some independents with movies are also good pullers in daytime hours. But, don't buck the networks in primetime on independent stations. Look to the late, late shows for your action.

Since there is no restriction on commercial time at these hours, you can buy the two minute (or more) segments with no problem.

Always check for deals in time buying. Talk with the rep about testing four or five commercials, then see what he'll offer for a 25 or 50 unit buy. Keep in mind that you want to advertise this over a two week period at the most, but want good daily frequency. At least one shot every couple of hours of air time on as many stations as you can use that get results. Sometimes you can make a deal with a station rep to get you a package deal on his and another station for a good time buy. Talk to them about a range of products you'll be advertising, and get the best price you can. If you are dealing with a strong station, you won't have much luck discounting the rate card, but if you are in a competitive market, you can often get a package deal for as much as 75% off the rate card by pushing for it.

How One Promoter Does It

Barry Helman is sometimes called the "Fad Man." He is a master merchandiser of fad products by TV promotion. He's made millions hustling fake diamonds, door pulley exercisers, Star Wars type illuminated swords, food processors, puka shell jewelry and now he's going to hustle roller skates.

He markets his products by "blitzing" big cities with two weeks of radio and TV commericals that lead up to three day sales of whatever he's pushing at selected stores. When the sale is over he takes his money and runs.

In a recent interview he was quoted as saying, "You have to know when to get out. You mark down near the end and close them out, otherwise you get killed."

Helman didn't create or invent any of the products he sells. He spots an item that is moving, hires a knock-off firm to produce a cheaper model, then through his corporation, JLA Inc., markets them via TV blitzing.

One item, the door pulley exerciser was so hot he leased planes to bring them in from Taiwan. He sold three million of them in four months. You probably saw the ads on TV for them.

He knocked off the Star Wars sword, called it "Force Beam," and sold a million and a half of them before the licensed Star Wars firms could get theirs to market.

He learned mass merchandising working for Thrifty Drug Stores, the Southern California promotional drug chain. He bought into JLA Inc., eleven years ago and his annual gross business runs from $5 to $25 million a year depending on how hot the items are.

He tunes into fads by reading a tremendous amount of newspapers, trade publications and visiting trade shows all over the world.

While he does not do direct marketing, his system is the same. I suggest you start with direct marketing, and as soon as you can supply the quantity needed, then switch to store sales.

This program works simple enough. You build the commercial that will sell the goods. Then you pick some high volume stores in the area your commercials will reach and stock them with the products. The TV pulls in the customers and makes the sales. When the program is over, you take what is left back, collect your money and go to the next market.

How One Man Did It

Bernard Saltz invented a hand held sewing machine and he wanted to market it himself. He took his idea to a Chicago Ad agency that specialized in direct selling promotions.

They reviewed the product and developed a commercial for it. They invested $4,500 in getting a commercial made and run on a Texas TV station, and the merchandise was placed in stores.

The first commercial sold almost $5,000 worth of merchandise at a time cost of $1,300. This was a nice response, so commercials were continued till they played out.

The next test was in Sacramento, California and a $2,850 TV spread sold $18,000 worth of merchandise. So, they were continued until they no longer pulled.

This market-by-market approach cuts losses quickly because if the ads don't pull, they are stopped at once.

The old deck of magic cards that had been around for fifty years was reintroduced on TV when magic enjoyed a new boom. They sold over $1,000,000 worth of those cards by calling them TV Magic Cards.

The point is that there is tremendous power in TV to make piles of money suddenly if you can find the right product, develop the right ad for it and hit the markets at the right time.

So, as a second step in getting your product in national distribution consider direct sales on TV, (or through local stores) it has made millions for others.

CHAPTER 23
SELLING THROUGH AGENTS

Selling By Mail Through Agents

This is the bottom of the barrel or bail out system. If you have not been successful in other forms of marketing this a way to dump your inventory and get your investment back with a little profit. Or, if you are not able to finance another form of marketing this a way to build your cash flow so you can afford to get into standard marketing channels.

The one advantage of this system is that you can really start it up for less than fifty bucks in advertising and the cost of some literature.

Taking a product to market, and getting national distribution can be done on a shoestring if you take a step-by-step approach to it. The key factor in starting on a shoestring is to create an immediate cash flow that will self-finance expansion out of income.

The market out there is immense. Some 230 million people who talk the same language, have more-or-less a common life style, use the same money and can be reached and sold in a variety of ways.

The market can make millions for you if you play your cards right, have some patience and stick with your plan. You have to attack a small segment of the market at a time. If you try to capture it all at once you will be crushed by its size. Even if you were lucky and got huge orders right at the start, your capital and productive capacity would soon flounder under the deluge. But, it is more likely you would never manage to even scratch the surface of the potential. It's like trying to kill an elephant by stabbing him to death with a toothpick.

The shoestring entrepreneur must enter the market in a manageable manner. This will result in your first efforts creating the cash flow you need and can handle, and give you the time to expand according to plan.

You Must Have A Saleable Product

You must have a product that is available in quantity, that can be sold to a satisfied customer for a profitable price.

The Unique Selling Proposition

If you are not skilled in sales, advertising or marketing, you will have to do some research in order to find the *unique selling propostion* for your product. The *USP* is the factor that sets your product apart from all competing products, and is the factor you advertise and promote to make sales.

If you have to do this research, you should gather up all the competing products for making this comparison to speed up the process of finding your *USP's*.

USP Checklist

- ☐ Is it personalized or customized?
- ☐ Is it electrified or automatic?
- ☐ Is it more convenient?
- ☐ Is it cleaner, filtered, self-cleaning?
- ☐ Is it safer? How?
- ☐ Does it taste, smell, feel, look or sound better?
- ☐ Is it cooler, hotter or both?
- ☐ Is it louder, quieter, noiseless?
- ☐ Is it lighter, heavier, stronger, weaker?
- ☐ Is it taller, shorter, wider, thinner?
- ☐ Does it have more or less vibration?
- ☐ Is it brighter, darker, more or less visible?
- ☐ Does it have more or less color, different color?

- ☐ Is it foldable,·portable, adjustable, modifiable?
- ☐ Does it cost more or less, terms shorter or longer?
- ☐ Does it last longer. Is it disposable, renewable?
- ☐ Does it have more or less parts, pieces, assemblies, uses?
- ☐ Is it easier to control, store, handle, ship?
- ☐ Are accessories available—more or less needed?
- ☐ Is it animated, revolving, reversible?
- ☐ Does it float, fly, self-propel?
- ☐ Is it guaranteed?
- ☐ Is it packaged better?
- ☐ Is package reuseable, or can be used for something else?
- ☐ Is it newer, more unique?
- ☐ Is it easier to fix, repair, replace?
- ☐ Is it easier to clean, adjust, maintain?
- ☐ Does it use less power, no power?
- ☐ Is it easier to use, easier to learn to use, easier to master?
- ☐ Can you use the waste or by-product?
- ☐ Is it approved, recommended, used by anyone who could influence others?

As you use this list you will find other points of differnce which will give you a USP. Make a list of all you find, and then put the list in the order of importance as a sales promotional tool. Number one should be the headline in your ads, your lead off statement when you sell. It should be the slogan on your package.

Pricing The Product

You will have a different price for each marketing method. Each will reflect the value of the product, its potential demand and the prices of the close competition.

In setting prices for agent marketing you should be working with a product whose retail price is ten times your price out the door. If you are selling to agents and the product costs you a dollar on the truck, you will want to be working back from a ten dollar retail price.

The reason is that you are going to be working on a multi-level selling program where a chain of discounts will be needed to produce business, and still give your agents a reasonable profit.

The second reason is that you will be financing your next marketing move out of cash flow, and need a high profit figure to keep the project moving.

Since your primary cash flow in step one comes from the agents, and you don't worry too much what the agents do with the product they order, your price is not of great importance. The agent part of your marketing plan is not a permanent program, but merely a starting point to get you on the next step with more cash flow and far less problems.

Product Liability Insurance

Don't overlook product liability insurance when you start marketing a product. Find out how much insurance those who sell you the product carry, and whether that covers you. When you have that information, talk to an insurance agent and a lawyer to see to it you are fully coverd. If additional coverage is needed, get it.

Getting Organized

I am going to assume you have very little capital to invest in marketing this product. I will attempt to show you how those few dollars can be the seeds for a bumper harvest. Even if you have adequate capital to market your product in normal channels, you should consider this system as it will teach you a great deal about marketing your product through normal channels.

The first step of selling through agents is sometimes called *sample selling*. This is a program that does not intend for a product to sell to consumers, but merely intends to sell enough to agents to make a nice profit. If any agents do manage to sell some of the product they ordered, the sample seller is pleasantly surprised and looks on that income as gravey.

The sample seller creates his cash flow, and net profit from agent orders, not from sales to the consumer. The value of this system is that it creates an instant cash flow on a very modest investment, and results in multiple product orders that build up cash flow fast.

The sample seller is essentially a short term operator who finds a product he can romance enough to interest agents, and when he has played out the field, drops that product and finds another one.

It is not my intention to show you this agent selling deal as a potential scam, but to use its advantages of quick entry and fast cash flow to get you moving toward your goal of national marketing through stores. I will show you a reasonable and logical method of offering your agents a real income from your product, without doing any of the belly-to-belly selling themselves. If the program is presented properly, you can expect a good many repeat orders and a high cash flow almost from the start.

Whom You Will Be Dealing With

I can tell you up front that you will not be dealing with the greatest sales people on earth at this level. You are largely dealing with four classes of people in this kind of program.

First, you get the professional sample collectors and literature freaks who write for everything. They may pay a dollar or two for a sample, but have no intention of trying to make any money with what they receive. These are always the first to respond as they comb the ads looking for something new to add to their collection.

Second, there are life's professional losers. These are largely ignorant, unemployable people who survive on chiseling, misdemeanors and small felonies. They will send you bad checks, pleading letters to send free samples so they can get to work and make enough money to cure their cancer, deformity, handicap, etc. If you answer, you've got a mooch on your back for years to come.

Third, you get the *coxie*. This is a person who is always looking for a new deal because the last one was a loser. He is a confirmed grasshopper who jumps from deal to deal because there is some hard work involved, and that is definitely not his bag. The coxies will make some sales for you, even reorder a time or two, but there's always a new deal coming along and they know it's got to be the easy one they are looking for.

Fourth, you get the amateur grinders. *These people are your treasures.* They like the product, the sales plan, and they go to work on it. They have little or no experience as a rule, but they have the guts to get out and pound doors or call on merchants on a regular basis, and they make money. You will find that only about 5% of those you start will be grinders, but they will produce more bucks than all the others combined.

I point this out to you so you won't expect too much from your agents. It is not an efficient method of marketing, and it is a method you should drop as soon as the cash flow from your next step permits.

Your Recruiting Ad

The first step in preparing to sell through agents is to pick your contact method. I would test the water with my toe before I plunged in. I would do this by taking a classified ad in one of the five salesman's magazines currently published. *Specialty Salesman, Salesman's Opportunity, Sparetime, Moneymaking Opportunities or Income Opportunities.*

Before you start writing ads and preparing sales literature you should think a little bit about who you are trying to reach and what motivates them to answer ads like these.

The Three Motivators

There are three basic things that will motivate people at this level. The first is reassurance there is no way to lose. Remember, by and large these people are losers, and the fear of further loss is their prime concern.

The second motivator is the hope for an easy gain, to make money without risk, and without a lot of hard work. If they can be convinced this is possible, they will act.

Third is peer group envy. Remember they have been losers all their lives. Their peers know they are losers, and they have this burning desire to drive up to the homes of the people they know in a new Caddy, wearing Gucci's and a two carat diamond so they can tell them they are jetting to Europe for a vacation.

You put these three motivators in your presentation and you will have action, cash flow and be on your way.

Your first contact will be your classified ad. Make it simple and intriguing. Keep the three factors we mentioned in mind when you write it. It should mention an income that sounds believable, no risk, no work and prestige. Here is a sample that does all that in a few words.

NEW PRODUCT

SOLD BY SIMPLE PROGRAM WHERE OTHERS DO THE WORK. EARN $20.00 AN HOUR SUPERVISING. SALES GUARANTEED, NO RISK. WRITE THE PACKARD STERLING CORPORATION, 1234 MAIN ST., SUPER CITY, USA 12345.

All the elements I discussed are in that ad, and it will bring responses. You start with one or two ads to test the water, then expand the number of ads, and their size.

Your Recruiting Package

When you get an answer to your ad, be ready to respond the same day by first class mail. Don't wait or delay, as this prospect is a fly not an elephant. His attention span is short, and his address is usually very temporary. He has also written fifteen or more other firms for information, and he may spend his last dollar on their stuff. *So get back to him at once.*

I would develop a package that could go first class in an envelope for one or two ounces. If you wind up with a big package, then send a teaser letter at once saying you are holding this $25,000 a year executive management post for him, and his appointment material is coming in a separate envelope.

The response package should consist of a short letter reminding him of the ad he answered, and the great proposition he is now being offered. Don't go into detail in the letter, just enough information to get him to the selling material.

The selling material should be organized in a booklet format. The booklet takes him step-by-step through the proposition. The reason for this is a very basic selling proposition many people seem to ignore. *Always establish value before you quote price.*

Most of the material I have seen from sample sellers comes in a bunch of sheets of paper crammed into an envelope with no real starting or finishing point, and no structure to the offer. I think this is a fatal mistake for a new boy to this field.

Let me give you an example of what I mean. If I came to your office or home and said I have this Cadillac outside I will sell you for $100, you might not even go look. In your mind's eye you see a rusty old pile of junk that would be more bother than it's worth. That is quoting price without establishing value. If, however, I said I have this 1978 Cadillac with just 1,000 miles on it, in mint condition outside that I will sell you for $1,000, you may very well be definitely interested. I am asking for ten times more money, but I established value before I quoted price.

If your prospect finds out that he has to invest $25 to $500 in your deal before he understands the deal, he very well may toss the whole deal in the round file. By using the booklet format you can avoid this, and get the value set in the prospects mind before he knows the price.

A Successful Format

I am going to give you an example of a successful format that worked for a promoter back before World War II. I haven't seen anything better.

It was a sample selling deal, pure and simple. The promoter had no hopes for the product going beyond the agents closet. So, he had to make the deal appear to be a real winner.

1. *It described the product.* He used a picture and a drawing of the package to show how classy it looked. The product was a silver polish that was mixed with a drop or two of cooking oil, and it did a nice job. He stapled in a small wax paper envelope with a sample of the powder so the prospect could try it out. He gave him all The USP's he had, and did a good job on selling the value of the product.
in a small wax paper envelope with a sample of the powder so the prospect could try it out. We gave him all The USP's we had, and did a good job on selling the value of the product.

2. *It stated the Income Potential*—He used the headline, "*YOU CAN MAKE MONEY NOW!*" then, continued with something like, "without wasting time with a long training program—without taking time from your job or family—without risking your money—just follow my simple plan for an easy $50 a week extra income." (Remember, in those days a lot of people were working full time for $20 a week.)

3. *It listed easy Selling Plans*—The next pages were devoted to the easy selling plans the agent could use. He developed a simple pitch for each plan, and told them what to say, and what to tell others they hired to sell the product to say.

His sales plans covered hiring sub-agents to sell door-to-door (primarily kids to earn pocket money and prizes in what was called "Trust Schemes" in those days); store consignment with the product placed on counter cards; store demonstration which was big in those days; and church fund raisers.

This gave the prospect some ideas on how to get others to sell for him or her, and made the program seem like an easy way to make money.

Next, he added something that was designed to really stimulate the greed glands. You recall I mentioned peer group envy as a big motivating factor for losers. He set up a "Set Your Own Goal" program. He offered them a chance to get a new car, all kinds of new appliances (very big status item then); a fully paid family vacation to Florida or California; fur coats, new suits, sports equipment and the like. All these were free premiums earned by ordering "Evershine," the product name.

None of these prizes were going to cost us anything as they all came out of the agents orders. He allocated $2.00 from every six dozen units ordered as premium reserve. In those days a new Ford or Chevy cost around $800. So the prospect could earn a new car accumulating 500 bonus points. He had to buy 3,000 dozen to get the points, and the profit to the promoter was $6,000 on that many dozen.

These free status symbols were prime motivators in getting initial orders.

5. *It had no risk*—The brochure explained that they could order and had two weeks to sell the goods or they could return it for a refund less shipping and handling costs. Thus risk of loss was removed, and hope of gain established.

6. *It told them what and how to order* — A bonus of 10 points was offered if the initial order was for the six dozen units. A tear out order form was provided with step-by-step instructions on how to fill it out.

7. The next page told them what to do while they were waiting for the shipment to arrive. How to start lining up sales people and groups to sell the product. Suggested ads they could run in the paper, handbills they could have printed and the like. A daily schedule was provided to keep them busy while they waited.

8. He told them how to set up their business, keep records and handle their taxes.

9. He told them exactly what to do when the order arrived. To reorder at once if all their stock was out to agents, etc.

10. He then recapped the whole deal, reminding them of what that extra money would mean and how the neighbors eyes would pop when they wheeled up in their new car, 100% paid for. Then he added a pro-forma statement of earnings and the premiums those earnings could bring.

Setting Up Your Own Program

With the same system in mind and brought up to date, you can develop a successful agent selling program. I am going to offer you a suggestion on how you can do it.

First, let's take a look at a possible sales letter to accompany your booklet. It should be brief and to the point. Don't try and sell the deal in the letter, just use the letter to introduce the booklet. I would write something like this:

A FEW GOOD PEOPLE ARE GOING TO MAKE A FORTUNE WITH THIS NEW PROGRAM

Your inquiry about our program indicates that you are one of them. I thank you for writing to me about this unique method of creating an income for yourself by showing others how to make money.

I want you to take 30 minutes of your valuable time to study the enclosed brochure. **It will be the most profitable 30 minutes of your life.**

We are manufacturers of "Good Stuff." It is a product that will (go on to explain why people will eagerly buy the product).

It is selling fast all over the country by people who are no better educated, financially better off or more experienced than you are right now—yet, they are cashing big checks everyday.

I want to remind you that we are not looking for door-knockers or peddlers. We are looking for executives who will show others how to make money from "Good Stuff." You will earn from $20 to $200 an hour supervising these people.

Please take the time to read the brochure carefully. **You will discover the money making opportunity you have always been looking for.** The one that will set you free from the rat race and insecurity, and you risk nothing to grab the opportunity of a lifetime.

The Booklet

I would set the booklet up in ten steps to systematically establish value and increase interest in the program.

1. *The Product*—Tout the product, its wide appeal, its great results. Use all you USP's here.

2. *How Income Is Earned*—Here's where you explain your sales plan. If you are simply a sample seller you will cover all the possible plans in brief explanations. Personal selling, sub-agent sales, fund raising sales, telephone sales, store consignment sales, cash sales to stores, mail order sales, party plan sales, flea market sales, demonstrater sales, fair booth sales, etc. This will leave the prospect cold. Remember you are not dealing with highly motivated experienced people here. You are going to have to tell them exactly what to do if you want any action.

I would suggest you concentrate on store sales since that is the ultimate goal of this program. You use consignment selling to stores as your key. The product is packaged in its own display and these are put in stores and paid for by the merchant after he has sold them. He risks some space in order to make some profits.

This system has a lot of potential, if you use it. For example, your agent can contact fund raising groups to make money by putting the display units in stores. They get a percentage of all sales made. They can tell the retailer rather than asking him for a donation, they ask him to sell the product, make 33% profit, and help the cause. The people belonging to the group can get easy placement in stores where they are regular customers and make money for the group without having to do any selling themselves.

You should also provide the agent with instructions on how to hire women who have sold Avon or other direct selling products to act as agents to place units in stores. You can show that they will make more money than they did knocking on doors and pitching at parties, and all they have to do is get a merchant to agree to take the units on consignment.

Why consignment? Because it brings in the cash flow. You are selling these units for cash up front, and you want action. This guarantees you a lot of product moving out, and since your profit is in your pocket, the problems of consignment selling are not your concern. I will just say in passing that there are a considerable number of problems with consignment selling, and you will hear about all of them from your troops.

If you concentrate on that plan, and that plan alone, you will get more action and a higher cash flow.

3. *The Premium Offer*—This is the "Set-Your-Own-Goal" program. You put pictures of the major premiums that agents can earn and explain how they come automatically from orders. You show them that when they earn $50,000 they get a free $10,000 boat, car or motor home. When they earn $25,000 they get a free vacation, etc.

This is a real motivater so think big. Offer prestige prizes to reinforce the fantasy the reader has about showing everyone he isn't a loser.

4. *Testimonials*—You must have these. The testimonials you want to use are those that show an uneducated clod went out and made a killing with this deal. People with no experience, no talent, no skills are cashing those big checks.

How do you get testimonials? You pump for them. When you send out the offer that the letters become your property to use as you please. Then, take the best ones and use them. The first time you get a big reorder, call the agent on the phone and and get a statement on how he got the order. Use that in your testimonials.
you get a big reorder, call the agent on the phone and get a statement on how he got the order. Use that in your testimonials.

When you are starting and don't have any testimonials, get one from your brother-in-law, a couple of friends, etc. I would not advise you to use ficticious testimonials as you might get ripped by some DA or the Federal Trade Commission. If you have the letters on file, then you can't be charged with making them up.

5. *Place Your First Order*—Strike while the iron is hot. You've talked money and prizes, you've stroked the greed gland, so ask for the money right here. Show the reader exactly how to use the tear-out order form. Offer free bonus points for prizes for placing the order fast. Offer additional bonus points for ordering more than the minimum. Stress your moneyback

guarantee, there is no risk. Don't ask for the order; demand it! The territory won't last, the prices are going up, bonus points can only be had now, etc.

6. *Tell Them How To Start*—Tell them what to do now while they are waiting for their order to arrive. How to get started contacting sub-agents, give them some classified ad copy to run in local papers—letter copy to send to fund raising groups, etc. Get them moving so that re-orders will start coming in faster.

7. *Business Information*—Give them some brief instructions on checking out business licenses, setting up records, handling taxes, getting business stationery printed—and what office supplies they will need. Give them suggestions on storing the inventory, selling to sub-agents, etc.

8. *What To Do When The Order Arrives*—Explain how to check it, get it ready for sale, etc.

9. *Reorder At Once*—If they have sub-agents lined up, then advise to place an order at once for more units. Tell them to divide their goal up by the number of months they will take to reach it, and place the reorder to meet that goal. Remind them there is no risk, and they can have plenty of stock on hand to take care of the business.

10. *Pro-Forma Statement Of Income*—Make up a pro-forma statement of the income they can make. Show them how much profit is possible if they keep adding sub-agents to place the units. Close by telling them they are now in the upper 5% of income in the country and they should enjoy their new status as a winner.

The pro-forma is the spike for the deal. It reinforces all you have said before, and gets the greed juices flowing and the order on its way.

A Word About Premiums

Don't stand short on offering premiums. You can offer a Rolls-Royce, an airplane, boat, travel to exotic places, etc. Make it look like a very big deal. After all, the money to buy the premiums comes out of their pockets, not yours, so why not.

Keep something else in mind. Most of the premium money you set aside will never have to be spent. You can expect that 90% of those placing the first order will never place another one, and even the best of them will dropout in a few months time. Few will ever earn any premiums.

To give your deal a shot of class and a lot of lesser premiums to choose from, contact the *Travelers Premium Company,* 110 5th Avenue, New York, NY, and ask for their package offer. They have a premium program designed just for the kind of deal we are working up here. There are ten different levels of premiums, and they will supply inexpensive four color brochures displaying the premiums at a small cost. By adding a couple of these brochures to your recruiting package you can build some real impact.

Handling Your Orders

There are two ways to handle orders. You can handle them yourself, in house, or hire an order filler to do it for you.

Handling them yourself has the advantage of total control of the program. However, if you are operating on a shoestring, and don't have a lot of space to store inventory, then, you can use the order filler quite profitably.

If you put an ad in the paper for someone with storage space in their home who would like to make some extra money evenings filling orders, you will get a lot of replies.

You set a per unit, or per order fulfillment price. The order filler takes the order copy, packs it, puts a label on it and ships it. They store the inventory at no cost to you and are paid as the orders are filled. You will have to get a bond on them if you have a lot of valuable inventory. You can add the bond cost and what you pay them to shipping and handling costs your agents pay. The new effect is that this cost does not come out of your end.

The Order Handling System

An efficient order handling system starts with the order form you receive. If you arrange it so that the agent fills it out in such a way that a shipping label is provided, and a photo-copy machine will provide the copies, you have little or no typing to do, and no special forms to prepare.

When the order arrives you check it, see to it that the proper amount of money is enclosed, make whatever notations are needed for your records, then make the necessary number of photocopies for files and shipping.

The shipping copies (two) are sent to the order filler. He fills in the proper places on the form showing when it was received, filled and shipped. He prepares any bills of lading that are necessary, and sends back the house copy with bills of lading, etc., attached. This is filed with the original order, and the paperwork is complete.

Work out this process carefully as it is of vital importance to keep it current and organized.

Include a constant check on inventory in the system so you aren't caught short.

Handling Checks

All checks should be treated like hot potatoes; held as briefly as possible. Deposit all checks at once. If there are checks for large orders you can put them through for collection (this speeds up the clearing process).

No matter how good an agent you have, do not ship until checks clear. Make this clear to the agents. For same day shipment, they must send money orders or certified checks.

You should become a VISA and Mastercharge merchant through your bank so you can offer your agents the right to charge on their bankcards. This gives them immediate shipment as you can check validity by phone from your office.

You can fool around with COD's if you like, but they are a pain in the butt. If you do ship COD get enough of a deposit to cover all your shipping costs both ways.

Set Your Cash Flow Goal

Keep in mind this program is a temporary step in reaching a total marketing effort. Set the cash flow point you need to reach before you begin the second phase of your marketing effort. In other words have a plan to expand your agent sale program into a higher cash flow and reach a much larger share of the market.

Getting Store Names

Here's one point in closing. If you are going after nationwide marketing through retail stores, then make sure your agents supply you with a list of all the stores where they have placed goods on consignment. You can use the excuse that you must have the list of names from them in order to protect them with your product liability insurance. Tell them if you don't have the names on file they could be sued or something like that. But, put in a system where the list of names comes back to you.

This will build a name file for your direct to retailer sales by mail. It will be worth a lot of high cash flow dollars to you, so be sure and get it.

The Failure Rate

There is no guarantee the agent program will be failure proof. There is a less likely chance of failure in starting with this program than in trying to sell by mail or direct to stores. But, there is no guarantee it will work.

Just remember, it's no sin to fail in product marketing. The biggest of corporations fail far more often than they succeed in getting a new product into profitable national distribution. So, you won't make it work everytime, but you won't lose much of anything either. In fact in the agent deal it's possible to fall flat on your face in getting a product sold to the consumer and still make money.

[illegible]

Getting Those Names

[illegible]

The Failure Rate

[illegible]

TACTICS

Guard your time closer than your cash!

Treat time like a basketfull of thousand dollar bills. Time is the one thing we are limited in. The richest man on earth cannot buy one more second—it has no price.

If you want to put a price on it you can think of it this way—if you are going to work an average of 40 years—you have about 350,400 total hours of time available to you. If you want a million dollars to retire on, you will have to make a net, bankable profit of $3.00 an hour, 24 hours a day for 40 years. If you want to be a millionaire in ten years—and you work about 10 hours a day, you will have to net $30 an hour after taxes—or $300 a day to do it.

If you decide that is your goal, then you have to value your time at $300 an hour—and spend it accordingly. The key is to multiply yourself—and have others working and earning that $300 an hour for you.

The key to time management is the list of ten—each day you put down ten things that must be done—and as they are done you cross them off. Any that are not done, are added to the next day's list and done first. This keeps your time profitable—your job manageable and your profits secure.

STRATEGY

Diversify your contacts to the extreme.

Build a bank of contacts with knowledge in all areas of human endeavor—help and ideas can come from anywhere.

Robert Heinlein wrote in "The Notebook of Lazarus Long" (published by Putnam) that "A human being should be able to change a diaper—plan an invasion—butcher a hog—conn a ship—design a building—write a sonnet—balance accounts—build a wall—set a bone—comfort the dying—take orders—give orders—cooperate—act alone—pitch manure—solve equations—analyze a new problem—program a computer—cook a tasty meal—fight efficiently—die gallantly. Specialization is for insects."

Build your resources so that you either know or can find out. Know people who would know what you need. The wider your access to diverse knowledge—the more successful you become.

CHAPTER 24
BUILDING A DYNASTY

How to Start a Dynasty With This Program

I'll show you how to turn this concept into a fortune of substantial size by organizing some service business ventures — you can hire sharecroppers to run for you — and have access to all the capital — research information — new ideas and concepts you will ever need to become a tycoon of the eighties and nineties.

First, I'll show you how to get access to all the capital sources in your area — by selling a service to people who need capital — and then have the sources available to you whenever you need capital for a venture of any kind. It's called the Capital Consultant's Service, and it analyzes loan and investment packages for people seeking capital — and puts them in contact with capital sources. You can set a sharecropper up in this service, and have $20,000 to $50,000 a year in net profits to split from the service to others. It's like owning a bank vault you can tap for funds whenever you need them. I'll give you a detailed explanation of how to set it up.

The Commercial Research Service

The second thing you need for any of your deals is information. I will show you how to set a sharecropper up in a commercial research service — make money selling the service to small business firms — and have the firm available to do your work at cost, and you can participate in substantial profits as well. Any time you need market research for a business takeover you can have the service do it for you.

You can use it to test product ideas — new business ideas on a professional level — all at no net costs because your profits from other services will more than pay for your work.

The New Venture Consulting Service

Next, I'll show you how to set up a cooperative consulting service for people wanting to start small business ventures. This is a badly needed service in every area of the country — and one that can put $100,000 a year of profits or dividends in your pocket while your sharecropper pockets a like amount. This is a simple business where others do all the work, and one that will also bring you many ideas and opportunities to set up sharecropper businesses in selling new products and services.

How to Franchise a Small Business

Finally, I'll show you how to franchise a small business, and show you how you can do it without registering a franchise with the state or federal government. By using a technique I explain, you can sell franchises anywhere in the country legally without any registration. And, I'll also give you the system for setting up the franchises and selling them quickly.

The New Venture Business Planner

Then, I'll give you a step-by-step planning guide for new ventures. How to quickly write a business plan that covers everything from the concept to the grand opening. Using it as a guide you can develop a comprehensive plan to sell the sharecroppers on a program — to impress bankers and other capital sources — and to get your ventures started quickly and profitable. You can also use this program in the new venture consulting program to develop clients. It will help you get 50 to 100 clients a month each paying $300 or more for the service.

The Opportunities are Limitless

Using the techniques I explain in the following chapters, and using the sharecropper technique rather than trying to run them yourself — you open the door to an unlimited choice of small business opportunities that you can capitalize on by being a professional entrepreneur. So read on — this is a map to the goldmine.

STRATEGY

Don't play for nickles and dimes.

You can't build wealth pitching pennies.

You have to get in the big game where:

- You have less competition.
- More opportunity to win big.
- And can play on other people's money.

The key is lack of competition!

Nickle and dime deals have millions of people competing for them—a job and a paycheck—little, easy to run businesses—small income properties—fad investments.

- A million dollar deal may have 100 competitors.
- A ten million dollar deal may have two or three.
- A hundred million dollar deal one or none.

The bigger the game, the fewer the players. The amounts of money involved are relative—the sums are meaningless—it's the potential return that counts.

Fact—the bigger the deal, the easier to use other people's money in getting control of it. Bankers and investors hate little deals—love big deals.

Fact—you need less capital of your own if you think big.

CHAPTER 25
CAPITAL CONSULTANT

The highly successful entrepreneur has access to capital—both investment and working capital whenever he needs it. The wider his capital contacts are, the greater his ability to put deals together. My knowledge whenever possible. The following will show you how to have the greatest possible number of capital contacts in your area for putting together your own deals and how to set up a service a sharecropper can run for you that will not only pay for the researching and finding of the contacts, but give another source of sharecropper income by providing a unique consulting service to those seeking capital. A by-product of this service will also be that you will be able to locate some hot takeover and sharecropper opportunities of which you would not otherwise know.
tunities of which you would not otherwise know.

The Concept

A Capital Consultant is an advisor to those who seek capital or loans, a trusted point of contact between money seekers and money lenders or investors.

The CC is a middleman who learns what is required to interest lenders and investors, and how to use that information to help those seeking funds.

The CC does not collect fees based on a percentage of the funds required, nor does the CC promise clients that they will get funds through his efforts.

The primary function of the CC is to do an analysis of the fund request and determine its potential, who would be interested in seeing it and what can be done by the client to make it more attractive.

Most people seeking funds do not understand the money markets, nor do they know who will be most interested in providing funds for the purpose they seek.

The CC does not operate as a finance broker. He does not represent anyone else, nor put loan offers into a daisy chain of other brokers and finders. He does not ask for a percentage of the loan as a fee.

The finance brokerage field is filled with phonies who infer that lenders and investors are happy to pay 10% loan fees to a stranger who sent them the information. **They aren't and they won't pay it.** They are interested in getting proposals from legitimate sources, and the CC will earn their trust and respect when they understand he or she is not collecting part of their loan or investment as a fee.

The Federal Trade Commission and other government agencies are prosecuting advance fee brokers who collect money up front, plus demanding a percentage of the loan or investment. A lot of them have wound up in jail.

The CC renders an honest service for a reasonable fee, and has no problems with the authorities. He is a consultant, pure and simple.

The History Of The Industry

Up to this time this service has been provided primarily by accountants and brokers of various kinds. Bankers are involved to an extent as are lawyers. But there are few serious specialists dealing with the public at large in this field to date.

There are some operations, including one or two franchises that offer this service at rather high initial investments—and there are some people doing nicely helping small business entrepreneurs prepare Small Business Administration loan packages. But, there has been so much hype in that field that the SBA finally put a limit on what a consultant could charge a loan applicant to prepare his package.

The field is being highly exploited by so called finance brokers who lure amateurs into the field by selling them lists of so called money sources and a brief explanation of loan packages. This causes many people seeking funds to get involved with these amateurs who send their loan packages to promoters who may or may not present them to money sources.

Third party presentation of loan or investment packages does not work. Anyone parting with money wants to deal directly with the source seeking the funds, and is seldom willing to deal with fee brokers to find them.

There are other sources who deal in loan packages such as mortgage bankers, real estate brokers, venture capital firms, etc. However, they are not involved in the preparation of loan packages, but in the marketing of them.

There is a genuine need for a legitimate service that puts the right package before the right source.

The Business Operation

The CC has some very worthwhile services to offer both the fund seeker and the fund provider. First, he knows the market for money. He knows who is lending and investing and who isn't. He knows what types of investments or loans each source favors, and what guidelines they set down for consideration of a loan or investment. He knows how to prepare packages and offers that appeal to them. Thus, he does not waste their time, nor does he send questionable offers to them. They appreciate this, and will act on those he does send with dispatch.

Since they know he does not participate in any way in the proceeds from the funds, nor does he represent either party in negotiations, they appreciate his service, and the courtesy he shows them.

He builds a strong and favorable relationship with fund sources.

Secondly, he offers his clients, the fund seekers, a valuable service at a reasonable price. He can show the strong and weak points of their proposals, have them improve the offers, aim it at specific fund sources and turn the odds for getting the funds from highly negative to highly positive.

His services are valuable to both sides of a deal, and this builds a substantial income from a consulting practice.

It is estimated there are at least $100 billion looking for an investment every business day in this country. The sources of funds are vast and varied and any seeker of funds with the proper help, and a legitimate proposition, has a good chance of obtaining them if he or she is properly counseled on where to go, and what to say. That is what the CC does.

The CC through advertising in various forms makes contact with people seeking capital. They answer the ads by calling a telephone number. This is an answering service or the CC's office. The caller is questioned about the type of funds he is seeking, the amount, what they will be used for and when they are needed. The caller is asked to leave a phone number where the CC can reach him.

The CC returns the call when he has time for a brief telephone discussion with a prospective client. He uses the information taken by the answering service, and adds more information from the caller. What security or collateral is offered? What terms is the seeker looking for? How long will funds be needed? And more details about the use of funds.

The CC is qualifying the prospect in terms of validity of the proposition and the level of financial sophistication of the seeker. If the CC feels there is a legitimate offer, and some prospect of getting funds for the prospect he invites the caller to his office. He explains he is a consultant with wide contacts in the money market, and he acts as a consultant in helping the fund seeker get the funds he needs from the proper sources. He explains, he takes no fee based on the amount of the loan, and does not get involved in negotiations for the funds. His only fees are for an analysis of the loan or capital request, and suggestions on how to improve it, and where to take it for the best chance to get the funds.

At that point the caller knows there is a fee involved and either agrees to come, or passes. If he agrees, the CC makes an appointment for him, sets up a folder with the information he obtained, and makes any pertinent notes.

When the appointment time arrives the CC refreshes his memory from the file, seats the client and the discussion begins.

The CC explains his basic service to the prospect. He will do a professional analysis of the package, and if there is no need for preparation (typing the request, gathering the facts, etc.), quotes him a price for the analysis and his help in submission to the money sources who would be most interested in the proposition.

If there is no formal application or prospectus, then the CC quotes a price for analysis and package preparation. He sets a time limit (usually 90 to 180 days) in which he will seek sources and arrange presentations for the client. If the prospect simply wants sources to submit the loan himself, the CC explains that he will never arrange for presentation of any offer to his sources without first analyzing it. He shows the prospect a sample analysis, and touches on the reasons an analysis can greatly improve the chances of getting the funds.

He spends no more than 20 minutes on this, and asks for the order. If the client agrees, he fills out the necessary forms, collects his fee in advance, and arranges for the analysis, or for additional information needed to make the analysis.

If the prospect is not interested, the CC thanks him for coming, and makes a couple of helpful suggestions and ends the interview.

The average CC will close half of those who come to the office, and with fees ranging from $250 up, he can generate a considerable cash flow if he keeps up the advertising to produce inquiries.

On a full time operation you should interview between 10 and 20 prospects a week. The 50% close rate gives you (with an average fee of $300) between $1,500 and $3,000 a week gross income. With proper management a substantial portion of that is net income.

You Don't Have To Be A Financial Expert

To operate a successful Capital Consulting service you don't have to be a financial expert yourself. There is an old saying among lawyers, "you don't have to know the law, just where to find the law." It's the same in this profession. You don't have to know finance, just where to find the right information.

For example, you don't do the analysis of loan or capital packages yourself. You hire moonlighting experts to do it for you. You can have bankers, accountants, builders, lawyers, brokers and others making these analyses, and you simply present the results. They are your "Ghostwriters." They go over the packages with you, explain the problems, the pluses and minuses and you pass the information along to your clients.

All it takes to get into this field is guts, and the ability to sell people a service they need very badly. All the expert help you need, can be hired when you need it.

After discussions with your freelance analysts and some study of books on the subject, you can become expert enough. Keeping in mind that an expert is someone who knows more about a subject than you do. And, you will know a lot more than your clients do about money sources and what plays and what doesn't.

This is a salesman's deal—you are really only a middleman selling a service that others need.

Location Of Your Practice

The choice of location is important. You should be in an area where commercial activity is growing, or at a high level. You should be in a trading area where you have at least a million people to draw from, and it should be filled with upward mobility aspirations on the part of the population in general.

There should be strong financial activity, lots of banks, savings and loans, commercial finance companies, mortgage brokers, etc. A run through the yellow pages of local area phonebooks under various headings such as Banks, Savings and Loans, Loans, Real Estate Loans, Mortgage Finance, etc., will give you an estimate of commercial fund sources. By checking listings for doctors, lawyers and dentists you can get an idea of the probable amount of private investment capital available.

Your Office Location

You can start in your home if you like. In most cases where you are based at home, you should have access to an office for meeting clients. Many phone answering services make such offices available, and there are some services now offering short term (a day to a week) office rentals. If, however you have a nice home or apartment in a good area with a well appointed office in it, there is no reason why you can't operate from it.

If you want an office for your practice, choose the best one you can afford. Take a good deal of care choosing furniture and fixtures (you can rent these at the start) to impress your prospects and clients. Much of your success in selling your services will be the impression you make on the prospects. A highly skilled professional has impressive offices, and charges accordingly.

Since your fixed overhead costs are low, primarily office and advertising, you should invest as much as you can in them.

Ideally your office will consist of a reception area, and one or more private offices for meeting with clients and prospects.

It is wise not to commit yourself to a long term lease when you start as there are several things that can happen. The obvious one is that you won't make it, and be stuck with lease payments or penalties you can't afford. The second, and more likely prospect is that you will quickly outgrow your initial office and need larger quarters. A long term lease may prove difficult to break. A third possibility is that you will find a better deal after you are started, and want to take advantage of it. For that reason, try for a month to month rental of your office at first.

Client Demographics

The prospects you see will represent a broad range of the economic spectrum. You will have highly knowledgeable business people with sound propositions seeking loans and capital. You will have backyard inventors with the mysterious black box seeking $50 million, and everything in between. You will have many people in the construction industry and many small business owners seeking working capital. Breaking them down, you have the builder, the small businessman, entrepreneurs with good ideas and the skills to make them go, promoters with wild ideas and no skills and the occassional nut with grandiose dreams.

As time passes you will learn who you can serve and who you can't and pretty much decide in the first phone conversation. You must limit yourself to those people who have a realistic proposition and the necessary skills to use the money successfully. If you send your money contacts the promoters and screwballs just to pick up a fee, you will lose them and destroy your business.

This means that you will have to turn away a lot of potential business that would pay your fee. The temptation is great, particularly at first, to accept this business because of a need for a cash flow. But, if you destroy relationships with fund sources by sending flakey deals to them at the start, you will have killed the goose that lays the golden egg.

Economic Analysis

You will want to keep abreast of economic conditions as they do have a substantial effect on your business. As money gets tighter you will have to develop sources of funds outside the standard commercial sources, and work harder to find them. The advantage of bad times is that you will have all the clients you need, but money sources will be scarce.

If you learn to read the economic indicators you can anticipate tight money, or high fund availability and turn that into surges of income working back on a client list. Many of your clients will have a long term need for funds, and when you can alert them to changing economic conditions, you can get additional business from them.

Choosing The Business Name

In choosing a business name, I would suggest you follow the professional practice. Use your own name followed by Capital Consultant, just as a lawyer uses his name followed by Attorney at Law. If you expand and take in partners or associates you add their names to the firm.

It gives your operation the profesional touch, and some additional advantages in your start-up. You don't need to open separate checking accounts, get a business phone number, file ficticious firm name reports,etc. You have everything in place except some business stationery.

Business Form

You have three choices: The sole proprietor, partnership and corporation. The sole proprietor is simple, quick and hassle free. Later on, you can form a partnership or professional corporation if required.

Bank Account

You can establish a second account in your own name for the business if you wish—or simply use your present account till you get a cash flow and something to deposit. When you are established you should have accounts in several banks for business reasons. It gives you leverage to get friendly with bankers who can help you a great deal in developing money sources.

Record Keeping

You will need to keep books. However, the concept of this business is that it is an advanced fee program so you will not be keeping accounts receiveable. They may crop up as your venture developes, and in that case you will need an accounts ledger and a billing system to handle them properly. In the beginning you should only have to use one of the simple bookkeeping systems you find in any stationery store. They have one designed for people in the professions. The trade name is "Ideal." It would give you all the record keeping you need to set up and start operating the business. In addition, you should have a receipt book for client payments, and some petty cash slips for your office. The bookkeeping system and your canceled checks are really all of the bookkeeping paraphernalia you will need to manage this operation. There is little point in having a CPA or high cost accountant to keep your records, as you can use a bookkeeping service to handle preparation of tax forms and give you profit and loss statements, balance sheets and other reports you may require. It is likely you will run across someone among your contacts who can keep a good set of books for you for a minimum fee.

Licenses And Permits

All you should need is a local business license—and if required, a sales tax permit. This is only needed if services are taxable in your state or locality. To my knowledge there is no special license for consultants, but some states may have such requirements and it would pay you to investigate them. It should be pointed out that you should in no way engage in giving investment advice, legal advice or in handling real estate transactions or do anything else that requires a special license from the state or federal government. Stay strictly in the field of analyzing financial statements and directing clients to possible sources of capital and you should have no difficulty in this area.

Communications

Pay some attention to your choice of telephone systems. You should have a button phone in your office, one on the receptionist's desk and any other offices where communications will be required. You should install at least two lines and have the intercom feature with the hold button attached to the phones. This insures your ability to call out and have conversations and leave one line open for incoming calls for clients and prospects. If you're going to leave the phones uncovered during business hours, use a hook up to a good answering service rather than an answering machine. It makes a better impression, and it makes sure you get messages that are understandable from those who called. You may want to add a document transfer device to your phone system. This transmits documents over phone lines from one unit to another anywhere the telephone will reach. This won't be a great necessity, but as your business develops and you establish branch offices or are dealing with financial institutions at long distances, the ability to transmit a loan package, a loan summary or other material in a few minutes time could be of great assistance to a client and to the potential lender or investor. If you branch out in your business beyond your own locality, you may want to investigate the possibility of having a WATS (Wide Area Telephone Service) line installed. This enables you to make either outgoing calls to any area covered by the WATS line or receive incoming calls from any area of the WATS line for a greatly reduced charge. It is only valuable when you will be using more long distance calling than the price of installation and the monthly fee would cover. For example, at this writing it is possible to get a national WATS line, either one that you call out on or one that clients can call you on, for $256 a month for ten hours of long distance calling. If you use it more than ten hours a month it would cost approximately $26 an hour for each additional hour. That is a minimum contract. An unrestricted WATS line in which you're free to call as long and as often as you wish starts at $1,800 a month up. The basic advantage of a WATS line is that it enables you to call anywhere in the country at a reduced fee, and in return receive calls from anywhere in the country at reduced fees. It would be particularly useful if you were advertising for prospects on a national basis and the prospects were able to answer your advertising with a toll free telephone call. It greatly increases returns and also gives the prospective client the impression he's dealing with a large successful firm. There are several other communications tools we will get into in the marketing section of this program. That will make it possible for you to get a good many more paying clients by proper use of your communications equipment.

Business Literature

Your business literature needs are modest. You'll need:

1. Letterheads
2. Envelopes
3. Business cards
4. A brochure, if you want one
5. Client information forms
6. Loan analysis forms
7. Purchase orders and/or statements
8. Letter of agreement

You don't need fancy designs or artwork. You should consider using standard professional formats for all your literature. It is the same as that used by doctors, lawyers, CPAs, etc. You may or may not need a brochure. We'll get into the pros and cons of that decision later.

The management section gives you specific examples of simple forms you can use in order to manage your business properly. All material you are sending outside your office to either money sources, clients or other business firms should be of top quality both in type of paper or printing stock used, format and reproduction. Trying to save money by using cheap materials or cheap printers is far more costly than the few dollars saved. In purchasing printing for this business, pay far more attention to the quality and the ability of the printer than to his price schedule.

Business Equipment And Fixtures

You will need the normal compliment of desks, chairs, filing cabinets and other business fixtures that normally are used in any office. These can often be rented or leased in the beginning in order for you to save capital for advertising promotion where it is far more productive. Your desks should reflect some degree of quality, and lend an air of dignity and authority to your office. Pay some particular attention to your own desk and make sure it is rather massive and heavy looking. There is a psychological advantage to your sitting behind such a desk in the same way a judge has a psychological advantage sitting on his podium in a court room. It puts you in a position of authority and gives your clients the impression that you are a substantial and knowledgeable individual.

In picking typewriters you should give serious consideration to leasing or renting a word processing typewriter. This is a machine that stores copy on magnetic cards, tapes or disks and will retype them at high rates of speed, without error, upon command. As your business develops you will find that many features of loan applications and loan packages have virtually the same content. By having this information stored on magnetic media, the typist can call up the appropriate material from the memory units of the equipment and have the machine insert the stock paragraphs in their proper place upon command. This saves hours of repetitive typing and thousands of dollars a year in typing payroll. It can also be used to store stock letters for prospects making inquiries, clients making inquiries, money sources making inquiries, etc. Again, as your business develops you will discover the same questions being asked over and over again, and a stock letter stored in an automatic typewriter system can answer these questions by having the typist prepare a personally typed letter in reply at the touch of a button that will be finished in a minute or two.

There are many of these systems on the market, and used equipment that is in good condition is just as useful and valuable as new equipment. You will find listings of firms dealing in this equipment under word processing in the yellow pages of your phone book, and in some cases, also under typewriters. More and more of this equipment is coming into the used market, and can be rented or leased quite reasonably.

If you have a nice office, and want to get use of some of this equipment without charge for a few days or a week, you can often call the firms selling the new equipment and ask them to leave some equipment on trial so you can test it out. In this way, you may be able to get the usage of word processing equipment for a short period of time at no cost, and if you convince enough salesmen you need a test this can run for three or four months before you have to make a buying decision.

It is also worth noting that the small microcomputers are now capable of doubling in brass as word processors when hooked up to a typewriter rather than a computer print out machine. You can investigate small computers such as TRS-80 from Radio Shack, Apple Computers from local computer stores and other similar small computers that have the capability of being both word processors and giving you additional computer functions. This can save you a considerable amount of money by not having to pay freelancers to analyze the simpler loan packages, and would very shortly pay for itself.

You will also need a good copier, one that handles both standard and legal sized documents and makes clean, clear copies. The best system is to investigate available brands, check the used market, watch for bankruptcy auctions where it is possible to pick one up for ten cents on the dollar, or if you don't have time for that then rent or lease one on a short term basis to make sure it will do the job for you. There are so many of these on the market that it is impossible to make any recommendations, and they are constantly coming out with new models that do better jobs for even less money. The one key to watch for is to make sure that service is available in your area for the type of machine you acquire. These often require service, and without it you are likely to get very short usage out of any machine you pick up.

Your filing system is extremely important. As your business grows you will be filing case folders almost daily, and you want a system that will give you a cross reference to enable you to locate a specific file when you need it, and for a loan source. If you have a computer on the premises, it can provide you with a cross-reference index that can be kept up-to-date daily, and enable anyone to locate any necessary file immediately. And when your business gets larger, and filing space becomes a problem you may want to investigate microfilm equipment. This reduces your filing space necessity by 95%, and systems are available now that can be cross connected with computers so that any file in your office would be instantly available by simply consulting the computer. But under all circumstances, be very careful about setting up and maintaining your filing system as it becomes very important to you as your business develops.

Supplies

There are no specific supplies other than normal office supplies and your printed forms required in this business. Since this is a service and consulting business, it's all done with paper, postage and conversation. If you have no commercial credit standing, one of the simplest accounts you can open is with a local stationery store for business supplies. Many give a 10% discount to people who purchase supplies for businesses, and will normally open an account for you with a banking and one other credit reference. This gives you one commercial credit source should you require credit from other sources.

The Marketing Plan

One of the good things about this business is that it is very simple and uncomplicated. The marketing plan consists only of small ads run regularly in local or area media, and your two-step telephone system of getting clients in your office.

You don't need any advertising literature. In fact, I would advise you not to make up a brochure to send out. There are three reasons for this. First, you take away the personal consultation, and to a degree, the professional approach of the program. Doctors and lawyers don't send out brochures. Secondly, you don't really know as you begin what direction your service will take. You will make several changes in your operations in the first few months, and wind up with a lot of useless literature. A third reason I don't like brochures for a venture of this kind is that they give people ammunition to come after you. If you make claims in the brochure that can be deemed to be false or misleading, or you infer that you are something more than you are, you can be sued by clients or badgered by authorities. If your only literature is your letters of agreement with clients, then what is said or inferred is a matter of oral statement, and difficult to prove in a court of law.

I don't mean to infer that you are going to be running a racket, but if you start enjoying a good degree of success you are going to have problems with people in government who hate to see other people make money.

So, you can prepare a brochure if you like, but I think it's a waste of time and money. It's a better idea to put those funds into expanding your advertising and making more contacts. If a prospect asks why you don't have a brochure, just point out that yours is a highly personal service, and each client requires different types of attention. You are running a consulting service, not a store.

Your advertising should be in every type of media that pulls results. The two best are the newspapers and yellow pages. An ad similar to the one below can be a starting point.

FUNDS AVAILABLE NOW!
FOR BUSINESS PURPOSES — START-UP CAPITAL — EXPANSION CAPITAL — CONSTRUCTION — INVENTORY — ACCOUNTS RECEIVABLE — LEASING, ETC. CALL 212-4356 FOR INFORMATION.

You can run variations of that ad, by offering funds for specific purposes such as — **$100,000 available for small business investment** — add the phone number — or **up to $5,000,000 for construction and development loans** — this brings in the small builders and real estate brokers. It is a wise idea to vary your copy, using different purposes for funds to attract new sources. You should run the ads on a regular basis in the best circulated newspapers in your area.

The yellow pages are a prime source of business and you should take listings in all categories that pull business. Loans, investments, mortgages, etc. In the one with the most listings, take a small display ad or bold face listing, and additional listings in the others.

The phone company has a new program where you can have listings in phone books in other cities, and have the call come to your phone. The caller doesn't know you are not a local firm, and you pay only the listing fee and distance charges used. You don't have to get a separate phone number in that community. This is worth looking into if you expand.

If you want a gimmick to build business, get a separate phone and hook it to an answering machine (you can rent one from the phone company). Put a daily 30 second report on tape about who's lending money, and interest rates. Run an ad something like this — **Want to know who's lending and investing? Call 123-4567 for recorded message**. This will get calls, and tell them where loans are being made (such as banks are tight, but there is still savings and loan money) — then give today's interest rates, and follow it with, "We are in constant contact with thousands of fund sources — if you need money for business or construction call (give your other phone number) during business hours." Repeat your number at least twice.

This will get action and get people talking about you.

Building A Base Of Private Investors

Contacting the Private Investor

The way to put your service ahead of any competition that might crop up is to build a stable of private investment sources no one else knows about. Anyone can contact the commercial fund sources, but no one can get at the private fund sources but you.

There are a couple of ways to do this. First, you can run ads in the paper something like this:

> **INVESTORS ATTENTION — FREE CONFIDENTIAL BULLETIN LISTING THE BEST LOCAL INVESTMENT OPPORTUNITIES — SHORE AND LONG TERM — NO SALESMAN WILL CALL, FOR SAMPLE COPY CALL (TELEPHONE)**

This will generate a small, but steady list of names. You can send out a bulletin (as part of your newsletter) listing client offers. They could read something like this:

> **LOCAL BUILDER WITH STRONG LOCAL TRACK RECORD SEEKS $150,000 FULLY SECURED — SHORT-TERM CONSTRUCTION LOAN TO FINISH OFFICE BUILDING. PERMANENT FINANCING IS ALREADY ARRANGED. PAY PRIME PLUS 3 POINTS, WITH A BONUS TAX CREDIT PASS THROUGH ON $80,000. PROJECT #747.**

Instruct the investors to call your office for a mini-prospectus on any item of interest. Then, they can get back to you to make an appointment to meet the principals of the deal they are interested in.

This brings you a lot of private money contacts and builds your fund source base much faster than personal contact can.

Another way to build private money sources even faster is to send out letters to top income people in the area offering them your free bulletin. It could read something like this:

The Best Local Investment Opportunities

> The Sam Smith Investment Bulletin is a free service to local investors that should interest you. Each issue lists interesting short and long term opportunities for better than average returns.
>
> We will be happy to send you a free copy of each issue on a confidential basis. No salesman or seeker of funds will bother you, and there is no charge of any kind to you.
>
> We are consultants to those seeking funds, and make detailed analysis of each venture so any investor may examine the program with detailed and verified facts and figures.
>
> We are not brokers or finders—we do not collect a percentage of any investment or lean, nor do we take any part in negotiations. You deal directly with the principals, and not with third parties.
>
> To get on the mailing list to receive the bulletin just call (telephone), and leave your name and mailing address. If you find something of interest, call our office and we will forward additional information on it, or make an appointment for you to meet with the principal if you wish.

You can include a copy of a bulletin with the letter if you have some good listings, and send it as often as you have enough listings to warrant it. Once or twice a month should be plenty.

This also helps you sell the prospective client when you show him the letter and tell him it's going out to a thousand or more money sources in a week or two.

The value of building a substantial list of private investment sources will become apparent to you as your business develops. In many cases you will have clients coming to you who have already tried all the local commercial sources of funds without result. Your ability to present their package after it's re-tailored for private investment will enable them to get funds. In some cases you will be able to interest one or more private sources in a larger deal and enable the client to form an investment syndicate to get funds that single sources could not provide.

When the commercial fund sources become aware of your large area of contact with private fund sources they will start telling some of the people they must turn down about you, and referring clients to you.

So, pay as much attention as possible to building up these contacts, as they will make thousands of extra dollars for you.

Getting Money Sources

Once you have decided this business is for you — then your first step will be to build a file of money sources. It will take some time, but you should have at least a hundred of them in your file before you begin to contact clients.

The place to start is with local bankers. Drop by and see them in person. Identify yourself as a small business consultant. Don't tell them you are going to be putting loan packages together, they will mistake you for an advance fee broker, and not tell you much. Tell them you help small businesses solve their problems, and often are called on to suggest forms of financing. You would like to get copies of the bank's business and construction loan forms if possible, and find out their basic criteria for making loans, beyond the fact of sufficient collateral, and ability to repay.

The bankers will tell you in general terms what bank policies are, and what types of financing they prefer.

Ask them specifically about commercial finance firms in the area, mortgage brokers and other fund sources. Get names of principals so you can contact them using the banker's name as your source.

Never ask permission to send clients with loan packages to them. It will brand you as an amateur. They have to look at loan requests, that is what they are hired for. They must make loans to survive, so they will see anyone who has a package, and if you send only those who meet their minimum criteria, they will come to appreciate your service, and be nice to your clients. But, at the start, only find out what you can about their policies, and the names of the people to see.

By using each contact you make as a source for other names, you can build your contact file fast. You can call many of them on the phone when you have a name to use. For example, you call the Commercial Finance Company manager in the area, and tell him Charley Banker gave you his name, he's going to be polite. Charley Banker sends him business and he's not going to get smartass with someone who knows Charley.

So, spend your time building your contact file, and make up cards on each of them with the information on this checklist:

1. Name of institution or organization
2. Name of main contact
3. Names of other potential contacts
4. Phone numbers of all contacts
5. Type of money source
6. Loan policies and restrictions
7. Correspondent relationships
8. Best times to contact
9. Personal interest in idiosyncrasies of your contacts

A file kept in a loose leaf notebook and added to as needed will be worth many thousands of dollars to you if it's developed and kept up-to-date at all times.

In general terms your file building will include these types of money sources:

1. Bankers
2. Savings and Loans
3. Commercial Finance Firms
4. Real Estate Brokers

5. Stock Brokers
6. Mortgage Brokers
7. Attorneys
8. Accountants
9. Insurance Agents
10. Venture Capital Firms
11. Factors
12. Private Investors
13. Mortgage Bankers
14. Pension Fund Managers
15. Insurance Company Investment Agents
16. Foreign Sources

The file is your gold mine. Most people know so little about fund sources, they will assume that you arrange things for them when you send them to see one of the sources. They don't understand the sources are more anxious than they are to find the kind of deal they can put money to work in. These commercial sources have thousands of dollars a day coming in that must be put to work, and not allowed to pile up earning peanuts.

Understanding Your Loan Sources

When you begin dealing with your fund sources you will have an advantage if you understand how they think, and how they look at loan or capital applications. First, most of the people you deal with are employees. They represent banks, savings and loans, commercial finance companies and other entities that lend or invest funds. As employees, they have no personal concern about the money involved. It is not their money, and therefore they have no vested interest in it. But, they have a serious concern about their jobs, their promotions and these are tied to how well they handle the company's funds. In every case their first concern is how will lending or investing in this deal make me look to my superiors. Making good loans or investments is the key to upward mobility, and making bad ones is the way out the door.

Thus, you are dealing with a personal concern of those who can approve or disapprove a package. Most of the people you will have as clients are small entrepreneurs of one kind or another, and they do not think like a corporate employee. The lender is looking at downside risk, while the entrepreneur is looking at upside potential. The lender or investor is first and foremost interested in the safety factor of the proposed loan or investment. A lender is concerned with safety to a higher degree than an investor, but both do not want to lose their money. So, the first key to a successful package is security for the fund provider. In every package you consult on, keep that point in mind. As the level of security drops, so does the probability of getting funds, and the probability drops much faster than the rate of security.

The second factor is profitability to the fund provider. The ratio of profitability comes not only from the direct return from the use of the money, but also from fringe benefits the provision of funds can supply. For example, a banker looks at a business loan as a way to create a profitable bank customer. The rate of return on the loan requested is not as important as future benefits such a loan might bring to the bank. If the banker sees the business as a growth situation, where the account will get larger, the loans larger and more profitable, the firm using other bank services, and becoming a high profit account for the bank, he will take more of a chance than he would if it was simply an in/out proposition where a few interest points were made, but little future propspects involved.

In the case of investors, the same thing holds true. The kickers in a deal such as convertible bonds, or warrants to buy stock at a low price, or other kicker arrangements to give investors more than a simple dividend return will create more potential for obtaining funds.

So the second point in developing your packages is to create the most future benefit beyond the original transaction as you can.

How Will Funds Be Repaid

The next question that must be answered is how the source of funds gets the money repaid along with the profit. This is the critical point in the package. If they can be assured the funds will be generated to repay, then the problem comes down to terms and amounts. But, if there is no valid proof the necessary funds will be coming in, the deal is dead.

In the case of lenders they are primarily interested in finding out whether the funds can be repaid out of cash flow, or whether it has to be out of profit. The cash flow projections in the package are the place they look to determine this. No short term lender will put up funds that have to be repaid from profits. That is the province of the long term lender or investor. The short term lender wants his money from cash flow whether there are any profits or not.

In the case of investors, it is understood their returns come from profit, or from sale of their holdings to others anticipating greater profits in the future. So, the packages will differ as to repayment in this respect.

To prove that the funds will be generated, a cash flow projection should show the funds coming in during the time limits of the loan to make repayment. This projection must be backed with enough information so the loan analyst can verify the projections and be assured they are both reasonable and probable. This is done by giving the lender a use of funds statement, showing what will be done with the loan funds, and how this application will generate the needed income to repay.

Let's go over these three critical points again:

Safety — the lender must be assured his funds are safe. He wants to see collateral, co-signers, subordination of previous debt, etc., in order to assure the safety of funds.

Profitability — the lender is interested in the best rate of return on this loan, plus future profits from further dealings with the borrower. By showing the lender more income for him down the road, the borrower greatly increases his chances of getting the original loan.

Repayment — verifiable proof of the use of the funds will generate the necessary cash for repayment within the allotted time for the loan. Give an accurate use of funds statement and a projected cash flow statement showing how that use of funds will provide the necessary cash flow. These assumptions must be backed up with reasonable proof that can be verified from other competent sources.

When you hire freelance analysts be sure they understand these three points, and that they are carefully analyzed in each package along with suggestions on how to improve the presentation in each area.

The Ratio Analysis

It is not the purpose of this chapter to give you a course in accounting or financial statement analysis. You can get that information from your freelancers or from the books I will suggest you obtain for your practice.

In all cases where lenders are presented with loan applications they use financial, marketing and operating ratios to determine the profitability and management skills of the applicant. These ratios are key factors in judging the viability of the business venture, and while some bad ratios will not negate obtaining funds, it will result in the lender asking the borrower for correction of the problem or additional security, etc.

Every business has problems, and anyone who needs funds will have them as well. These ratios tend to quickly point up what those problems are, and what needs to be done to rectify them.

I am going to give you a checklist of these ratios, and you will want to be sure your freelancers understand them and can read into them what the fund providers will see.

They are:

- Percent of net profit to net worth
- Percent of net profit to net sales
- Net sales to fixed assets
- Net sales to net worth
- Current ratio
- Acid test
- Receivables to working capital
- Inventory to working capital
- Collection period (days)
- Net sales to net inventory
- Net sales to working capital
- Long-term liabilities to working capital
- Debt to net worth
- Current liabilities to net worth
- Fixed assets to net worth
- Average amount of sale
- Number of customers
- Number of customers gained/lost
- Average size of accounts receivable
- Percent of sales in cash
- Percent of sales on credit
- Number/amount of bad debts
- Dollars in sales for each ad dollar spent
- Dollars in sales divided by number of employees
- Dollars in sales per sq. ft. (retailers)
- Profit per sq. ft.
- Profit earned by item sold
  a. largest volume item
  b. next items in order of volume
- Average pay per hour
- Employee turnover rate

All these are not always required, but, if they are in the package, they impress the sources of funds that the borrower has a firm feel of his operation.

Another form of ratios that is checked is what is called the operating ratios. These are the percentage of various expenses to total gross sales. For example, rent may represent .03% of total gross volume, and cost of goods sold 45%. These ratios give the fund source a clear key to the management skills of the operator. There are standards in each industry to which they can compare figures, and often these ratios will show that a business is spending too much or too little in given areas and help the sources of funds get some corrections made in operations that will give them a greater margin of safety.

One point about making up these ratios . . . it's a natural for a small computer. Since all these figures are obtained by adding, subtracting or multiplying and dividing, a computer can whip through them at the speed of light. It only takes a simple program, and you can save a lot of hours of figuring for your freelancers — a lot of fees for their time — by doing the ratios on a computer and giving them the printouts. You could also do them on a Texas Instrument or Hewlitt Packard programmable calculator.

Dealing With Clients

Let's go over the process of dealing with your current prospective clients. Their first contact will be a phone call to your answering service or office girl in response to an ad. The caller will be asked what amount of money they are seeking, for what purpose they require it, and how soon they need it. They will be asked to leave a number and a time you can reach them by phone. Under no circumstances should the people taking these calls discuss any of your services with the caller. You don't want any preconceived notions in the prospect's mind when you return the call. You should return the call at the agreed time if one was given. When you have the prospect on the phone, give your name and ask for his or hers. Tell them you represent many sources of funds looking for good lending and investment opportunities. Mention the amount of the loan on your call slip to verify it. Then ask what the funds will be used for. Ask if the prospect has a figure in mind (percentage rate on loans, percentage of ownership on investment) he would be willing to pay to obtain the funds. Ask how long the funds will be needed, and how he intends to repay. Ask if there is any security offered to lenders or investors. Are there any added inducements such as a piece of the action or a bonus offered? Where will the funds be used, that is, where will the office be that receives and disburses them be located? What business is the caller in? What experience has he had in the project the funds will be used for? Are any others involved in sharing the proceeds from the venture? If so, who are they, and what specific functions do they perform?

If the caller provides all this information, then you are in control of the situation. If they balk, or want to know just who you are, and what you're selling, don't tell them. Explain that you must get an idea of what they want, what they have to offer, and who is involved before you can even decide if you want to get involved. If they don't want to give you the essential facts then you can't help them. You must only deal with people you can control. If you let them push you around on the phone, you will be wasting your time in trying to sell them later. Don't be too eager on the phone, act like you are the one with the money, and let them sell you.

When you have the facts, then you have to decide if you want to proceed further. If the caller is a backyard inventor who wants a million dollars to put his 500 mile a gallon secret fuel on the market (and you will get calls from people just like that), you can pass. But, if it's a local builder who needs construction financing for a new apartment house, you can proceed to the next step.

You can say something like this: "On the basis of the information you have given me, I have some people who provide funds that would be interested in seeing your package. I am a consultant, and I will analyze your package for my sources — then I will sit down and go over the analysis with you pointing out the good and bad points from the standpoint of the lender or investor. I will help you develop your package so it has the best chance of being accepted, give you some help in how to negotiate with them, and provide you with contacts to as many of our sources as you wish for a 90-day period. We do not charge you a percentage of the amount you require, nor do we take any part in your negotiations with the fund sources. All you pay us is a small fee to analyze your fund request and give you our help in making sure that it will be something our sources will be interested in.

If you are interested I will make an appointment for you to meet me in my office, and we can discuss the matter to determine for sure whether we can help you.

When you are through with that statement, there will usually be one of three responses — first, "How much is your fee?" Second, "I'd like an appointment." Or, "I'll think about it and get back to you."

In answer to "How much?", don't hesitate. "Our fee varies with the complexity of your package, but our average fee for analysis and consultation of a loan package is around $250 for 90 days of service. It runs somewhat higher for investment packages as we need up to six months to properly reach all the fund sources on investments."

That's all you say. He now knows that $250 is the bottom figure, and he will either agree to come in or back off. Don't try to sell him, or suggest there can be easy terms or later payment. You've got what he wants — sources of funds. If he wants them $250 worth, he's a client. If not, he either doesn't have $250 or won't part with $250. If he says something like that's a lot of money, or something to that affect, and you want to zing him, you can use this one. You answer in a casual off-hand manner, "Since we represent our fund sources, and must protect their time and interests, we must analyze each loan application before we submit it. The small fee we ask is less than you would pay for a small ad in the Wall Street Journal, or even your local paper that would run at best, a day or two. But, if you consider it too much, I can certainly understand your position, and I wish you good fortune in finding your fund source. Goodbye Mr. Smith." Then you hang up. If your zinger worked, he'll call back.

In response to "I'd like an appointment", make one for him as soon as you can. When they're hot, they're hot, so don't let them cool off. This answer is almost always a sale.

In response to, "I'll think it over, etc. ..." Don't try and make a sales pitch — just say, "Fine, Mr. Smith, you've got my number, goodbye" and hang up. Never let the phone discussion get beyond the question of making an appointment. Don't try and explain what a loan analysis is — or what kinds of sources you represent — or how long you have been in business, etc. Either make the appointment or end the conversation. You cannot come across as a salesman trying to sell them something. You've got to come across as a source of funds. After all, the banker doesn't have to sell the loan applicant, even if the banker if going to make a fat profit from the loan, and you don't have to sell your contacts either in the sense of asking them for business. You have to convince them you have the key to the vault, and they will sell themselves.

The Office Interview

When the prospect arrives for the interview you take your file folder with the preliminary information and refresh your memory about the deal and any notes you made about the conversation.

When the client arrives in your office, seat them and get down to business at once. Don't get involved in chit chat, you want to give the impression your time is valuable. Ask him or her for their package of information and look it over to see what shape it is in. If it has the necessary financial statements, the personal information, the summary of request for funds, how they will be used and how they will be repaid, then you can get down to business. If there is only a financial statement, or some rough draft figures and a package will have to be prepared, then you will need to take a different tack.

Let's take the complete package first. Look it over, make any notes about missing parts, or unclear statements, then say something like this. "Mr. Prospect, your package looks to be complete, ready for our analysis. We will go over it just as the source of funds would and give you a detailed breakdown of what the strong and weak points are. I will make some suggestions of how you can present this offer to the fund sources, and will contact those who are interested in acting on propositions of this kind. The analysis will take about seven to ten days, and will be made by our Mr. Brown, who is an expert in this area. As soon as he has finished, I will arrange for a consulting appointment for you, and we will take an hour or so to go over it with you. When you are ready, I will make as many appointments as possible over a 90-day period, or until you get the funds.

If the prospect asks you what you think of the package, or asks any specific questions about it, you say something like this — "I make it a practice not to comment on these packages until I have the analysis. It would take me two or three hours of study to give you any reasonably accurate answers, and that is why we do the analysis.

When you have fended off all the questions, then you quote the price. A $250 fee for analysis and your consultation on the results, plus making appointments with fund sources. If all goes well you can have the prospect meeting sources of funds within 15 to 21 days.

If the prospect says he doesn't want an analysis and will pay you just for contacts, you should come back hard . . . you wouldn't submit a deal to your fund sources without prior analysis. The only reason you can provide the service you do is that the fund sources know you have made an expert analysis of the deal, and that you consider it worthy of their attention. If you simply sent people out without knowing what they were offering, you would soon be wasting everyone's time, and fund sources would no longer be willing to see the prospects you send them.

There are two reasons for being adamant about this feature. First, once the analysis has been made, the $250 is yours. As you will see in your agreement, that is what the client pays for, and that is all he pays for. The rest of your services are free, based on the favorable results from the analysis. If you find the offer will not stand the test of lenders and investors, and suggest changes to make it meet the minimum requirements to qualify for funds, and the client refuses to do so, then you are out of the deal, and earned your $250 analysis fee. Once you make the analysis you are in the driver's seat.

The second reason is exactly the one you gave the client. If you send every turkey with a wizard deal around to these sources, they will simply refuse to talk to them. But, if they get your analysis statement, and a call for an appointment, you will be able to put clients in front of them, and many of them will get the funds because you did the job properly.

If the client gets on the "You've got to guarantee I'll get the funds before I pay" — or, "I'll pay a 5% fee when the funds are raised." — push them out the door. You don't work on the come, or on a percentage. If they can't pay the price of your service, then they have nothing you can use, and don't waste time with them.

The Client With No Prepared Package

This is a different problem. You have a prospect with some rough figures put together and not much else. This is either a $500 client, or a time waster, and you might as well find out up front. You tell this client that you will need to prepare a package for him that will be acceptable for review by your fund sources. Your fee to prepare the package for a loan application is $500, plus expenses — for an investment package $750 plus expenses.

If the client is agreeable, then you will give him a loan application form to fill out, a questionaire to answer and some other material. Once these are completed, you can prepare and analyze the package, and start processing fund sources for him.

There is an additional problem here many times. The prospect doesn't know how to fill out even a simple loan application. In this case, you will fall back on the expenses part of your quotation. You will give him over to your analyst, who will ask the necessary questions, help him to find the answers, and then turn the results over to your office girl for typing. The client is charged by the hour for this service, and makes a deposit large enough to cover costs for a minimum package.

Your job in selling this service is to demonstrate to the client that the major reason people fail to get loans or raise capital is that they don't prepare proper applications, that your service guarantees him a complete and proper application, that fund sources will agree to review if the offer is basically sound.

These sales are easier to make than those who have complete packages, and produce far more income. So, concentrate on them, and develop a nice pitch to sell them. Show them an example of a completed package and how fund sources use it. Explain something about financial and operating ratios, cash flow projections and how fund sources look at loan and investment packages. They can see the difference, and grasp the need for your service.

The Letter Of Agreement

Here is suggested copy for your letter of agreement with your clients.

> **TO SAM SMITH & ASSOCIATES**
>
> This letter confirms our conversation, and I intend to retain you in the matter of raising funds for (name of project).
>
> I understand you will make a complete analysis of my proposal; then consult with me concerning the results. You will make suggestions for changes which I may accept or reject.
>
> For this service I pay herewith the sum of $ ___________
>
> Upon completion of the consultation you will provide me with source information, and/or appointments to present the package for financing.
>
> I understand there are no other charges, and you are not to receive any fees, commissions or payments other than the retainer paid herewith, unless I specifically designate in writing approval of additional charges for extra service ordered.
>
> Signed ____________________ Date ____________________

The above letter is for analyzing a prepared package brought in by the client. If you are going to prepare the package, the following paragraph should be used instead of the one above.

> I understand you will propare my package from the figures and information I give you. You will then consult with me concerning the results and how it might be improved to secure immediate funding. For these services I agree to pay $ ________ , plus expenses. It is agreed the expenses will not exceed $ ________ , and you will render an itemized expense statement. If the amount is less than covered by my deposit, the difference will be refunded. Upon that understanding I pay herewith the sum of $ ________ .

Loan Analysis Staff

To get freelancers to do analysis of your loan packages, you simply advertise in the newspaper for people with specific skills in fields you may have to deal with. In other words people that have dealt with construction loans, small business loans, start-up business investment packages, loans for agriculture, manufacturing, wholesaling, retailing, etc. As you get responses to the ads you pick those you feel are most likely to do the best job and sit down and build an analysis system (they do all the work you simply make suggestions), so that each package gets a specific type of analysis based on financial ratios, operating ratios, cash flow projections, etc. You agree on a price for each analysis and then call them in when you have clients.

You should build a substantial list of these freelancers as one or two will not suffice. It is much better to have a larger group with widely diversified experiences so you get people to analyze loans that have had specific experience in the business they are analyzing.

In developing analysis forms, the easiest way to build an analysis package is use the forms used by your local banks for commercial loans. By following these step-by-step, you will be doing an analysis in the same manner the local bankers would do it. And by having their loan firm as your check list guide, you'll come up with a complete analysis package with a minimum amount of effort.

You want to keep one thing in mind as you develop your marketing plan for this business. You are going to be making a great deal of money from this service if it is organized properly and carefully thought out and prepared. If you try to slop your way into it, and bluff your way along with your clients, you're going to get that reputation in the area and both clients and fund sources will simply not respond to your service and you'll be out of business. You have to consider yourself the general of the army. You don't have to make the battle plans, you simply have to plot the strategy and acquire the people who will carry it out. You have to be completely aware of what you are doing and how you're going to do it in order to be successful.

Package Checklists

There are a group of checklists that your analysts can use to develop loan packages and prospectuses for your clients. By developing the information indicated they will end up with complete packages ready to present to fund sources. In some cases the outlines call for more information than might be needed in every case, and good judgment on the part of the analysts can determine what to leave out.

Here is the information needed to be supplied by the client. You have to remember your analysts are moonlighters for the most part, and can't spend their time doing research. They simply tell the client what is needed and he finds it and delivers it to them.

General Descriptions Of Business

1. What is the general nature of the business? Give brief description of the product line and the market it serves.
2. How big is the company? Latest annual sales figures in dollars, and value of total gross assets.

History Of Company

1. Obtain as much information as possible concerning date formed, by whom, where organized, and amount/source of original capital.

Structure Of Company

1. Corporation, partnership, or proprietorship.
2. Financial structure—amount and ownership of common stock, preferred stock, bonds, and notes.
3. Organization chart-lines or authority and numerical size of personnel in various categories.

Financial Status

1. Balance sheets with supporting detail of appropriate items.
2. Income statements including trends in sales, gross margins, and profits.
3. Cash and working capital requirements.
4. Inventory data by category and including slow moving and obsolescence factors.
5. Credit reputation with supporting Dun & Bradstreet reports, bank references, and supplier relationships.
6. Property mortgages and notes.
7. Accounts receivable and bad debt situation.

Products

1. Description of products and product lines. (Including catalogs and circulars.)
2. Price and cost data.
3. Any new products on the drawing board and their potential.
4. Patent and license situation.
5. Quality, style, and price in relation to competition.
6. Risk of substitution in material and style of present product.
7. Possibility of product diversification.

Distribution

1. Characteristics of Sales Department.
   a. Number of people and method of selling.

   b. Territories and coverage.
   c. Branch offices.
2. Use of distributors and manufacturers' agents and contractua relationships, if any.
3. Markets.
   a. Domestic and foreign.
   b. Market background information.
   c. List of major customers.
   d. Estimate of potential market.
   e. Geographical concentration.
4. Sales Analysis.
   a. Itemize products and product lines.
   b. Itemize markets and major customers.
   c. Order backlog and size.
5. Advertising program.
6. Customer relations and reputation for service and quality.

Competition

1. Names of major competitors.
2. Description of competitive products.
3. Competitive position in total market.

Purchasing

1. Principal materials used.
2. Sources of supply.
3. Purchasing methods—discounts, etc.
4. Importance of inbound freight costs.

Manufacturing Processes

1. Comparison facilities and processes with competition.
2. Patentable processes.
3. Degree of automation.
4. Flexibility to meet possible changes in requirements.
5. Ratio of material to labor.
6. Maintenance requirements.
7. Type of quality control.

Research And Engineering

1. Comparison of size and quality of laboratories and staffs with competition.
2. Amount of research work contracted to outside engineering firms.

Employee Relations

1. Union situation and labor contracts.
2. Wage rate comparison with competition and community.
3. Labor supply in area.
4. Fringe benefit plans.
5. Labor turnover statistics.
6. Number of shifts of operation.
7. Appraisal of working conditions.
8. Group insurance program.
9. Retirement program.

Evaluation Of Personnel

1. Special skills, abilities, education, reputation, and income.
   a. Top management.
   b. Administrative personnel.
   c. Plant supervision.
   d. Maintenance personnel.
   e. Engineers and scientists.
   f. Sales force.
   g. Office force.
   h. Production employees.

Future Prospects And Problems Of Any Kind Which Might Be Predicted

Evaluation Of Physical Assets

1. Land.
   a. Market value, assessments, easements, adjoining property, and space to expand.
   b. Tax rates.

   c. Accessiblity to roads, streets, and railroan terminals.
   d. Adequate parking areas.
   e. Landscaping.
2. Buildings.
   a. Market value.
   b. Age and type of construction.
   c. Fire protection.
   d. Shipping and receiving facilities.
   e. Amounts of insurance and rates.
   f. Taxes.
   g. Systems—light, hear, water, ventilation, aisles, and conveyors.
   h. Lockers and wash rooms.
   i. Cafeteria and lunch rooms.
   j. Building codes and zoning laws.
   k. Sewer and waste disposal.
   l. Inventory storage facilities and shelving.
3. Machinery and Equipment.
   a. Complete list of all equipment identified by original cost, manufacturer, age, net book value, condition, and replacement value.
   b. List of obsolete or unused equipment.
   c. Arrangement for work flow.
   d. Machinery on order.
   e. Machinery designed by company itself.
   f. Lift trucks and other material handling equipment, including tote boxes.
   g. Tractors and trailers, officials' cars, panel trucks, pick-ups, etc.

The Property

1. General Description.
2. Legal Description.
3. Locations.

4. Location Sketch.
5. Aeiral Photo.
6. Location Benefits.
7. Location Drawbacks.
8. General Statistics.
   a. Demographics.
   b. Average rent.
   c. Traffic count.
9. General Site Data.
   a. Legal.
   b. Size and square feet of land and site coverage.
   c. Use of site.
   d. Zoning.
   e. Utilities.
   f. Access.
   g. Sketch of lots sharing building location.
   h. Survey.
10. Land Value.
    a. Estimated value of site.
    b. Comparable land sales and values.

The Developer

1. Name.
2. Address.
3. Occupation.
4. General Data.
5. Net Worth.
6. Supporting Documents (not included, but will be on forms, institution supplies).
   a. Net worth statement.
   b. Schedule of assets.
   c. Schedule of liabilities.
   d. Reference.
   e. Position of employment.

   f. Verification of salary.
   g. Estimated annual earnings.
   h. Credit report if applicable.
   i. Other forms supplied for application.

Accounting Policies And Procedures

1. Inventories.
   a. Categories.
   b. Costing practices.
2. Fixed asset or property record accounting.
   a. Type of appraisal cards.
   b. Grouping of categories.
   c. Straight line or accelerated depreciation.
   d. Guidelines and investment credit.
3. Type of cost system.
   a. Job cost.
   b. Standard cost—absorption or direct.
   c. Selling price determination.

Construction Or Development Loan

Outline For A Construction Or Development Loan

The Project

1. General Description.
2. Site Plan.
   a. Breakdown of project to square footage of improvements.
   b. Use of project.
   c. Stages to be built or developed.
3. Economics of Project.
   a. Cost estimates.
      (1) Builder's bid on other supporting data.
   b. Operating expenses.
      (1) During development.
      (2) Marketing expenses.

   (3) Preleased agreements (if applicable).
  c. Cash flow—expense vs. income chart.
4. Feasibility of Project.
  a. Economy of area.
   (1) Aerial photo showing location of similar projects in competing area.
   (2) Description of competing projects.
   (3) Economics of competing projects.
   (4) Future growth proposed and documented.
   (5) Future demand on type of project (including supporting documents).
   (6) Summary of economics of competing projects.
  b. Opinion of use based area economics.
5. Value of Completed Project.
  a. Estimated potential cash flow on finished project (if income property shows operational statement, 12 month estimate after project completed).
  b. Market value based on cash flow (capitalize at current investor demand rate).
  c. Value of existing projects of similar nature (refer to same projects covered in earlier description of competing projects).

The Loan Request (for end loans)

1. Recap value of finished product.
2. Recap development cost.
3. Add land cost to development cost.
4. Show relation to total estimated value and total cost to develop.
5. Amount of loan requested.
6. Terms and conditions requested.

The Loan Request (for construction or development loan)

1. Recap value of finished product.
2. Recap development cost.

3. Add land cost to development cost.
4. Show relation to total estimated value and total cost to develop.
5. Copy of end loan commitment.
6. Amount of construction or development loan requested.
7. Terms and conditions requested.

Supporting Documents

1. Full set of working plans (if available).
2. Typography (if needed).
3. Preleased documents (if applicable).

Mortgage Or Income Property Loans

Outline For Mortgage Loans

The Property

1. General description.
2. Legal description.
3. Location.
4. Location sketch.
5. Aerial photo.
6. Location benefits.
7. Location drawbacks.
8. General statistics.
   a. Demographics.
   b. Average rent.
   c. Traffic count.
9. General site data.
   a. Legal.
   b. Size and square feet of land and site coverage.
   c. Use of site.
   d. Zoning.
   e. Utilities.
   f. Access.

   g. Sketch of lots sharing building location.
   h. Survey.
10. Land value.
   a. Estimated value of site.
   b. Comparable land sales and values.

The Improvements

1. Description.
2. General statistics.
   a. Date built.
   b. Year remodeled.
   c. Type of construction.
   d. Other structural and mechanical data.
   e. Floor area.
   f. Parking.
   g. Other data.
3. Sketch—for each floor if floor plans vary.
   a. Show tenants.
   b. Show square feet.
   c. Show approximate sizes.
   d. Building plans (if new building, or if lender is not in area, or if requested).
4. Personal property.
   a. Inventory.
   b. Value.
5. Statement of condition of property.
6. Replacement cost of structure.
   a. Original cost.
   b. Replacement cost.
7. Comparable sales of improved property of similar nature in the area.
8. The economics (actual).
   a. Income.
   b. Expense.

    c. Net operating income.
    d. Economic value.
    e. Rent roll.
    f. Sample lease.
    g. Past records of income and expense.
9. Opinion of economics.
    a. Relationship to average square foot rent for area.
    b. Average of square foot for this building.
    c. General opinion.
    d. Estimated future income.
10. General summary of value.
    a. Land values.
    b. Replacement value.
    c. Personal present value.
    d. Estimated present value.
    e. Economic value at present income.
    f. Comparable value.
    g. Contract price.
    h. Copy of contract.
    i. Value justified.

The Person

1. Name.
2. Address.
3. Occupation.
4. General data.
5. Net worth.
6. Supporting documents.
    a. Net worth statement.
    b. Schedule of assets.
    c. Schedule of liabilities.
    d. References.
    e. Position of employment.
    f. Verification of salary.
    g. Estimated annual earnings.

h. Credit report of applicant.
i. Other forms supplied for application.

The Loan Request

1. Amount
2. Terms and conditions.

Office Interview Form

On the following pages you will find a suggested form for taking information during your office interview. By getting the information indicated, you will have a fairly complete picture of what the client has to offer, what he needs and what shape his proposal is in. This is useful when you discuss the project with your analyst, and gives you a place to get a quick refresher on the project when you need it.

Office Interview Data

Name ____________________
Phone ____________________
Company Name____________________
Mailing Address____________________
City ____________________
State____________________
Zip____________________

Type of Venture

☐ Service Firm
☐ Manufacturing
☐ Agriculture
☐ Accommodation, Entertainment, etc.
☐ Products or Inventions
☐ Franchise
☐ Mining, Resources, Minerals, etc.
☐ Real Estate, or Construction
☐ Institutional or Professional
☐ Marketing: Sales, Wholesale, Retail
☐ Other (describe) ____________________

____

Amount Requested $ ____________________

Brief Description of Proposal______________________________

____

____

Explain steps to be taken to minimize risk to lender or investor, prime collateral and valuation, interest rate and term of loan or investment yield:

____

____

____

____

Describe any additional collateral you wish to offer (including co-signer(s):

____

____

____

____

Is part ownership, stock etc., offered to lender or investor? If yes, give brief description:

____

____

____

____

Describe the purpose of the loan and how it will be used:

____

____

____

____

List your estimated (projected) capital recovery or net profits in a given period of time:

____

____

____

____

Products or services provided now or proposed in the future:

____

____

____

____

Geographical coverage and description of where products or services will be marketed:

____

____

Check appropriate caption that describes the ownership if this is a present functioning business

☐ Proprietorship ☐ Partnership ☐ Corporation

Give brief description of any experience, background or education in this field:

____

____

____

____

Present package checklist—use it to indicate what is now in the package, and those not checked will show what might be needed:

- ☐ Balance sheet
- ☐ Operating statement
- ☐ Cash flow statement
- ☐ Use of funds statement
- ☐ Pro-forma statements showing use of funds
- ☐ Personal financial statement
- ☐ Personal background resume
- ☐ Income tax statements
  - ☐ Business
  - ☐ Personal
- ☐ Collateral list

- ☐ Leases, mortgages, contracts specimens
- ☐ Incorporation papers
- ☐ Statement of ownership
  - ☐ Major stockholders
  - ☐ Partners
  - ☐ Bond or note holders
  - ☐ Options
- ☐ Business history summary

Current amount of capital to be provided by you and/or the firm — money:

____

____

____

____

Are you and/or your firm rated by Dun & Bradstreet? ____________

Give brief summary of why you feel a lender or investor should feel your case would warrant advancing funds in your behalf—return on investment, tax shelters, etc.

____

____

____

____

Transportation

The use of your car in the business is a deductible expense. You will want to keep accurate track of all expenses involved in use of your car for income tax purposes. If you have two cars, use both of them in the business in alternating two week periods so you can claim deductions for both.

When your practice grows, and you have a branch office, you should consider leasing a car for the business, and deduct all costs for its use. You can discuss these alternatives with a tax advisor to get the best tax deal on transportation.

Dues And Subscriptions

When you establish your practice you should join the local Chamber of Commerce, and any other civic group that will give you exposure and a measure of prestige. The dues you pay are, in effect, advertising costs.

Books and Periodicals

You should subscribe to, and read, certain publications that will keep you informed about financial markets and business conditions.

First, read The Wall Street Journal. It's the daily newspaper of the financial world. This is a must.

Second, subscribe to Business Week, published by McGraw Hill, 1221 Ave. of Americas, New York, NY, 10020. It's a weekly magazine with news of the business and financial community that is must reading for anyone in business.

In addition to those two publications you can choose others as you feel the need. I would suggest, Forbes, Fortune, US News and World Report, Barrons, Mergers and Acquisition, American Banker, Bankers Magazine and any local or area business publications where you are in business.

You will want a library of books that you can refer to, and as a start I would suggest these:

Financial and Executive Handbook, edited by Richard F. Vanci. Published by Dow, Jones, Irwin. **Complete Guide to Real Estate Financing,** by Jack Cummings, published by Prentice Hall. **How To Find Out In Banking And Investment,** by N. Burgess, published by Pergamon. **Handbook Of Investment Products And Service,** by Victor Harper, published by McGraw Hill. **The Interpretation Of Financial Statements,** by Graham, Benjamin & McGorlick, published by Harper Row. **The Meaningful Interpretation Of Financial Statements,** by Donald E. Miller, published by American Management Association.

These basic books will provide you with information as you need it. There is no need to sit down and try to read or study them. A simple system for turning them into an instant reference library is to hire a high school or junior college kid to make a card file from the indexes, by subject matter. Then, when a question arises, you can find the answers quickly by referring to one or more books. The card file is like having a consultant in the office with you. You should add to your library as you go along, as it will be one of your most valuable assets and will teach you what you need to know.

Here are two forms to use in opening files for clients, and giving work assignments to analysts.

File Opening

Name of file__________________________________

Address __________________________________

City/State/Zip__________________________________

Phone/Home/Office__________________________________

Date opened__________________________________

Type of file

- ☐ Loan — Client Package
- ☐ Loan — In House Package

Client Prospectus

- ☐ Investment — In House Prospectus
- ☐ Other __________________________________

Consultant Assigned__________________________________

Date Assigned__________________________________

Consultant Phone #__________________________________

Date Completed__________________________________

Date File Closed__________________________________

Here is a form you can use for assignments to your freelance people

Freelance Assignment

To__________________________________

Client Name__________________________________

Address __________________________________

Phone ________________________________

Best time to contact__________________________

Analyst Assignment

Assignment ______________________________

Type of work_____________________________

Fee payable______________________________

Maximum hours available____________________

Expected completion date____________________

Opened by_______________________________

Closed by_______________________________

Expenses total $__________________________

☐ Expenses receipts attached

Fee paid by check #________________________

Expenses paid by check #____________________

On the following page you will find a pro-forma financial statement for 12 months operation of a capital consultants service. It is based on an average of 1 new account per day, 5 days a week, with a minimum sale of $250 per package. It allows you a $2,000 a month salary, and takes 20% of the fees for commissions for your analysts. As you will note, salary plus profit gives you a gross income of over $40,000 on this minimum operation. If you wish, you can charge higher fees, and handle fewer accounts.

DATE: 12/31/81 PAGE 1

SAM SMITH & ASSOC
INCOME STATEMENT
PERIOD ENDING 12/31/80

ACCT DESCRIPTION	CURRENT	%	YEAR-TO-DATE	%
••••••••••••••••••••••••••				
**GROSS SALES				
••••••••••••••••••••••••••				
3001 SALES	0.00	0.0	72,000.00	80.0
3002 CREDIT SALES	0.00	0.0	18,000.00	20.0
**TOTAL GROSS SALES	0.00	0.0	90,000.00	100.0
••••••••••••••••••••••••••				
**COST OF SALES				
••••••••••••••••••••••••••				
4001 ADVERTISING	0.00	0.0	9,000.00	10.0
4002 COMMISSIONS	0.00	0.0	14,000.00	15.6
**TOTAL COST OF SALES	0.00	0.0	23,000.00	25.6
••••••••••••••••••••••••••				
**GENERAL OVERHEAD				
••••••••••••••••••••••••••				
4003 OFFICE HELP	0.00	0.0	7,200.00	8.0
4005 MANAGEMENT SALARY	0.00	0.0	24,000.00	26.7
4006 DUES AND SUBS	0.00	0.0	300.00	0.3
4007 AUTO EXPENSE	0.00	0.0	2,400.00	2.7
4008 RENT	0.00	0.0	7,200.00	8.0
4009 TELEPHONE	0.00	0.0	2,400.00	2.7
4010 UTILITIES	0.00	0.0	350.00	0.4
4011 WORD PROC LEASE	0.00	0.0	2,400.00	2.7
4012 ACCOUNTING SERVICE	0.00	0.0	360.00	0.4
4013 TAXES AND LICENSE	0.00	0.0	600.00	0.7
4014 POSTAGE	0.00	0.0	600.00	0.7
4015 SUPPLIES	0.00	0.0	600.00	0.7
4016 OFFICE EXPENSE	0.00	0.0	300.00	0.3
4017 REPAIR & MAINTENANCE	0.00	0.0	300.00	0.3
**TOTAL GENERAL OVERHEAD	0.00	0.0	49,010.00	54.5
TOTAL INCOME	0.00	0.0	90,000.00	100.0
TOTAL EXPENSE	0.00	0.0	72,010.00	80.0

NET PROFIT ....$ 17,990 19.9

STRATEGY

Get a license to steal.

Know more about a deal than the other person and you are in the position of a burglar in an unguarded bank.

Get to know how to get information.

Consider this—suppose you could get up a poker game where only you could see your cards—others could not look at theirs—they did not know what hands won or lost—you told them when to bet—and how much to bet—and you told them who won and who lost. Would you like to play?

Everyday people invest in the stocks of companies they know nothing about, based on a tip from someone else who knows nothing either. They buy land without seeing it. They buy art, coins and stamps without ever knowing what the real market value is. They buy businesses without knowing how to run them—and lose billons of dollars.

These are people you can buy from and sell to—all you have to do is know more than they do about the deal.

Every fortune ever made from scratch was based on superior knowledge of the entrepreneur about potentials, markets, financing, etc.

J.P. Morgan knew nothing about making steel—Andrew Carnegie was a genius at making steel. J.P.

Morgan knew everything about selling stocks—Carnegie knew nothing. Morgan offered Carnegie $300 million for his steel company. Carnegie took it—Morgan formed U.S. Steel, and sold a billion dollars worth of stock in it—later Carnegie said to Morgan I think I should have asked for $400 million. Morgan said, "I would have paid it."

Knowledge is power—which can be converted to a fortune.

CHAPTER 26
COMMERCIAL RESEARCH

Marketing information is your key to picking the right sharecropper opportunities. Here is a sharecroppers service you can set up that will enable you to market surveys whenever you need them—and by setting up a sharecropper to run this service—pay all your costs—and provide extra income as well. A successful small business research agency can become a million dollar gross business by doing work for clients and by creating and selling its own products.

This is an interesting business that can be started anywhere on a small investment and produce a sizeable income if it is properly managed and promoted. The concept I am going to offer you is to organize a commercial research service that will hire others to prepare and carry out all the research assignments on a percentage of the fee basis. *Your job is to develop concepts and solicit business.*

The Concept

The concept of this business is to sell unknown information. You dig out facts that develop into a body of knowledge that no one else knows. You provide your clients with this information to help them in making decisions concerning projects or ventures they are planning or are involved in.

You are really selling *advantage.* The information your clients receive gives them an edge in their operations because they know something no one else knows, or learned something others knew but would not reveal.

This information has *tremendous value* if it is accurate and timely. The cost of obtaining it is the best investment the client can make.

That is the reason commercial research is one of the highest dollar-volume-per-person employed industries in the world. Price is not important in terms of what it buys—the making or saving of millions of dollars in one aspect; in other aspects, the ability to do something, get elected to an office or create something that would have been impossible without the information.

It Is Relatively New

While commercial intelligence is as old as the Phoenicians who sailed the seas in the centuries before Christ and brought back news of markets and prices from the four corners of the known earth, commercial research as an industry really didn't get started in this country until the 1930's.

It was developed as companies grew and needed to increase their markets and find new products. Until commercial market research was developed into a more or less exact science, new product introduction had merely been a matter of entering the market with either no competition, or coming in at a lower price or a better designed copy of an existing product. It would capture its share of the market or fail with no one really understanding why.

If you had a grocery product, it was sold through grocery stores, a drug product through drug stores, auto products through auto stores, etc. But, in the early 1930's the supermarket was born and self-service retailing became the wave of the future. Stores began carrying other product lines. Supers put in cosmetics and toiletries, drug stores sold batteries and motor oil, and discounters came along and sold everything. The market became huge and complex, and the need to find out how and where to market a product before it went into full production became mandatory.

This created a need for commercial information, and firms

sprang up to fill that need. They developed surveys and programs to find out in advance which products, packages, advertising, promotion, etc., would appeal to the marketplace. They developed methods of identifying the market—sex, age, income status, area of residence, family size, etc. They found out what the public read, listened to on the radio, saw on billboards, what was done with mailings received, etc. They determined which colors were liked best, which designs the public liked, which packages were liked, which prices sold best, etc.

These surveys began to have great impact on the marketing methods and ad media of this country. It was only a short step to find out how many people listened to each radio show—and later watched each TV show—how many people actually looked at magazines and newspapers, how long they spent reading them, which ads they noticed, etc.

As marketing becomes more complex and expensive, commercial research becomes more in demand. It is a growing industry grossing billions of dollars a year, and one in which you can get started on a shoestring.

Start Where You Are

This is a business that is not better in one place than another. You can *start right where you are now* and do it all by mail and phone if you wish. You can promote your surveys and sell them by mail.

Keep in mind you are not going to get hired by Proctor and Gamble or General Motors when you start out. In fact, there is a very big opportunity in this field dealing with small business because no on is really concentrating on it. By developing concepts and ideas for small business firms you eliminate most of the competition and build a nice cash flow at once.

What You Need To Know

You don't have to be an expert researcher to get started. You will have to understand the basics of the business and learn some of the terminology, and know where to get information.

If lightning strikes and you get an assignment that requires some real expertise to put together and manage, you can hire it done for a percentage of the fee. There is a large supply of qualified moonlighters available everywhere to do this kind of work. Everything from librarians to college professors are happy to pick up some extra money from a research assignment. Notices in college papers, contacts with local library people, and ads in the paper for people to do part time research work will get you a long, well qualified list of people you can call on when needed.

Areas of Commercial Research

Here is a list of the types of commercial research most commonly used today.

Product and Service Profiles
Consumer Profiles
Brand Surveys
Test Marketing
Marketing Characteristic Surveys
Distribution Channel Surveys
Store Audits
Split-Run Tests
Media Surveys
Advertising Audits
Readership and Audience Surveys
Inter-Media Exposure Tests
Public Opinion Surveys
Concept Tests
Consumer Attitude Surveys

Consumer Profiles
Marketing Forecasting

I shall give you a brief explanation of what each of these types of commercial research involves so you will have an overview of what is being done, and what can be done by you.

Product and Service Profiles

These are also called market studies, concept tests or consumer attitude surveys. They seek to determine how the client's products or proposed products compare to existing products, how they might be improved by asking consumers about their likes and dislikes, determining consumer buying patterns (how often and how many), the prices the consumer expects to pay, packaging the offer, etc. These products can be toothbrushes or million dollar computers. It's all done by asking questions of known consumers of these products and tabulating the answers.

This type of survey is also used for services to determine the same things. These services can range from banks and country clubs to people who mow lawns.

Consumer Profiles

These are also called discrimination studies or prospect surveys. They are used to draw attention to it. The researcher checks on the sales through store audits and questions buyers about their attitude toward the product, age, sex, family status, family size, income range, home owner, renter, etc. The result of this profile is to identify the composite target of the product and advertising. For example the composite consumer of a cosmetic brand might be 28 years old, married, one child, works, husband employed, family income $27,000, buying home, two cars. From this target information the seller can identify the size, location and potential of his market.

Brand Surveys

These are also called identified product tests. These use a survey of a targeted group to determine how many recognize the brand, how many use it, how long they have used it, what they like and don't like about it, why non-users have never tried it, and how it fares against the competition.

Test Marketing

This is also called market testing. The manufacturer picks a small trading area with a composition pretty much like the nationwide market (usually a city) to test sales potential of a new product or service. The product is placed in the regular channels of distribution, and advertising and promotion are used to draw attention to it. The researcher checks on the sales through store audits and questions buyers about their attitude toward the product, price, advertising, package, etc.

Market Characteristic Surveys

Market characteristic surveys are those used to determine the existing market for a product at a given time. Market size, the best way to divide up sales territory, and allocation of sales quotas are used to determine how profitable a product or line of products is in a given area. This information is developed by interviewing those selling the products as well as those buying them. It also determines the extent and degree of competition.

Market Share Surveys

These are also called market segmentation surveys. They are used to find out how much of the total market can be captured by a product or service. The researcher identifies the size of the market, the users are located, and a sampling is made to determine what share of the market each product or service enjoys.

Distribution Channel Surveys

These are also called distribution means analysis. They are usually commissioned by wholesalers, distributors and sales managers of large firms. The survey is made to determine if products are being sold in the most efficient manner, and to locate other outlets that might sell them.

Store Audits

This is a method most commonly used to check the movement of products off the shelves. The research service goes into the stores (with manager permission) and checks stock at the beginning of the period. He returns in a week or two and checks stock, plus amounts ordered, to determine how much was sold. This gives the client a turnover rate on products.

Marketing Forecasts

They are also called sales forecasts, market studies or estimates. This service is usually done by polling salesmen, managers, retailers, purchasing agents and distributors. Ask how much they expect to sell or buy in a given period of time (usually a year). The information gives the client an estimate of the total future market for that period.

Advertising Audits

These are also called advertising effectivity, retention, and recognition surveys. These are conducted among consumers to determine how they see and react to client's advertising—how well they can recall it, what they liked or disliked about it, where they saw it, etc. It gives the client a readout on how effective the advertising is, and where it is most often seen and remembered.

Split-Run Testing

This is a program designed to determine which advertising message is the most effective where there is more than one to choose from. The advertisers run two or more ads in the same issue of publication, or different ads on the same day in broadcast media, and the researcher contacts consumers to determine which ad was most effective.

Media Surveys

These are also called advertising penetration analyses. They are conducted to determine the best media for an ad campaign. They target the media that reaches the target group most effectively. They also determine which media is most cost effective in delivering the largest target audience for dollars invested.

Inter-Media Exposure Tests

These are also called alternative media surveys, sometimes reach and frequency analyses. They are surveys of the amount of time people spend listening to, watching, or reading various media. The longer they take, the better chance the advertiser has to get his message across.

Public Opinion Surveys

This is part of the political polling you hear so much about. They are generally issue or candidate oriented and are taken from a valid cross section of the public.

In commercial use they are used to get reactions to programs, campaigns, or images of companies, groups or associations.

That Is The Business

This gives you an overview of the business, and the different assignments you might get. There are other types, and new types will be developed. It goes along with the old saying, "*we are getting to know more and more about less and less all the time.*"

In truth the range of services you can offer is only limited by your own imagination as we will show you further on. You don't have to wait for assignments. You can create your own, and sell them before you do the work.

Finding Clients

Now that you have an idea of the kinds of research that are being done, how does this translate into getting business for a new boy on the block? I am going to give you a list of potential clients by type of business or operation and an idea of the kinds of research they buy.

Department and Discount Stores

You can sell them customer profiles, media use and interest surveys, advertising recognition tests, sales promotion effectiveness and kinds of promotions liked best.

Supermarket and Drug Stores

Consumer profiles showing products wanted in the stores and the products not wanted, how well coupons work, what kinds of coupons work best, what customers like and don't like about advertisements, complaints about service, store layout, checkstand lines, etc.

Shopping Centers

Shoppers' profiles, shopping habits, frequency of visits, kinds of new stores wanted, kinds of events and promotions they like and would like to see, how it compares to other centers, best media for advertising and best use of media.

Retail Stores

Store recognition surveys, advertising effectiveness, customer opinion about merchandise, sales staff, and service in general, comparison of the above with competition, market share survey, competition survey (what are the strengths and weaknesses of the competition), in-store surveys of customers to determine where they live, what brought them to the store, amount purchased, and reactions to store, shopping service to get reactions from sales people to various created situations and test competence.

General Business Firms

Surveys of market, advertising, sales programs, finding new prospects, competition survey, etc.

Manufacturers—Wholesalers—Distributors

Store and consumer audits, distribution channel surveys, concept and new product tests, market share and characteristic surveys, consumer profiles, all advertising and media surveys.

Advertising and Public Relations Agencies

Virtually every test named above is usually commissioned for their clients. This is a difficult area to do business. My advice is to stay away from these agencies unless and until they contact you. When dealing with them, be very precise about what you will and will not do. Make sure they understand that you report what you find—good or bad—and are to be paid regardless of how it turns out. Many times the researcher will find that the agency simply wants him to go out and bring back good news about their project, and if it's not good, they won't use it and won't pay.

Financial Institutions

Banks, savings and loans, and finance companies are prospects for research services. They need to know what people want, what services they offer that people are not well informed about, consumer profiles of present and lost customers, and all types of media surveys.

Trade, Professional, and Civic Organizations

These will use public opinion polls, surveys of membership to see how they feel about the group and what it should and should not be doing, and surveys to test the best way to conduct new membership drives.

Political Groups

Surveys on candidates, issues, voter registration, voter profiles of candidate or issue, survey of special interest groups (minorities, labor, business, women, etc.) and during campaigns, snap polls (a two to three hour telephone survey) to give voter preference in given areas.

In addition to these there are churches, social and sports groups, charities and foundations, trade unions and schools, and government agencies that use research services.

Lots of Prospects for Your Service

As you can see, there is no shortage of prospects for your service. The job is to get organized so that you can develop a following among the users of research services, and business will come to you almost faster than you can handle it.

Gathering Information

Since you are going to be in the information business you need to understand where information can be found and how to obtain what you need. This is a nation that is classified down to its teeth. There is information about everything, if you know how to look for it.

Primary and Secondary Sources

The information in the research game is classified as primary and secondary. Primary information is what you gather yourself directly from those you contact. Secondary information is what is published by someone else.

When you are starting on a research project, it is best to gather secondary information first. Many times you will find what you need has already been done by someone else.

In terms of using the available sources, you should work from your own community outwards. That is, start with what is available closest to home and continue to expand your search until you have what you need.

Here are twenty-five sources you can work with:

1. The Public Library
2. The Chamber of Commerce
3. The City Government
4. The County Government
5. Local Directories

6. Local newspapers/media sources
7. Local area universities and colleges
8. The State Government
9. The Federal Government
10. Public utilities and large companies
11. Local groups and associations
12. State and regional groups and associations
13. State libraries
14. National associations
15. Books about the subject
16. National periodicals
17. Trade periodicals
18. Data bases
19. Major corporations
20. National directories
21. Specialized libraries
22. Foreign embassies and consulates
23. United Nations
24. International organizations
25. Other research services

By working through the list you will find what is available to you and how you can use it.

Using The Public Library

You should learn the resources that are available in your public library. Your key spot is the "Reference Library." In the larger libraries this is managed by a trained reference librarian, who is a skilled researcher. Some of the big city libraries have specialists in reference service. They can lead you through the maze of material to find the sources you are looking for.

The library will usually have reference material in the following areas:

Directories of:

- Manufacturers directories
- Associations directories
- Individuals directories
- Corporations directories
- Government agencies
- Economic and marketing information
- Local, state, and federal government information
- Guides to commercial publications
- Book and publisher directories
- Periodical indexes
- General information sources
- References to all major disciplines

From these sources you find additional sources until the search is narrowed down to your specific needs.

Interlibrary Loans

If there is a book that you need, and the local library does not have it, they can usually obtain it through an inter-library loan (ILL). A needed book can be traced through publications such as the National Union Catalog, the Union List of Serials, or through a computer data base being installed in most major libraries. For example, the Ohio College Library Consortium links 1500 libraries across the nation. There may be a charge for this service but it is usually nominal.

I am going to give you a basic list of references you can tap in most public libraries for information you may need.

REFERENCES

The Chamber Of Commerce

The Chamber of Commerce is a business organization devoted to increasing the numbers of business firms in a community and improving business conditions. To do that, they keep a good deal of statistical information about the area and the industries in the area.

Here is some of the information they can usually provide:

Company names and addresses
Names of management of company
Number of employees and gross payroll
Products and services statistics
Local maps
Membership directories
Historical data
Information on events
City and county government statistics

Chambers of Commerce are not in the business of doing research work. If they have information in published form, they will usually provide it. They are more often a source of sources.

The City Government

The city government can usually provide population, and some business and industrial data such as the numbers of business permits, building permits, etc. Some have a lot, some very little, but it is a source to be identified and the type of information available noted and filed.

County Government

Lots of tax base information can be found from the county government, usually some business and industrial statistics, court house sources of information, sources of property information, source of election information, schools and other institutions. County information is usually more up to date than similar information from other sources.

Local Directories

Such things as city directories, membership directories, telephone books, and privately published directories can all be used from time to time by a researcher. It is a good idea to make a list of all local directories and sources of them to use when the need arises.

Newspapers And Other Media

Almost all newspapers (dailies) have demographic information on their subscribers, and payroll and other facts on the community. This information is very useful to a research service. The primary use for it is to help the newspaper sell advertising. They have had surveys done to determine the family size, income, housing status, and other data on their readers. You can usually get this material with a phone call.

The same type of material is collected by radio and TV stations in a community. They will usually send it to you on request. Just tell them you are making a survey to determine the best media for an advertiser. To get the material always call the advertising manager at the media.

The State Government

The State Government will have a wealth of data on all aspects of business and population in the state. It is simply a matter of identifying the sources. To do this use the office of your state legislator—that's part of his job. Try to build a source file on all the sources of information in the State Government.

The Federal Government

This is where it's at in the research business. I will make no attempt to try and show you where you can get information from the Feds. You can get it everywhere. It would take a 50,000 page book just to list it all.

You can get information from every office of the Federal Government—the White House, Congress, and all the Cabinet offices, Judiciary and the Military. The best way through the maze is to write the Government Printing Office, Washington, DC 20401, and ask for their catalog of catalogs of publications and periodicals. Then when you have a specific problem, call your Congressman or Senator's office and ask them to find out where you can find what you need. Things change so quickly, and sources come and go so fast, it is impossible to print a list that wouldn't be outdated in 90 days.

It is a fair guess that whatever research you are doing, the government has done it before, and has the results stashed somewhere.

The key agencies for commercial research are the Department of Commerce, Bureau of Census, Small Business Administration, Department of Agriculture, and the Department of the Interior.

Public Utilities And Local Companies

These businesses usually have some statistical and demographic information about the community that you can obtain. It will pertain to their particular needs, but often can save you a lot of time by asking what is available.

Local Groups And Associations

These are often sources of specific information on subjects the groups and associations are interested in. Many times they have published papers and reports on their work that has information you can use. A phone call can often save hours of research work duplicating what they already have.

State And Regional Groups

The same is true here. These groups, whether professional groups, industrial, political, social, or religious, often have made surveys or compiled information you can use. Again, a phone call or letter can bring the information they have.

State Libraries

Often these are in the State Capital and are small editions of the Congressional Library. Placed there for the use of the State Legislators and their staffs, they are crammed with statistics, historical data, and current information on a wide variety of subjects. They have well trained research librarians who can be of immense help in locating information.

National Associations

These are goldmines of information. They live to prepare reports and information for their members. You will find almost every library carries a copy of the Directory of Associations, and you will find the name, address, phone, and services they provide listed. They are usually very cooperative with research people, particularly if the researcher assures them the source will be credited in the final report.

Books About The Subject

Finding books to get information is easier than any other type of information. First, librarians know how to locate books of all kinds. Secondly, you can go to Bowker's Subject Guide To Books In Print and locate all current books on any subject, and they also have more specific guides published from time to time such as Subject Guide to Business Books In Print, and their major guide, Books In Print, which is arranged alphabetically.

If you want to find a book printed in English and published anywhere in the world, you can look through the Cumulative Book Index. It lists every book published since 1898 anywhere in the world. If you want a book that is out of print, you can usually get it by running an ad in the Antiquarian Bookman stating title, author, publisher, and date of copyright if known. This publication is read by used book dealers and collectors who will quote you a price on what you want.

National Periodicals

All major magazines have made studies of their readers to help sell advertising. You can usually get this information on request. It can be very useful as you will discover later in this report. The same is true for TV networks.

If you want to research articles from national periodicals, the library has various indexes to assist you. Some are for specific publications, such as the Wall Street Journal and New York Times, others are indexes of groups of periodicals—general interest, business and trade, science, engineering, etc. You can look up needed material by subject in these indexes. Other information provided on periodicals that may be helpful is Standard Rate and Data, a set of manuals broken down by type of media. It covers newspapers, consumer magazines, trade magazines, radio, and TV.

Trade Magazines

These are goldmines of business information. The publishers have a great deal of data on the industry they serve. Almost all of them publish special editions each year on specific subjects, and most have an annual that gives the names, addresses, products handled, etc., of all the firms in the industry.

You can get specific information about these trade publications in Standard Rate and Data (most libraries have it).

Data Banks And Bases

Here is where almost all secondary research will be done within the next ten years. Computers are being fed everything mankind knows, and it can be located and used within seconds.

There are now data base services available to find information on almost any subject you would be researching. There is a major directory of them published by Gale, titled "Encyclopedia of Information Systems and Services." It covers just about all the data resources available.

There is some terminology you should understand when you are working with computer retrieved information. A data base is an index system, like the card file that locates books in a library. It locates sources of information, giving you titles, authors, dates of publication, etc. A data bank is a computer that has the actual information stored, and can print it out on request. For example, a data base would refer you to a data bank to get a report.

Another term you will notice when looking at descriptions of data sources is "interactive." This means the data source can supply you not only with the information in its computer, but its computer can call up other computer bases or banks and see what they have to offer. In other words, an interactive source has access to many sources.

The terms "on line" and "off line" will also come up. When you use a computer terminal to call up another computer you are "on line." As a rule you are paying for the long distance call to reach the computer, plus the charge made by the computer owners to use it. If you find some data you want printed out, you can order it "on line," which means the computer will deliver it through your printer on request. This is expensive. Data travels at the speed of light, but printers run at the speed of a mechanical device. So, it takes time to print what you want. This means you pay phone charges, plus the computer time. If you order the material printed "off line" then the source computer prints it out when it has time in its own office, and the material is mailed to you. This saves a lot of money.

Finding A Computer Terminal

To use the data base service you must have a computer terminal that has a telephone modem to call other computers. These can be rented or leased, but it is possible to find one that you can use less expensively, or even free.

For example, some colleges and universities have them for student use. You can enroll in a class, become a student, and use the computer there. You may even be able to use it without enrolling. It is possible a local firm has a terminal you can rent time on at less cost than you would pay for a rental or lease. A lot of individuals have computers at home that you might rent time on, or hire the owner to search for you. Look around, call up computer sellers—IBM, Texas Instruments, and others—and ask a salesman if he knows of a computer customer who might rent time.

To give you an idea of what is offered, check the listing for the Lockheed dialogue information retrieval system as it appears in the Gale Publishing Research Co. directory. (Write for the current price of the encyclopedia of information systems and services.Book Tower, Detroit, MI 48226). This will give you an idea of what is offered.

Major Corporations

Every major corporation has information and statistics that a researcher can use from time to time. All you have to do is write to them, care of their Public Relations Department and request it. The key to getting a quick response is to be specific. If you are writing an oil company, don't request all information on the oil industry. Ask for any data on the specific facts you need. A point about this—you can usually get a lot quicker and better response if you call rather than write. For one thing, you can define your request if necessary, and the phone call gets the machinery in action at once. A tip—on all phone calls you make to large firms or government agencies, call 1-800-555-1212 first, and ask information if they have an 800 number. This is a toll free number, and many firms have one, but don't advertise the fact.

To find the addresses, and in some cases the names of the people in a large company that you wish to contact, use the Standard and Poor Directories—your library has them.

Specialized Libraries

Many libraries in this country have subject specialties. That is, they have more books and information on a given subject than other sources. Some are complete libraries by themselves. Your librarian has reference sources to locate these libraries and determine how you might obtain specific information from them.

The biggest and the one with the most sources is the Library of Congress in Washington, DC. You should contact them for lists of publications and services.

Foreign Embassies And Consulates

If your research involves getting information from foreign sources, your best starting place is with the embassy or consulate in this country. Write your specific request asking for either the information or the sources of the information to them. You can look them up at the library, or just address an envelope to the named country embassy, Washington, DC.

United Nations

The U.N. is full of statistics and information about projects and countries all over the world. To get at the right sources, simply write United Nations Office of Press and Publications Division, Room 376, United Nations, New York, NY, 10017.

International Organizations

These are multi-national groups such as the World Bank which have members from many countries. You will find many of these representing all disciplines, and your librarian can help you locate them.

Other Research Services

Other services can be contracted to do work for you, or you can buy some of the work they have already done. If you look in Gale's Directory of Associations you will find all types of research service information under "research."

Make A Source File

When you discover a source, make up a 3 x 5 card and put it in your source file. Instruct all of your researchers to do the same and turn them in. This way you will be building a valuable source file that will speed up you operations as you go along.

Organizing Your Business

The first step is setting up your office. You will want the usual desk, file cabinet, chair and typewriter. You should also consider getting a microfiche reader. Much material is available on microfiche at far less cost than paper prints, and you can file what would fill a whole library of paper reports in a shoebox if the material is on microfiche.

There are many firms selling readers, and a check in the yellow pages of your phone book (Microfilming Services and Supplies) will put you in contact with sources.

You should also consider a computer when the cash flow will permit. It can keep information (for example, your source directory), keep your books, store and write your reports, do calculations necessary to interpret the reports, etc.

You will, of course, need a phone. Your home phone will do just fine to start.

Choosing Your Business Name

You have two choices here. You can pick a fictitious firm name such as Research Associates, the National Research Service, or something like that. There is no advantage to this, and it involves a lot of extra start-up expenses. You'll need to register the name or file a fictitious name report, get a new bank account, have a new phone put in at business rates, etc.

The best known firms in the field, A.C. Nielson, Roper, Gallup, etc., are all named after the founder. If you just use your name, John Jones, and then on your stationery add "and Associates" under the name, you have as good a name as you can find, and you can use all the phones, addresses, bank accounts, etc., now listed as John Jones.

Getting Research Moonlighters

Your next step will be to get part time help when you need it. You will need field interviewers, someone who can interpret and manipulate statistics, someone who can write reports, someone who can act as a research manager on a larger project, and someone who can work with a computer.

You can find all these people with small ads in your local paper, through associations you join or contact, and simply from contacts you make in the course of business.

One place you can get some competent help at a reasonable cost is from the Association of America Library Schools, 417 Park Lane, State College, PA 16801. Get the association's annual Directory of Schools and contact students or faculty to moonlight for you at agreed rates. All these people are competent and well-skilled researchers.

When you locate people who want to work for you on a per project basis, find out how much they want to be paid, then make up a card file with their skills, name, address, phone, and available times. When you have jobs, you can contact those with the appropriate skills and make a deal with them for the job. Always make them quote a per job price; don't pay by the hour. This makes them independent contractors like freelance writers, so you don't have payroll taxes, unemployment insurance, etc. They agree to do the work using their equipment, at times of their choosing, and you exercise no control over their activities. This meets the standards of independent contractors.

How To Get Business

Getting business is a matter of contacts. Your first step should be to prepare a brochure of the services you intend to offer, and a sales letter asking for assignments. These should be sent to business firms and organizations in your area on a regular schedule.

To find out what to say and how it is done, write or contact existing agencies as a potential customer. See how they handle your inquiry, what they send, how they follow up, etc. This is a free education in how to market your research service.

Free Advertising

Now, I'm going to tell you the big secret in this business. You can get a tremendous amount of free advertising by sending out publicity releases with summaries of your surveys, or by making some public opinion polls on your own. All media like to use stories of public opinion polls. All you need is a creative slant to your information, and you get your name listed in the story as the source. This builds recognition, and you can use reproductions of the clippings in your sales material to potential clients.

Find a book that tells you how to write a publicity release at your library, then contact all the media and find out who to send press releases to on various subjects. Some papers have editors for various departments of the papers, and each has a deadline and a preferred time and way to get releases. You find this out by asking, and by following instructions you can start hitting the papers, radio and TV stations on a regular basis. This builds your image and brings in business.

For example, during an election campaign there are all kinds of polls about candidates and issues. So, you make a survey based on this question: "If you were elected Mayor, Councilman, Governor, President, or whatever the current campaign is for, and you were able to give one order and have it carried out, what would it be?" This is a different slant, and you can have a list of five to ten things that were said more often than all the others, along with a couple of humorous or ridiculous statements. All the media will pick this up as it is a new slant with definite news value. So be a little creative in your polling, and you can get free advertising.

In addition, always send a press release with a summary of any survey that is not confidential to the media. They will run it as often as not.

How Do You Learn How To Make These Surveys

You do some research. There are many books on the subject giving detailed information on how to do all the types of surveys and polls we have mentioned. You can find them listed in Subject Guides to Books in Print under research, marketing, and other appropriate headings. Get some of them through the library, and you can buy some if you wish. You can learn as much as you need to know to discuss the programs with a client, and you can hire the expert help you need to pick targets, make up questionnaires, analyze and manipulate the results for the client, etc.

You can get a list of these books from the American Marketing Association (Directory of Associations) and John Wiley, McGraw Hill, Prentice Hall Publishers (Subject or Guide to Books in Print for addresses).

The Solicitation Letter

I am going to give you an example of a solicitation letter that brings inquiries and business. It should be accompanied by a brochure outlining your services. It should be mailed out to all prospects in your area at the rate of 10 to 20 a day.

Here is the letter:

> Could you make more profit if you had tomorrow's newspaper today?
>
> Sure you could — and now you can!
>
> We can find out how you can anticipate the needs and wants of your market — how you can know what will sell best in the future.
>
> You can find out how the market views your business to-

day, and how you can improve their perception tomorrow.

You can learn what ad media, ad message, or what type of promotion you can plan today for use in the future that will increase your share of the market.

The total market share in this area last year was $35,000,000 — how much of that was yours? How much of it would you like in the future?

By knowing what your competition does not know you can build your market share fast; that is what a tailor-made market research program can do for you.

Give me 20 minutes of your time — I'll prove it.

That letter, or a slight variation of it, sent to all the prospects in your area, will bring some results for specific assignments. It will take time, and nothing will happen overnight, but just keep sending letters along that theme, and you'll get business.

Handling The First Interview

When you get a response to your letter, make an appointment to see the prospect. Look up his name in your file and note his business. Then, go to your source file and find out where you can get some fast information on that business or industry. This is to familiarize you with the general situation in his business, and give you some facts and figures to use during the interview.

Don't go to the interview with the idea you are going to drown him in facts and figures. Just have some facts to show that you know what you are talking about if they are needed. The idea of the first interview is to find out what he or she needs to know. Then you can make a proposal on how to provide that information at the second interview. Never try to sell at the first interview; you are too inexperienced to do it properly, and you may be too eager. You will have to figure out how to get the information and how much you will charge for it. You will need to consult with some of your moonlighters and check some of your reference texts to come up with a viable plan.

Go to the interview to take notes and listen. Only talk when it is necessary to find out something that is not clear. After you know what is on the prospect's mind you can make your proposal. You will develop a suggested program to get the proper information and come back with it, and the cost. If the client tries to press you for a price, just return the favor by asking how much he can allocate to the research. Usually he'll say he's not sure, and you tell him that you aren't either. You will have to work it out and get back to him.

Pricing Your Services

Pricing your services is not complicated. You start out by placing an hourly value on your own time. Then you add up all the costs of the program (you'll find a list following), and you add in a profit figure for the job. The total is what you should get for the job. Keep in mind that your hourly rate is not profit; that is what you are paid for working on a project. Profit is what the business makes after all costs are covered. You should earn money for your time and a profit for your business on each project.

Secondary Research Cost

1. Cost of writing letters for information
2. Cost of making phone calls for information
3. Cost of using data bases
4. Cost of time at libraries or reading material
5. Cost of purchase of any material to be used
6. Cost of time of moonlighters
7. Cost of time to organize data received

Primary Data

1. Cost of preparing questionnaires
2. Cost of reproducing questionnaires
3. Cost of mailing questionnaires
4. Cost of envelopes and reply postage
5. Cost of moonlighting interviewers
6. Expenses of moonlighters—gas, lunches, etc.
7. Cost of organizing results
8. Cost of checking the questionnaires

Final Report

1. Cost of preparation and writing
2. Cost of reproduction and delivery

Overhead

Determine costs of all fixed overhead. The job must pay the percentage of time costs. That is, if you had ten jobs in the month, and this job took 15% of the time, it must pay 15% of the overhead.

Profit

Allocate your profit, not including the costs of your time. The profit is for the business; your time is a business expense, not part of the profit.

In practical terms, you will change what the traffic will bear. Research has great value over and above the cost and profit in developing it. You can and will often get far more than a formula price for your work. It takes experience to recognize the pricing opportunities.

How To Be Paid

The standard practice should be one-third paid with the order, one-third paid when the data has been collected and it's time to prepare the report, and the final third upon delivery.

I would suggest that you make it 50% with the order, the balance on delivery of the finished report. Some prospects may decline this way, but it is better to walk away than to finance their research for them.

Preparing Your Offer To The Prospect

When you discover what the prospect wants to find out at the first interview, you go back to your office and determine how you can do the research and what you can find out for him.

You estimate how you can use secondary data to build the foundation of the project and what kind, if any, primary research will be needed.

With that information you can come up with a list of benefits for the client and a price.

How You Might Do It

Let's look at an example of an assignment you might get. Your prospect is a dentist who is thinking about opening some coin-operated laundries in the area, and has three specific locations in mind. He wants to know how well they might do, and if the areas are the best places to open.

With that information, you go back to your office and figure out what you can find out for him.

First, you look at the U.S. Census file and using the Standard Metropolitan Statistical Area Census of Selected Service Industries, you can determine how many laundromats are operating, how much business they do, how many employees they use, the average payroll, etc.

Next, you contact manufacturers and trade associations to get a profile on the average person using a laundromat—how often they use it, and the average amount spent for washing machines, dryers, purchase of soap and other incidentals. You can find the manufacturers listed in Thomas Registry of Manufacturers, or get a list from the association.

From these same sources you can find out what the average investment is—the cost of construction of a building or average rental paid, the cost of equipment, its installation and average maintenance costs.

With your profile of the average user you can use the bureau's Census of Housing and Population for the proposed areas to determine the number of potential users in the area.

You can get an estimate of potential business by finding out how many people it takes to support a laundromat within a trading area from the Association of Manufacturers. If there are laundromats there now, you can do some primary research by interviewing customers while they are waiting for their washing to find out how they like the place, what complaints they have, what they would like to see added, and if they would consider using one at the proposed location.

If there is no laundromat in the area, you would locate a profile group in that area and interview them by mail or phone about their thoughts on using one if it were available.

Now Prepare Your Package

Now that you know what you can do, figure out the costs and come up with a price. Then prepare a list of benefits the client will get for his money. In this case the benefits would look like this:

1. Determine how many coin operated laundries there are in the area
2. Total gross volume of business for the market area

3. Average gross volume of business for each
4. Average gross volume for those with employees
5. Average number of employees
6. Average gross volume for those without employees
7. Profile of average customer of laundromat
8. Average amount spent per visit
9. Average number of customers per year for all operating units
10. Average number of customers for large and small units
11. Areas where most prospective customers will be found
12. Sources of equipment and supplies
13. Average investment to lease an existing building
14. Average investment for start-up, building your own building
15. What present users like and dislike about the facilities they use
16. Number of potential customers at each proposed location
17. Projected gross volume of business at each location
18. Cost of maintenance and overhead at each location
19. The projected growth or decline of each location in terms of potential customers
20. Estimated profits for each location

There you have offered twenty benefits the dentist can obtain using your research service. You present these at the second meeting, and let him read them. Never write the price in your written proposal, make him ask you the price.

All of the above information is easily obtainable, and is almost all manipulation of figures. For example, you find from Census Bureau figures there were 40 laundromats two years ago doing a million a year gross. Divide 40 into the million and you have $25,000 average gross. You find there were 10 with employees doing $400,000; dividing 10 into $400,000 gives you $40,000 gross for those ten. This leaves 30 doing $60,000, or the non-employee units gross $20,000 a year.

Most of the report is made up of that type of figure manipulation.

As you can see, it is not really all that difficult when you know where to find facts and figures.

The Research Entrepreneur

Here are some ideas on how to create your own cash flow. You think up a research project and sell the concept at a reduced price to a number of clients. In other words, you become a research publisher. The limits of opportunity in this field are only those of your own imagination. You can think up almost any idea, and decide whether a group of firms or organizations would pay to find out the results, and make them an offer by letter. If enough go along, you have the money up front to do the research. If not, all you lost was the cost of sending out a few letters.

Organize Your Plan First

The first step is to figure out your concept. Then organize a plan to do the research for it and decide on the list of benefits. Write a sales letter to those you think would pay for the information showing them the list of benefits your research offers. You tell them that the cost of such research paid for by an individual firm would be $5,000 to $10,000, but since the material is currently available, they can have it for $100, or whatever price you pick. Ask for the order, and tell them it will be four to six weeks to put the material into report form.

If you get 40 orders from your mailing, you have $4,000 to do the job. If you only get a couple of orders, return their checks and go to your next idea.

The Yellow Pages Program

Many service business firms do almost all of their advertising in the Yellow Pages. They would have a great interest in how their ads rated against the ad that consumers judged to be the best of all those in that category. The list of benefits would look something like this:

1. What is the best size ad in each category per customer response?
2. What ad does a consumer panel feel is most representative of an honest and reliable service firm?
3. What ad does a consumer panel feel is from a firm that is not reliable?
4. What information does the consumer most look for in a yellow pages ad?
5. What information would they like to see most visible in the ad?
6. How does your firm's ad compare with the other ads in the book?
7. How does your ad compare with the best ads in your category?
8. Which heading do consumers most often and least often turn to in seeking your service?
9. What do consumers most dislike about yellow pages ad (print)?
10. What is an example of an ad they would respond to best?

There can be more benefits listed, but those should be enough. If you offer that research report to service business firms ranging from beauty parlors to washing machine repair services, say at $50 each, you can expect some orders—probably a lot of them.

How To Get The Business

The program is simple. You assemble a panel of consumers who indicate they are heavy users of the Yellow Pages and have them look at ads, judging them from the various standpoints you have indicated in your benefits.

Use out of town phone books with the names of the companies, but no addresses so that the panel does not know which town is involved. You can go through three or four phone books per panel sitting, so that you have a lot of prospects.

Each panel should only judge one category of ads. Let's say you get Houston, Denver, Los Angeles suburbs, and Washington, DC.

You use beauty shops as your category. Reproduce the ads on yellow paper with addresses removed and prepare a questionnaire for the panel. Direct them through the process which might go something like this:

> First, pick out the ad in each of the four sections you think is best. Then pick out the second, third, fourth, fifth, sixth, etc.
>
> Then show them the ads of the people who have ordered your reports and get their opinions on them. Have a discussion of what is good and bad about each one. Tape the discussion.
>
> Now, get them to design an ad with the things they would most like to see when they wanted to pick a service.
>
> Prepare a mail questionnaire with the ads of your clients, the best ads the panel chose, and the ad the panel made up, and get responses in terms of which is best, etc. If you have 50 clients, break up the ads into 5 units of ten client ads each so you get one to ten ratings on their ads. Mail out 1,000 questionnaires in five units of 200 each. Here is how to get nearly 100% response. Offer a prize, to be picked from a drawing of returned questionnaires. The person receiving the questionnaire has a chance to win $100 if they return it filled out.

To summarize, take four or five Yellow Page sections (note—do not use large metropolitan area phone books, use suburban books where the most ads of varying sizes appear) and pick a service category. Make up a sales letter with a list of benefits from your research; always indicate their own ads will be used in the research against both competing ads in their own area and those from around the country. State your price, include an order blank, and see how much you receive. If the money comes in, first do a panel research with 10 to 15 people present to rate and talk about the ads. Then do a mail test to verify the results. Ship the finished report to each client.

You can do this for all types of small business. You can do it for shopping centers and downtown shopping areas. The only limit is your own imagination.

The New Industry Research

There is another way to make money from your research, and build it into a steady and sometimes substantial income. That is to spot new industries as they are getting started. In recent years we have seen solar energy, video tape recording at home, electric cars, do-it-yourself law, and others get started. If you spot one, research all of the sources of products and information, and advertise your reports in appropriate publications. You will get orders, and if you set up ongoing research for these industries you can keep adding new information to sell your buyers as updates, thereby building a nice cash flow. You can become a headquarters for industry information, and wind up with a newsletter, magazine, annual almanac, etc.

The County Almanac

Here is one that can keep you in the chips for life. You publish a county almanac and update each two years with a new edition.

You compile all the statistics for the county from the Bureau of Census material and what you get from state and local sources. Organize it by subject and put all of your data on a computer.

Then go community-by-community with a telephone campaign getting names and addresses of all the business firms, the organizations, the public offices, schools, churches, etc. Sell copies as you make the calls. After getting the information, the person on the phone gives a brief pitch on the book and asks how many copies the person would like to order.

This gives you a cash flow as the material is organized. You can get the orders and show them to your local banker, or advertise for an investor to finance the invoices for a share of the profits. Let's say you will sell the almanac for $10.00. The bank or investor buys the order for $8.50, and gives you the cash to operate. When the books are published, the billings go to the bank or investor directly, and you make good on any unpaid invoices.

Once the orders for books start coming in you can sell advertising. Hire a commission salesman to sell ads for a 30% commission, and factor those through your investor or bank as well.

You can make money on this right from the start, and once the first one is out, you can sell it through book stores, newsstands, etc., giving you an extra income all year long.

You can run it for several counties in your area, and have a little goldmine from your research knowledge.

To Sum Up

A commercial research service is a genuine opportunity. If you start with small business, there is little competition. You can dream up all kinds of projects that will bring the cash rolling in, and expand the service as you wish.

There is plenty of moonlighting help available to make your research valid and well worth what you charge. To put the value of commercial research in perspective, think of it this way: Every day businesses and organizations go into a room with money scattered all over the floor. Most of the money is dollar bills, but there are some 50's, 100's and 1,000 dollar bills scattered around as well. Almost all those who enter are blindfolded. They pick up the money at random. But, those who have researched the market go in without blindfolds, and they pick up the big money every day.

How To Learn About This Business

Here are some sources you can use to learn what you need to know to plan and operate a successful research service.

Associations

American Marketing Assn., 222 S. Riverside Plaza, #606, Chicago, IL 60606, has books, periodicals, and other pertinent data on all forms of marketing research.

American Management Assn., 13 W. 50th St., New York, NY 10020, has some material relating to marketing research.

Market Research Assn., P.O. Box 1415, New York, NY 10017, primarily for field research people, publish a manual for research interviewing.

Books

Do-It-Yourself Market Research, by George Edward Breen, 1977, published by McGraw Hill.

Professional Mail Surveys, by Paul L. Erdos, 1970, published by McGraw Hill. Tells how to prepare and conduct research surveys by mail.

Handbook of Modern Marketing, by Victor P. Buell, 1970, published by McGraw Hill. Compilation of information on all phases of marketing.

Handbook of Marketing Research, by Robert Ferber, 1974, published by McGraw Hill. Eighty chapters on everything you ever wanted to know about market research.

Market Research, 4th Edition, by Luck, Wales & Taylor, published by Prentice Hall. A standard text on market research.

Periodicals

Journal of Consumer Research, Chicago, Quarterly
Journal of Marketing, American Marketing Assn.
Journal of Marketing Research, American Marketing Assn.
Information Manager, Box 13240, Philadelphia, PA
Free subscription when requested on letterhead.

The addresses given here were accurate at press time, but they may need updating. To find association addresses, use the Directory of Associations at your public library. To find publishers' addresses, look in the index in Guides To Books In Print in your public library. To find periodical addresses, look in Ayer's Directory of Periodicals, or Ulrich's Directory of Periodicals.

STRATEGY

Never work for less than you are worth.

Set a dollar value on your time.
Don't do jobs others can do for you at less cost.
Maximize your time and talents.

There is a story about the man who was driving a Rolls Royce through New England. He was having trouble with the engine—it was coughing and sputtering as he drove. He stopped at several garages and gas stations but no one was familiar with the car and he struggled on. Finally, in desperation he stopped at a small country store with a gas pump in front and honked his horn. An old man came out, walking slowly and listened to the driver's problem. The old man opened the hood, tinkered with the engine for a few minutes then slowly walked back into the store and came out with a paper clip. He bent the clip in an odd shape, inserted it in the engine and told the driver to start it up. He did, and it purred like a kitten.

The driver was delighted. "How much do I owe you?" he asked.

"Ten dollars," was the reply.

The driver frowned, "Isn't that a lot of money for a paper clip?"

"The paper clip was a penny," the old man replied. "The nine dollars and ninety-nine cents was fer knowin' where to put it."

Point—"Knowin' pays better'n doin'."

CHAPTER 27
NEW VENTURE CONSULTANT

As you develop your sharecropping program you will find tax shelters of income becoming a problem. This zero cash takeover program is designed to show you how to acquire real estate investment properties with little or no cash down—and provide you with high number depreciation figures to write off against your income.

This is a program to acquire assets that grow in value tax-free while producing little or no income.

There is a bust or a big downward adjustment due soon in the money real estate market and you can use this zero cash investing technique that we will explain to you to acquire many solid properties to add to your assets' base—and give you maximum tax shelter at the same time.

Concept

The concept of the New Venture Consulting service is a cooperative consulting program whereby those seeking help in starting small businesses share the costs of detailed consultation on their projects and problems.

It is designed to be a series of meetings covering all the required steps of business start-ups. The clients attending these meetings are getting detailed information they can use to write a business plan for their ventures as they go along.

Provide Real World Consultation

The difference between this service and the courses they can take at local colleges, or seminars promoted by the Small Business Administration and others, is that the help they get here is real world, small business operational help. In the courses presently offered there is a lot of theory, and more particularly a lot of techniques used to run corporations palmed off as the way to run a small business.

For example, in current courses when it comes to accounting, you are advised to hire an accountant. In this New Venture Consulting program the clients are shown how to start out by keeping their own books as a way of keeping score and conserving capital. The new entrepreneur seldom has all the capital he or she needs, and the worst advice they can get is to squander their seed money by hiring a lot of so-called professional experts to do things they should be doing themselves. The small business entrepreneur has to wear many hats and learn how to do many things in order to be successful. The consulting course is designed to show him those things, and give him enough information so he can either do them himself or at least know what needs to be done so he can intelligently hire others to do it.

Dealing In Specifics

The NVC service is intended to deal in specifics of small business management and operations. One of the first things that will be discussed in some detail is the concept of the business, and the possible conflict between business and personal goals. You seldom see any of this in books simply because corporations don't have that problem.

One of the major reasons for failure in small business is that the entrepreneur did not understand the priorities of his enterprise. He or she assumed that the business was a means to an end, a method of reaching a personal goal. But once the venture was launched it became clear that the commitment of time, effort, thought and plain old sweat was far greater than he assumed. This brings up some serious problems at once—whether or not the entrepreneur is willing to do what is necessary to make the business succeed.

Here is an example of this. John starts a shoe store and his personal goal is to net $50,000 a year operating the store as manager with two employees. The business begins and it becomes evident to make $50,000 a year John is going to have to work 18 hours a day, hire more people, open a second store and stay open seven days a week.

John had been an advertising manager for a large firm before he launched his business and led an active social life. He had a boat, went skiing on weekends in the winter, and took three week vacations each year to nice places. The shoe store was to support this lifestyle and improve it with more income.

Here is where the conflict between business goals and personal goals arose. John could make his $50,000 if he gave up his social life for a period of perhaps five years. If he didn't give up his social life the business would earn him a modest living but would not support the social life he was accustomed to.

The consulting service is designed to bring this problem to the attention of the clients right away. Owning a business is like owning a cow. You've got to attend to it every day or it quickly gets sick and dies. That is the real world and the client who wants to start a business should understand that his goals must mesh. He must be prepared to give the business what it needs in terms of time and attention, and the family and social life will suffer to whatever extent those demands become.

From this starting point where you begin to show the client the real world of small business, you take him through each step of his start up business plan. The idea is not so much to educate him in the sense you can make him an expert at everything, as it is to tell him how and where to get the help he needs to solve problems and be successful.

You are not selling education, you are selling techniques for getting things done.

Business Detail

The major problem with books and courses in starting small businesses is that they do not help the entrepreneur with what he needs most—**specific detail.** For example, most courses and books mention the need for a business license or permit. In the New Venture Consulting course you can give them the specifics—what licenses are needed for various businesses, local business licenses, sales tax permits and anything else. You give them specific instructions on where to get the necessary forms, how to fill them out, when they need to be turned in, and the costs—complete detail on something they might take hours of time trying to figure out by themselves.

In another meeting you discuss shipping costs. Show them how to figure postal rates, motor freight rates, railroad rates, air shipping rates, express delivery rates, UPS rates, etc.; how to fill out a bill of lading; how to file claims for damage or lost shipments, etc. In other words, pay attention to **detail!** This is the real value of the NVC program.

How It Operates

The program works like this; you have a marketing program to meet with prospective clients, and sign some of them up for the service. They come to meetings three nights a week, two hours per meeting. A meeting unit should be from ten to twenty clients. They pay $10 per hour ($20 per meeting) for the program. There is one consultant who handles each unit, goes through the start-up process, and uses guest speakers in some meetings on subjects where expertise is needed. Each meeting covers a specific subject, and the clients write their business plan as they attend. At the end of the 32 plus hours of consulting meetings they will have a completed business plan for their venture.

Advanced Consultation

At the end of the business plan program, some clients will want to sign up for the advanced consultation program. This is a cooperative consulting program with fewer clients per unit, perhaps three to five. This series would be designed to go one-on-one with them as they implement their business plan and start operating their ventures. This consultation series would be for three months, meeting once or twice a week, and you could get $25 per hour per client.

It Can Be Very Profitable

If you take the time to organize it and hire good people to handle the clients in a classroom setting, you can build a very profitable venture. Your income with a program designed to produce four basic business plan consultation programs a year, and four advanced programs, would be well in excess of $100,000 a year.

Information Required

The first thing you will have to know is how to put a cooperative consulting program together. We will give you an outline of the program as it could be organized at the end of this chapter. Take that outline and flesh it out with specific detail as it applies to your local area, and build a program that will be well worth the client's time and money.

You will need to develop "teaching plans" for your consultants—how each subject will be handled in a group session and how control of the flow of information is maintained. In each session you should plan for a fifteen to twenty minute lecture by the consultant or a guest speaker on the subject covered, then some further discussion of the detail of doing what is needed to make the necessary choices and decisions. This should be followed by questions and answers from the clients, and each meeting should end with a ten minute summary of what was learned and how to include that in the business plan.

You will want to structure the course so that each meeting results in the clients being able to include what they learned in their business plan. Question and answer sessions sometimes get out of hand and off the track, so the closing summary of what was learned is vital.

You will also need to compile source books, reports and data on business operations. There should be a library for client use, based on the lending library concept where they rent books by the day.

Skills You Will Require

The major skill you should bring to this program is the ability to organize a plan and manage people. You will be hiring people to be unit consultants for your clients, and you will have to provide them with an organized program they can present intelligently and understandably to the unit. You will have to motivate and inspire them to some extent to do a good job. When you have more than one consultant working for you, you will have the problems of keeping peace in the family when they begin bickering over who gets to use what piece of equipment. You will have a staff of clerical help and one or two people involved in selling the program. So, like the clients you will be helping, you need a plan to organize and manage the operation.

Perhaps the most useful skill you can acquire for this program would be to find information you need. There is an old saying about lawyers, "They don't need to know the law, just where to find the law." This is true of this business too. Learn how to find information and you'll keep your program moving ahead.

Area Of Operation

You should start this program in a metropolitan area. This gives you a broad enough market to keep operating in one place without running out of potential clients.

You also have the option of running this program in several areas by organizing a staff in each area to keep a high cash flow. Simply put, this is not a business that will work in a small town.

Business Location

The location of your office is not of major importance. It should be in an area where your clients can find you easily, and since there will be evening meetings, an area where they won't get mugged.

You can actually start with your office in your home, and hold your meetings in a rented motel meeting room. This has the advantage of easy access for clients, and all the amenities (rest rooms, food and parking) already available.

At some point you can move into a suite of offices in a good location with the office and meeting rooms.

The Competition

In the classic sense you will have no competition unless someone else reading this chapter starts an operation. In reality you will have competition from local schools and colleges who present these courses, and from seminars and other consultants.

This program is cooperative consulting, where a group of people are paying the consultant for help and advice. It is not a course or a seminar.

However, you will find that if you are as successful at this as you should be, you will get some competitors doing pretty much the same thing making a run at you. Your first competitor will likely be one of your own consultants who has conducted the program and counted the money you were taking in.

While imitation is a sincere form of flattery, it is a pain in the ass when it is from a former employee. But, you are first, and while the competitor may think it's going to be easy to compete, he'll find out the facts of life in a hurry. If you are running a sound, well organized program, you don't have to worry about competition.

Economic Climate

When times get tough, this business will suffer like all businesses do. But, you have a singular advantage with this program in bad times. Many people who can't find jobs will try to start a business to make an income. This will increase interest in your program, and keep your income at a higher level than otherwise might be possible.

Choosing A Business Name

You should use your own name followed by associates—John Jones and Associates, Business Consultants. This is the professional approach and creates more confidence than something like the Small Business Sudden Success Institute.

Form Of Business

I would seriously consider forming a corporation to operate this program. To some extent your fate is in the hands of other people, and anything can happen. A corporate shield against your personal assets is a good idea when you are dealing with as many people and situations as this program requires.

Banking Connection

The right banking connection can be a big help to you in this program. A banker who likes you and your program can steer a lot of clients your way. He runs into people every day wanting to start a business who don't know which way to put the key in the lock. He could suggest they investigate your program to help get organized and get their venture started on the right foot.

You will need VISA and Mastercard programs from your bank, and you can investigate the bank handling your payroll.

Another possibility, if you are offering terms on your program is that a bank could lend you funds against your receivables if you needed funds. So, do a little banker shopping when you have the program organized, and the banker whose eyes light up when he sees it is probably the one you are looking for.

Record Keeping

You will need a standard set of books. A cash journal, payables ledger, ledger cards for students, payroll records and the usual accounting reports—operations statement, balance sheet, cash flow, etc.

You can have an accountant set them up for you and reconcile them monthly.

Licenses And Permits

You will need a business license as a consultant, a retail sales license if you sell books and course materials, and a sales tax permit.

Non-Marketing Literature

You will need business cards for yourself and your staff. Letterheads and envelopes, employment forms, client enrollment forms, receipts, invoices and purchase orders. You will also need some standard housekeeping forms such as inter-office memos, telephone message forms, petty cash forms, etc.

Business Equipment

To start, a typewriter, desk and a filing cabinet are about it. As the business develops you can look into computers, word processing equipment, copiers, etc. Keep in mind that it can be a lot easier and more profitable in the long run to farm out some work than to buy and maintain expensive equipment that will only be used for short periods of time and then sit silent for the rest of the time.

I think a small computer could be useful, not only as office equipment, but could be used in demonstrating what computers can do to clients in one of the meetings on the subject of business equipment.

Employees

You will need consultants to handle client meetings. You will need some office help and some help in selling the program.

The meeting consultants ideally should be people with a background in small business start up and operation who are good communicators. They must have an outgoing personality that will generate response and participation from clients, and be able to follow a structured plan for teaching the program. Your ideal consultant would be a good public speaker with a small business background who knows how to teach.

Your office help will manage routine office duties, with one acting as bookkeeper. At the start you will probably only need one full time person, and hire temporaries when new programs are being sold and organized into meeting sessions.

Phone traffic will largely be from clients with questions about meeting times and procedures. There will be inquiry calls from prospects that need to be handled properly, as well as the normal traffic any business handles with its suppliers and business contacts.

The key person is the marketing manager. He or she will be selling the program, and they have to be reliable, good and enthusiastic about the program. As you will discover when we get into marketing and operations plans, this person can be a part timer. This person should be one with great personal magnetism on a speakers platform, and a person who understands selling. It's a job for someone with some snow on top but fire in the belly. In other words, a middle-aged man or woman who knows the score and likes to talk and sell.

The reason for the older person in this position is that they will be making a presentation on small business operations to people with a lot of miles on them. They would resent a 20 year old kid telling them he can show them how to start a successful business. So, look for some maturity and ability to pitch a crowd and make them listen.

Marketing Program

The marketing program for this service is a two step operation. To get interested clients you run ads in local papers in a metropolitan area similar to the one shown here. Prospective clients come to the seminar and are given a one hour lecture on the perils and potentials of small business ownership. The key to the presentation is that the difference between success and failure is having a complete business plan written before investing time and money.

It is a fact that over 90% of all small business failures come from lack of adequate planning and management. The reason most often given is lack of capital, but the truth is it is lack of management of that available capital that causes the failure.

Your seminar speaker will go through a series of stories showing how small businesses became large because the managers knew what they were doing and where they were going.

The Structure Of The Seminar Presentation

There is a definite progression in the presentation at the seminar. Follow the old sales adage, "Always create value before you quote price."

The prospects who attend are interested in owning a business of their own. But, they are not in business now because they are both unsure of themselves as business owners, and they are not quite sure how to proceed. The first step is to prove that success in small business is not only possible, it is certain if certain procedures are followed.

The often quoted fairy tale based on statistics from Dun & Bradstreet concerning business failures is that 90% of all new ventures fail. The speaker will point out that D&B failure figures come from the number of businesses that are not operating under the name they used at the start. So, some businesses simply change their names and are included in the out of business figures, and the new name pops up in the new business figures. No failure was involved. The owner, for his own reasons, may have changed the name. He may have incorporated under a different name. He may have sold the business and the new owner changed the name, etc. The second reason for a business to quit may not be failure, but simply that the owner didn't want to do it anymore and couldn't sell it. The business may be very successful, but the owner wanted to do something else. Still, it shows up as a business failure in the statistics. Still another reason is the owner moved from one city to another, and took the business with him. It shows up in the statistics as a business failure in one city and a new business in another. So, there are many reasons for businesses showing up in these figures besides going broke—the owner dies, a natural disaster wipes it out, a divorce ends it, etc.

Other studies have been made of the opportunity versus risk in a well organized and planned small business venture, and found it to be better than five to one in favor of the entrepreneur.

This theme gives the prospect a different look at risk, and a positive reinforcement that there is not as much risk as he or she supposed.

Each segment of the presentation should be reinforced by a war story about small business success—the story of Paul Galvin of Motorola who failed twice in the battery business, then started Motorola on $500 the year the big depression started in 1929; the story of Colonel Sanders who saw his restaurant go broke because a freeway took away all the traffic, and who used his Social Security checks as capital to finance the sale of the first Kentucky Fried Chicken franchises; the story of Henry Ford, and the Detroit coal dealer who actually went out and sold stock to finance the Ford Motor Co. start-up; the story of Ray Kroc, a milkshake salesman who got the rights to franchise McDonalds fast food operation and made business history; the story of Hugh Hefner who started Playboy magazine on a $600 bankroll and a business plan; the story of Mary Kay, who wrote a business plan for party plan selling, and liked it so much when she finished she started her own company.

All these stories represent one thing—a business plan was turned into a fortune by people with widely diversified backgrounds, educations, and abilities. They were able to start a small business, more or less on a shoestring, and having the plans to make it work, build their fortunes.

The next phase of the presentation should discuss the era of small business opportunity in the 1980's as the decade of the small business entrepreneur. This is the future opportunity, as opposed to past opportunity you talked about before. You can show them the new area of opportunity, and relate them to the growth in population and demand.

Now You Begin To Sell

The first part of the presentation was to set a solid premise that opportunity to succeed is reality, not fantasy. Now you begin to build on that base to show the prospects how this program can make their hopes and dreams a reality.

The first sales points should be made by using the analogy of building a house. Before a house can be built, an architect must draw up a set of plans. The second step is for the builder to follow those plans by putting up the structure. The third part is for those owning the structure to live in it and get both shelter and pleasure out of it.

A small business is the same process. First, there must be a plan. Second, the structure of the business must be put together. And finally there is the operation which provides economic security and a lot of enjoyment for the owners.

The Cooperative Consulting Program

The cooperative consulting program puts that formula into action. First, the role of the business architect is necessary. The coop consulting program takes you step-by-step through the planning stage, so when you have completed the program, you have a fully developed business plan.

It is not a course of instruction—it is a consulting program. It does not deal in theory and book, it deals in real world reality for small business operators.

The cost for an individual to get this type of consultation would be $3,000 or more from a practicing business consultant. By using the cooperative program it reduces the cost to the point anyone can afford it.

An example of just how valuable the program can be is given here. Take one small part of the total program—the part where business licenses and permits are discussed. In books and courses they mention the entrepreneur should obtain them, but that's all. In the consultation program the clients are told which business licenses to obtain, how to fill them out, where to obtain them, when and how to send them in, how much to pay and anything else that is pertinent. All pertinent licenses and permits are covered. This takes an hour or so, and it **is guaranteed to save the client as much or more than the cost of the course in time and money.** The point is that everything is explained in real world terms. Nothing is assumed, and the client will save hundreds of hours and thousands of dollars by using this program.

A brief discussion of the outline of the program follows to reinforce the value of the program, and the speaker ends with a statement something like this:

"You can invest thirty-two hours of your life in the New Venture Consulting Program and reap the benefit of having the freedom to choose your way of life for the rest of your life."

At this point the speaker should close the proceedings like this:

"I'm sure some of you who are interested have some questions to ask, and I'll be happy to answer them. However, there are probably some people here who are not interested and would like to leave. So, we'll have a ten minute break and those who are interested can come back and we'll sit down together and I'll answer any questions you might have.

This lets those not interested out of the room, keeps them from getting up and walking out in the middle of a question and answer session, and brings those who are interested eyeball-to-eyeball with the salesman.

The question and answer session should be joined by the consultant who will be handling the group. He or she and the presenter can handle the questions, and a clerk from the office will be there to take deposits and enrollments in the program. If your presentation is powerful, and the closing is done well, at question and answer time you should get from 5 to 15 signed up at each seminar, assuming your ad pulled 100 or more attendees.

A Look At The Money

Let's take a look at the possible income from this service. We will estimate it two ways—first, as a part time do-it-yourself project, and secondly, as a full time operation in which you hire the work done and manage the operations.

The do-it-yourself program involves holding your own seminars and selling the program. You will want to get 20 clients per class at a price of $320 per client for 32 hours of consultation. We shall estimate that it will take two free seminars to get the 20 clients you need.

Seminars—two at $300 each	$600
Rental of meeting rooms (at $30 a meeting)	$480
Pass out material to clients	$800

20% drop out after down payment (4 clients at $220 each)	$880
Office and clerical help	$500
Total expenses	$2,540
Net profit	$3,860
Hourly consulting income	$120

You can repeat this cycle four to six times a year as a part time business if you like. And, you have an additional source of income here as well. After you complete the 32 hour planning session, you can take some of the clients on as personal clients at your $100 an hour rate, or put two to four of them in a cooperative program where they pay $25 an hour each and meet once or twice a week.

The Promoter's Approach

If you want to make this into a big money operation here's how to do it.

First, you eliminate any costs for seminars to get clients. You hire a good salesman who can motivate a crowd to promote the seminars and sell the program. You raise the price of the course to $400 and pay the seminar salesman $100 per client. Thus, a good salesman can sell 15 clients at a seminar with 100 to 150 attendees. He will gross $1500 per seminar, pay out $300 to $400 in seminar costs, and net $1100 to $1200 per seminar. If he holds 100 seminars a year he will have an income of over $100,000 a year.

You group the new clients into classes of 20, and hire a consultant to handle them. You pay your consultants $50 per meeting, so they make $800 for each completed course.

On that program with new units being formed on a regular basis in one or more cities, your program would look like this:

Gross Income per unit	$6,000
Cost to hire consultant	$800
Cost of meeting room	$480
Pass Out material	$80
Clerical and office help per unit	$500
Dropouts 20% (4 at $300 loss)	$1,200
Total expenses per unit	$3,060
Profit per unit	$2,940

If you sell 100 units (2000 clients) a year in one or more cities, you would generate an income of nearly $300,000 a year on this program alone, plus any advance consulting programs or sales of miscellaneous materials.

Operations Plan

The first step in operations is to prepare your program. Work out the details of how the business plan program will be presented, and the timing of the presentations.

You can use guest speakers on specific subjects—lawyers, printers, office equipment people, computer people, bankers, accountants, etc. They will be willing to give their lectures free of charge in return for the exposure to possible future customers or clients.

You will need to hire your group consultant, present him with your program, and together sit down and develop a teaching plan for each segment of the program. It could start with a fifteen or twenty minute lecture from the consultant or a guest. That could be followed by questions and answers for another 30 minutes, and then a ten minute summation of what was brought out and should be included in the business plan. A ten minute break follows, and the second subject of the meeting is handled the same way as the first one was.

The size of each unit taking the program should be 10 to 20, with fifteen probably ideal. Any more than that with one instructor will not allow enough participation from some of the group. You must remember that these people will be writing business plans for different ventures, and will have slightly different questions to be answered, so the group must be small enough to allow for this.

Meeting times are optional. Three times a week for two hours is probably best, but it can be programmed any way you wish to do it. The six hours a week for five weeks gives you a tight program with not too much shoved at the clients at once. The final two hours should be party time for congratulations and awards of certificates of completion.

If you wish you can establish a book and equipment sales center for the clients. You can get deals to display equipment, have a stock of books the clients can buy through you at a discount. This is an alternative profit center with a couple of advantages. First, it makes money. Secondly, it provides some equipment for the clients to see in operation and judge the value to their proposed ventures.

Office procedures for handling the business will have to be established. A system for handling client enrollments, collection of fees, scheduling classes, and preparing and handling any course materials you will use.

The office procedures for the marketing people will be to schedule seminars and seminar advertising, getting all the needed materials to the proper locations, and doing publicity work such as making speeches to groups and organizations upon request.

Insurance

Check with a good insurance agent about the coverage you need. Since anything can happen in a group of people, up to and including murder, you want to be covered. You will need coverage for seminars, for meetings of your clients, and for your office and company vehicles. You may also want to bond your money handlers. So, get all you can afford, as you will need it sooner or later.

Tax Planning

A successful operation of this kind can balloon your income quickly and you should have some kind of tax planning program in place. You will need to look into shelters, how to use your corporation to shelter some income, the best salary dividend plan, etc. Just don't get caught with a $100,000 or more that will be directly taxable because you didn't have time to do some tax planning.

Setting Up Your Consulting Program

Before we get into detail about setting up your course, it is important that you understand something. This is a consulting program, **not a teaching program**. You are not giving instructions on how to be an accountant, purchasing agent, advertising writer, etc.; you are showing your clients what they need to know and do in order to start and manage a small business.

Let me give you an example of what I mean. Let's take the hour given to setting up books and records. There is no way you can teach bookkeeping and accounting in an hour, and it is not your purpose to do so. The accounting program should consist of showing the clients the kinds of books they will need—journal, ledger, payroll, etc. Go into the systems that are available—Ideal, Dome and one-write check systems. The discussion is about the usage and values of these items. In discussing book entries, you can show them post binding systems, looseleaf systems, bound books, etc., and discuss the advantages and problems of each. You show them the record keeping tools they need, show them comparative costs, and where they can buy them.

In the same hour you can discuss the use of an accountant or bookkeeping service—comparative costs, advantages, problems, etc. In the summary you will have them indicate in the plan their options, and after they investigate they can write their decision.

Let's take another example—insurance and security. You

discuss the kinds of business policies that are available, the costs and benefits, and general terms and conditions of business insurance.

For security you discuss prevention of burglary, shoplifting or armed robbery, external security threats, embezzlement, employee theft of inventory and under-ringing at the cash registers. Then you suggest ways to get help in solving the problems—prices of burglar alarms and security systems. You tell them where to find the information they need and give them bibliography sheets with sources listed.

Two Kinds Of Business Plans

There are two types of business plans—first, the one you most commonly see is the one used to raise money, either investment or a loan. This is heavy in pro-forma financial statements with personal resumes and some business data. The second is the type we are discussing here—the start up operating plan that gives the client a blueprint from which to build a going business.

In the session on capital and capital sources, the consultant should get into the financial plan, but not in great detail.

A Suggested Program

I am going to give you an outline of a suggested program to help your clients write an operating business plan. The trick to handling this program is to make the program fit all types of businesses. You will have clients who want to open stores, sell products, manufacture something, become wholesalers, sell services, go into mail order marketing, etc. To meet the different needs you can use the pass out material as your variant. Each client gets pass out material pertinent to the type of business they are interested in starting. The general discussion of the consultant will cover the subject, and the question and answer sessions can be used to cover any specific points of varying types of businesses.

The Course Outline

First hour—**The Concept of Your Business.**
The business you are entering.
What are you really selling?
Who will you sell it to?
The concept in 30 words or less.

For this first section I'll give you a brief example of the kind of lecture the consultant will give on the subject. This would be followed by the question and answer session. Each client will have pass out material with the outline of what the consultant is discussing, and his summary, then space for the client to write in his decision or answer to be put into his final business plan.

The Structure of the Sessions

Here is a suggested method of handling the client meetings. Each meeting is two hours of consultation with a ten minute break between hours.

The first subject should be introduced with a 15 to 20 minute lecture by the consultant introducing the subject and what options and decisions are needed to write it in the plan. This is followed by 20 to 25 minutes of group discussion, questions and answers on the subject, and then a final 5 or 10 minute summary of what should be written in the plan. Each subject should have some pass out material for the clients. These can be lists of sources, prices, places to get further information and instruction with a summary sheet on each subject listing the decisions that have to be made. This material serves to refresh the client's memory about what was discussed along with any notes made, and the summary sheet gives him a place to put down his decisions, which in turn makes the business plan.

First Hour—**Concepts and Goals.**

This first session is designed to lay the foundation for the business plan by showing the client what he will be doing and the kind of a commitment he will have to make in order to be successful.

The first hour is a discussion of the concept of the business. The questions to be answered are:

1. What business are you planning to enter?
2. What will your customer be buying?
3. What kind of customer will you be selling to?

Here is a brief example of the lecture that the consultant might give on this subject so you can understand how the program will work.

Your Business Concept

The key to successful business planning is to first lay a foundation for the plan. The foundation can be called, **"The Concept."** It is a brief statement of what the business will be selling and who it will sell it to. This statement will give the entrepreneur a clear view of what is going to be accomplished, and will represent the philosophy of the venture.

It is not as simple as it sounds. For example, you might say, "I'm going to open a shoestore and sell shoes." That is not the concept of the business, it is the explanation of the product you will sell.

Sure, your customer will pay you and walk out with a pair of new shoes. **But they did not buy shoes per se.** They bought either foot protection, style that gives them a better self image, comfort, or perhaps only the spiritual lift buying something new gives us all. Those are the things you sold the customer, not the shoes. Any product or service you sell is only a means to an end for a buyer. The values and perceived benefits of the product are what the customer buys. Elmer Wheeler wrote a book a long time ago and is best remembered for one statement, "Sell the sizzle, not the steak."

Therefore, to understand the concept of your business you must understand why people will buy what you sell. You must analyze what you offer, determine the benefits it brings those who buy, and then you will understand what you have to do to make sales.

The setting down of the benefits you are going to sell will give you a basis on which to decide which of the benefits you deem the most saleable. The choice of benefits will give you the second part of the concept, to whom you will be selling.

For example, if you decide that style and self-image are the most important benefits in the purchase of shoes, you will open a high fashion shoe store. If you decide that foot protection at low prices is the better benefit, or at least the one needed most in the area, you will open a discount shoe store.

We can perhaps best demonstrate how understanding what you are selling determines your approach to the market by using the automobile industry.

First, we have the benefit of personal transportation that all automobiles offer. Then we get into psychology and perceived benefit.

If you wanted to sell cars to those people who care nothing about price of the car or cost of upkeep, but must drive the ultimate status symbol in personal transportation, you would want to be a Rolls Royce dealer, or sell the most expensive sports car.

If you wanted to sell status symbols, but want to make as much money as possible, then you would deal in Cadillacs, Lincolns, Porsches, etc. This gives you a status symbol with mass production behind it. You can get as many as you can sell, unlike the Rolls dealer who gets only limited numbers.

If you decided that you wanted to reach a broader part of the market, but still sell cars with some status symbol recognition, you would sell Buick, Pontiac, Chrysler, etc.

If you wanted the largest part of the market, and wanted to sell those to whom a new car is a status symbol as opposed to a used car, then you sell Chevy, Ford, Plymouth or the low end imports.

If you want to sell strictly on price to the low income area, you become a used car dealer.

Each dealership has a different market, and each has a place in the pecking order of automobile marketing.

So, concept will give you two things: knowledge of what you are going to sell and to whom you are going to sell it. That is the foundation for your business plan.

Writing The Concept

In writing your concept, you should keep it to twenty-five or thirty words. If you need more than that, you probably are not sure enough to write one.

For example, if you were going to open a high fashion shoe store, you might write your concept like this: "I will be selling foot beauty in flattering styles of the very best quality shoes to those people whose personal appearance is of paramount importance. My store will be of striking appearance and have a well-trained staff."

If you were going to open a discount self-serve shoe store it might read something like this: "I'll sell shoes at rock bottom prices on self-service displays to those who are strictly price buyers, no service, no credit, no exchanges."

Turn to your summary sheets and you will find a place to list the benefits of the product or service you will offer. When you have listed them, choose the benefits you feel you can sell best. That choice will dictate the market you are going to be serving.

It is important to remember one thing about selling. There are few products or stores that appeal to everyone. Some products are used by almost everyone, but they buy them from different stores or sources, and pay different prices. Don't make the mistake of thinking you can be all things to all people.

That was a suggested outline of the talk your consultant would give at the opening of the hour. When he was through he would ask some questions of clients if they had none for him. After the discussion lasted for 20 minutes or so the consultant would summarize something like this:

"Now, ask yourself what are the benefits my product or service offers those who buy it? Write your answers down on the summary page we passed out to you. Now, pick the benefits that you feel you can sell the best and then determine who will buy them. Are they men or women or both? What is their average economic status, where do they live or work? What type of store or sales program would most appeal to them?

Second Hour—**Business and Personal Goals.**

What are your business goals?
What are your personal goals?
Is there a conflict between them?
Can you subordinate personal commitments for the venture?
Are your goals realistic?

Third Hour—**Business Format and Name.**

Visualize your business premises.
Store—size, location, interior, exterior.
Office—colors, furnishings, layout.
Plant—offices, production areas, interior and exterior.
The business name you choose.
Does it fit your concept and your premises?

Fourth Hour—**Legal Formation.**

Sole Proprietor.
Partnership.
Corporation.
Advantages, disadvantages of each.

Fifth Hour—**License and Permits.**

- Local Licenses—fees.
- Sales tax permits.
- State Licenses.
- Federal Licenses.
- How to prepare them, where to get them.

Sixth Hour—**Choosing Location.**

- If people come to you—
  - Traffic flow study.
  - Parking.
  - Neighborhood stores and residents.
  - Cost per sq. ft., versus estimated gross.
- If you go to customer—
  - Central location.
  - Shipping facilities.
  - Traffic congestion and parking.
  - Sq. foot versus gross volume test.

Seventh Hour—**Equipment and Fixtures.**

- Make a list of what you need.
- Compare costs—depreciation between new and used.
- Is service and repair available?
- Buy—rent—lease options?

Eigth Hour—**Records and Accounts.**

- Basic records and retention.
- Books of account.
- Accounting systems.
- Accounting services.
- The CPA.

Ninth Hour—**Printing and Business Forms.**

List the printing required.

Types of printers and printing.

Saving by preparing copy for printer.

Finding the right printer.

Business Forms—stock or custom.

Local printing sources.

Tenth Hour—**Purchasing.**

List items to be purchased.

List available suppliers.

Compare goods, terms, shipping costs, etc.

Purchase order use and design.

Inventory purchasing procedures.

Supplies purchasing.

Equipment purchasing.

Purchasing system for firm.

Eleventh Hour—**Inventory Management.**

Who will be in charge of it?

How will records be kept?

Who takes inventory and when?

How are withdrawals made?

What paperwork required?

LIFO or FIFO for tax purposes.

How will security be maintained?

How will it be insured?

12th Hour—**Security.**

Burglar and robbery security.

Shoplifting security.

Internal theft security.

Underrings at the cash register.

Embezzlement and conversion.
Patrol and guards.

13th Hour—**Insurance.**
Basic premises insurance.
Inventory insurance.
Employee bonds.
Theft and burglary.
Liability policies.
Workman's compensation.
Vehicle insurance.
Key man insurance.
Health and accident.
Replacement income riders.
Specialized policies.

14th Hour—**Pricing Your Goods or Services.**
How to figure prices correctly.
How to price against cut rate competition.
How to know when you are underpricing.
How to know when you are overpricing.
How to raise prices without losing business.

15th Hour—**Shipping Methods and Costs.**
Postal rates.
UPS rates.
Bus rates.
Motor Carrier rates.
Railroad shipping rates.
Air freight.
Shipping by water.

Air Express.
Freight Forwarders.

16th and 17th Hour—**The Marketing Plan.**

What market will you serve?
Do you know who will buy?
Do you know where they are?
Do you know your competition?
How will you compete with them?
What is your unique selling proposition?
How to do your own market research.
Identify your primary market.
The size of the market.
The dollar volume of the market.
Your estimate of market share.
Write your marketing plan.

18th and 19th Hour—**Advertising and Publicity.**

How will you advertise?
What media will you use?
What percentage of gross will you spend?
What other media or methods will you use?
Who prepares ads?
Who schedules ads?
When and how often will you advertise?
What will be your main theme?
Will you try to get publicity?
Writing publicity releases.
Creating publicity events.

A planned publicity program.

20th and 21st Hours—**Personnel Management.**

Writing job descriptions.
Salary levels for jobs.
Temporary versus full time.
Independent contractors.
Employee benefits.
Employee working rules.
How to hire.
How to terminate.
Fair employment practices act.
Occupational health and safety.
State and local regulations.
How you will manage your people.

22nd Hour—**Management Techniques.**

Time management.
Management by exception.
Installing systems and records.
Designing systems.
The art of decision making.
Use of records for management decisions.

23rd and 24th Hour—**Credit and Collection.**

Who will grant credit?
How will credit applications be checked?
What are credit limits to be?
Can receivables be financed?
How will accounts be aged?
What collection procedure will be used?
When will accounts be turned over to outside

collectors?
What is average collection time in industry?
What are common credit practices of industry?
Who will make credit decisions?

25th and 26th Hour—**Raising Capital.**
How will capital needs be estimated?
The sources of capital.
The loan application package.
The SBA loan application package.
Raising private capital.
Bank services to small business.
Other government fund sources.
Using factors.
Selling stock.

27th and 28th Hour—**Forecasting and Financial Projections.**
How to forecast sales
How to forecast profits.
Pro forma statements.
Balance sheet.
Income statement.
Cash flow statement.

29th and 30th Hour—**Finding Information and Writing Your Plan.**
How to find information.
How to write your business plan.

The 31st Hour—**The Cocktail Party.**

To Sum Up

In summary, this opportunity is a genuine service, needed by many people, and if it is properly organized, marketed and operated as a real benefit to those paying for it, you have a business that can provide a six figure income for you in a relatively short time.

It will take time to organize it, and some time to get it right once you start, but the opportunity is there, and the need is there. **Go for it!**

CHAPTER 28
FRANCHISE IT

Franchising is a way to expand business rapidly, but the regulations and cost of registering franchises is becoming prohibited for small business. There is a way to get the same results as with franchising without registering as a franchise with state or local authorities.

You set up your pilot store, and prepare an operating manual just as a franchiser does. Then you set up a company to lease the fixtures and equipment needed—a second company to sell supplies — a third company to handle record keeping, tax planning, advertising, and promotion.

Next, you find a capital invester who will fund up a unit in a location you choose. The business is established and starts operating. After a few months it is offered for sale to a local owner. The owner takes over the leases and supply contracts, the capital investor gets his money back plus a profit from the buyer, and you have the net effect of owning a franchised outlet without calling it a franchise. To make sure it has no franchise recognition, use different names for each business—make no agreement that the owner must buy the services you offer after the initial contracts run out, and allow the owner to sell the business to anyone at anytime.

Your three companies are competing for business—they have different corporate structures with different stockholders other than you—and since there is no common name, state and local authorities have no way of calling it franchising. You get the same results as getting a share of the gross profits as payments for the business over a long term—the leasing of equipment and fixtures bring more long term profits—the sale of supplies and of bookkeeping services adds still more profits from the unit.

One way to keep the bureaucrats from discovering it as a franchising scheme under another name is to have each of your companies organized in different towns—and even different states if possible. With your sharecroppers as owners, you will have no problems with franchising registration. You can work the details out with your CPA and lawyer, and come up with a program that will give you the same income that a franchiser makes without the bother of all the registration and extra expenses involved in franchising.

While it is true that you don't have the same ironclad control over a franchisee that a franchiser has, if you run a fair and honest operation, you should have no trouble making a great deal of money from this program with a lot less upfront expense.

Franchising Is An Old Game

Franchises are nothing new. They have been used for centuries in one form or another. Kings gave franchises to nobles for lands, castles and the serfs who worked on them. Emperors gave entire nations to favorite friends. Kings also granted commercial franchises, the British Eash India and Hudson's Bay Company are two examples. The original Jamestown settlement was a commercial venture franchised by the King of England. The American government granted franchises and land to railroad builders. Local governments gave franchises to utilities and banks. Taxi permits, broadcast licenses, licenses to sell liquor and others that are restricted by law, are in fact government franchises to do business against limited and controlled competition. Commercial franchises are also as old as man's history. The landlord gives the right to use land for a share of the crop—sharecropping is a franchise.

In the U.S., the first small business franchises were granted by the Singer Sewing Machine Company in the late 1800's. In the early 1900's Henry Ford recognized the need for a nationwide network of dealerships to sell his mass produced cars. He lacked the capital to set them up, so he sold franchises. The rest of the auto industry followed his lead, and today auto dealerships are all franchises.

In the 1930's the oil companies wanted faster expansion of service stations. Up to that time all stations were company owned; they launched franchising and covered the nation with gas stations.

So, franchising is nothing new. What is new is that the higher standard of living we have achieved since the second world war has made it possible for many more people to invest in franchise businesses. This brought on the big boom in franchising during the 1960's, where everything a promoter could dream up was offered as a franchise, and the boom collapsed. It has started to grow again, this time with somewhat more stability and better controls over how franchises are offered for sale.

The Purpose Of Franchising

The name of the franchise game is cash flow. The purpose of franchising is to expand a business operation by selling the rights to do business to investors instead of selling stock. The franchiser uses the capital obtained from franchisees to expand his business, just as the company that sells stock would.

Now, consider the difference in selling franchises rather than stock. The company that sells stock is diluting ownership. The stockholder is partowner, and has a claim on assets. In addition, each year he is entitled to a share of the profits in the form of dividends. The franchiser, on the other hand, sells no right of ownership in his company, and instead gets an investment in the form of a franchise fee as a right to do business. All he gives up is a geographic area to the franchisee. Instead of paying dividends to his investors, the franchiser collects dividends from them in the form of royalty payments. So, the franchiser can build his business without diluting ownership and creates a cash flow from his investors instead of the investors creating cash flow from him.

What is a Franchise?

The current definition of franchising goes something like this: *Franchising is a system for the selective distribution of goods and services under a brand name through outlets owned by independent businessmen, call "franchisees." Although the franchiser supplies the franchisee with know-how and brand identification on a continuing basis, the franchisee enjoys the right to profit and assumes the risk of loss. The franchiser controls the distribution of his goods and services through a contract which regulates the activities of the franchisee in order to maintain an acceptable standard of quality, service and profit for all concerned.*

The International Franchise Association states a true franchise must contain three essential elements. They are:

- A written contract between both parties which obligates and guarantees both parties' rights and privileges.
- A continuing relationship between the parties which includes all necessary product, equipment, training, advertising and counsel on a joint basis.
- A common name, used by both, and controlled standards of operation in specified territories.

In essence it is simply a matter of rights and know-how in exchange for money.

What Can Be Franchised Successfully?

Almost anything can be franchised. But to successfully franchise a business today, there are some key points to consider. The first and most important is whether or not the business is viable. Not only will it make money where it is starting, but will it play on the road? Some businesses can do very well in some areas, but outside that area would fail quickly. As an example, a cornbread and grits fast food operation may be a winner in Mississippi, but will it play in Peoria?

The second point—is the business a long term proposition? This is not important in the context of this chapter, as you will see, but for the person looking for the long haul, it must be considered. For example propositions like skateboard parks, trampoline centers, theme restaurants, discos, car washes, motivational programs, miniature golf courses, etc., are fads. They have short lives and come to swift ends when the public tires of them.

In real terms the small business franchise should have these qualities to make it saleable:

- A unique selling proposition.
- A business average skills can manage.
- A potenial for many locations.
- Does a reasonable volume of business.
- Can be franchised for a reasonable investment.

The unique selling proposition is the key. What does the business offer that gives it an advantage over the competition? McDonalds grew on fast service, low prices and adequate satisfaction with the product. Prices for hamburgers were starting to go up when McDonalds came along with a 19 cent hamburger; that was the unique selling proposition. Chicken Delight was the first big franchise for fast food chicken. They decided to promote delivery to the door instead of take out. Kentucky Fried Chicken came along, picked better locations, more uniform product, less overhead, lower prices, and ran Chicken Delight out of business.

The unique selling proposition is nothing more than a competitive edge that creates business or takes business away from existing competition.

The business must not be so complex that a person with average intelligence and reasonable skills cannot manage it. There have been many cases where people have taken franchises to market high technology products, and discovered that they needed to know how to install and service the products and that was beyond their abilities. The most saleable franchise is one that the franchiser can teach a person of average intelligence to operate successfully in a short period of time. McDonalds operates a training center they call Hamburger U. A franchisee must take their course and pass it or he doesn't get his franchise.

Location potential simply means that the business does not require the population of half a major city or state to support it, that it has a large potential for locations because a relatively small number of people can support it. For example a small grocery store or deli can prosper with under 1,000 people as a trading base. These are stores such as 7/11 or a mom and pop grocery. By the same token, a bike shop needs a trade area with no competition of over 100,000 people to be successful. So, you are looking for a business that can be supported by a reasonable number of inhabitants so locations and franchise sales wil' not be a serious problem.

The business must do a reasonable volume of business to assure the franchiser his royalty on gross sales will be large enough to make it worth his trouble, and the franchisee can earn enough money to make the investment worthwhile. In other words, a small store or service business doing $40,000 to $50,000 a year in volume would not make an attractive franchise unless half or more of the income was profit.

Finally, it needs a reasonable investment to make it saleable. And, some or most of the investment should be financeable. That is, there should be a source of financing for land, buildings, equipment leasing and the like, so upfront cash from the franchise is not so high you eliminate 99% of the potential prospects.

Franchising is most successful in the retail area for the above reasons. The franchising of small stores and services is a valid concept, and one that you only have to look around you to determine the potential.

The Law Of Franchising

The laws covering the sale of franchises have become quite strict due to the abuses of the past. It is not the purpose of this chapter to go into detail on laws and legalities. The laws vary from state-to-state, and the Federal Trade Commission has issued new regulations on how a franchise can be offered for sale.

Before you prepare a franchise offer you will want to use an attorney familiar with franchise law to help you put your offer together. In almost every state there is some agency you will have to clear your offer with, and in many places with local government as well.

The main thing to keep in mind in this maze of laws and regulations is that if your offer is sound, and represents a genuine opportunity, it can be sold. But, **do not proceed without legal clearance.** If you do, you can wind up in the slammer, or in civil court fighting lawsuits from all sides.

Finding A Franchise Opportunity

This report is designed to show you how you can get into franchising without any great risk on your part, and nothing more invested than your time. To do that, you must become an astute observer of the contemporary scene.

The key to finding a franchiseable concept is to keep the unique selling proposition in mind while you are looking. Ray Kroc was selling milk shake machines in 1954. A small chain of drive-in hamburger stands in San Bernardino, California, called McDonalds bought a machine from him, then several more. He became curious about their operation and came to town to visit their stores. He saw crowds around them everywhere, and figured here was a hot concept. They were selling fifteen cent hamburgers, fries, milkshakes and cold drinks in tremendous quantities given the size of the community in which they were operating. Kroc envisioned a nationwide chain of these stores, and told the brothers about it. However, they were happy and were not interested in expanding beyond San Bernardino. So, Kroc got the rights to franchise their operations, and they kept their own stores. The rest is history. Kroc was a franchise promoter, spotting a hot concept and taking it to market.

The franchise promoter who wants to get into this business on a shoestring has the opportunity to follow Kroc's example. Here are the things that create franchising opportunities:

- Changing lifestyles.
- Changing methods of business operation.
- New technology.
- Changes in the economy.
- Fads that have national appeal.

Changing lifestyles have made some of America's great franchise operations possible. Howard Johnson and Holiday Inn boomed when the great highway system was built and travel on it filled their motels. Hertz saw a need for people traveling to strange towns on trains and planes to rent cars—his franchises are like money in the bank today. The rush to suburbia and home ownership after the second world war created needs for renting tools and equipment. Tool and equipment rental stores turned into franchises. Fast food for an out and about population was another.

The point is, the observant person watching lifestyles can find many opportunities to create businesses that cater to it, or, like Ray Kroc, find one with a concept he can take to market.

A good example of this in current terms is the boom in running and jogging. Franchised stores now sell shoes, clothes and literature. They have become hot franchises. An outfit called Phidippides, out of Atlanta, opened a pilot store selling jogging and running gear in 1976. In three years they have sold 56 franchises for a $5,000 franchise fee, plus 4% of gross sales royalty. There are others popping up to take advantage of the new sport created by the fitness craze.

Changing methods of doing business are another area to watch. In the 1930's the grocery store was manned by clerks. You went to the store, handed them a list of groceries you wanted and they got them off the shelves and rang up the sale. When the depression hit, most of these stores went bankrupt because they extended credit.

The use of help, extension of credit and general methods of doing business kept food prices high. Two men in New Jersey got an idea. They rented an abandoned auto factory, built rough wooden shelves, stocked it with food and put out some circulars. Come to our new grocery store. Serve yourself, pay cash and save 20% on your grocery bill. This was in the very depths of the depression. In one weekend they sold out to the walls and a new industry was born—the supermarket. Self service retailing was born, and it spread to every line of business. New types of franchises popped up. Rexall and Walgreen went out and franchised existing drug stores, allowing the use of their name and greater buying power to add more products. The drug store that sells everything was begun there.

With the advent of big government, new opportunities sprung up in selling insurance as tax shelters, handling paperwork, doing income taxes for businesses and individuals. Firms needed extra office help from time to time, and Manpower and Kelly Girl came along as franchises to fill that need.

So, methods of doing business change, and bring opportunity with them for the alert observer.

New technology creates instant opportunities. The automobile created the biggest industry on earth. The computer is another automobile in terms of its potential for society. Many opportunities for franchising exist in it today, as it is still an infant.

Video tapes and discs are just now starting to get into homes. There will be many franchise opportunities in this field, and another Radio Shack will grow out of it.

The invention of an instant printing plate maker spawned the start and growth of quick printing franchises. One of the pioneers of this field, Postal Instant Press, just reported an income from franchises of over $13 million a year. Energy, security products, electric cars, and home building systems are all technologies with tremendous future potential that bear watching.

Fads are always with us. While fads seldom last for long, it is possible to open a business based on a hot fad and get your entire investment back in a matter of weeks, even days. In many ways they are the easiest franchises to sell because they have no competition in the classic sense, and they produce high cash flows at once. Fads are not predictable, but one just has to read the newspapers and periodicals, watch TV and look around to spot them. They are ideal for the franchise promoter because they are easy to sell.

So, finding a franchise opportunity simply takes observation and a readiness to act when you see an opportunity.

Here are some current areas you might start investigating:

- Computer services.
- Diet food lunch rooms.
- Energy saving device stores.
- Security equipment stores.
- Instant lube and oil change stations.
- Underground home building.
- Moped sales and service.
- Video discs and tapes.
- Reclaimed motor oil.
- Rebuilt auto parts.
- Used car lots.
- Office centers for small business.
- At-home recreation equipment and supplies.
- Singles clubs.
- Alternative delivery services.

These are just a few of the areas you can investigate.

Getting Information Fast

When you spot a concept that you think can be franchised, here is how to find out in a week or two if it's known around the country. Employ a clipping service to clip all the printed stories about the subject for you. If you are dealing with a fad item, or something that you think might have potential, the clipping service is the fastest way to find out about it. Have them also clip ads if it is for a certain type of business and see what others are doing with it.

Go to the library and look into the various indexes of periodicals they have there and see if there is any action on the subject. These indexes are tables of major periodicals in the country. There are also indexes for the New York Times and Wall Street Journal. Check them out, as they are more current.

The value of this research is that you will find out just how far out in front you are with your concept. One important thing to remember in starting a new venture—if you are too far ahead of the public or your potential customers, you'll fail. If there is no action anywhere on your concept, then proceed with caution. But, if there is activity elsewhere, and it's getting media attention, then you are probably on to something.

The Franchise Promoter

The franchise promoter is just what the name implies: an individual who promotes business ventures into franchised operations. It can be done by anyone with some moxie and a willingness to plan carefully. You don't need a lot of money of your own. But, you do need to have ideas and enthusiasm for putting them into action.

There are two ways a franchise promoter can get started. First, he can develop a concept of his own and raise the seed capital to start a pilot business operation with the goal of franchising it. This gives him complete control of the planning and development of the program.

The second way is to find an existing business that has franchising potential and get the franchising rights from the owner. This is the way Ray Kroc started McDonalds, and others have done the same thing. It is a quicker way to franchise selling because you already have a proven operation as a base from which to work.

Promoting Your Concept

The first step is to write a business plan for your concept. You will find a check list further on that will make it simple to do this.

The next step is to raise private capital for your concept so you can begin a pilot operation to prove the concept will work, and build a base from which to launch your franchise sales. It will take a year or so of operation to reach the point where franchising is possible.

The advantage of this approach is that you can plan the business for franchising from the start. You develop systems for operations and marketing that will make the business successful for others. You write your operations manual as you go, from the grand opening plan right on down to how many times a day the rest rooms or parking lot have to be cleaned up. You will keep a daily diary of operations and learn what works and what doesn't. You'll have the opportunity to evaluate equipment, learn about suppliers and pick up on hidden costs you were unaware of. The best way to keep this diary is to take 15 minutes at the end of each business day to talk into a tape recorder about what you did, what you learned and what you plan to do. You can have a typist transcribe these dictated thoughts every so often, and from that information can easily compile an operations manual for franchisees.

Franchising A Going Business

The second way is to find a business with a unique concept that has franchising potential and get the rights to set up a franchise selling program based on it.

When you spot a business with this potential, go to the owner and tell him or her you want to buy the business and ask them to name a price. The reason for this is that as a potential buyer you have the right to look at the books, watch the operation, and learn all the details from the owner about the business to determine if there is franchising potential.

If you decide the concept can be franchised, then go back to the owner and tell him you have a better idea, that you and he or she can make a lot of money by franchising the operation. You will set up a franchise sales program and split the profits on a mutually agreeable basis. If the owner has an average amount of greed and ego this will have a terrific impact, and you will have little trouble setting up the deal.

In this case you have the owner use the dictating machine to give a daily, blow-by-blow account of the operation from when the key is turned in the door in the morning till the place is locked up at night. This will be transcribed into an operations manual. His business will be the training facility for new franchises.

Setting Up Operations Systems

The key to successful franchise operations is to have understandable and workable systems for franchisees to follow. They will need systems for:

- Keeping records.
- Hiring and managing help.
- Purchasing inventory and supplies.
- Advertising and promotion.
- Taxes and government forms.
- Security—internal and external.
- Quality control on anything they make.
- Management techniques.

The way to work out systems for small businesses is to plan for management by exception. That means you put in programs that work automatically. The only time the owner-manager has to make decisions is when something happens that is an exception to the system. For example, the business has a policy of only taking checks for the amount of the purchase. But, a good customer wants to cash a check when the banks are closed. This calls for a management decision. Thus the manager is freed from making decisions about every check to be cashed. The management by exception technique keeps the manager from being drowned in detail that destroys his ability to manage.

The Franchise Agreement

This is the key to success or failure of a franchising program. The agreement must specifically set out the duties and obligations of both parties, and be the basis on which disputes can be solved.

There are different types of franchise agreements. Some make franchises easier to sell than others, and you will have to decide which way you want the program to go when you choose your agreement format. If you want to sell franchises as fast as possible, and then sell the franchising company—take your money and run—you will want an agreement that tilts in favor of the franchisee. If you want to build the franchise into a profitable operation you will need a much tighter agreement that tilts in favor of the franchiser.

Fixed Franchise Fees...A fixed fee is a one time payment for the rights granted to the franchisee. It may be an annual payment of a stipulated amount, or simply a once only fee for rights and training to operate the business. This is the quick seller fee.

Territory Based Fee...This is a fee charged based on the size (population) of a territory in terms of numbers of potential customers or clients.

Percentage of Gross Fee...This is the most common fee, and the one that builds the franchising company into a cash machine. The fee runs from 1% of the gross up. This needs a bookkeeping system that can be audited by the franchisor to determine the proper fees owed by the franchisee.

Obligation to Purchase...This is a sticky subject. In the beginning, franchisers made most of their money by selling the inventory and supplies to franchisees. They had locked-in customers who had to buy from them, and made fortunes overcharging franchisees. The courts have ruled this practice to be in violation of anti-trust laws, and is no longer enforceable. But the franchiser can demand the franchisee purchase inventory and supplies to meet minimum quality standards set by the franchiser, and he has the right to refuse to allow a franchisee to purchase below standard quality items. Of course, that has to be written into the agreement. In practice the franchiser sells some or all of the supplies to franchisees.

Equipment Leasing...Franchisers frequently arrange for leasing or installment sale of necessary equipment to franchisees. This is another area where franchiser abuse caused the courts to strike down some agreements as in violation of anti-trust laws. In practice, the franchisee usually buys a package in which leases or installment sales are included, and if the terms are not unduly harsh, it causes few problems.

Accounting and Consulting Services...A franchiser who receives a fee based on gross volume will want to have his own accounting service handle the accounting and tax work for franchisees. This protects his interest, and is a help to franchisees because the accounting firm is fully knowledgeable about the operations.

Capital Provided by Franchiser...If the franchiser is lending funds to franchisees he can of course earn interest on the money, as well as receive fees, and the only limits on interest rates are the usury laws.

Competition Protection...The key to the franchise is that the franchisee has territorial protection against other franchises being granted in that territory. But, always include a clause that gives you some flexibility if there is a sudden population boom, or the franchisee does not exploit the total territory as he should.

Choice of Location...If location is a key factor in the success of the venture, the franchiser will want control over the choice. The franchiser will usually have realtors select several locations, and then make a survey to determine the potential of each. The franchisee will be offered the best of them. If the franchisee picks the location, the franchiser reserves the right to refusal.

Design of a Structure...If the franchise is going to operate from its own building, it is usual for a standard building to be designed and built for the business. It is part of the package and there is no negotiation on its construction or appearance. If the property is leased or purchased and an already existing structure used, the franchiser will provide the necessary materials to make it uniform in signing, fixturing, etc., with other franchises. If the franchise is terminated, then the franchiser can retain the right to remove all identifying materials from the premises.

Maintenance Requirements...Setting up standards for maintenance for both interior and exterior structures and equipment is very important. Proper maintenance of the premises is vital to the reputation of the entire franchise. The franchiser should enforce this provision at all times among all franchisees.

Financing...The agreement must clearly state which financial obligations each party to the agreement are liable for. Leave no gray areas here; stipulate who pays for what, and when it is to be paid.

Management Requirements...The franchisee should be obligated by the agreement to use the techniques and systems provided by the franchiser. Failure to do so would be grounds for termination of the franchise. It is imperative that the franchise operation be as uniform as possible in management policies. If there are recipes, formulas or other items to prepare, they should be done exactly as instructed by the franchiser so uniform results are obtained.

Manuals Supplied by Franchiser...These are confidential manuals and should be treated as such. A substantial replacement cost should be set for replacing any lost manuals other than by fire or other acts of God. If it will cost the franchisee $500 to get another manual, he will be very careful with the one he has. All manuals should be constantly updated and revised as times and conditions change. The franchisee should be made aware that he is expected to follow the manual in all cases where decisions must be made.

The Company Representative...At some point the franchiser needs to employ a consultant to meet with franchisees at their place of business. His job is to both inspect their operation from the standpoint of maintaining the franchise image, and to help them solve problems. Some franchise operations hire successful franchisees to do this work;

others hire outside managers. The person who does this work should be a communicator, one who can both instruct intelligently, analyze problems and find solutions that help both the company and the franchisee. His pay comes out of the royalty fees paid by franchisees.

Advertising...Advertising and promotion should be done from the home office. In some franchises an additional percentage of the gross is charged to cover this cost. There should be a constant flow of ad layouts, in-house promotional banners, signs and point of purchase (POP) displays. This is more than just a business builder, it ties operations together and increases gross business, which increases company income.

Training Programs...This should be spelled out in the agreement. The standard practice is to have a new franchisee work in the pilot store for a period of time to get the feel of operations, and there is a company representative on hand when he opens his business to help with the grand opening and initial work load.

A second point to cover is who bears the cost of the training and assistance. In practice the initial training is covered by the franchise fee, and if additional help is needed this cost is borne by the franchisee.

Price Controls...The setting of uniform prices is good business for franchises. People know what to expect. However, the franchiser cannot enforce strict price compliance due to anti-trust laws. General practice is to provide a suggested price list and let the franchisee price to meet competition if he wishes.

Materials and Supplies...The agreement has to be loose on this. Any attempt to make the franchisee buy only from the franchiser will result in a lawsuit and damages awarded to franchisees. Controls can be established so the franchiser can require certain quality levels in the inventory and supplies purchased by franchisees.

If you have a secret formula or certain branded trade items, you may require franchisees to buy them. The key is not to overcharge, take kickbacks from outside suppliers who get exclusive contracts to supply your franchisees, or otherwise try to restrict the freedom to purchase in order to make excessive profits.

Personal Guarantees...If the franchisee is a corporation, particularly one formed for this venture, the franchiser will want personal guarantees on debt and compliance from the stockholders. Without it, he is helpless to enforce the agreement.

Audits of Franchisees...The franchiser will want the right to audit the books, or require income tax statements from franchisees where a royalty payment based on gross business is paid.

Franchisees Right to Assign...The franchiser will want the right to approve of any assignments of rights in the franchise, either by an individual or corporation. The common practice is to simply make an assignment of rights reason for termination, unless approved in advance by franchiser.

Termination...The right to terminate the agreement is important to the franchiser. While franchisees are protected by law against unreasonable termination, the right to terminate for cause is vital to the success of a franchising program. Here are some of the causes to be included in the agreement.

- Violation of any terms of the agreement.
- Improper use of trademark or franchise name.
- Failure to file reports or maintain records.
- Failure to operate as instructed by the manual.
- Failure to meet performance or quality standards.
- Failure to follow instructions of franchiser's representative.
- Attempt to sell or transfer interest without franchiser's consent.
- Bankruptcy or insolvency.

Termination Procedure...The agreement should spell out what happens when a franchise is terminated. List who gets what, or pays for what. In all cases the franchiser should have first right of refusal on all assets.

Term of Franchise...The agreement should spell out how long the agreement is in force, and terms for renewal. If any franchisee terminates a franchise there should be a non-competition clause that bars him from entering a competitive business for a period of 2 years after termination.

Preparing Your Contract...You will need an attorney to prepare your franchise contract. To save time and money you can use the check list that follows to cover all the points, and let the attorney put it in contract form. You will find sample franchise agreements in books and sources given in the bibliography in this report. You can refer to them, but don't try to make up your own contract from them. Times and conditions change, and those agreements are past history.

Agreement Checklist

☐ Name of franchiser.
☐ Name of franchisee.
☐ State of domicile of franchiser.
☐ State of residence of franchised business.
☐ Specific location of franchised business.
☐ Form of franchise.
   1. Fixed fee.
   2. Size of territory.
   3. Gross business.
   4. Other.
☐ Amounts of fees and how formulated.

Other Fees:

☐ Purchase of supplies.
☐ Minimum quantities.
☐ Equipment lease.
☐ Accounting/auditing fees.
☐ Other services.
☐ Interest on loans.

Insurance:

☐ Types required.
☐ Who pays the premiums.

Grounds for Termination:

☐ Violation of any term of agreement.
☐ Improper use of name or trademark.
☐ Failure to file reports.
☐ Failure to maintain records.
☐ Failure to follow operators manual.
☐ Failure to meet sales quota.
☐ Attempts to sell or transfer franchise.
☐ Sale of stock in corporate franchise.
☐ Bankruptcy or insolvency in either party.

Opening Costs:

☐ Franchise fee.
☐ Business license fees and permits.
☐ Building and land costs.
☐ Utility and other deposits.
☐ Training costs.
☐ Equipment costs and installation.
☐ Payroll.
☐ Grand Opening costs.
☐ Other costs.
☐ When can books be audited?
☐ Rights of franchiser representative to require compliance.
☐ Time period of agreement.
☐ How it can be renewed?

- ☐ Procedures under termination for any reason.
- ☐ Use of trade name and symbols.
- ☐ Use of inventory.
- ☐ Use of structure.

Territory Assignment and Limitations:

- ☐ Location of territory.
- ☐ Boundaries of franchisee control.
- ☐ Can franchisee open other units in area?
- ☐ Can franchisee sell franchises in area?
- ☐ What are limits of units in area?

Location and Building:

- ☐ Who chooses location?
- ☐ Who owns location?
- ☐ Who approves of location?
- ☐ Who owns building?
- ☐ Who leases building?
- ☐ Who constructs building?
- ☐ Who remodels building?
- ☐ Who designs building?
- ☐ Who approves of building?
- ☐ Who sets prices?

Costs:

Who bears costs for the following:

- ☐ Utilities and Heat?
- ☐ Advertising?

☐ Maintenance and Repairs?
☐ Taxes, state, federal, local?
☐ Legal and accounting fees?
☐ Normal business expenses?
☐ Freight?

Marketing:

☐ Franchiser's contribution.
☐ Franchisee obligation.
☐ How costs are shared.
☐ Use of signs.
☐ Use of equipment.

Note—it is common practice for the franchiser to have right of first refusal on all assets of franchisee at termination. Payment is value less depreciation. If the franchise is operating, then payment is the fair market value of a going business.

In Summary

So far, we have given you the general idea of franchise promotion, what you need to know to give it a shot.

At this point I want to summarize what this opportunity represents. First, while it is unlikely you will come up with another McDonalds or Kentucky Fried Chicken, it is still possible. Both of those concepts were started by men probably no better off than you are right now. Colonel Sanders had gone broke in the restaurant business in Kentucky, and instead of sitting back and living off his social security checks, he used them as capital to finance his travels in selling KFC franchises. That was about thirty years ago, and there are now nearly 6,000 outlets.

Since fast food represents the highest possible number of locations, we checked a franchise directory to see how many outlets those listed had. There were 150 franchises listed, and 80 of them had less than 25 franchises sold. But, there were 23 with over 300 franchises, so the odds are far from impossible. A hundred established franchises with good volume mean wealth for the promoters.

The key to it all is in your planning and carry through. You don't really need anything radically different or new. A couple of professors who studied the field discovered that the successful franchise was one in which customers were willing to expend some extra effort to do business with the franchise. So, any concept that gets the customers excited enough to come back and tell their friends about you is a potential franchise. In this day and age just a little common courtesy and pleasant conversation with customers may be enough.

Think about it from the standpoint of just getting an edge on the competition. Something just different enough to make it go.

BIBLIOGRAPHY

Associations—**International Franchise Association,** 7315 Wisconsin Ave., Suite 600, Bethesda, MD 20014, has many books and publications on franchising, and most franchisers are members.

Books—Mathew Bender & Co., 235 E. 45th St., New York, NY 10017, has a complete legal guide to setting up franchises. It is provided with updates covering new laws and regulations.

Fransworth Publishing, Inc., 78 Randall Ave., Rockville Centre, New York, NY 11570, is another source of books on franchising. The publish **The Report of the Annual Conference on Franchising,** sponsored by the Boston College Center for the Study of Franchising.

Franchise Opportunity Handbook, published by the U.S. Department of commerce, and available from the U.S. Government Printing Office, Washington, DC 20402, is a book that lists most of the current franchisers, along with sources of additional help and information.

Boston College, Center for Study of Franchising Distribution, Chestnut Hill, MA 02167, is another source of information.

Financing Franchise Systems and The Franchise Game is Basic Operations, The Cornell Hotel & Restaurant Administration Quarterly, August 1971 issue (reprints $1.00) has some tips for prospective franchisors.

Newsletters—**IRA Franchising World,** news of the franchising world put out by International Franchising Association (see address above) — free to members, otherwise write for subscription rate.

Continental Franchise Review, Box 6360, Denver, CO 80206. Published twice monthly on franchise industry. $75 a year.

Note—Check **The Subject Guide to Books in Print** at your local library for latest books on franchising.

TACTICS

Manage by exception and keep your sanity.

Small business operators have too many hats to wear—this makes it impossible for them to make every decision everyday in a business operation. The way to avoid this is to manage by exception. Managing by exception is to develop specific systems and procedures for running the normal business day. Set up these systems so that normal operations require none of your attention—it is only when an exception to the norm crops up that you must make a decision.

If you set up standard procedures for handling:

1. Sales
2. Credit
3. Inventory
4. Returned goods
5. Cashing checks
6. Filling orders
7. Shipping and receiving
8. Handling the mail
9. Making bank deposits
10. Opening and closing the business
11. Answering phones and handling most callers

You will have systems in place that do not require your time and attention. This leaves you free to see salesmen, visit with your banker and other businessmen, analyze your books, do your purchasing, and plan for the future.

CHAPTER 29
THE BUSINESS PLANNER
Section I — The New Venture Planner

Personal Goals

Before you start planning for any venture you must have a clear idea of what you want from this risk and effort you are about to undertake. Your concepts of what you want in terms of personal satisfaction, material gain and lifestyle are the keys to the type of operation you are going to have. You want to get these personal goals clear in your mind so you can make the business decisions that will bring them about.

This Personal Goals section is for those who are using this manual to plan their own ventures. If you intend to write a plan for sale to others you can leave this section out. You will have to assume those who buy the plan know their reasons for getting into the business.

In terms of setting personal goals, you will first want to examine what you are bringing to this venture, and what you will have to do in order to reach your goals.

First, what experience do you bring to this venture? Have you ever done anything like this before? Do you have a first hand knowledge of any aspect of running a business? Are you willing to do to learn what you need to know to be successful? There is a price you are going to have to pay if this venture is going to be on the job training. That price is time, and the cost of the mistake you are going to make. The acid test is this, if you owned this business and were going to hire a manager, would you hire yourself?

Many people are frightened by the word business and what it connotes. They have a conception of it as some highly complicated and mysterious system of marketing goods and services that is difficult, if not impossible to master. This is both true and false. You will discover as you use this New Venture Planner, that there is a great deal to learn — and a lot of decisions to make. But, you've got to keep it in perspective. Taken as a whole, it is complicated, but broken down into individual segments it is not.

As a matter of fact you have been in business most of your life. I call it the "self-business." You have a service or product you sell — you have to sell it at a profit — you have to cover your overhead — pay your taxes and do your personal bookkeeping. It makes no difference whether you are a housewife who manages a family business or an executive working for a large corporation. Your product or service is your time and your skills. You market to an employer who pays you a gross income. From that income you must pay your overhead, your food, your clothing, your shelter, your transportation and medical care. Added to that you must pay for grooming essentials and perhaps some tools or equipment. You could call these expenses, "cost of goods sold." Beyond that you need a profit to provide for your family — to give to church and charity and pay your taxes. This "self-business" is almost exactly the same economic system used to operate General Motors or the corner gas station.

You can judge your business management potential pretty well be examining how you handle your self-business. Do you pay your bills on time? Have you managed to accumulate assets that exceed your liabilities? Can you save by giving up some immediate gratification to invest in a future benefit? Do you have a sound credit rating? Do you have a personal goal to improve your standard of living? Do you have adequate insurance? All these questions will give you the answer as to how well you are likely to do in a small business of your own.

If you have answered them in the affirmative for the most part, you have an excellent chance of being successful in a business venture. If, on the other hand, the answers are negative, I would suggest you either get an associate with management skills, or you take some time to get your affairs under control before launching a business venture.

ANSWER THESE QUESTIONS:

Yes	No	
☐	☐	When you decide on a course of action do you follow it through to a decision?
☐	☐	Do you face problems head on and solve them?
☐	☐	Are you in good health?
☐	☐	Can you take criticism and handle the hostility of others?
☐	☐	Do you work well under a lot of pressure?
☐	☐	Do you hate to lose?

Those are six simple questions, and if you answered any one of them no — you should hesitate to get into a small business. First, you must be willing to follow through on decisions. You can't keep changing your mind, or putting off making them. It leads to quick failure. Secondly, you must face problems in business at once. You can't let them fester and turn into heavy losses. Third, you must be in robust health. You are in for a severe test physically and emotionally, and poor health just won't stand up under it. Fourth, you will get lots of criticism from your customers, your employees and your business contacts — it goes with the territory. Some will be deserved and some won't. If you are thin-skinned, and easily upset by it — business may not be your bag. Fifth, you will have almost constant pressure from many sides in a small business. There is seldom enough money, there are late shipments of goods your customers are hounding you for — there are errors, accidents and misunderstandings almost daily. It all puts pressure on you, and you have to handle it and keep going. Finally, you have to be a winner by nature — losing is not something you do easily. You go into business expecting to succeed, and will compete to succeed till the last dog is hung.

The Risk Of Failure

There is a serious risk of failure in any business enterprise — big or small. It's like a man-eating tiger prowling the economic jungle waiting to pounce on the careless, stupid or unwary entrepreneurs. Anyone who has ever started a new venture can tell you they have seen him many times, late at night, when they were pouring over their books trying to find a way to stay afloat. The point is that you must consider the consequences of failure from a personal point-of-view. What will it mean to your family? How will it affect their lives? What do you stand to lose besides the time and money you invested? Can you start over? How will it affect your personal relationships with friends and neighbors? It is only prudent to assess the effects of failure, because in truth, you are more likely to fail than to succeed. So, consider the other side of the coin before you commit yourself. As you are examining the possibilities and ramifications of possible failure, keep this point in mind:

> "Total commitment to success is the only way you can beat the odds. So, if you find that you are afraid to fail — don't start."

You can't play scared cards in business. You have to take risks—enjoy the action—and when you must place your bets, you place them willingly and with the full expectation you are going to win.

Creating the New Venture

The entrepreneur finds the creation of a new venture similar to that of becoming a new parent. First, there is the ecstasy of conception, the thrill of the idea, the concept of the venture. Then, the gestation period occurs when the raw idea is formed into an organization. And, finally the day of birth happens, when the business is launched and begins life. The early days of its childhood when it takes its first stumbling steps, then becomes self-sufficient and can stand alone are gratifying. This sense of accomplishment is what makes the entrepreneur proud and content. Money is only the way to keep score, to mark the progress. But, it's the pride of the creator and the fulfillment of a dream that is the real reward.

The Three Steps To Success

Success is always achieved in three steps. First, there is acquisition of knowledge. Knowing what you are doing and why you do it, is important. So is knowing what to expect and how to react, learning the methods, the techniques and the skills required to accomplish the tasks that lead to success are all vital. When you have the knowledge and know what you are doing—you automatically move to the second step—self-confidence.

Self-confidence comes from knowledge. Think about the first time you got behind the wheel of a car; you were certainly nervous, possibly frightened and perhaps terrified. Here you had to manuever a ton of metal at relatively high speeds in a confined space without hitting anything. Your first attempts were clumsy, but as you gained the knowledge of how to control that car, and acquired the skills to do so—you became confident, and now can jump into your car and go anywhere without any problem. Self-confidence then creates the psychology for the third and final step—perseverance.

There is an old and true saying—"winners never quit and quitters never win." Overnight success is luck—and rarely happens. The only way to be sure of success is to persevere—to hang in there and do what needs doing each day. Everything we do that's worth a damn has a price. You want to understand that before you start a small business. No matter how carefully you plan—things will not work out the way you expect they will. There will be mistakes—disasters over which you have no control. There will be fraud and deceit practiced on you, and set-back after set-back will happen. You will have to operate under Murphy's Law:

> Whatever can happen will happen. And, add Mrs. Murphy's Law, it will happen when you can least afford it.

So perseverance is the final step, and backed with knowledge and self-confidence—it will bring you the success you seek.

Setting Personal Goals

You must take some time to consider what it is you want from this venture. First, list the personal satisfactions you seek:

- To be a winner
- To be free to choose you own way in life
- To be recognized as a leader

Second, list your goals in terms of financial rewards:

- Financial security for yourself and family
- Achievement of wealth to some degree
- Making some fast money by building up a venture and then selling it
- The start of a business empire

Keep in mind that there are no bad goals per se—so choose your goals honestly and they will form the basis of your planning to reach them.

Lifestyle Considerations

There are certain benefits, or trappings, if you will that go with business success. The large home, with swimming pools, tennis courts and a staff of servants, is one. Others are the fine car, the boat, the airplane, etc. There is ability to travel in style anywhere on earth, the clothes, jewelry and other status symbols that the successful entrepreneur enjoys. When you make your list of personal goals you can also make up a list of these material things that you would enjoy having and even make timetables for the acquisition of each of them. It will give you something to shoot at in planning and operating the business.

Decision Point

Think about what you want, and make a realistic estimate of how soon you want them. This gives you a set of personal goals and a time frame for reaching them.

Make a list on a separate sheet of paper of your goals, then put it aside, but refer to it from time to time as a reminder of the reason you began this journey.

Section II — Find the Concept

To fully understand what you are going to be selling, and how you can best go about selling it, you must understand the basic concept of what you intend to do, to know what the customer is buying, and who those customers will be.

For example, if you asked a locksmith what he sells, you would expect him so say locks and keys. The one who understands the concept of his business will reply "I'm selling peace of mind." The product or service you deliver is not what the customer buys.

They Buy Benefits!

A housewife who buys a dishwasher buys automatic dishwashing—less work and clean dishes. You deliver a dishwasher, but she wants the benefits—not the machine.

For example, if someone selling shoes was asked what he or she sold—the person who understood the concept would say:

I sell:

- Foot protection
- Foot comfort
- Style and eye appeal
- Quality and long life of the shoe

These are the benefits—and all are wrapped around the price and the method of selling.

For example, let's say you open a shoe store that will feature the best brands and styles of shoes—the highest quality of materials and and workmanship — you will be catering to the upper class market. You will choose your location and the decor of your store accordingly.

If you decide to try and sell the broad middle market or shoe buyers, you might open a family type shoe store. You will have shoes for both adults and children, with the most popular styles and sizes in middle ranged prices.

If you decide that you want the low end of the market, you want to set up a discount operation, with shoes set up for self-service—no clerks—no service and low prices. You sell foot protection pure and simple.

The Concept Identifies The Market

As you can see from the examples, the concept will tell you which market segment you will be serving. Once you know the marketing target, you will have to consider, as part of your concept, why the customer will buy what you have to sell, other than just for the benefits. After all, your competitors will be selling the same benefits. You can now try to develop your concept of doing business.

For example, will you have:

- A better location?
- Offer better service?
- Better designed store or office?
- Exclusive brands they cannot buy elsewhere in the area?
- A wider choice of styles and sizes?
- Do a better advertising and promotion job?
- A better trained sales staff?
- Product at a lower price?

You can add more reasons why customers will buy what you sell.

The benefits you choose to be your primary selling points will identify your market. The reasons customers will buy from you rather than your competitors are the keys to how much business you will do.

To write your concept, you need to answer three questions:

1. Which benefits will you be selling?
2. Which will you feature in your business?
3. Why will customers buy these benefits from you?

Let's try this with shoes and come up with some sample concepts.

First, what are the obvious benefits all shoe buyers want?

1. Foot protection.
2. Foot comfort.

What are the special benefits they look for?

1. Style and eye appeal.
2. Quality and name brands.

And, they all will only pay the prices for perceived values.

The concept for a store that will stress style and quality states: "Our store will be located in the exclusive Brentwood shopping center, featuring the three best brands of high style footwear, with a wide range of styles and sizes. Our store will be luxuriously furnished and fixtured, with a highly trained and competent staff to serve our clientele."

For a family shoe store your concept might read something like this: "We will open a store in the community of Suburbia. It will feature the most popular styles and sizes of middle-ranged price lines. A well-appointed store, with a heavy promotional advertising campaign, will create business."

For a pipe rack, discount shoe operation: "We will have a discount—manufacturers close-out shoe store operation, with a well-traveled highway location. There will be one clerk at the register, and terms will be that all sales are final."

The three concepts set the stage for the plan. You know which benefits you will stress, which segment of the market you will reach, and know where you should locate your store.

If you are developing concepts for other than retail businesses, you will use the same process. If you are going to sell office copiers, remember the benefits are what the customer will buy. These benefits could be clean, clear copies; high speed; low service and maintenance costs; easy to use; lower costs per copy; takes up less space; etc.

The Edison Concept

Let's say you were going to develop a concept for the electric light. First, the benefits.

- Inexpensive, long-lasting light source.
- Quick to light or turn off.
- No flame or flammable oils to use.
- Can be in ceilings or in lamps.
- Clean to use, no dirty walls or curtains.

There are more. But, Edison took the product, and using those benefits as his selling points, drove coal oil lamps, gas lamps and candles out of the lighting business, except for emergencies. The concept might have gone something like this:
generating company, and sell electricity to industry, homes and farms to use for lighting. The cost will be cheap, the dangers of fire from flame light sources eliminated. Eventually every home, factory and farm will use my electric light."

Think about your concept. On the following pages you will find a helpful guide to developing your concept. Take some time to do this, because it is the foundation of your total plan.

The Concept of Your Venture

Make a list of the benefits you will be selling.

1. ____________________
2. ____________________
3. ____________________
4. ____________________
5. ____________________
6. ____________________
7. ____________________
8. ____________________
9. ____________________
10. ____________________

Arrange them in the order of their importance to the type of customer you will be catering to.
To help you, consider what you will offer them as a retailer:

- ( ) The location of the business?
- ( ) Ambience of your store and facility?
- ( ) Superior service to customers by skilled staff?
- ( ) Better selection of products and services?
- ( ) More convenient hours of business?
- ( ) Offer only top line brands and styles?
- ( ) A unique advertising promotion program?
- ( ) Lower prices—self-service?
- ( ) Better terms—easier credit?
- ( ) Other?

If you are going to be selling direct to consumer with non-store marketing, will you have:

- ( ) Unique product with new benefits?
- ( ) Better marketing and promotion?
- ( ) Lower price—same price with more accessories?
- ( ) Strong buyers guarantee of satisfaction?
- ( ) Better credit or payment terms?
- ( ) Better after sale service?
- ( ) Other?

If you are going to be selling your product at the wholesale level, will you have:

( ) High profit resale lines?
( ) Exclusive source of hot products?
( ) Quick efficient delivery?
( ) An exclusive line of product with high customer loyalty?
( ) Price or credit term advantages?

Some Sample Concepts

Retail

We will feature exclusive designs in jewelry and objects d'art created with the finest gems and findings in a beautifully appointed store, with a highly trained staff to serve those who appreciate the finest in these products. Our name will become a symbol of quality and superior workmanship.—Tiffanys

We will feature promotional lines of jewelry, small appliances and luggage from stores in high traffic locations. We will sell on easy credit terms to blue collar people.—Credit Jewelry Store

We will feature jewelry and gift items at low cash prices in a catalog store where samples are displayed and catalogs sent to consumers who will pay discount cash prices.—Catalog Store

Product

We will standardize production methods and use mass production techniques to produce an automobile we can sell at a low enough price so our workers can afford to buy what they produce.—The Ford Motor Company

We will produce the ultimate in luxury personal transportation using master craftsmen, the finest components and sell it to those who can afford the finest.—Rolls Royce Motor Co.

Keep in mind the concept is the base on which you will build your plan. Once you understand what you will be selling and who you will be selling it to, you can write your plan to develop that kind of business.

My Concept Is

____

____

____

____

____

____

____

____

Section III
Setting Your Business Goals

The next step in your planning is setting your business goals. It is important to do this because you must decide if the goals you are setting for your business are compatible with your personal goals. Many times the new entrepreneur assumes that running a small business is a 9 to 5 job, just like the one he or she had, and because they own the business, they can take off whenever they wish. Reality, is quite different. Owning a small business is like owning a cow. It must be attended to daily, or it will die. A business owner puts in far longer hours than an employee, and vacations in the first few years are wishful thinking for the most part. So, in making plans, and setting business goals, you must assume that 12 to 16 hour working days are going to be common place, and the higher your business goals, the more time and work will be required.

In general terms there are four stages to business success:

- The break even point
- The survival point.
- The expansion point.
- The wealth building point.

There is a time frame required to reach these points depending on the skill of the manager and the type of business. Again, in general terms, it takes less time to reach break even in a small business that has a known market, and known products or services. This includes small retail stores, service businesses and direct selling of some types of products. The time to reach the point where the business is going to survive is also somewhat less. But, these types of businesses seldom go beyond those points. On the other hand, the new service, product or program will take longer to reach break even and survival in most cases, but is far more apt to go past those points to expansion and wealth building.

Here Is The Definition Of Goal Points

THE BREAK EVEN POINT — This is when the business is generating enough income from sales to pay all of its costs of doing business, plus enough salary to the owner so he can continue to run the business without dipping into his savings or other sources of income to maintain a modest standard of living. As a rule, this is only a matter of months in well planned and managed small businesses, but in some cases, such as manufacturing and marketing a new product, it can take two or three years.

THE SURVIVAL POINT — This is where the business is not only covering all the costs of doing business, including a salary for the owners that maintains a respectable standard of living, but also gives the owners an acceptable return on investment. This usually takes a year or more, and it is a point at which 95% of all small businesses stop growing.

THE EXPANSION POINT—This is the point where the business is showing a gross sales increase (with comensurate profits) of 20% a year or more, and can command the borrowing capacity to carry on a sustained expansion of marketing either to new geographical areas (branch stores or offices), or to expand with new lines of products or services in the present market. This is the point where the entrepreneur starts managing his managers, rather than managing the business.

THE WEALTH BUILDING POINT—This is the point where the expanding company either goes public with a stock issue, or is merged with a larger company, and the entrepreneurs turn their interests into marketable stock that would be worth seven or more figures if converted into cash.

In making a realistic business plan there is no precise way to create a time table for reaching these goal points, but in the case of the first two, the entrepreneur has a built-in time limit—and that is how long he can survive without having the business provide enough personal income to maintain his standard of living.

In writing the business plan it is important for the entrepreneur to examine his assets and judge his staying power in terms of how long it will take for the business to provide him the personal cash flow he or she needs to keep food on the table and a roof over the head.

Your first and most immediate concern in planning is time. You must reach the survival point before your personal resources are exhausted. It is exactly like starting across a desert with a limited supply of food and water. The food and water, if properly managed will last ten days. If you can't reach a water hole by the tenth day, you are in trouble. You will start to founder on the 11th day and probably die on the twelfth. The food and water represent your available personal capital to keep going while the business develops into a necessary source of income. So, planning to reach breakeven, where you don't have to put any more money in the business, and can actually take some out is the first step to your survival plan. Then, the time it will take for the business to start paying you a salary that reflects your worth, and give a return on investment is more a matter of how long you want to sacrifice with a lower standard of living to keep the business going. There is no mathematical formula for making a precise estimate of this time, but the planner needs not only to determine the time the business will take to reach these points, but also his position in being able to stay with it until it does.

Some Reasons Why Small Business Fail Fast

Why They Fail in 90 Days or Less:

- The entrepreneur gambled on a bad idea without first determining who would buy what he was selling.
- The founder went in on a shoestring without a proveable plan for a fast buildup of cash flow to support lack of initial capital investment.
- The founders knifed and forked up the business capital. Instead of using the capital to generate sales—it was used for personal draws, expensive trappings and prestige transportation, etc.
- The failure of a promise to materialize, more capital from another source—a license for an exclusive product, a piece of equipment, or credit—whatever. A business was started on a promise, not a contract.
- Chaos from founder indecision—changes of direction or putting off decisions and resulting chaos.

It is not too dificult for a new retailer of known products or services. Location is the key—if there is a large enough population in a three to five mile radius and not too much competition, then the concept is a definite go.

But, if you are going to market a new product, or a new service, you've got to make a market survey to determine the demand, if any, and the potential market share.

If you want to know how to do market research on your own, there is a book that will give you the necessary information. It is titled, **Do-It-Yourself Market Research,** published by McGraw Hill, written by George Edward Breen. You can probably order a copy through your local library, (the inter-library loan service), or a copy for yourself through your local book store.

It is important to do a feasibility study of some kind to be sure you are on solid ground.

Thinking About Business Goals

Below you will find your goal planner. You will note that there are two spaces under each goal point. One for your estimated time, and one for the absolute time for Break Even and Survival. You will want to give some serious thought to both estimates. In most cases your estimate time is going to be too optimistic because things never go as planned — there are always setbacks you can't foresee. The absolute time based on how much personal capital you have to sustain your living standard without a guaranteed paycheck. The business will contribute some income, and should increase month-to-month, but to be on the safe side you should have at least six months of living out of your personal funds without taking a dime out of the business. If this is a problem, then you should plan to organize the business as a part time venture, keeping your present source of income until break even is reached.

The second two goals are strictly long range goals, and are not important other than setting a future timetable. In most small business ventures, these would be ten or more years in the future.

Your Business Goals

1. To Reach The Break Even Point — The time the business no longer requires additional personal capital. It is paying its own way and providing a living wage for the entrepreneur.

Estimated Time____

Absolute Time____

2. To Reach The Survival Point — The time when the business is in a position to pay the entrepreneur a chosen (within reason) standard of living wage — and provide a return on investment of at least the average in the industry. In short, the place where the entrepreneur is willing to continue the business or can sell it for a profit.

Estimated Time____

Absolute Time____

3. To Reach The Expansion Point—Where the business is producing sufficient profits in an expanding market which will allow it to expand market share by increasing market coverage, introducing new products or increasing store or production capacity.

Long Range Goal________________________________

4. The Wealth Building Point—Where a public stock offering is made, or the business merged with another business resulting in the entrepreneur's interest being converted to cash or stock in seven or more figures.

Long Range Goal________________________________

Note! If you are writing a plan to sell, give the estimated average time for reaching the first two goals, and indicate the option to the plan buyer of setting his own goals for the last two.

Section IV
Choosing Your Business Name

Choosing a business name can be important, or unimportant depending on the kind of business you are going to enter. For example, a publishing company is usually named for the principals. McGraw Hill, Scribner, Harper Row, etc. When they produce a best seller no one knows or cares who they are. Few people know who published "Gone With The Wind," or "Jaws." A company that markets products can pick just about any name they wish. Their problem is finding names for the product.

The entrepreneur starting a new venture in most lines of business should give serious thought to picking a name that will generate public recognition of what the company does. Just as the cigar store wooden Indian of past years was a symbol that gave instant recognition to the business the store was in—or the barber pole was instant recognition of that service. While it is true that some of the best known business firms in America are named after people — Macy, Sears, Wards, Hewlitt-Packard, Ford, McDonalds — if they were new, small businesses today no one would know what business they were in. Imagine if you were coming from another country and saw the name Sears—it would mean nothing. When you start a new business you have to remember there are 230 million people who never heard of your business.

If you decide to use a family name you should consider the problems of educating the public as to what business you are in when they see your name. As an example, if you came from another country and wanted to buy a hamburger and you looked in the phone book and found names like Wendy's, McDonald's, Jack-In-The-Box, and saw Burger King, you would know from the names only one for sure had anything to do with hamburgers. If you consider that your name is going to be displayed many places, on the outside of envelopes, on letterheads, lisings in phone books and other directories, you have many places to tell people what business you are in. So, if you list Ford Motor Company, Macy's Department Store, Getty Oil Company, Smith Brothers Cough Drops, Kraft Candy Co., etc., you are getting information across as to what you have to sell. This is no small matter for a new company. The market is large, you have tremendous competition for attention and anything that you do that causes confusion in the minds of your potential customers costs you business. Your business name should identify your product or service.

Generic Names

The generic name is often used by business firms. Greyhound, Royal, K-Mart, Jack-In-The-Box, Catapillar, etc. In and of themselves they have no meaning to a potential buyer. As in the use of your family name, you should use the product or service name as well. Greyhound Bus Co., Royal Office Machines, Jack-In-The-Box Restaurants, Catapillar Tractor Co., United Airlines, Home Savings and Loan, etc. The generic name also has another consideration. The uses of animal life names can cause problems if you intend to export products. In some cultures these names may be offensive to the people for various reasons. The best use of generic names is an allegorical use. That is, Greyhound runs fast for a bus company. The catapillar can crawl over anything for a tractor. Lightning Express is the name for a truck company.

The Initials For A Name

We have all heard of IBM, ITT, RCA, 3M, TRW, ABC and the

like. These are current favorites of large corporations who have many different businesses, or in some cases are simply the initials of their original titles. It may be a great idea for them, but it is a lousy idea for the small business entrepreneur for a couple of reasons. First, the initials don't tell prospective customers what business you are in, and secondly, they are hard to remember or keep straight. When you become a conglomerate you can change to initials, but until then best to forget it.

Contrived Names Can Be Useful

The contrived name can be a good choice. It gives you a unique name, hopefully one that will be easy to remember and can be trademarked easily. Manpower, Burger King, Pizza Haven, Computerland, U-Haul, Newsweek, etc., all indicate what is being sold. On the other hand contrived names can also mean nothing in terms of what they represent. Exxon, K-Tel, Safeway, Xerox, Tron-co, etc. They may mean something now because they represent large companies who have spent billions educating the public, but for the small business man the best contrived name will be one that names the product or service.

It is important to go about choosing a name not for your own ego satisfaction, but to sell more goods or services. Every advantage you can get at the start is a plus, and means you won't have to waste capital in education of your prospects.

Geographical Names

This is another favorite of many businesses, and is a particular favorite of retailers. Examples are the Seattle Furniture Store, The Southwestern Savings and Loan, The Miami Printing Co., Eastern Airlines, Denver Department Store, etc. The idea is to give your business some instant status by tying it to the name of a city, county or region.

Your Choices

In general terms then you have five choices of a business name.

1. Your Family Name.
2. Industry or Product Name.
3. Geographical Name.
4. Generic Name.
5. Contrived Name.

Here are the points you want to consider in choosing the name.

1. It tells people what I have to sell.
2. It is easy to pronounce.
3. It is easy to remember.
4. It is not offensive to anyone.
5. It is legal for me to use it.
6. It will wear well.

I want to touch on the sixth point, wearing well. Too many new entrepreneurs spend a lot of time working up cutsie-pie names that they think will tickle people. For example, Pee Wee Town, a childrens shop; Toys R Us, a toy franchise; Frans Fantastics, a dress shop; Neato, a diner. These names tend to cheapen the image of a business and seldom attract any attention. While Toys R Us has been a succesful franchise, I would say it is in spite of the name. You want a name that will stand the test of time, wear well in the community and can be something you won't find yourself becoming ashamed of.

Take some time in choosing your name, and look through phone book yellow pages for ideas — make some lists and pick the one you like best.

Choosing Your Business Name

You have five general types of name from which to choose:

1. Family Name — Jones Company.

____

____

2. Family and Industry or Product Name — Jones Shoe Store or Kaiser Steel.

____

____

3. Geographical Name — Los Angeles Golf Shoe Co., Miami Appliance Co.

____

____

4. Contrived Name — Shoeland, Kwickfix Appliance Service

____

____

If you are writing a for sale plan — check yellow pages for suggested names in various categories in the type of business you are developing the plan for — this will give the plan buyer some immediate choices without doing research.

Section V
The Choice Of Legal Structure For Your Business

When you start consideration of the structure of your business, you will have to make a decision as to the legal form of ownership. You have three choices — the sole proprietorship, the partnership or the corporation. Each has advantages and disadvantages.

To some extent your choice may be dictated by your needs in organizing the business. If you need outside funds, and perhaps extra help in managing it, then you should consider a partnership or corporation. If you can supply your own funds, and supply all the managment skills, then you will be better off to go it alone.

You will read in some books that a corporation will protect your present assets by limiting your liability for the debts of the corporation. In a small business this won't work. All lenders and suppliers who extend credit to small business corporations without a strong credit rating will require the owners to take personal liability for all corporate debts, so the corporation will not provide the protection.

In almost every case a small business should start either as a sole proprietorship or partnership in the formative and initial stages of development. The only real advantage a corporation would provide a new venture is some tax sheltering of income. If this need appears, a corporation can always be formed when needed.

However, if you need to raise capital to fund the business start-up, The Sub-Chapter S corporation is an ideal business format on which to raise funds.

The Sole Proprietorship

This format requires no special forms or agreements, other than those required by local licensing authorities. You get into business at once. You march to the beat of your own drum. You make all the decisions and have total control over business operations. All the profits are yours and you can move at your own speed.

The Advantages Are:

- Ease of getting started.
- Total control over the business.
- No sharing of the financial returns.
- Ease of changing course — expanding or closing up.
- Ability to take in a partner or incorporate later if you wish.

But, there are also disadvantages. You are alone, risking most or everything of what you now have, and if you should become ill or have an accident — the business could suffer or fail.

The Disadvantages Are:

- Everything you have is at risk.
- Illness or accident can wreck the business.
- Death can be a disaster for the family.
- There are few options for tax shelters.
- Credit line restricted to your net worth.
- The pressure on you is constant — no management help.

Except in cases of partnerships formed to provide more working capital, or in professional practices, the sole proprietorship is the best format for the new, small business.

The Partnership

This is a legal entity formed by one or more persons who operate the business in a general partnership as co-owners. The partnership pays no income of the partnership and distribution of profits to the partners, and the partners pay their own taxes.

The Advantages of Partnerships:

- More capital can be invested in the business.
- Responsiblities and work can be shared.
- More partners can be taken in without changing business format.
- The Uniform Partnership Act gives partners protection in disputes.
- More credit can be obtained.
- A larger volume of business can be managed without additional help or wage costs.

The Disadvantage Are:

- All partners in a general partnership are liable for the acts of all other partners.
- There is always an unequal contribution to profits that creates dissention among partners.
- Death or dispute can dissolve the partnership.
- One partner can force dissolution.
- Management by committee is difficult and often unsuccessful.

In real life, partnerships are a hard way to go in non-professional operations. Personality conflicts crop up in many areas of business operations, and after a time, partners are operating under strained relationships. Partnerships in professional fields can work because each member is primarily doing business with his own clients, and shares out are generally pro-rata to income in. What you have primarily is a sharing of expenses and not of income. But, in other businesses. (Selling businesses such as manufacturers reps and brokers excepted.) The income comes from a common pot. It is a rare situation where each of the partners considers they have made equal contributions to the profit they will share. Then there is always the problem with working hours and time off. One partner may be a married person and require weekends off with the spouse or children, the other may be put in the position of working longer hours and at inconvenient times. Another problem is that where duties are divided up and each partner is responsible for his own department or function—problems will occur when any action is taken by other partners that seem to infringe on that area. This is human nature, and nothing anyone can do will change it.

Choose A Partner With Care

Remember when you are thinking about taking in a partner that it's a good deal like getting married. You are going into a close relationship with another person and the financial welfare of both of you is at stake. There will be many pressures on both of you. The first test is to sit down together and make up your partnership agreement. You can use the outline at the end of this section. If you get into hassles over the agreement, you are going to be in trouble in the enterprise very quickly. The second test is to see if your partner can get along with your spouse. Not that you will be doing all that much socializing, but you really don't need to go home at night and hear what a no good bum your partner is.

The best answer is to write out the agreement so that the partnership can be dissolved without closing up the business. Make it possible for either partner to buy the other one out in some reasonable manner, and the decision of who goes and who stays is decided automatically when the time comes. It can be a cut of the cards, a flip of the coin, or which one makes the best offer to the other.

The Corporation

This business format is something the new entrepreneur should stay away from until the business has reached the survival point. It is a complicated procedure, you can look at the check list in the back of this section and see how many decisions you will have to make on a subject you know nothing about.

In addition, the corporate format creates an incredible amount of paperwork. You have federal forms, state forms, county and city forms to file at regular intervals. You have to hold meetings, keep minutes of those meetings, maintain a complicated set of books, and pay higher fees and taxes in most states. Since a new venture is seldom a tax problem in its first year or two, the tax advantages of a corporation are of no value, and the expenses of maintaining it can be a problem. A corporate format for a sole proprietor is seldom anything more than a status symbol.

The Special Situation

There are some start-up situations that call for the corporate format. If you have to raise capital, particularly seed capital, to get started — the Sub-Chapter S and Rule 1244 corporation are needed. Briefly, these two choices of corporate formation allow the seed capital investors to choose to take losses by the company as personal income losses to them, and to be deducted from their personal income. And in a later year, they can choose to have the corporation be taxed as a corporation, and pass through dividends to them, or sell their stock and pay capital gains taxes. It is the corporate format designed to help the entrepreneur raise capital for new ventures.

The second situation is when you are in a business where you risk large damage suits. For instance, some examples are serving or selling food or drugs, a new product that could bring class action damage suits that would overwhelm your insurance. A corporate shield for your personal assets is good planning. While you will have insurance, if circumstances should cause judgments beyond your insurance protection, the corporate shield is your second line of defense.

The new, small business will not get any protection against debt with a corporation. Banks, major suppliers and others will require the corporate founders to take personal liability for debt until the corporation is sound enough financially to stand on its own.

One other point about corporations. If you are selling through agents in other states you can be required by that state to pay income taxes on all business you do in the state, or a percentage of your gross income for all sources. So, be very careful about incorporating until you have examined the full cost.

Take Great Care In Incorporating

The primary purpose of a corporation is to raise capital and protect the assets of the corporate owners through shielding them from liability for corporate debt, and through tax reductions and tax free benefits.

In order to make the corporate shield secure you will need to take some steps to make sure there is a legal shield established. This comes both in the manner in which the business is incorporated and how it is operated after incorporation.

You need good legal advice in both sequences. Any lawyer can run a set of incorporation papers through his word processing equipment and charge you $500 to a $1,000 for doing it—and leave you wide open for lawsuits and personal liability. You need a lawyer who knows corporation law, and can tell you exactly how to proceed to set up a valid corporate shield against personal liability.

You must follow his instructions to the letter, because if you fail to hold the necessary meetings, keep the minutes, file the necessary papers, and other procedures, another lawyer can sue you and prove your corporation was a sham, and you, and your stockholders are jointly and severally liable for corporate obligations.

You should also use the services of a qualified accountant to show you how to save money taxwise when you incorporate, and the best time to form the corporation.

Incorporation Decision

Below you will find the outline of decisions and steps you will have to take to form a corporation. It is important to remember you can do this after your business is operating, and do it more or less tax free. You will want to be clear in your mind as to the purposes of incorporation—what advantages you expect from it—and how you will use it. If you need the corporation to raise seed capital, then consider the Sub Chapter S corporation, as it has the structure to appeal to investors, and still provides the corporate shield.

The Corporation—Advantages:

( ) Limited personal liability of stockholders.
( ) Tax advantages in corporate incomes.
( ) Business life is perpetual.
( ) Free transfer of interests through stock sales.
( ) Corporation does not have to allow public trading of stock— it can be closely held.
( ) Can acquire and operate other businesses through sale or transfer of stock.

Disadvantages:

( ) Difficulty of initial formation.
( ) Expense of initial formation.
( ) Obtaining credit—getting loans difficult for new business unless owners personally guarantee them.
( ) High degree of regulation by state and federal agencies of corporate enterprise.

The corporation also offers the entrepreneur the vehicle with which to raise additional capital from a wide range of sources by selling stock—rather than borrowing or selling assets.

The Sub-Chapter S Corporation—Requirements

1. It cannot have more than 10 (15 in some cases) stockholders—all must consent to Sub-Chapter S declaration.
2. It can issue only one class of stock.
3. The stockholders must be indivuduals, estates and in some cases a voting trust.
4. It must be a domestic corporation with stockholders who are USA residents—and cannot have over 80% foreign income.
5. No more than 20% of its income may be from rents, royalties, interest, dividends—so called passive income.
6. It must be organized as a corporation before it can elect Sub-Chapter S status—using approriate IRS tax form.
7. What organization provisions should be included in the charter and bylaws.
8. Will it need to qualify as a foreign corporation doing business in other states—or to get rights to sell stock in other states.

Here Are The Steps To Incorporating:

1. Check availability of chosen name and reserve it.
2. Complete and execute pre-incorporation agreements.
3. Draft and file incorporation papers in chosen state.
4. Pay filing fee and organizational tax.
5. Hold first meeting to organize the corporation.
6. Get subscriptions to stock.
7. File the necessary papers.
   a. Who will be agent for corporation?
   b. Statement of paid in capital.

    c. Officers oath.
    d. Local city or county filing.
8. Draft the by-laws.
9. Make sure it is legal to issue securities without special authorization.
10. Get stock certificates—corporate seal—stock register and minute book.
11. Hold meeting to elect directors.
12. Authorize issuing stock certificates and accept the stock subscriptions.
13. Receive payments from investors.
14. Authorize setting up of corporate bank account with directors resolution authorizing deposit and withdrawal in the bank.
15. Set schedule for future meetings to meet legal requirements.

Incorporation Of A Venture

What you need to know before you file your papers:

1. What are the purposes of the corporation and what business activities will it engage in?
2. The proposed name of the corporation, and importance of a specific name to the business—if any—a search to determine the legal right to use that name.
3. Name of incorporators, addresses and details as to age and present occupations.
4. Functions of the incorporators in the business operations—if any—and compensation to be paid.
5. Capital investment of each participant—what they are investing, cash, property, equipment, patents, processes, trademarks, inventory, etc. How value of each is adjusted?

6. Estimates of corporate profits for first 5 years.
7. How profits are to be divided by incorporators?
8. Where will voting control rest?
9. Are any incorporators getting employment contracts with the corporation—and what are they?
10. The state where incorporation will take place.
11. The capitalization of the corporation:
    a. Shall common shares be par or no par?
    b. How many shares will be authorized and issued?
    c. Will there be preferred shares?
    d. Will bonds be issued—what type?
12. If preferred shares are to be issued—make these decisions:
    a. Face value?
    b. Shall they be redeemable?
    c. Shall they be convertible into common?
    d. What dividend rate is guaranteed?
    e. Will it be cumulative?
    f. Will a sinking fund be maintained for dividends?
    g. If dividends not paid do holders get voting rights?
13. For what considerations shall shares be issued?
14. Should shareholders have pre-emptive rights?
15. What kind of voting rights will be offered?
    a. Cumulative voting.
    b. Quorum provisions for voting.
    c. Special meeting provisions.
    d. Annual meeting provisions.

Essence Of A Partnership Agreement

Articles to be included.

Article I—

The name and purpose of the partnership. The location of the business operation.

Article II—

Duration of the partnership—Usual statement is that it will continue until dissolved under terms of the agreement.

Article III—

How capital is invested.

How much contributed by each partner?

What form investment takes—cash of other assets?

The firm will maintain a separate capital account for each partner.

The definition of what the partners consider to be capital contributions—and what are expenses?

There will be an annual audit of physical assets and cash and securities held by the firm—and individual capital accounts will be adjusted accordingly.

Article IV—

Devotion of time to the firm.

What amount of time each partner will contribute to the business.

All compensation received by the partners for sales and services for the firm will be accounted for.

The length and number of vacations the partners will take.

If either is incapacitated—how will he share in profits?

If a partner fails to give the time to the business that is required by this agreement—he will have to take the amount of compensation the other partners judge to be fair.

Article V—

Management.

Each partner shall have an equal voice in management—all management decision noted legated to each partner shall be decided by a majority of partners present at any meeting of partners of which all partners are aware of the time and place to be held.

Admission of new partners shall be only by affirmative vote of

a majority of all partners.
Decisions on expulsion of a partner shall only be by unanimous vote of all partners.
Decisions to call meetings may be made by any partner—but the management partner shall schedule the regular meetings.
All partners must be notified of meetings—time and place with reasonable time allowed to make necessary arrangements to attend.
A quorum shall be a majority of partners.
Day to day affairs directed by managing partner:
Carry out firm policies.
Hiring and firing of employees.
Control and training of employees.
Supervising records and office duties.
Handling or supervising collections and credit.
Scheduling and notifying of partner meetings.

Article VI—
Bank Accounts.
Open and maintain bank accounts by agreement of all partners—two or more signatures on checks as agreed on by partners.

Article VII—
Records And Accounts.
An adequate partnership accounting system to be used.
All books and records open to all partners at all times.
Separate income account maintained for all partners.
Setting of the fiscal year date.
An outside auditor or accountant shall be used as directed by the partners.

Article VIII—
Profits—Losses and Draws.
Each partner shall receive a semi-monthly draw as agreed by all partners.

Profits and losses shall be credited or debited to each partnership account each month.
All partners agree to not draw against their accounts if funds are not there—and to repay the partnership within 30 days for any excess draws—or repayment will be made from future profits and no draws can be made.
At the close of the fiscal year all profits will be distributed to all partners—less draws and borrowings of each partner.

Article IX—
Limitations of Partners.
No partner shall:
Borrow money in name of partnership without consent.
Assign, transfer, release or adjust any claims or debts due the partnership except on payment in full.
Make, execute or deliver: Any assignment for benefit of creditors—and bond, confession of judgment, guaranty, indemnity bond; surety bond or any contract to sell, lease or mortgage any part of partnership assets.
Make any purchase or expenditure—not related to business operations in excess of $50, without consent of all partners.
No partner shall engage in any other business or corporation other than passive investments not requiring business time.

Article X—
Purchase of Interests.
First option to buy interest goes to other partners.
Set rule for retirement of partners.
Set purchase plan in case of partner death or incapacity.
If other partners do not wish to purchase interest set rules for purchase by outside party—what are minimum acceptable qualifications of purchaser?
If no acceptable outside buyer can be found, the partnership is dissolved—set time limit for dissolution to be triggered.

Valuing the Partnership Interest:

Value shall be sum of any unpaid loans due, his capital account, any balance in his income account, a given percentage of the accounts receivable at withdrawal date, less any obligation owed the partnership by withdrawing partner.

Set terms of payment of interest by the firm—giving time allowed to pay, method of payment, and recourse in case default is made in payments.

The withdrawing partner is to be held harmless from all past and present obligations of the firm—except for discovered fraud or error on part of the withdrawing partner.

Remaining partners shall have the right to sell the withdrawing partner's interest to a third party at their discretion.

All files and records are to remain with firm.

The remaining partners shall have the right to use the present name of the firm if they wish—even though it may contain the name of the withdrawing partner.

The withdrawing partner or his representative shall have the right to examine the books until full payment is made.

Set rules for each partner on how interest is to be repaid (and to whom) in case of death or incapacity.

Article XI—

Continuation of the firm after dissolution.

When a partner withdraws according to the terms of the partnership agreement—the purchase partners shall continue operation of the firm till those interests are satisfied—or shall pay him full amount due if business is discontinued.

Article XII—

Expulsions—

Set the rules for expulsion from a partnership. They can be fraud, violation of agreement, or personal actions that seriously affect the operation of the business. Expulsion can occur upon unanimous vote of other partners.

The remaining partners are obligated to pay the full value of the expelled partners interest at the price and terms stipulated in Article X.

Article XIII—

Liquidation of Partnership.

All matters in process to be completed or completion assumed by one or more partners with consent of customers if such consent is necessary.

Assets shall first be sued to pay all debts, reserves for taxes, leases, etc., set up. Repayment to be made in the following order:

1. Repay any loans to partnership by partners.
2. Pay all balances in income accounts.
3. Pay all net balances in capital accounts.
4. Distribute petty cash or other cash.

Determine who will maintain necessary records as required by law.

Article XIV—

Admission of New Partners.

All partners must agree on admission of new partners.

What financial requirements are for the new partner.

Amount of cash to be invested—how much to be paid at once—can notes be issued for some part—how they are to be repaid, etc.?

New partners are to become parties to the partnership agreement and bound by its obligation.

COST OF BUSINESS FORMATION

Sole Proprietor	$
Making a Will	
Partnership	
Legal cost of Partnership Agreement	
Registering Agreement with county or state	
Making of partner Wills	
Other costs	
Incorporation	
Search to determine legality of name use	
Reserving name use with the state	
Legal fees for preparing incorporation papers	
Notary fees	
Copying costs of incorporation papers	
State license fees	
State tax on capitalization	
Other state fees or taxes	
Legal fees for preparation of corporation by-laws	
Other legal fees	
Costs to register as a foreign corporation in other states	
Costs of copying by-laws	
Cost of corporate seal	
Cost of printing stock certificates	
Fees for registering corporation with city or county	
Cost of a corporate agent	
Cost of a transfer agent	
Prepayment of taxes or fees	

Other expenses ____________________________

Total Expenses ____________________________

The Decision of business format is:

Section VI
Choosing the Right Business Location

In setting out to find a location for your business your plan should be to find the best possible location not only for the first year or two of business, but for the future as well. This is particularly true for businesses where the customer comes to you.

In many cases the new entrepreneur will find a location that has just what he needs in terms of space, outside parking and other amenities and will sign a long term lease. To his or her sorrow the location was in an area where rapid changes were taking place, and that great location became a disaster. Location is the key to success in businesses of many kinds, and careful evaluation of prospective locations is vital.

Two Types Of Locations

There are locations where you go to the customer to make sales. There are locations where the customer must come to you. There are different criteria for each type of location.

The seller of goods and services to the end user, the retail and service businesses, need locations where customers can find them, park their cars, move about in safety and not be subject to unusual traffic problems.

The seller of goods and services to consumers in their homes or places of business needs locations where he can safely store the goods he sells—or equipment he uses—and that is centrally located in the territory he intends to serve. His concerns are also with shipping and receiving goods—with ease of movement on streets and highways and adequate space to manufacture, store, assemble and otherwise handle goods or service work necessary.

In some cases there are businesses that have dual functions. A seller of some types of goods may also need a showroom where wholesale or retail customers can come to buy, but also needs a warehouse or plant as well. This location seeker has to find some of both advantages in a chosen location.

Picking The Territory

The first decision is the territorial decision. Is the area you have chosen to serve going to be able to support a business of the kind you propose? Will it have the stability and growth patterns your business needs to survive and grow? If you have done the feasibility study suggested earlier, you know that answer. If not, you have some questions to answer now.

1. What is the size of the area?
2. What is the dollar trading volume of the area?
3. Is the size and dollar volume growing or declining?
4. How is the purchasing power distributed?
5. Total retail trade—and trade by types of businesses.
6. The size and quality of existing businesses.
7. The size and quality of your direct competitors.
8. The projected growth or decline of the trading area.

You can get this information without trying to do the research yourself. First, try the Chamber of Commerce. Next, try the local newspapers and TV stations—the radio stations all have this kind of information as part of their sales pitch. Write your Congressman, your State Legislator asking for the information. Check with your local librarian, the public utilities, city, county and state governments. It's all there waiting for you.

One thing to be careful of in selecting your territory. Don't select it on the basis of it's where you live. It may be that a few miles up or down the road is a territory that will be growing rapidly, while your area may be suffering a decline. A few miles of daily travel may be the difference between success and failure.

Your primary interest in territory is present and future growth, and the nature and state of existing competition. One more business of the kind you plan in that territory may be one too many. You may have to drive out some competition, or go under yourself. It's best to find a territory that has the growth pattern to support your new venture as well as those already in business.

To give you a rule of thumb estimate of the potential of a territory, here is a chart with national averages of the number of inhabitants it takes to support one business. This is somewhat outdated, but most associations have this type of information. As an example 667 people can support a small grocery store, while it takes over 100,000 to support a bicycle shop. But, you must keep in mind that changes in lifestyles and in demand change these numbers dramatically. The chart you see here was developed before the boom in adult bike riding, so those figures would change accordingly.

[National Averages]

Kind of business	Number of inhabitants per store
Food stores	
Grocery stores, including delicatessens	667
Meat markets	7,266
Fish (seafood markets)	39,926
Fruit stores, vegetable markets	13,653
Candy, nut, confectionary stores	9,847
Dairy products stores	22,711
Bakery products stores	9,006
Eating, drinking places	
Eating places	754
Drinking places (alcoholic beverages)	1,057
General merchandise	
Department stores	54,875
Dry goods stores	19,630
Variety stores	8,243
Apparel, accessory stores	
Shoe stores	7,089
Women's clothing, specialty stores	3,882
Children's infants-wear stores	23,500
Furniture, home furnishings, appliance dealers	
Furniture, home furnishings stores	3,181
Household appliances, radio TV stores	4,227
Music stores, records and musical instruments	21,725
Automotive groups	
Passenger car dealers (franchised)	4,493
Automotive groups—Cont.	
Passenger car dealers (nonfranchised)	6,839
Tire, battery, accessory dealers	8,284
Aircraft, boat, motorcycle dealers	33,763
Household trailer dealers	56,411
Lumber, building materials, farm equipment dealers	
Farm equipment dealers	9,114
Lumber, building materials dealers	4,969
Paint, glass, wallpaper stores	15,530
Heating, plumbing, equipment dealers	26,392
Hardware stores	4,997
Drug stores, proprietory stores	
Drug stores	3,367
Proprietory stores	36,212
Other retail stores	
Fuel, ice dealers	6,066
Hay, grain, feed stores	10,323
Farm, garden supply stores	21,470
Jewelry stores	7,294
Book stores	60,048
Stationery stores	26,518
Sporting goods stores	17,620
Bicycle shops	100,720
Florists	9,034
Cigar stores, stands	32,466
News dealers, news stands	22,979
Gift, novelty, souvenir stores	12,386
Camera, photographic supply stores	49,624
Luggage, leather goods stores	122,344
Optical goods stores	58,330
Antique stores, secondhand stores	8,189

In general terms, if you find well established competition in an area where one more store would have far less than the number of needed residents to support it, you have good reason to look for another territory.

Finding The Specific Location

Since the retailing location is of key importance to the success of the business—we'll take up finding a store location first. The first thing you will have to determine is how much you can afford to pay for a location. There are figures called operating ratios which tell the entrepreneur what the average successful business in his chosen field allocates for rent. These are called operating ratios. You can obtain a list of them for most retail service and wholesale businesses from Dun & Bradstreet. Call their nearest office and ask for their list of operating and financial ratios from small businesses. They are usually sent free of charge. You can also obtain a more detailed book of ratios for all types of businesses from Robert Morris and Assoc., 1432 Philadelphia National Bank Bldg., Philadelphia, PA. 19107 (Phone 215-563-0267). Contact them for the current price.

When you find out the average amount of rent paid on gross business in the type of business you will be in; you can determine how much rent you can afford to pay. You estimate your gross business per year (over a 5 year period), and multiply the average sum by the proper percentage of rent.

For example, the average rent in retail trade runs between 3% and 6% of annual gross. If you project your annual gross volume over your first five years will be $200,000, then you should pay somewhere between $6,000 and $12,000 a year. This gives you a dollars and cents figure based on an informed guess as to what you should pay. It will save you a lot of time and trouble looking at properties you could not afford, and lets you focus on investigating those you can.

The Location Search

The first thing to do is survey your territory. One smart retailer I knew who made a handsome living starting womens dress shops and selling them as going businesses, always hired a helicopter to fly him around the territory during the best shopping hours, between 10 a.m. and 2 p.m. so he could see traffic flow on the streets, check the number of cars in shopping center parking lots, get an idea of which streets carried the traffic and could spot all the potential business locations in the area.

Next, cruise the area in a car. Look for possible locations with for rent signs. Talk to merchants in various locations about business in general. Get a feel for those locations with potential.

Then, contact real estate offices for any listings they have of potential locations. Watch for ads in the paper, and build a list of locations where you will want to do specific investigation and analysis.

The Location Area Evaluation

When you have found suitable locations, you will want to make an evaluation of the immediate area to determine the future prospects of that location.

- The power of your proposed store to attract business.
- The nature of the competition in the area.
- The traffic patterns coming into the area.
- Nature of zoning tendencies in the area.
- Direction of expansion.
- General appearance of the store.
- Number of independent stores.
- Number of stores pulling your type of customer within a block or two of your proposed location.
- Number of major or regional chain stores pulling traffic.
- The number on your side of the street.

- How difficult it will be for people to cross the street.
- Number of vacancies adjacent to your location.
- Foot traffic flow past your location.
- The availability of parking in the general area.
- The promotional tendencies of stores in the area.

To determine the power of your store to attract business you break retailing down into three types of goods—consumer or convenience goods, shopping goods and specialty goods. If you are going to open a drug store, a small hardware and variety store, a delicatessen, a bakery, liquor store, etc., then you sell convenience goods and you want locations with the highest possible foot traffic.

If you are going to be selling appliances, apparel, shoes, furniture, gourmet cookware, jewelry, books, etc., you will want to know how many shoppers pass your doors. Shoppers are those who are looking for specific kinds of goods and will visit more than one store as a rule. For example, if your store is located where you have heavy foot traffic from people going to and from work—convenience goods sell well—but shopping goods, not so well. The shopping goods retailer wants a location where people pass when they are on shopping trips, not on other business.

Specialty goods retailers can locate away from high traffic areas because they are selling goods that consumers want and will come and get. Franchised operations fall into this category, as do retailers selling specific kinds of services such as repair and parts for vacuum cleaners or applicances, etc.

Competition in your area can be a good thing. Two stores will draw more shoppers into an area, and if you can get your share of the business—you will do more business—particularly if you offer alternative lines and different services.

Traffic patterns are important. If you find your location is on a fast street, that is, traffic moves swiftly, then stopping and parking can be a problem, and getting across the street most difficult. If stop lights are timed to move traffic along at 30 miles per hour or more, you are going to have a real problem. Look for areas where traffic is slower, lots of parking and foot traffic of the kind you need.

Be sure and check zoning in the area. If you find that the character of zoning is changing, for example, single family dwellings into multiple unit housing, or light industrial is moving in the area, you are seeing changes of buying patterns beginning to form. Find an area that is stable and expansion is along the same lines as present zoning. Many times you will find that housing in the area is starting to deteriorate, and within a few years the character of the area will be entirely different. Also be careful to check out any planned major shopping centers coming in that can pull away most of the shopping trade.

Pay close attention to the present commercial activity in your location area, the numbers of stores within a few blocks who are pulling the kind of customer you need. How long they have been there and how well they are doing? Check the number of chain stores—major and minor—and how well they are doing. If there are vacancies other than your choice of location find out how long they have been vacant. What kind of store was in them? Pay particular attention to this. Did the stores go out of business or did they move? If they went out of business then the problem was probably in the operation of the business—but if a number of them moved to new locations—track them down and find out why. Move outs are an indicator of changing activity in an area.

Talk to present merchants in the area. Find out what is good and bad, and by all means get the opinion and cooperation of your proposed wholesale suppliers on location choices. They know which are best and which are not—they have a vested interest in your success—and will help in every way they can to see to it your location is the best possible business getter.

If you are selling shopping goods pay a lot of attention to parking—it's the life blood of store traffic. Make sure there is plenty of parking, not only for your location but for all locations in the area.

Making A Traffic Study

Make your own traffic study. First, study the foot traffic past the location. Count the number of people at the best shopping hours. Get a clipboard and ask every 10th person if they are on a shopping trip or on other business. If they are shopping, ask them if they ever shopped for whatever you intend to sell in the area. If they say no, ask them if you put a store in that location if they would shop for those items. That's all you really need to know.

It will tell you how many people passing the store location are potential customers, how many now shop the area for what you sell, and how many might shop in your store.

If you want to refine it a little you might also ask them how often they passed that point—in other words did they pass by several times a week or month—or was this an unusual trip that would not be repeated. This eliminates the person who would not be a potential foot traffic customer. Just be sure there was no special event in the area that day which pulled a lot of people past the door who would not normally be there.

When you tally your figures, you have a total count of per hour traffic past the door, you have the percentage who were shopping (possible customers), the number who had shopped for what you sell in the area, and the number who stated they would shop your store. While this is not exactly scientific, it does give you a point of reference in determining your best potential location.

To study automobile traffic, try and get on a roof where you can see up and down the street. I've done that by getting permission from a building owner to get on the roof by telling him I was a photographer and offering him pictures of his building. This gives you a better view of the street, and makes it easier to count cars. Check the number that park in the area, and check activity in other stores along the street. Check the number of passing cars—and the type of cars. If you are opening a dress shop with exclusive lines you want to see the upper-middle class vehicles on the street. If it's going to be an Army-Navy store you want pick-up trucks and older cars with young people in them. Get a percentage that stop, and drivers or passengers get out, compared to the number that pass. This gives you a value ratio per passing vehicle, and a way to estimate potential future business.

It is important that you do this if there is a difficult choice between locations. The results will probably give you a clear answer to your best choice. Don't take anyone's word for it—do it yourself.

The Rental Location Analysis Formula

When you have finished your research into possible locations you will have some specific information on which to base a decision. You can put that information into a mathematical formula and come up with a specific answer as to which is the best location.

You need to know:

1. The flat rental or guaranteed rental cost.
2. The percentage of gross charged to rent.
3. The costs of location preparation.
4. The estimated amount of business the locations will generate.
5. The selling square footage of rental space.

To show you how to use the formula let's assume you have narrowed your search down to two locations. One is 3,000 square feet with 2,500 sq. feet of selling space—the second is 3,500 square feet with 3,000 sq. ft. selling space. We will call them Unit 1 and Unit 2.

Unit 1 rents for $9,600 a year plus 2% of gross sales. Unit 2 rents for $12,000 a year flat rental. The costs of preparing the units (remodeling—lighting installation—signing, etc.) will be $8,000 for unit one and $4,000 for unit two. We shall assume a ten year lease on both units—and shall amortize the cost out over the full term of the lease for purposes of comparison.

From your traffic studies you estimate that Unit One will produce 60% of your gross business from walk-in trade and that Unit Two will pro-

duce 30% of your gross business. You assume by advertising and promotion you can do $200,000 a year in either unit.
Which is the best deal?

	Unit 1	Unit 2
Flat or guaranteed rental	$9,600	$12,000
Percentage of gross rental	4,000	—0—
Total Rental	13,600	12,000
Add amortized cost or prep.	800	400
Adjusted rental cost	14,400	12,400

Now we want to determine the annual per square foot cost of selling space in each unit. To do that we divide the selling space cost into total rental cost.

Unit One has 2,500 sq. ft. of selling space so we divide 2,500 into 14,400 and have $5.75 per sq. foot cost for our selling space. Unit Two has 3,000 sq. ft. of selling space at 12,400 annual rent or $4.13 per sq. ft. of cost for rent.

Next we estimate the percentage of business at 60% for Unit One — taking 60% as the contribution to gross business we have $120,000 that is generated by walk-in business from the location. To determine the net cost per square foot of selling space we will deduct 60% of 5.75 per square foot and come up with a allocated cost of $2.30 a year. For Unit Two we estimate it will generate 30% of our business for the year — so we deduct 30% from $4.13 and come up with $2.89 per square foot cost. We can also generate another comparison figure — Unit One will generate $48 per square foot of sales— Unit Two will generate $20 a year per square foot.

So your location analysis would prove that Unit One was the better location based on costs and income generated.

Here is the formula:

1. Add guaranteed rent, percentage rent and amortized costs of preparing the site.
2. Estimate the percentage of total business the location will produce.

3. Divide the square feet of selling space into the total rents for each unit. Get an annual cost per square foot.
4. Subtract the percentages of total business for each location from 100 — and multiply the results by the square footage costs of each unit.
5. The results give you adjusted costs per square foot.

Admittedly this is not a precise and scientific method of doing things — but you are interested in some kind of measure that represents educated guessing rather than letting yourself be talked into something without really making a comparison.

Since location is vital to a retailer, take your time, do the necessary looking around, talk to other people, get a feel for what is true and use the formula to help you make your decision.

Shopping Center Locations

To begin this section let me say that the average person who is starting in business for the first time should not start in a shopping center, unless it is some type of food specialty or novelty item, and a short term lease can be negotiated.

The hot shopping center will not lease to a new entrepreneur unless he has something very unique. The centers that will are either established, and are losing business — or are new and having problems renting. The hot center has a waiting list of well-established and experienced people. The problem for the newcomer is that he hasn't the merchandising experience to handle center volume. All his promotional eggs are in one basket — the lease is a huge burden — he will be operating out of cramped quarters and must carry exactly the right merchandise mix, or business disappears.

You must operate your business the hours and days the center is open — you must contribute to the promotional fund — you must maintain your store as the center dictates, and if business is bad there isn't much you can do about it.

The Types of Centers

The Strip Center...Is usually a neighborhood center with a large anchor store such as a supermarket — a K-Mart or other large store that pulls good traffic. The anchors are usually at one end — sometimes two ends of the center — and the smaller merchants located in strips of stores along the sides. This type of center usually serves an area of 10,000 to 20,000 people in a five mile radius — and is the best center for the newcomer.

The Community Center...This is the name of your town or community center. This will serve from 30,000 to 100,000 people in a radius of five to ten miles. Here you will usually find a large department store or two, some chain specialty stores, food and recreational facilities, etc. These centers take many configurations — some are enclosed malls — some are scattered in large parking areas — some are anchored by major stores at either end, with the smaller shops between. It is worth noting that there are some real dog locations in these centers — and you have to survey proposed locations carefully. These centers have lots of promotional activity — a manager who works full time on developing center traffic — and well-managed businesses prosper in them.

The Regional Center...This is the shopping center big leagues. This is where all the retailing heavyweights gather in one place — and suck in business from a fifty mile radius. Here are the multi-level malls — your miles of parking — your action everyday. You've got to be successful and loaded to get in here — and it's another center with some hideaway locations that you would lose your assets renting. The competition in these centers comes from the best in the business — the major chains — the local superstars and smart specialty goods people. Stay away from here 'til you know your business.

Finding an Office Location

Finding a suitable office location is a good deal less complicated than finding a retail location. There are two types of location — where the customer comes to your office — where you go to the customers.

Finding the Office Where the Customer Comes to You... Your choice should be based on the ambiance of the location and ease of customer access. The first step is to determine how much rent you can afford to pay. Since there is no foot traffic problem with an office — you have to pull all your customers in. There is no contribution to the business to consider. But, consider carefully the parking in the area, its cost and the type of tenants now in the building.

Rentals are quoted by the month or by annual square foot cost. To determine what you need go to a stationery store and get some graph paper and a template (made from plastic) of office furniture. Draw in an estimated square footage for an office, then, using the template, arrange your furnishings. This will give you a reasonable idea of how much space you need — and then based on the rent you can afford to pay, you can look for what you need. Your method of choice here is really one of personal preference based on your observations and what you can realistically afford.

Finding the Office Where You Go to the Customer... This is a choice which can be more complicated than it might seem. There are some hidden costs involved in this location evaluation you should consider.

The key points of a selection here are:

1. Your access to the market.
2. Employee access to the location.
3. Security of the location.
4. Cost of the location.
5. Travel costs to and from the location.
6. Time costs.

The usual choice for the office or facility where you go to the customer is the industrial park. These are designed to provide the necessary parking — buildings are zoned light industrial — shipping and receiving is planned for — security is usually better than in solo locations.

Costs of preparing these locations can be considerable if you need offices, warehouse space and location of equipment, etc. Utility and telephone costs are also to be considered. Check phone rates; you could be in a zone where most of your calls to your customers would be toll calls. Also check traffic flows at peak periods to see if it is badly snarled. This situation often gets worse rather than better. Make sure the location is not such that employees you might need will find it too far to consider as a job location.

The checklist on the following pages will give you a guide to the costs of preparing your unit for business. It is best to get prices from several sources for any of the work needed to be done.

Get advice from your wholesaler and fixture supplier — but don't take any of it until you have checked it out with other sources. Make your own decisions, but keep an open mind on anything they suggest even if it seems to cost more that you think you can afford.

Estimated Cost of Preparation of Unit . . . . $________
Total Costs of Rental and Preparation . . . . $________

Comparative Cost Evaluation

There is a system for estimating the true costs of office locations where you must go out to get business. You need the following information:

1. Total square feet rented.
2. Annual rent.
3. Average utility cost.
4. Telephone and communications costs.
5. Estimate mileage to and from per day.
6. Time per mile expended.

Let's take an example of two units both 5000 sq. ft., Unit One at

$6.00 annual per sq. ft.—Unit Two at $4.00 per sq. ft. Utility costs for #1, $3600—for #2, $2400. Estimated mileage per day: Unit One 20 miles per working day, Unit Two is 40 miles.

Comparative costs:

UNIT ONE		UNIT TWO	
Rent	$30,000	Rent	$20,000
Utilities	3,600	Utilities	2,400
Preparation Costs	5,000	Preparation Costs	1,500
Mileage Costs Per Vehicle	1,500	Mileage Costs	4,500
Time Costs	6,250	Time Costs	18,750
TOTAL	$46,350	TOTAL	$47,150

Use this analysis system and you get some interesting answers. If you were analyzing locations and considered only rent, utilities and preparations costs Unit Two would be far and away the best choice. But you add two things: cost of mileage to reach your customers, and the time it takes.

In the case of Unit One average mileage to and from the territory, is 20 miles. In the case of Unit Two, it is 60 miles. If you take 30 cents a mile as the cost of driving—and 250 days as the number of days you drive—mileage costs per vehicle are three times as high for Unit Two. But, the heavy cost is time. If you figure time at $25 an hour, with 20 miles an hour driving time in the territory, your costs for Unit Two become higher than Unit One. Each representative can spend one to two hours more in the territory producing sales and business from units which could increase the difference even more.

Don't overlook the hidden costs in picking locations, often they can make a big difference in actual costs.

Negotiating Your Lease

There is a term in the real estate trade used for bad income property; it's called an "alligator." You don't want to become the tenant in an alligator, and often the terms of your lease are what makes it an alligator for you. Any time you are taking on a long term lease — use a lawyer who is willing to help you get a better deal, one who is willing to contact the landlord or his agent and get some terms and conditions changed on your behalf. Almost all leases you are offered are standard — with all the clauses put in to give the landlord all the advantage. Never sign one of these leases — always try to make them give up something, do something, etc. because in most cases they will if you work through a lawyer.

When the attorney looks over the lease there are some points you will want to discuss with him:

1. An absolute definition of what constitutes gross sales and receipts. (See summary.)
2. The diligent operation clause. The landlord with a percentage lease will try and put in this clause — which makes him a partner in your business. Simply put, it means that you must keep all your business sales at his location and not divert them to other locations — that you will give full time to the business. Don't sign a lease with that clause in it.
3. If you are taking a long term lease you will want the right to sub-lease in case your business fails — or needs larger quarters. Get your attorney to put in the needed clauses, including the requirement the landlord's stating specifically the types of businesses he won't accept — all others being acceptable.
4. Some leases make the tenant liable for all repairs regardless of cause. Make sure your lease only requires you to repair that which you are responsible for damaging.
5. In some office buildings it is the policy to charge the tenants rent for use of hallways, rest rooms, walkways, etc., that are adjacent to their units. Don't pay it — pay for the space you occupy — nothing else. Offer at the quoted rate per sq. ft. on the size of your unit.

Get the best deal you can — never accept and sign a lease until you have read it — let your lawyer read it — attempt to get the changes you want — and negotiated over the terms. You don't know how desperate the owners are, and how much they might give up to get the space rented. Always assume you are going to make changes in any lease offered to you — you won't always get them — but you will more often than you might think.

Finding a Business Location

Picking Your Territory:

1. The population trends in the area.
2. The size of the trading area.
3. Total purchasing power and its distribution.
4. Total trade in your line of business.
5. Number, size and quality of direct competition.

This information can be obtained from the following sources:

1. The U.S. Dept. of Commerce Census of Population.
2. The U.S. Dept. of Commerce County Business Patterns.
3. The U.S. Dept. of Commerce Census of Manufacturers — Wholesale Trade Area Statistics — Retail Trade Area Statistics — Selected Service Industry Area Statistics.

You can find out growth or decline patterns in the territory from these sources:

1. Chamber of Commerce trade statistics.
2. Bank clearings from Fed Reserve Board.
3. Utility hookups for residential and commercial use.
4. School enrollments.
5. Building permits.

Picking an area in your territory:

1. Number of potential customers in the area.
2. Purchasing power of these customers.
3. Growth or decline in business activity.
4. Business climate from government tax and regulatory considerations.
5. Number of direct competitors within the area.

6. Any future plans that would change business patterns in the area.

This information can be found from these sources:

1. Potential customers — U.S. Dept. of Commerce Census of Population and Housing.
2. Same source as number one.
3. Chamber of Commerce and bank statistics for growth.
4. Business Climate — checking licenses, regulation and talking to other small business owners — pay attention to voting trends for future estimates.
5. U.S. Dept. of Commerce General Statistics by Industry for Standard Metropolitan Statistical Areas will locate number and type of competitors. Also a check of the latest yellow pages phone book.
6. Check with government agencies and Chamber of Commerce concerning possible building of shopping centers or other projects that would radically change business conditions.

Picking a Specific Location:

Retail:

1. Determine what you can pay for rent by projecting annual volume and take average for industry percentage of sales operating ratio.
2. The number of independent stores in the area.
3. The number of direct competitors in the area.
4. Number of major chain stores in the area that will pull traffic that would buy from you.
5. Number on your side of the street in walking distance.
6. Number of vacancies around your proposed site.
7. Traffic flow past your location — type and quantity (write the Small Business Administration Office in your area and get a copy of Small Marketers Aid # 152 "Using a Traffic Study to Select a Retail Site").
8. Location problems that could affect business.

9. A specific study of the store site using the checklist at the end of this chapter.
10. The history of the site — check with former tenants and other merchants in the area.
11. Check promotional activities of other stores in area.

Shopping Center Locations:

1. Strip Centers.
2. Community Centers.
3. Regional Centers.

Finding an Office Location:

1. Access to the people or firms you will be serving.
2. The physical layout that suits your needs.
3. Plan your needs on paper.
4. Find your square footage and estimate rent you can pay.
5. Check with present tenants about management of building.
6. Check with management on policy of who they rent to.

Locations Where You Go to Customer:

1. Centrally located in your market area.
2. Security is good.
3. No problem with labor turnover in location.
4. Check utility and other costs not included in rent.

Negotiating the Lease

Use a lawyer to try and get some breaks from the lessor. Here are the types of leases:

1. Flat rental.
2. Step-up lease — rents tied to Cost of Living Index.
3. Escalator — this ties additional payments to a flat rental payment to cover increases in taxes — insurance, etc..
4. Re-evaluation lease — allows landlord to reappraise property from time to time and set new rates.
5. Percentage lease — commonly used in retail rentals — a minimum rental paid plus a percentage of gross business done. These come in two types — fixed rent plus percentage and fixed rent and percentage — but percentage does not

add on until base rent percentage is covered.

6. Straight percentage lease with no minimum rate.
7. Minimum rent with a percentage — but a maximum rent is also included. Your lawyer should also have this put in a percentage lease.

Here are the things to watch for in leases and make sure they don't come as surprises:

1. What constitutes gross sales or receipts? For example, sales taxes can't be counted — or sales of assets or sales of a sub-lessor or concessionaire, etc.
2. How will gross sales be tallied? Usual store method is by cash register tape.
3. Watch for the so-called diligent operation clause.
4. The landlord disclaimer clause.
5. What form and how will advance deposits be handled?
6. Under what terms are deposits returned or forfeited?
7. The right to sub-lease property.
8. Define reasonable consent by landlord to sub-leasing.
9. Default protection if a tenant is ready to move in.
10. The right to use adjacent facilities.
11. Non-competitive rental clause — won't rent to a direct competitor in same complex.
12. Who makes alterations?
13. Who makes repairs?
14. Rental space and useable space — pay for space used not corridors and sidewalks.
15. Who pays utilities — how are rates fixed?
16. Who pays for maintenance — parking, etc.?

LOCATION ANALYZER

Location Address ______________________________

Flat Rate Rental — Per Year . . . . $______

Percentage of Gross Added to Rent . . . . ______

Estimated Additional Rent on Percentage . . . . $______

Additional Costs . . . . $______

Square Foot of Rental . . . . ______

Annual Cost Per Square Foot . . . . $______

Percentage of Business Volume
Contributed by Location . . . . ______

Net Cost Per Square Foot . . . . $______

LOCATION COST ESTIMATOR

This is your cost estimating form — you will find an office checklist to estimate costs of preparing the location for occupancy.

Cost Sheet

Cost of Rental (Flat Rent) . . . . $______

Security Deposit . . . . $______

Advance Rent Deposit . . . . $______

Legal Cost for Lease Negotiation . . . . $______

Advance Utility Deposits . . . . $______

Estimated % of Sales Rental Cost First Month . . . . $______

Other Costs . . . . $______

Section VII
Getting the Licenses and Permits

Since the days of Rome the bureaucrats have been sticking it to the merchants. Operating on the "deep pocket" principle, stick it to those who have money, but no political clout. The fees and permits for operating businesses have been prime targets for the raising of funds.

The fee or permit payments you must make to start a business do not put one dollar in your pocket, nor provide you with any benefit over and above what you are entitled to as an individual taxpayer.

For that reason, it will pay the entrepreneur to do some shopping around concerning the need for various licenses and permits, and the cost of same. The bureaucrats who issue these are only interested in how much money they can extract from you — and will always quote the maximum rate if you ask them. You will find in most cases the clerk manning the desk that takes the money has no idea of what the right permit or fee should be. They will not offer you any choices, and unless you ask for specific licenses and permits, you'll get and pay for the ones that cost the most.

Local Business Licenses

In almost every community the city fathers or county commissioners sell business licenses and permits as a fund raising venture. These are always raised first when the need for more funds arises, and in some cases new types of permits invented to get even more.

The first step is to get a list of their fees — what they charge for different types of businesses and professions, and then pick the type that costs the least.

For example, I was going to sell carbon paper in a large city. The license for a sales agency was $250 a year. The license for a peddler was $10 a year. I had a friend who ran a five million dollar a year business in the same city on a $10 peddler's license. The point is not to be a sucker and pay for a high cost license if you can get by on a cheaper one. In most cases, the bureaucrats have no idea of what you are doing, all they need to know is that you have a business license. If they find out you have the wrong license you can always tell them that's what the clerk said you should have, and then get the higher priced one if they insist.

If you are not running a store you can probably operate without a license in most large cities until the business produces the cash flow to pay for the proper license.

The key is to get the list of their fees before you apply for the license, and apply for the one you picked and don't discuss the reasons with the clerk. If it's a peddler's license say you are going to be peddling something door-to-door or office-to-office.

Shop Your Territory

Another thing to do is to check out the permit and license fees in different areas or jurisdictions. In some places, you have to buy a license in an incorporated city, but no license in the county. So, if you can find a location in the county, you'll be better off. This may not be possible for a retail location, but if you are going to have an office or warehouse — then your location is not important from the standpoint of having customers come to you. This territory shopping is very important for high gross volume businesses where the city charges a percentage of gross volume as part of the license to do business. Often the permit will only be a few dollars, but you've taken in a partner who shares in your gross business from then on.

So, get a list of the costs of licenses and permits — how many you are required to have — and pick out those that cost the least and apply for them specifically.

The Fictitious Firm Name

Some states require that a business doing business in a name other than that of the owner must fill out a fictitious firm name application, and have it published in a newspaper of record for a period of issues or weeks. This establishes a record of who the owners of the business are, their addresses, etc. to allow other businesses, credit agencies and financial institutions time to check out the new owners.

There are firms, or attorneys who handle this chore, and most papers qualified to publish legal ads have the necessary form. In metropolitan areas this filing and advertising can cost several hundred dollars if done by an agency or lawyer. However, if you check around in the county, you can find small, weekly papers who are legally entitled to publish these ads, and will run them for you for half or less of what city papers or legal papers charge.

If you use your own name as the title of the business, then you can eliminate this step. If you start a business without filing, you may not be able to open a bank account or sue on debts owed you, etc.

In some states, it is required that you renew publication of this fictitious firm name periodically. If you fail to do it, someone else can legally steal your business name, and you can no longer use it. That is another scam pushed through by newspaper publishers to suck money out of the pockets of small business, along with the bureaucrats. Be sure to make a note of when this refiling must be done so you won't forget. There is a great little racket in picking off the business names of owners who forget to refile, and selling them back for a nice ransom.

State Licenses

Many skills and professions are licensed by states. This ranges from doctors, lawyers and CPA's to beauticians, contractors, insurance and real estate brokers and salesmen, collection agents, etc.

In these situations the state may require the applicant:

- Pass an examination.
- Furnish a bond or other security.
- Meet certain pre-requisites of experience or training without a test.
- Furnish proof of good moral character.
- File information on background and business methods of the founders — such as in franchise selling.
- Furnish proof of financial responsibility.
- Meet other qualifications.

These licenses are issued for a specified period of time (usually annually), and subject to cancellation for various breaches of conduct.

In cases where alcoholic beverages are sold, or dealers in automobiles, cash registers, tobacco products, fireworks, etc., you also have to get state licenses. Be sure and check these out as failure to get them can bring on stiff fines or closure of your business.

Sales Tax Permits

In all but a few states the seller of goods has to have a sales tax permit to sell to end users or a permit that allows him to exempt his sales from taxes in the case of wholesalers and those selling tax exempt items.

There is usually no charge or a small fee for the permit, and in some cases an advance deposit against future collection of taxes.

You remit your collected taxes to the state — usually on a quarterly basis.

You want to get this permit as soon as you start making purchases for your business. Wholesalers will not sell to you as a rule without a resale license number, or will charge you sales tax.

The Pre-deposit

Some states will require you to make an advance deposit on future sales when you apply for a permit. This is a legal scam to grab money from new businesses, to put the state in the position of eating their cake and having it too.

The best way to handle this problem is to tell the state you are going to be running a little hand-to-mouth business which will only do a few hundred dollars in business. This way you get the permit without a deposit.

One tip, in getting this permit don't walk in wearing a $1000 suit and Gucci loafers, go in wearing old clothes and look like you just came off the bread line. Remember, you are playing a game with these bureaucrats to conserve your start-up capital. Keep your seed capital out of the hands of the tax eaters as long as you can.

Federal Permits

If you are going to have employees, you will have to apply for your employer identification number from the IRS. There is no charge, and it puts you on the feds' list as an employer. They will send you quarterly forms to fill out listing your employees, how much you paid them, how much you withheld for income tax, and for social security, and then you will have to deposit the withheld funds, plus your own contributions through your bank.

It is best to have your bookkeeper or accountant handle the filling out of these forms and the filing of them with the feds, and the state on the proper due dates.

Other Federal Permits

In some lines of business, handling alcohol, firearms, bowling alleys, billiard rooms, oleo margarine and certain types of butter and cheese, coin-operated amusement or gaming devices on your premises and bookmaking, require a federal occupational tax or license. These are issued by the Internal Revenue Service.

The producers of crude petroleum, tobacco dealers and sellers, manufacturing certain types of matches, importers of gasoline and lubricating oils, theatre operators, and other places of entertainment, manufacturers of playing cards and those in the business of hauling freight or moving property for hire including freight forwarders and express companies, require special federal licensing.

Dealers in animal and animal products in interstate commerce need federal licenses, as do some dealers in agricultural products.

Makers of drugs, and allied products need licenses from the Public Health Service.

Postal Permits

If you wish to take advantage of certain post office services such as bulk mail, business reply postage, pre-sort first class postage rates, using pre-cancelled stamps, etc., you will have to obtain a permit for which there is an annual fee in most cases. These can be obtained at your local post office.

Foreign Trade

Importers and exporters have to obtain a variety of licenses and permits depending on what type of goods they are involved in. The Department of Commerce — Bureau of Customs can provide you with the needed information.

You must approach the licensing of your business in a pragmatic manner. Pay what you need to pay to start operations, and avoid paying anything until is necessary. If you have to take some tests to be licensed, be sure you have allowed enough time for the results of the test to be certified and a license issued. Don't be paying rent, utilities and other overhead and not be able to do business because you are waiting for a state license.

You will find a listing chart below that you can use to note all the permits and licenses you will need — and the cost. List them, and total them up so you will have your complete upfront costs for licenses and permits.

BUSINESS LICENSES AND PERMITS

Use this form to get costs of licenses and permits — and to compare costs in different locations.

Name of License or Permit	Issued By	1st Cost	Annual Cost
Local Business License			
Fictitious Firm Name			
State Occupation			
Federal Employment No.			

Section VIII
Buying or Leasing Fixtures and Equipment

When you are ready to buy or lease the fixtures and equipment for your business, you will want to put them into two categories:

1. Those that produce income.
2. Those that cost income.

The equipment that produces all or part of your product and the fixtures that move merchandise are income producers. Cost is only a factor in relation to what they can produce. As an example a printing press makes money — an office copier costs money. The fixtures that display merchandise make money — the racks in the storeroom used to hold inventory cost money.

When you are shopping for fixtures and equipment keep those two categories in mind — in general terms you will pay any reasonable price for fixtures or equipment that will produce more income — but you will be highly price conscious about the income costers.

The costers are judged on their time saving and organizational functions — and price is of great importance. Your start up capital is needed to promote business not buy expensive products or fixtures that produce no income.

It is best to shop for the income producers first. After you have secured what you need — you will know how much is left for non-producers. You have the option of buying or leasing your equipment. As a rule of thumb — leasing is always more expensive than buying — so you should consider leasing your production equipment and buying your non-producers. There are some tax advantages to leasing — but in a small business start up situation they would seldom apply.

The main advantages of leasing are:

1. Acquiring the equipment with modest capital.
2. Better service on the equipment.
3. You have the latest model.
4. You are not stuck long term with obsolete equipment.
5. The full cost of the lease is deductible from income.

To determine the cost of leasing use this formula:

1. Total of your lease payments . . . . $________
2. Total estimated cost of insurance, maintenance and property taxes you must pay . . . . $________
3. Add line 1 and line 2 . . . . $________
4. Multiply line 2 by your income tax rate . . . . $________
5. Subtract line 4 from line 3 . . . . $________
6. Amount of investment tax credit passed through to you by lessor if any . . . . $________
7. Subtract line 6 from line 5 . . . . $________

Line seven gives you the net, after tax cost of the lease. To get a comparison of the cost to buy the equipment use this formula:

1. Cost of the equipment . . . . $________
2. Total interest paid on loan or installments . . . . $________
3. Total depreciation over life of machine . . . . $________
4. Estimated cost of insurance, maintenance, repairs and property taxes for life of machine or equipment . . . . $________

5. Total of lines 2 + 3 + 4 multiplied by your income tax rate . . . . $_______
6. Subtract line 5 from line 1 . . . . $_______
7. Amount of tax credit allowed . . . . $_______
8. Subtract line 7 from line 6 . . . . $_______

This gives you the net after tax cost of purchasing equipment.

Let's take a comparative example and show you how it works in practice.

1. The machine costs $10,000.
2. Lease payments will be $13,800 ($230 a month for 60 months).
3. Estimate $100 a month for maintenance, insurance property taxes, etc. Total of $6000 over 5 years.
4. Our income tax rate will be 40%.

Leasing Chart

Total of lease payments	$13,800
Estimated cost of insurance, maintenance, etc.	6,000
Total costs	19,800
Total of 40% income tax rate	7,920
Balance after tax rate applied	11,800
Amount of tax credit passed through	-0-
Net cost for leasing	$11,800

Buying Chart

Total cost of machine	$10,000
Total interest paid on the loan to buy	1,500
Cost of insurance, maintenance, taxes, etc.	7,000
Total depreciation on life of machine	9,500
($17,500) multiplied by tax rate of 40%	7,000
Net depreciated cost of machine before credit	3,000
Tax credit allowed 10%	1,000

Net cost for purchasing 2,000

So, you can see in terms of net dollars in your pocket, purchasing is a better deal. This does not show the down payment made on the equipment (usually 10% to 20%), which would have to come out of capital. You will find a form at the end of this chapter to use in listing comparative costs for leasing or buying equipment.

How To Buy Equipment For A Dime On The Dollar

If you have some time, and are willing to do some legwork, you can save up to 90% of the costs of buying much of your non-productive equipment, and even some fixtures and other equipment as well. Make a list of what you need and shop the sellers of new and used equipment to see what they offer and the prices they charge. At the same time keep watching ads in the paper offering equipment for sale — you'll find it under office equipment and store fixtures in the classifieds of most daily papers. When you spot an ad that isn't from a dealer go look at the equipment. You want to keep something in mind while you are doing this. The private parties who are selling this equipment see it as a problem in most cases. They have no further use for it — it is taking up space — and their price is therefore negotiable. If you have shopped the new and used dealers you have a pretty good idea of what the equipment is worth. Offer them what you estimate a dealer would pay for it — ten to twenty cents on the retail dollar. Always carry the cash — and take it out of your pocket — count out the amount — and offer it to them. You'll be surprised how many will accept.

You can also watch for bankruptcy auctions and attend them to pick up equipment or supplies. If you go to genuine bankruptcy auctions (not those that are augmented) — you will be bidding against dealers — and often can get both equipment and supplies at 10 cents on the dollar.

The point is to invest some time to save your capital by finding what you need at bargain prices. If you remember that it takes twenty dollars in sales to make back every dollar you spend on getting started — you can see the advantage of saving as much as you can before you open for business.

Understanding Depreciation Schedules

Depreciation is a cash flow you put back in the bank or in the business. All the machinery, equipment, fixtures, buildings, vehicles and other equipment you use in the business can be depreciated. There are different schedules for different items. A vehicle can be depreciated in three years — a printing press in seven years — normal office fixtures (desks, chairs, etc.) seven to ten years. The schedules change as the laws change.

First Year Write-offs...When you buy equipment you are entitled to take up $2000 over your regular depreciation schedule the first year. A corporation can get 20% deduction in the first year of property investment of up to $10,000.

Straight Line Depreciation...This is the schedule where you take the cost (less salvage value) and divide it by the number of years it will take to fully depreciate — thus if you were to depreciate $100 for 10 years straight line — you will take $10 per year.

150% Declining Balance...You take one and a half times straight line the first year and multiply the remaining balances by .15 taking the balances and rounding them off to the closest dollar.

200% Declining Balance...You multiply the remaining balances by .20 and round off to the nearest dollar.

The Sum of Digits...This is the schedule where you add up the numbers of depreciation years — for example if you were going to depreciate over 3 years you add 1 + 2 + 3 = 6 — then the first year you take 3/6th of the total — the second year 2/6th and the final year 1/6th.

Asset Depreciation Range (ADR)...This is a newer system that permits 20% faster depreciation by reducing the useful life of the asset and disregards salvage value — and provides much faster write-offs. It is not a schedule by itself — but is used in conjunction with straight line, declining balance or sum of digits. It also supplies annual repair allowances for different classes of assets — this avoids hassles with the IRS over whether a repair was actually a capital investment or an expense.

To give you an idea of how the various depreciation schedules work out in practice — here is a comparative schedule for 10 years on $1000.

Year	S/L	150% D/B	200% D/B	Digits
1.	$100	$150	$200	$180
2.	100	130	160	160
3.	100	110	130	150
4.	100	90	100	130
5.	100	80	80	110
6.	100	70	70	90
7.	100	60	50	70
8.	100	50	40	50
9.	100	40	30	40
10.	100	30	30	20

As you can see straight lines gives you a steady rate, and provides higher depreciation rates in later years when you may need the tax deductions. The other systems get your money back faster, and provide little help in later years.

Keep in mind in addition to the depreciation schedule, you are entitled to a 10% investment tax credit on equipment purchases. This is deducted directly from the amount of taxes you owe, not figured as a standard business deduction. You can also take an extra 20% depreciation the first year along with your regular deduction.

When you are developing your business plan, talk to an accountant about the current depreciation schedules — they are constantly changing — and decide whether you want your investment money back fast — or will need tax deductions in later years to offset higher profits you will be making. You will probably not have a high profit — most likely not any profit your first year, so large depreciation deductions are of little help. Use the tax credits and depreciation wisely, and get professional help with your decision.

Be Sure You Are Dealing With Needs — Not Desires

When you are making your decisions on fixtures and equipment be sure you are getting what you need and not buying status symbols or equipment with a lot of bells and whistles that add to cost, but don't fill any real needs. If you can get what you need from older, used equipment, then look for that type.

A good example of this will be when you get involved in computers or computerized equipment. The sales people will paint beautiful pictures of what the equipment will do for you. There is no question that the proper use of this equipment will make your operation highly productive, and in some cases can actually provide the help that will make the difference between success and failure. But, you must take a long hard look at the cost effectiveness of the equipment—and pay particular attention to the programs or so called software that is the key to proper use. In most cases it will be a wise move to buy from a supplier who will rent you the equipment with the proper programs for a short period of time so you can determine its real value to you. Don't rush into any purchase that you have not fully evaluated.

One final point—always buy equipment—never let yourself be sold equipment. Never make your decision with the salesman present—always take time to think it over. If this is your first venture this rule is very important. Always check with present users about reliability, service and how the company lives up to the claims they make. Many equipment sellers have effective sales forces and no service—they oversell the equipment and users are left holding the bag.

Always ask yourself this—DO I REALLY NEED THIS THING?

Buying Or Leasing Equipment And Fixtures

Two concepts—

1. Only lease equipment that makes money
2. Only buy equipment that costs money

How To Determine Costs of Leasing:

1. Put Down Total of Lease Payments .... $________
2. Total estimate costs of insurance & maintenance .... $________
3. Add line 1 and line 2 .... $________
4. Multiply line 3 by your income tax rate ..... $________
5. Subtact line 4 from line 3 .... $________
6. Amount of investment tax credit (if any) .... $________
7. Subtract line 6 from line 5 .... $________

Line 7 gives you the net after tax cost of your lease.

How To Determine The Costs of Purchasing:

1. Cost of equipment .... $________
2. Total interest paid on loan installments ..... $________
3. Total depreciation over useful life of equipment .... $________
4. Total cost of insurance, repairs, maintenance, taxes.................... $________
5. Total of lines 2 + 3 + 4 .... $________
6. Multiply line 5 by income tax rate .... $________
7. Subtract line 6 from line 1 .... $________
8. Amount of investment tax credit allowed ... $________
9. Subract line 8 from line 7 .... $________

Line 9 gives you the net after tax cost of a purchase.

Use these systems to compute costs and make a decision about lease or purchase of fixtures and equipment.

LEASING SCHEDULE

FIXTURES OR EQUIPMENT	TOTAL LEASE	NET LEASE	LEASE DEPOSIT	MNTH PAYMNT

PURCHASING SCHEDULE

TOTAL COST	NET COST	DOWN PAY	MNTH PAY	TYPE OF DEPREC.	YRS	ANNUAL $

Section IX
Setting Up Your Bookkeeping Records

When you are ready to install your bookkeeping system keep one thing in mind. Make it as simple and non-time consuming as possible. While accurate records are vital to your operation, you don't need to spend hours of your time fooling with them.

If you have bookkeeping or accounting experience then you can set up your own. If you are starting a simple cash in—cash out business with no accounts receivable—no large inventory—such as a small mail order business—then you can go to the stationery store and pick up one of the stock systems they sell (Ideal or Dome are the two best known). If you follow the instructions given in the books you will have an adequate bookkeeping system.

Hiring The Accountant Or Bookkeeping Service

If you are new to business, or are going to be involved in a great deal of work in creating business, then you should hire an accounting service to care for your records—make out and send in your tax forms—and give you monthly statements on how you are progressing.

The top of the profession is the CPA (Certified Public Accountant). He is the most expensive, and supposedly the most knowledgeable — which may or may not be true in the case of the small business client. A good many CPA offices are nothing more than computerized bookkeeping services—but they charge CPA rates. The work is done by so called junior members of the firm, and you are expected to deliver and pick up your paperwork. Unless you are operating a complicated corporate set up, you really don't need a CPA.

The Bookkeeping Services

There are many good bookkeepers and services that the small business person can use, and use profitably. The bookkeeper is often listed as an accountant, and one with experience in working with small businesses is ideal. He understands the problems, knows what needs to be done, and can handle the tax forms and paperwork for you. This person comes to your place of business to do his work on the books, and delivers your reports. You will find these people listed in the phone book under Accountants or Bookkeeping Services.

It is important the person you employ for this service be reliable and does not have more clients than he or she can really handle. You want to remember these people are not creative thinkers or skilled in all forms of tax law and sophisticated corporate tax shelters. They are technicians, who know how to do the job you need done, and can help you in your planning by showing you where you are springing profit leaks. You will have to keep certain daily records for them, and they come in and either pick them up, or do the work in your office. It will be a big help if the person you choose has had experience in the same line of business you are entering, or one very much like it. Interview more than one, and choose one that seems competent, and more importantly, one you will get along with on a personal basis.

These are usually computer based systems—something like the systems you buy at the stationery store. You keep certain forms and records—send them to the service, and they return computer printouts of the results. Operators of these services are almost always oversold in terms of personal service, so you won't get much personal advice or help as a rule. One point—stay away from the franchised small business consulting services—they put anyone with the franchise fee in business—and they sell a so called consulting service along with bookkeeping services. Check with established small businesses in the area and get some names from them as a starting point. Also check with your banker, he may know of a good person or service. Always get references from the people you interview and check them out. And a final tip, when you are interviewing ask them what types of businesses they now serve. Steer the conversation around to how well firms in that type of business are doing. See if the person tells you any war stories about his past or present accounts—not naming names, but revealing what should be confidential information, even in a general way indicates you have a blabber mouth, and you don't need one doing your books.

Be sure and discuss costs completely—how much to set up the books—how much to balance them—to prepare tax reports, etc. Give the accountant an estimate of your volume and what you want to find out from your records. There is a list at the end of the chapter to help you decide this point.

The Small Computer Systems

This is another route you can go—buying or leasing a small computer and keeping your books, your inventory and other records on it. The Apple and TRS-80 (Radio Shack) now have small business computers with software programs that can keep a fairly sophisticated set of records for a small business.

The computer system is not difficult to master, and it allows you to do your own books with the aid of part time office help. You can still hire a service to do your taxes and tax reports. It is worth investigating these systems as part of your decision process in planning your record keeping.

The Expense Budget

The new entrepreneur will need some controls and guidelines as he or she begins operations. The most important job is to manage the capital and income so the business stays solvent and growth goals are being met. The new businessman or woman is going to be exposed to a lot of sales pressure to buy all manner of things that are guaranteed to increase business or business efficiency. The best way to control impulse buying is to have a budget for each function where ongoing buying decisions are made—inventory—advertising—dues and subscriptions—office supplies and equipment—telephone—travel and entertainment, etc. Allocate funds month to month based on business volume, and stick to them. This makes it easy to say no, and keep expenses under control.

Set aside some time everyday to do your bookwork. Make it a time you won't be interrupted, and do all your number crunching, ordering and other paperwork, then. Many small business operators find the morning hours—before opening is the best time for this. Just don't let things pile up on you. Daily attention keeps the job manageable—but left undone for a few weeks and you'll never catch up.

The checklists on the next two pages will get you starting points for your thinking about what you want from your record-keeping systems. Keep in mind, too much detail is as bad as too little. If you hire a competent bookkeeping service, they do all that for you.

Setting Up Records And Accounts

What kind of records will you need?

1. How will sales be recorded?
   ( ) By cash register tape.
   ( ) Sales slips or written orders.

( ) By contracts with customers.
( ) Charge card slips.
( ) Forms for telephone orders.
( ) Purchase orders sent to you.
( ) Entries on ledger cards.
( ) Other.

2. How will purchases and payouts be recorded?
( ) By issuing purchase orders.
( ) By use of voucher checks.
( ) By signing contracts.
( ) By receipts for cash purchases.
( ) Receipts for payments on account with cash.
( ) Slips to record petty cash withdrawals.
( ) Method of recording owner cash withdrawals.
( ) Method of recording owner or employee mechandise withdrawals.
( ) Issuing promissory notes.
( ) How will barter or exchanges be recorded?

3. How to record refunds—discounts—shortages—customer exchanges:
( ) Credits to an accountant.
( ) Cash payouts.
( ) Check payouts.
( ) Recording cash shortages and overages.
( ) Goods exchanged by customers.
( ) Bad checks.
( ) Bad debts.

4. How to record deductible expenses:
( ) On checks—how entered and noted.
( ) Accounts journal.
( ) Cash receipts.
( ) Credit Card Purchases.

5. How to record long and short term liabilities:
( ) Notes payable ledger.
( ) Payment books.
( ) Other.
( ) How to get division of interest and principle for tax deductions.

6. Depreciation:
( ) Record of items and rates of depreciation.
( ) Type of depreciation taken.

7. How will taxes due be recorded?
( ) When they are due on the calendar?
( ) How funds are to be held or maintained for tax payments?
( ) How and when are payments to be made?

8. How will payroll be handled?
( ) How often will it be met?
( ) How will deductions and witholding be determined?
( ) How will payroll be recorded?
( ) How will W-2 and other forms be handled?

9. How will inventory records be maintained?
( ) Setting up initial inventory records.
( ) Records of inventory reorders.
( ) How will they be valued for accounting purposes—LIFO or FIFO?
( ) How often counted and checked?
( ) How often will shortages and overages be handled?

10. Financial Statements
( ) Balance sheet—open for business—then how often.
( ) Operating statements—how often.
( ) Cash flow statements—how often.
( ) Financial ratio analysis—how often.

( ) Operating ratio analysis—how often.
( ) Tax reports—who prepares.

11. Setting up budgets:
    ( ) Cash budget.
    ( ) Financial budget.
    ( ) Expense budget.
    ( ) Sales budget.
    ( ) Advertising budget.
    ( ) Research and development budget.
12. Credit records and accounts:
    ( ) Ledgers for accounts receivable.
    ( ) Aging reports on accounts—how often?
    ( ) System for triggering collection action.
    ( ) When and how will accounts be written off as bad debts?

What information do you want from your recordkeeping?

1. What income was received—what expenses incurred?
2. How do they compare with successful business operations?
3. How can expenses be reduced or eliminated?
4. How is the inventory—too high—too low—about right?
5. What are the assets—liabilities and net worth of this firm?
6. What is my return on investment?
7. What is the value of my non-liquid assets at this time?
8. How is cash flow doing?
9. How are my accounts being collected—average or better?
10. How productive is my staff?
11. Are my prices producing the best profit possible?

Cost Of Recordkeeping

Item	Annual Cost
Cost of Initial Books and Supplies	
Accountant's Charges to Set Up Books	
Cost of Accountant's Services	
Cost of Tax For Preparation	
Cost of Preparing Payroll	
Cost of Postage and Duplicating Tax Forms	
Other Expenses	
Total-Pre-opening Costs	
Total Monthly Costs	
Total Annual Costs	

NOTE—Pre-opening costs are not considered business expenses for tax purposes—but as capital investment. So, if you use an accountant—have him arrange his work so that he is not finished—and does not bill you for services until after you have started business—then it's fully deductible.

NOTE—Divide annual costs by 12—to get monthly costs of operating expenses for recordkeeping.

Section X
Buying Your Business Printing

One of the first purchasing decisions you will make is buying your printing—your letterheads, envelopes, business cards, invoices and business forms.

In the first blush of enthusiam, and as kind of an ego kick, a lot of new entrepreneurs spend too much money getting fancy artwork, paper and high priced printing of these things. In some types of business it is worth the investment if your literature has to impress people in order to do more business, but in most businesses it is a waste of money.

Your job in organizing the business is to make your capital go as far as possible, and there is no point in spending money just to make yourself feel good.

There are firms who print for other printers—who produce high quality work at reasonable prices, as well as retail mail order printers who use stock formats and turn out very nice stationery at prices considerably lower than you would pay a local printer, and they print in small quantities as well.

If you want to get the lowest possible prices on your printing then here's a way to get price lists and catalogs from "trade printers" (printers who print for other printers). Get some note heads printed up at a local quick printer with your name and address at the top—and a line across the bottom of the page—"printing broker." Use this to write to Graphic Arts Monthly, 600 5th Ave. NY NY 10019. This is a printers trade magazine. Ask to be put on their mailing list.

Then checking advertising in their classified section, and some display adds you will find trade printers for everything from business cards to business forms.

For example:

Summit Thermography, 8171 So. Grant Way, Littleton, CO 80122—who do trade printing of business cards, letterheads, etc., at about 50% less than printers charge.
U.S. Tag and Ticket Co., 2219 Robb St., Baltimore, MD 21218 — if you need tags or tickets.
Label Art, 23 Riverside Way, Wilton, NH 03068 — if you need mailing labels, product lables, etc.
Nationwide Stock Business Forms, 75 7th Ave., New York, NY 10011 — if you need business forms such as purchase orders, bills of lading, invoices. They have over 75 stock designs to fit most needs.
Dexter Press, Rt 303, West Nyack, NY 10094 — if you need four color catalog sheets.

And there are many more in each category in the magazine. I found it easiest to call these firms on the phone and tell them I was a printing broker and would like their catalogs or prices as I had accounts wanting the products they printed.

The advantage of using these firms is they are specialists in what they do—and they produce a quality job at a reasonable price. The one problem is time—you must order far enough in advance to allow four to six weeks in some cases for your order to arrive.

If you don't want to go to that much trouble, then you can write Drawing Board, Box 505, Dallas, TX 75221 for their catalog. They are retailers of all types of business printing in small quantities, and they do excellent work.

The advantage of doing business with these firms and others who sell by mail is they achieve economies of scale. As a rule they can charge less than local printers because they use stock forms—limited choices of type styles and gang-runs on the presses to deliver a good product at a lower price.

If you are going to use local printers, then shop around and check prices—the look of the shop and quality of work. Almost all local printers are oversold from time to time. They sell more than they can produce in the promised time. The one thing you want to avoid is to deal with a printer who is always in that situation. His prices may be lower, but the problems become far worse than the savings are worth. These days the quick printers can do most of what you need done and are geared to getting out the work.

If you are going to buy artwork for your literature, and you talk to a couple of commercial artists and they toss around estimates like $100 and hour, or $500 for a small design, don't pay it. Put an ad in the paper under Help Wanted for an artist with the experience to draw what you need—you'll find all kinds of talented people who will do a good job at a most reasonable price.

If you are planning on printing some brochures and using a couple of colors—then write to Champion Printing Co., Box 148, Ross, OH 45061. They will send you a pricing catalog that also has a short course in how to paste-up your copy for proper reproduction.

If you take some time to develop your sources, particularly if your business calls for a lot of printed matter—you will save a considerable amount of money and get good quality work.

Item to be printed	Date Required	Quantity	Price

Section XI
Setting Up A Purchasing System

When you begin to plan your purchasing keep one cardinal rule in mind—"ALWAYS BUY—NEVER BE SOLD." This simply means your buying decision is not the result of what some sales person says or does—but on careful analysis of your own needs. This is a vital point for the new entrepreneur to keep in mind—and why it is so important to write a business plan that you can follow. If you plan properly, buying decisions will be made on the basis of the plan—the budgets and what your goals are.

The Salesmen Are There To Sell

Salesmen are working for their company and their own income. They want to sell as much as possible in order to improve their own situation. You, on the other hand want to spend as little as possible in order to make your income larger. So, you must not let them sell you anything—you always buy after careful consideration of their offers.

Some old hands will spot a new entrepreneur and try to load him or her up by telling them all successful stores or businesses must carry the amount they recommend. On the other hand, some of the salesmen from large suppliers, particularly those who will be selling inventory items, will give you sound advice about your needs because they have a long term interest in your success. The people to be wary of are those that have no such interest, and the sale they are making is a one time shot. Often a broker or rep will call on you with offers of heavy discounts for some off the wall stuff which you can price lower than the market and supposedly sell at once. Unless you know you can—forget it. And another source of wizard deals comes in over the phone. Some coxie in a boiler room somewhere calls and lays a story on you that sounds logical—and he may even roll out some name brand stuff at heavy discounts—but don't bite. If the deal was as good as he is painting it—he wouldn't have to call you. These people are flat liars—don't believe a word they say. And, if you are tempted, tell them to make the offer in writing, send samples of the goods, you will examine it, and if you like it, accept it on 30 day terms. That will end the conversation.

Anytime you have a sales person with a one time deal—a special inventory deal—equipment or fixture sale—special advertising or promotion deal, etc., do this before buying:

1. Tell the salesman to come back tomorrow.
2. Check out the deal with someone else.
3. Check you budget to see if you can afford it.
4. Make a counter-offer for less money when the salesman returns. If he accepts it—back off again as he was overcharging you the first time. See if he will come down more.
5. Only buy if you decide it's worthwhile.

Now, one important point—

- Never chase prices on inventory items.
- Always chase prices on expense items.

You are buying inventory items for their profit potential in terms of volume and turnover—not to save money on costs. The key to inventory purchasing is resale potential—not price. It is to your advantage to develop strong relationships with wholesale sources who will help you build more business, than try to find one who will sell you a few cents less.

You will find some of your suppliers to be great assets to you, and it is to your advantage to give them the lions share of your business.

But, beware of putting all your purchasing in one basket. In today's world things can change overnight. A good supplier can be taken over by a major corporation and terms of sale and policies changed to your disadvantage. Always have other sources who can replace them if necessary.

Your main sources of supply in most cases will be obvious. When considering other sources, be sure and check them out with other retailers in the business. How well organized are they? Do they deliver on time? Do they stock enough inventory so you don't have constant back orders? Are shipments or shipping methods a problem?

In purchasing expense items, always chase prices. Every dollar you can save in expense purchasing, is $20 less gross sales you have to make to get that dollar back, or it's a dollar you can put in your pocket.

Types of Sources You Deal With

Depending on your line of business, you have several levels of marketing sources to deal with:

- The manufacturing source.
- Full line wholesaler.
- The broker.
- The manufacturers' rep.
- The specialty wholesaler.
- The importer.
- The jobber.
- The cooperative buying group.

Some manufacturing sources maintain their own sales forces and call directly on the trade. These are usually high ticket items, and in many cases factory franchises are granted for exclusive territorial rights.

THE FULL LINE WHOLESALER is the usual major source for retailers. They carry broad lines in the trade, and give good support to their customers.

THE BROKER is a commission salesman who represents manufacturers or other original sources—and does not handle, ship or otherwise deal with the products—and seldom has any system for helping customers build business.

THE MANUFACTURERS' REPRESENTATIVE is also a commission salesman who sells for a group of manufacturers of different products. The Rep can often be of great help to the retailer, and it pays to see them when they come around.

THE SPECIALTY WHOLESALER is one who stocks a narrow range of popular items in great depth. It is most common in the apparel trade. He can, as a rule, deliver faster on hot items.

THE IMPORTER is just what the name implies. He imports goods from overseas and sells them to retailers and wholesalers.

THE JOBBER, or SERVICE WHOLESALER is the one who puts in racks and services them on a regular basis. They keep the racks stocked and organized for you.

THE COOPERATIVE BUYING GROUP is an office representing a group of small retailers who combine their purchasing power to get better prices, delivery, etc. These are most common in the apparel, drug, grocery, hardware and some specialty trades.

You can see you will have many types of sellers offering you their goods, and at first, it will tend to overwhelm you. But, if you have developed a good plan, and know what you intend to do, your buying decisions will be based on that plan, and the decisions, yes or no, are made virtually automatically. As you gain more experience, you will be able to judge offers far better, and will find times when you have genuine buying opportunities that you will want to take advantage of despite budgets or plans.

If you are writing a plan for the wholesale trade, or are going to manufacture products, you will be dealing with the manufacturers or producers of raw materials, manufacturers' reps, importers and brokers. The key decision on purchasing here for wholesalers is turnover. While a retailer may do well turning inventory 6 times a year—a small wholesaler will have to move it 50 times a year because he is working on small margins. The manufacturer is interested in cost and delivery to meet his production schedules for raw materials and components. The problems with sellers are the same as with retailers—develop a purchasing plan and stay with it.

Develop A Precise System

You are going to have a thousand details to attend to in organizing and managing the business. It is very important you set up a simple and precise system for your regular purchasing. If you don't do this you will be in a constant state of aggravation over where things are when you need them; whether things have arrived from the suppliers or not; whether you received everything you ordered, etc. There will be delays, wrong goods shipped, shortages, back orders, overages, wrong billings, overcharges, etc. All these must be taken care of—and they should be done automatically.

It is important that you keep one thing in mind. As your business develops, you get into an adversarial relationship with your suppliers. They make mistakes, miss shipping dates, ship the wrong goods,—change prices without notification, ship too many or too few, etc. The people who work in the shipping department of suppliers are not the brightest people on earth, and mistakes are common. These errors cost you time and money—the suppliers still try and collect from you because shipping does not tell billing about errors. These mount up and you begin to understand the real world. By installing a purchasing system these problems are handled automatically and instead of fighting with your supplier, you will be respected by them, and they will make adjustments in your favor on request.

The Purchasing System

The key to this system is to trigger an automatic response to whatever happens after a purchase order is issued. Most small business people do not understand what a purchase order really is. It is a contract, once accepted by the supplier, it is enforceable in the courts. For this reason it is important for the issuer of a purchase order to specify the terms and conditions of the order.

1. The quantity of each item ordered.
2. Color, styles, sizes, brands, etc.
3. The exact item by supplier order number.
4. The price, per unit, doz., gross, etc., and any discounts.
5. The date you must have the order in house.
6. Whether you will accept substitutes.
7. Whether you will accept back-orders.
8. Terms of payment.
9. Shipping instructions.
10. Packing instructions.

In most cases common practice will eliminate most of the instructions, but keep in mind unless you specify, it amounts to an open contract that the supplier can do with as he pleases. As an example, in some trades it is common for a supplier to substitute items when they are out of stock. A smart buyer will not allow this, as it is an open contract for which he is liable.

When you decide to order from a supplier, get their order form and any instructions on how the order is to be placed. Put this in a master file book with your notes on how the orders are to be placed—and terms you want to specify. When you are ready to place an order you open the file and have your information before you. This automates your ordering function.

When you have the purchase order written, you can mail it, call it in over the phone or hand it to a salesman. You should make triplicate copies, the purchase orders should be numbered. You can order them printed with your business name, address and phone, or you can buy them in stationery stores—stock forms on which you can rubber stamp your name and address, etc. Keep in mind that purchase orders don't need to be status symbols unless you are using them to try and promote orders on credit. If you are, then one tip, start your numbering at 10251 or some such number—high numbers indicate a long time in business. The purchase order below is a sample of Rediform stock forms you find in stationery stores. If you decide to buy these, buy a year's supply with consecutive numbers—you may have to buy several packages—so make sure the numbers run consecutively. If you buy one package and have to go back to get another one, you won't have numerical sequence in your PO's.

Setting Up Your Tickler Follow-Up File

When the Purchase Order has been executed, you send the original to the supplier. You put your first duplicate of the PO in a receiving book—this is a book with all you PO's filed in numerical order that is used to check the incoming shipments. The third copy goes to your tickler file.

The Tickler File is 31 file folders numbered 1 to 31, representing the days of the month. When you place an order, you put your triplicate copy in the file on the date the order should arrive. Each night at the close of business you take all orders from the file that have not arrived—and follow-up on them the first thing in the morning. You call the supplier, and find out the status of the order—when you get a new date, put the PO in your tickler on that date for a second follow-up.

This automates your purchasing system. You know at all times the status of undelivered orders, and can cancel them—place them with another source—or prod the supplier for faster delivery.

When The Shipment Arrives

When the shipment arrives, check the PO in the receiving book to make sure it has been ordered. At the first opportunity, check the order to make sure you got what you ordered, in proper quantities, sizes, styles, etc., according to the PO.

If all is as it should be, sign off the PO in the receiving book, and pull the PO from the tickler. Attach the packing slips and other paperwork to the PO, and put it in your payables file, or you can use the tickler file for paying as well by dropping it in the day you need to pay to get your discount—or 30 days, etc. This way you also have automatic control over payables.

If there is something wrong, then set up a procedure based on your first contact with the suppliers. Get the name of the party you have to deal with, his phone and extension number. Get the name of any assistant who handles the job when the superior is not around. Find out from them, exactly what you do, and when and how they will issue credit, and who and where the person is who will issue the credit. The reason you want to do this is that buck passing is the great American business game. You won't have time to play it, so you want specific names of the people responsible. Put all the information on 3 × 5 cards, and keep them in a file on your desk.

If a credit is to be issued, then make a note of when it should arrive (and that's before the current bill is to be paid)—and put that in your tickler file for follow-up.

If part of the shipment is damaged, then learn exactly what you do. If you have to deal with the shipper, or someone at the supplier office. Put that information on your 3 × 5 card and file it. Keep names, phone numbers and office hours for all the people involved.

When you file a damage claim, then tickler file the date of expected response—follow it up if it has been delayed. This system will keep you on top of things—relieve you of worry about what is going on—and leave your time free for things that create more cash flow.

Finding Your Suppliers

The easiest way to find your major sources of supply is to talk to people already in the business—those in nearby communities you will not be in direct competition with. You can begin with the names they give you. Call the suppliers on the phone and arrange to have them get their catalogs and price lists to you. Chances are they have a salesman in the territory who will be assigned your account, and he will deliver the price information. He can also give you the names of sources of products that he does not handle.

You should also check with other merchants as to Trade Magazines. (You can also get your librarian to help you look up trade magazine sources in Ayers Directory of Periodicals, and in Standard Rate and Data.) Write on your business letterhead for subscription information—some will send you their issues free—others charge an annual rate. You will find other sources of products and a lot of valuable information about running your business in these publications.

One thing you should do, preferably before you go into business, is to attend a trade show featuring the kinds of merchandise you are going to carry. You can find out the dates of these shows from the Trade Associations—or the trade magazines. (You can find the phone numbers of these associations by looking through the Directory of Associations in your library.)

If you want to know when all trade shows and exhibitions are being held all over the country—you can order a copy of the Exhibit Schedule directory from Successful Meetings Magazine, 633 Third Ave., New York, NY 10017.

Watch the Shipping Costs

High fuel costs have exploded shipping costs, and they have to be watched carefully. When a supplier quotes FOB the factory, that means you pay shipping costs from his dock to your door. When damages occur, it's your problem — you have to contact the shipper for restitution. Damage and theft are increasing, so this is a serious problem.

Shipping Rates And Carriers

One important thing you should have is a schedule of rates using various types of shipment available. There are United Parcel Services — U.S. Postal System — Air Express Services — Motor Freight — Rail Freight — Sea Freight and shipment by bus. It will be a wise idea to get the costs for various weights you might be receiving from each source and make up a chart of costs using various systems. Each method has its own time schedules, and range of prices. One thing you want to watch very closely when shipping by motor carrier or rail and that is the class of goods being shipped. There are differences in costs of shipment by class of goods being shipped. If the supplier is shipping to you FOB factory, his people are not overly concerned how the shipper rates the goods being shipped since you pay the cost. So be sure you specify the class of goods when it is being shipped by carrier.

In practice most small businesses use UPS. They have a limit of 200 pounds, however, and will ship in most areas either by air or ground. In case of loss, they can quickly check out the reason, as all goods are signed for, and they have automatic insurance of $100 per package. UPS both picks up and delivers if you have to return something.

As your business develops you will learn which trucking firms are the most reliable and you can specify them as the firm the carrier will use to ship your goods.

Some suppliers will pay part or all the shipping charges if orders come in certain types, sizes or times. If this bonus is offered make note of it in your tickler file so you can take advantage of it.

PRIMARY SUPPLIER LIST

Name of Firm	Address	Phone

Section XII
How to Purchase and Maintain Your Inventory

One of the key skills the small business person must develop is the ability to maintain a profitable inventory. In a business where you will be selling goods the ability to maintain the proper inventory balance — to meet fluctuating demand — is essential. There must be a delicate balance between enough inventory to meet most demand without being overstocked or overinvested.

On the one hand, having constant shortages or stockouts will lose customers and cut your volume — and on the other hand, too much inventory keeps you making markdowns, cutting into profits and failing to produce enough net income to stay in business.

The first thing to understand is there is a cost to carrying your inventory. It is not an obvious cost, and is often overlooked by the new entrepreneur. First, you have funds tied up in inventory that could be earning an income somewhere else — next, you have the physical costs of handling the inventory, storing it, counting it, putting it on display, dusting and arranging it, etc. You have depreciation and obsolescence costs for goods held too long. You have taxes to pay on it, insurance premiums to pay, you have the costs of the space needed to store it and display it, and you have shrinkage — the inventory lost to shoplifters, employee theft or accident. The average retailer places a 20% cost on the average amount of inventory carried during the year.

There are two ways to look at your inventory. First, look at in units of stock — second, in dollars invested. Your problem is to keep enough units on hand to meet customer demand within a dollar investment limit you can afford.

The first step is to determine your investment in opening inventory. Your prime wholesale sources have model inventory plans you can draw on for help. You can also check with trade associations who often have such plans to offer.

The next step is to estimate your inventory turnover.

You will learn the average turnover of the industry from your wholesaler, and can use that as a base. This will give you your first estimate of average inventory investment. For example, if you expect to do $200,000 in sales and the average inventory turn is 5 times — you divide five into $200,000 and find that your average inventory should be $40,000. One point to remember is that sales levels fluctuate in most businesses from month-to-month or season-to-season This has to be taken into consideration when planning inventory. But, the major point is that the greater the turnover of inventory, the smaller the investment in it has to be.

I'm going to show you a table to help visualize how to determine the best level of inventory for a store. It shows you the annual sales figure — the number of inventory turns and the carrying cost.

Turns	Average Inventory	Annual Carrying Cost
1	$120,000	$30,000
2	60,000	15,000
3	40,000	10,000
4	30,000	7,500
5	24,000	6,000

It would seem from this that the trick is to carry the lowest possible inventory to keep carrying costs down. But, there is also a cost for running out of inventory and losing sales. If it happens too often — you also lose your customers. Experienced retailers estimate the cost of losing a sale because of stockouts is 150% of the selling price. The probability of losing sales due to stockouts rises with the rate of turnover. Here is a table that takes the cost of stockouts into consideration:

Turns	Annual Cost	Stockout Cost	Total Cost
1	$30,000	-0-	$30,000
2	15,000	$ 3,000	18,000
3	10,000	$ 9,000	19,000
4	6,500	$14,000	21,500
5	6,000	$24,000	30,000

You can see from this table the costs come full circle when stockouts are considered. By looking at the total cost column you will note the least cost of carrying inventory is at two turns — or in the case of this example — $60,000 average inventory.

It is important to keep in mind that a high turnover rate draws down the inventory much faster than total dollar costs might indicate — because some items are sold out faster than others, and the most lost sales coming from being out of the most popular items.

Another way to determine your inventory needs is on a month-to-month basis. You project a desired inventory level at the end of the month to begin the next month's sales. Here is how you would figure that:

Desired EOM inventory	$30,000
Planned or expected sales	40,000
TOTAL	70,000
Inventory at the start of month	$20,000
TOTAL	50,000
Markdowns during the month	1,000
Total inventory at end of month	49,000

If you are working on a 40% margin, then your inventory purchases would be 60% of $49,000 or $29,400. This is called your open to buy figure. You will purchase $29,400 worth of inventory in order to have a $30,000 retail value inventory at the end of the month. Note — the $1,000 markdown figure is what you estimate you will lose to shrinkage or reduce in price to sell some items.

The Retail Method of Valuing Inventory

		Cost	Retail
Beginning inventory		$ 54,000	$ 90,000
Purchases		99,000	152,000
Freight and receiving costs		920	
Net additional markups			2,000
Goods on hand for sale		153,720	244,000
Markup minus retail cost (Obtained by multiplying 37% by $244,000)	$ 90,000		
Net sales	100,000		
Markdowns & shrinkage			6,000
Goods sold at retail or missing			106,000
Ending inventory at retail value		86,940	
Cost of goods sold		67,920	
Gross margin		33,220	

This system gives you a complete costing of your inventory, and of costs to land goods in your store. It also takes in consideration your losses to theft, breakage, etc., and your markdowns on cost. Finally, you know what your gross $ margin was for expenses and profit at the end of the month.

As your business develops you will find you have the problem of figuring the proper inventory levels for many products or types of products. This cannot be done with any degree of accuracy until you have had experience in operations and get a feel for how products move in various categories.

The first decision is the range and depth of your inventory for various items. Some sell faster than others — some are more profitable than others. The question is, how many of each size, color, style, etc. will you carry in a product line? For example, you have a selection of small flower vases. They come in a selection of colors — red, yellow, white, green, blue, pink and orange. You decide to stock four colors, deciding the white will be the big seller, green and yellow second best and blue the question mark. So you plan your inventory on a two dozen order this way.

Model #123 Vase
1 - 2 - 3 - 4 - 5 - 6 7 - 8 - 9 -10-12-13-14-15-16-17-18-19-20-21-22-23-24
W W W W W W W W W W W W G G G G Y Y Y Y B B B B
- 12 White - - 4 Green - - 4 Yellow - - 4 Blue -

Let's say that this is a staple item in your store, and you don't want to run out of them — and it takes ten days for a new order to arrive in your store. How can you be sure it will be unlikely that you will run out. We shall say this vase turns six times a year and we sell 12 a month. White sells two to one over colors. We need a safety buffer to be sure we don't run out. There is a simple formula you can run through your pocket calculator which will give the number of units you should keep in inventory to be sure you don't have stockouts.

Now, you would assume that you have a two month's supply of this item on hand, and you could reorder at the 20th day of the second month and not be likely to run out. But, that assumption is all wrong. It is wrong because there is a cost involved in placing an order. You must make out the purchase order, send it in or call it in — you must put it in your tickler file to follow up — you have to inspect the order when it arrives, put it in stock or on shelves in the back room. There will be an occasional damaged item, there will be shortages, wrong colors, or wrong style — all this costs time and money. So, you have to consider this cost per order in deciding how often to order. The average small retailer spends about four dollars per order.

There is a formula you can run off on your pocket calculator to determine how often you should order these items and how many you should carry in stock for the least cost. To do this you first need what is called a multiplier. To get this you multiply your cost per order by two.

Cost per order = 4 times 2 = 8

Next we have a carrying cost for inventory which is 20% — so next we divide 20% into 8 and this gives 20/8 = 40. Now hit the square root key on your calculator and you get 6.32 (we use the square root to reduce the margin of error). We will use 6 as our constant — and as long as your order costs stay at $4.00 (the average for small business) — you can use 6 in these calculations.

Next we estimate the annual total sales of the product. We have 144 (12 items per month x 12 months) sales. Next we take our cost per unit which we will say is $2.50 and we divide it into 144 — 144 ÷ 2.50 = 57.6. Now we take the square root of 57.6 which is 7.5. Now to get our best quantity we multiply 7.5 by our constant 6 — 7.5 x 6 = 46 (rounded off). So, the quantity we should order is 46 (or 48 to keep it in even dozens). In other words, twice as many as we assumed.

You can use this formula for all your inventory decisions. Now, it's not engraved in stone that you have to do it that way, but it does give you a clear reference point for keeping your inventory at the proper level.

When To Reorder

The second thing you must consider is how to establish a method of reordering inventory items so you won't run out — but also so you won't carry too many. There is a formula you can run off on your calculator that will tell you how to do that so there is a 96% chance you won't have a stockout.

Some merchants mark a box on the shelf in the back room as a reminder to reorder. Others keep tally sheets and make educated guesses. But, here is a formula that gives you a safety margin by keeping enough goods in stock while you wait for the new shipment to arrive. We need a multiplier for this formula and we will use 1.8 — it is an arbitrary number, but gives us 96% protection against stockouts.

First, we take our weekly sales (4 per week) and it takes two weeks to receive a new shipment from the day we place the order. We multiply 4 units by 2 weeks (4 x 2 = 8) and get 8. We store the figure 8 in our memory in the calculator or write it down as we have to use it again. Now we take the square root of 8 which is 2.82 and multiply this by our multiplier 1.8 (2.82 x 1.8 = 5 rounded off) — this is our safety margin which we add to 8 (8 + 5 = 13) to get 13. So, anytime our stock gets down to 13 units, we reorder.

So, now you know how to determine how many of each inventory item to order — and when to reorder so there is little chance you will run out of stock.

You will want to set up a system to keep a perpetual inventory control. You can use the cash register — they will handle up to ten departments and give you daily totals — or price tags with item and style (size — model, etc.) on them. For example, in our vases you could mark the tag — X123W — the X would identify the source you order from, 123 is the model number, and W stands for white — the color. You collect these at the end of each day's business and mark off your inventory on your tally sheets, or in your computer. Each tally sheet or computer memory will have the automated reorder reminder to alert you.

If you are starting a wholesale business you can use the same formulas. Turning inventory is the name of the game in wholesaling — you are operating on such a small margin that goods can't be held. Inventory control is the whole ballgame. You can't be out — but you can't carry too big a load. A computer system for a wholesaler is almost a necessity.

If you are going into manufacturing you need a two track inventory control — one as a buyer of raw materials and components to keep your lines moving, and one as the seller to keep the finished products from piling up.

Here is one important thing to remember about inventory — it's money — cash — the hard stuff. It is amazing how closely a small business person will guard their cash and pay little attention to their inventory. Think of your suppliers as your interest-free bankers and let them carry as much of the load as possible. Keep the inventory moving, markdown or give away the dogs. Your space is expensive and only the goods that pay their rent should be kept. Evict all the others.

Understanding inventory management and control will make more money for you than any other operation of a business except selling.

Dealing With Suppliers

When you are open for business, you are a target. Sales people will begin making calls — new products and programs will be offered to you on an almost daily basis. Frankly, you won't have time to deal with all of them. So, right from the start you have to make choices.

There is a set of criteria you can use to determine the value of what they offer to you.

1. Does it make money or cost money?
2. Is there money in the budget to buy it?
3. Is this to be a regular caller — or a one timer?
4. Do I know enough now to make an intelligent decision?

First, does it make or cost money? If you are just getting started and the product is some kind of insurance, or fixtures, or printing, etc., you should cut the conversation short, ask for his card, and call him later if there is anything of interest. If it is something that makes money, ask if there's money to buy it. If you are interested, make an appointment at a more convenient time. Is the salesman a regular caller, one that represents a supplier? Then take some time to hear the offer. If it's a one timer, selling something — make him come back when it's convenient, if you're interested. And, finally, even if your are interested be sure you know enough to make an intelligent decision — I repeat what I said before — "never be sold — always buy."

You are not going to like everything a supplier does — nor are you going to like every representative of your suppliers. You have one advantage you can use. If you keep organized, know what you are doing, and can keep clear and accurate records of transactions, you will be in the driver's seat. Once, you get sloppy, let sales people start selling you, and issuing verbal orders for products, you are in trouble. Don't let petty personal annoyances or animosities cost you money. Keep your supplier relationships sound and as friendly as possible. Then, if you get in trouble, need extra time to pay, need more inventory on longer terms, etc., you can get it.

On the following pages are some suggested forms you can use to keep track of your inventory — to decide on your first inventory buy — and determine when you need to reorder.

This control sheet gives you a method of knowing when to place your reorder, how well an item is moving, and what is on order. You can make these up on a typewriter, keep them in a looseleaf notebook arranged by departments. (Have a quick printer run off 200 of them).

STOCK CONTROL

Item *Flower Vases* Stock # *X 123-W-G-B-Y*

Supplier *Jones Wholesaling*

Reorder Quan *48* Delivery Time *2 weeks -*

DATE	SALES	ON FLOOR	STOCKROOM	ON ORDER
		15	36	
6/18	9	18	24	
6/19	11	19	12	60
6/21	10	15	66	
6/30	10	17	54	

Have one of your clerks take the day's sales tickets, or the cash register receipt and enter the information — either after the doors close — or before opening in the morning. Give the clerk some method of alerting you to any items that should be reordered.

If you need to keep track by size and color put a depth chart on the back of each sheet indicating the size and color assortment. Marking off the sales on your depth chart will keep track of those needs without having to keep a separate form for each size, color or model.

The following chart will give you a control over model, size, style, etc. inventory. By checking off sales as they are made you can control the selection in your inventory.

You may make these with a typewriter and have them printed, and can run them on the entire page. The numbers on the left can be for single units, dozens, grosses, twos, sixes, etc., whatever you decide — print form on the back of your stock control forms.

STOCK DEPTH CHART

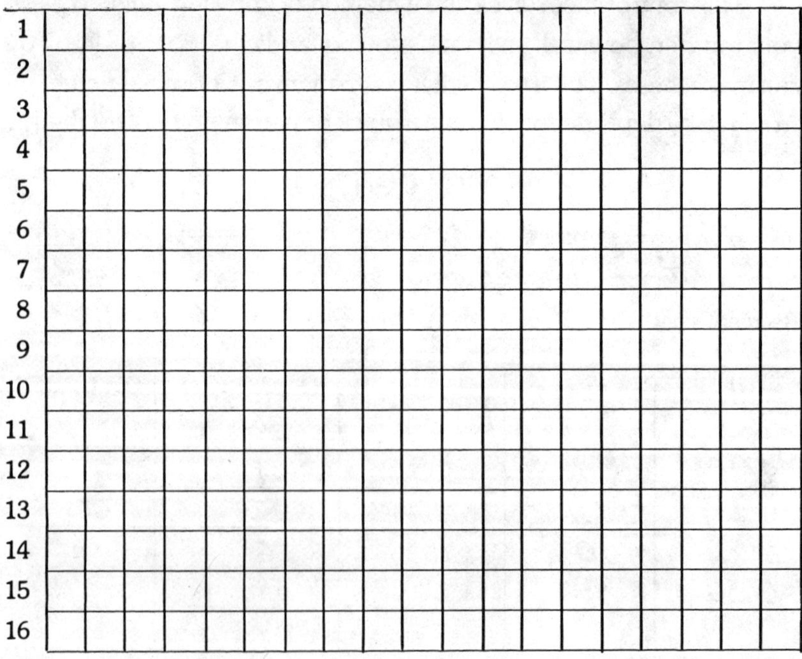

Code the squares with price style or model — then mark in the number of each in opening inventory — and X them out from the top down as they are sold. One glance at the chart shows your inventory by selection and depth.

A glance at the chart above would show that you had sold 14 white vases — 2 yellow — 3 green and 2 blue. You know where you stand with depth and selection.

If you don't have time, or it isn't critical to do a daily entry to inventory records — then set up a time during the week to do it — and make sure it is done — and that all needed records are kept in one place.

Inventory Investment

	Cost	Retail Value
Beginning inventory investment	$ ______	$ ______
Freight and receiving costs	______	______
Any extra markups on normal mark	______	______
Costs of checking, marking and stocking	______	______
Total costs of inventory		$ ______
Total retail value of inventory		$ ______
Gross margin		$ ______

Put down your total inventory investment — then put down the retail value of the inventory.

Add up all the freight and receiving costs — put them in cost column — then add up the checking, marking and stocking costs and put them in cost column.

Now add up all the costs. Then put retail value of inventory on indicated line below. Now, subtract costs from retail value of inventory to get gross margin of profit in dollars.

Section XIII
Pricing Your Products and Services

Price is a vital part of business success. The entrepreneur will learn soon enough that it is more of an art than a science. The person starting a new business tends to want to undercut existing competition by pricing below them — this is a great error. You must remember the most important thing about price—"it is a perception of value." For example, there is a value in convenience. A person buying a package of cigarettes out of a vending machine will pay half again as much for a pack as they would pay at a store, but they want the cigarettes at once, and the convenience of the machines creates the value. The perception of value also comes from a belief in superior quality. Take Bayer Aspirin; it has pretty well been established that any aspirin will help relieve pain, and given the same quantity of ingredient there is no difference between brands, but Bayer has spent millions of dollars creating a perception of superior quality in the minds of consumers — and it is the leading seller.

The perception of value is the key to pricing. If you were to start up a cut rate "tiffany's" you would go broke. The people who buy fine jewelry won't buy it from a cut rate store. Sears found that out when they tried to market mink coats. A woman who can afford a mink doesn't want one with a Sears label on it.

Perhaps the best example of perception of value I have ever heard of was from a story in the paper about a very successful antique dealer who got his start on the Boardwalk at Atlantic City—in those days Atlantic City was a carnival with cheap souvenir stores and hot dog stands as its staple businesses.

This man was rapidly going broke trying to sell cheap antiques. One day, as a kind of joke he took a bowl he'd paid $10 for, and put is on a velvet cloth in his window and priced it at $1,000. He sold it for that price the same day. The next day he had nothing in his store that sold for less than $100, and he had discovered a gold mine. In fact he became one of the most successful antique dealers in the country.

So, price is really a positioning mechanism in the market place. In planning your prices, consider that. Go back to your concept of this business and decide the perception of value a customer will have. Or, if you are marketing a product, decide which segment of the market you are after and what price will be most profitable in terms of those who buy the product for use or consumption—and for those who will be the retailers of your product.

Here is a checklist for pricing decisions:

- Buyer perception of the product or service.
- Comparative products and their selling prices.
- Psychological appeals as a part of the price.
- Cost of production or of selling the product.
- Volume anticipated at various prices.
- Relation of production capacity to cost.
- Break even points at various price levels.
- Estimated market share at various prices.
- Estimate of servicing costs after sale.
- How competitors will respond to pricing decision.
- Estimate of servicing costs.
- What margins can be given sellers of products.
- What cash flow will be produced at various prices.
- Do prices vary on a seasonal basis?
- Cost of guarantees.
- Discount structure on volume purchases.
- Cost of allowances—co-op advertising—premiums etc.

These are some of the factors in pricing decisions. One or more may have to be considered in making the pricing decision. In making your original estimates of pricing keep in mind that it is easier to lower prices than to raise them. So, if you are going to make an error in your pricing—you should err on the high side rather than the low side unless you are bidding for a job.

There are several methods of pricing for the entrepreneur to consider. They are:

- Full cost pricing.
- Going rate pricing.
- Gross margin pricing.
- Marginal costing pricing.
- Weighing the wallets pricing.

Full cost pricing involves all costs to the producer or seller in acquiring or manufacturing the product. Then, the fixed overhead costs are apportioned to the product on a basis of percentage of sales. Viable selling costs are added, and a predetermined amount or percentage of profit added. While this method guarantees a profit on every sale it does not take the real world into consideration; if the competition cuts prices, or inventory moves too slowly at the full cost price, it reduces profit.

Going rate pricing is probably the most common in the retail business and in service businesses. Prices are set by what everyone else is charging. There is no real analysis made of the true costs of doing business—only an assumption that if my competitors can make it at those prices, so can I. It is a foolish and often fatal way to arrive at prices. The neighborhood convenience store who tries to match selling prices with a supermarket will go broke.

Gross Margin Pricing is the common method used by retailers and wholesalers. They add a markup to their cost by a given percentage to arrive at a selling price. The markups will vary by the type of merchandise—it's rate of turnover and seasonal factors.

Marginal Costing Pricing is similar to full cost pricing except it is more commonly used by service firms to determine the actual hourly cost of each service to which a profit figure is added.

Weighing Their Wallets Pricing... This is "Santa Claus comes every day" pricing. It is used by professionals and is a price based on what the traffic will bear. In times of shortages, the guy who has the goods, names the price. In case of patent protection of a hot product that eliminates competition—the producer names the price. This is usually a short term proposition, buy while it lasts it's something else. A current example of this is OPEC oil prices.

The most common method of pricing is gross margin pricing. There are two methods—markup on cost and percentage of selling price. Either way you come out with the same price, but they are expressed in different forms.

As an example—if the product costs a dollar and you add 50% to cost—your selling price is $1.50. If your percentage of selling price is 33⅓% you also arrive at $1.50 for the selling price.

It is important to keep the two percentage figures separate in your mind. While you can use the markup of cost as a method of pricing, it poses some difficulties in estimating margins. If you bought your product for $1.00 and sold it for $1.50, how much profit have you made on $10,000. You have to know the number of units sold to figure it out. But if you express your margins as a percentage of selling price—when you want to know how much margin you have in $10,000 in sales, you multiply $10,000 × 33⅓% and get your answer without having to know how many units were sold.

The formulas for the two pricing systems are:

To get percentage of selling price $\dfrac{\text{Markup \$}}{\text{Selling Price}} = \text{Percentage}$

To get percent of markup over cost $\dfrac{\text{Markup \$}}{\text{Cost of Goods}} = \text{\% of Cost}$

At the end of this section there are a series of calculations for various combinations to arrive at percentages and prices.

There are tables and hand calculators in stationery stores to quickly find prices expressed either as markup over cost or percentage of retail—and they are much simpler to use than trying to do mathematics.

One important thing to remember in pricing with gross margin systems is to not set an across the board markup for all types of goods sold. Markups on slow moving items will have to be larger to compensate for the cost of carrying inventory—faster moving goods, priced with lower markups to meet competition. The key to smart pricing in gross margin is to get average target markup for your whole store or operation.

If you are pricing products you make and sell—then you will want to consider full cost pricing. In working up selling prices for manufacturing businesses you have four considerations:

1. Direct Costs.
2. Manufacturing Overhead.
3. Nonmanufacturing Overhead.
4. Profit.

Using this approach you start with known figures and use them to determine the price. Assume that the material and direct labor are $6—these are your direct costs to produce the product: You set a price of $10. The difference between $6 and $10 is $4—and $4 is what would be termed gross margin in retailing—but in full cost pricing it is called "contribution." So, you know that any price above $6 provides a contribution to covering your other costs of doing business and your profit.

It is important to remember this in thinking about price. The amount of contribution you get from each sale is directly related to the price you charge. The lower the price, the smaller dollar amount of contribution. But, we have to recognize volume of sales; a lower price can produce more total volume, and thus, a larger total contribution.

Another important thing to remember in developing prices is that there are two types of demand. Elastic and inelastic. When the price of an elastic demand item is lowered, it is like flipping off the top of a jack-in-the-box, demand explodes. But if the item is inelastic, nothing happens.

For example—if you cut the price of new cars with discounts and rebates—demand is elastic, and sales increase at once. But, if you had a sale on rat poison demand would increase very little. The new entrepreneur will find it profitable to recognize the difference between the two types of products or services. There is no point in trying to increase sales with inelastic demand, and cutting prices will only reduce the profits.

The aim of pricing is to produce the price that will make the greatest contribution of fixed overhead, variable sales costs and profit.

For example, if you sell 10,000 units at $10 each, your gross is $100,000. Your cost is $60,000 and contribution is $40,000. If you lower the price to $9 and sell 30,000 units your gross is $270,000—your cost $180,000 and contribution is $90,000, a 125% increase. But, if you only doubled the volume with a $9 price—you would sell 20,000 units at $180,000 gross, at a cost of $120,000—giving you $60,000 for contribution. But, the increased sales expense may well eat up the additional $10,000. The point is that volume is desireable up to a point—but many times a higher price and smaller volume produce more net profit.

As you develop your full cost pricing you have other things to consider. The cost of materials can vary, and in inflationary times is constantly rising—this must be considered in setting prices where you don't have the option of changing them every few weeks. So, a pricing decision on this type of product must include inflationary expectations on both material and labor costs.

Let's assume you establish your contribution percentage at 40% of the selling price. This means materials and labor will represent 60% of the selling price. If the materials cost you $2.70 per unit, and the direct labor cost was $1.00 per unit, your direct costs are $3.70 per unit. Now, you want to find the absolute minimum price at which you must sell this product. There is a simple formula:

$$\frac{\text{Direct Costs \$3.70}}{\text{60\% of Selling Price}} = \text{Selling Price \$6.16}$$

The contribution at this price is $2.46 which is obtained by multiplying the selling price $6.16 by 40% the contribution percentage.

But, there is more fine tuning to be done by the manufacturer. Labor costs should be standardized in figuring your prices—that is, labor costs must realize the same contribution to overhead and profits regardless of the cost of materials. So, you need mark on percentage for labor costs, which will give you the standardized labor cost contribution. Here's how you do that—in our example above, we had $2.70 for materials and $1.00 for labor—divide $1.00 into $2.70 and you get 2.7 or 270%. This gives you the standardized labor contribution. All you have to do now is find out what the materials cost, and divide that cost by 2.7

$$\frac{\text{Materials Cost \$2.70}}{\text{Labor Contribution 2.7}} = \$1.00$$

Now let's say that material costs rise to $3.00 how does that affect your direct costs. You divide $3.00 by 2.7 and you will see your labor cost rises to $1.11 per unit and using our pricing formula the selling price rises to $6.85.

There are more fine tuning formulas which involve the pricing by profit per product per machine hour—and figuring out how many machine hours are used for various products, etc. But, for the purposes of writing a business plan, the use of setting a gross margin, and then pricing by cost of materials, and using the labor percentage multiplier, will give you a price that should have the necessary profits to begin business.

The Pricing of Jobs by Bidding

If you are going into business where you must bid to get work, construction, printing, etc., you will want to have a pricing mechanism which will show you the best bidding price in terms of keeping a steady cash flow and have funds to pay your ongoing overhead.

To do this you need to know three things. First, the estimated gross profits on the bid price—second, the amount you will bid—and third, the estimate of your probable success in getting the job. Let's take an example where we can put in bids at five different prices:

Bid Amounts	Estimated Profit	% of Winning
10,000	1,000	95
15,000	3,000	75
20,000	6,000	25
30,000	12,000	02

To determine your best bidding price take the estimated profit and multiply it by the percentage of winning the bid. Here are your results. These show you profits on a continuing basis, keeping in mind that every bid you lose means you have to pay your overhead out of profits on former work done.

Bid Amount	Average Profit
10,000	950
15,000	2250
20,000	1500
30,000	600

As you can see the high and low bids produce the lease average profit—in this case the $15,000 bid is the best. Of course it will take time to be able to judge the possibilities of submitting winning bids—but experience teaches that skill rather quickly.

The Pricing of Services

Pricing of services is best done by determining the hourly costs of services performed, and add your profit to those costs on a gross margin basis. That is, if you want to earn 10% net profit on operations, you determine the hourly costs, and add the 10% to that figure. The problem is to determine the costs of different services. Most service firms offer more than one service, and need a system to determine the real cost of each service in terms of fixed overhead expenses and direct costs in performing each service.

We will take a consulting service as an example and say there are three services rendered—one is client consulting, the second is preparing reports and the third is research. First we will determine the fixed expenses of this operation:

Fixed Expenses	Total	Consulting	Prepare Reports	Research
Manager Salary	$2500	$1000	$ 750	$ 750
Rent	1500	500	500	500
Equipment Leases	1000	—0—	1000	—0—
Furn. Rental	1500	750	500	250
Advertising	2200	2200	—0—	—0—
Other	2000	1000	250	750

You will note that the total costs are spread among the three services according to their needs. The next step is to add in the direct costs of each service.

Direct Costs	Total	Consulting	Prepare Reports	Research
Report Salary	2400	—0—	2400	—0—
Research Salary	2000	700		1300
Consulting Sal.	3000	3000	—0—	—0—
Payroll Taxes	2772	1225	987.50	562.50
Materials	1500	300	1000	300
Totals	**22,475**	**8675**	**9187.50**	**4612.50**

Now you have to determine the hours per month available to you.

Then, discover what percentage of time is actually used to produce income, that is, none of the service areas are 100% employed, so you estimate the level of productivity. Divide the number of productive hours into the cost of each of the three services to get an hourly cost figure.

	Consulting	Reports	Research
Hours per month per service	172	172	172
Hours of active production	70%	90%	90%
Net hours of production	120	155	155
Hourly cost	$79.59	$62.20	$32.75
Rounding off the figures	$80.00	$65.00	$33.00

You add your net profit percentage to each of these cost figures to come up with an hourly charge for your services. If you decide on 20%, then you have $96.00 an hour for consulting, $78 for report preparation and $39.00 for research. This assures you of full cost pricing, plus 20% net profit.

FORMULAS FOR FIGURING PRICES AND PROFITS

Here are a group of formulas you can use on your pocket calculator to get the answers you need.

INDIVIDUAL MARKUP WHEN FIGURED ON RETAIL PRICE

1. Cost + $ Markup = $ Selling Price
2. $ Markup ÷ % Markup = Selling Price
3. $ Cost ÷ 100% – Markup = Selling Price
4. $ Selling Price – $ Markup = $ Cost
5. $ Selling Price × 100% – % Markup = $ Cost
6. $ Selling Price × % Markup = $ Markup
7. $ Retail – $ Cost = $ Markup
8. $ Expenses + $ Net Profit = % Markups
9. $ Markup ÷ $ Retail = % Markup

INDIVIDUAL MARKUP WHEN FIGURED ON COST PRICE

1. \$ Markup ÷ % of Cost = \$ Cost
2. \$ Retail ÷ 100% + Markup of Cost = \$ Cost
3. 100% + Markup of Cost × \$ Markup ÷ % Markup of Cost = Selling Price
4. \$ Cost × % of Markup of Cost = \$ Markup
5. \$ Markup ÷ \$ Cost = % Markup of Cost

SALES FIGURES

1. \$ Markdown ÷ % Markdown = \$ Net Sales
2. \$ Maintained Markup ÷ % Maintained Markup = \$ Net Sales
3. \$ Sales at Markdowns ÷ % Sales at Markdown = \$ Net Sales
4. \$ Shortages ÷ % Shortages = \$ Net Sales
5. \$ Gross Margin ÷ % Gross Margin = \$ Net Sales
6. Capital Turnover × Average Inventory at Cost = \$ Net Sales
7. Stock Turnover × \$ Average Inventory at Retail = \$ Net Sales
8. \$ Net Profit ÷ % Net Profit = \$ Net Sales
9. \$ Average Sale × Number of Transactions = \$ Net Sales
10. Stock Turnover at Cost × Average Inventory at Cost = Cost of Goods Sold

TURNOVER

1. \$ Net Sales for Period ÷ \$ Average Retail Inventory for Period = Stock Turnover
2. \$ Cost of Goods Sold for Period ÷ \$ Average Inventory at Cost for Period = Stock Turnover at Cost
3. Stock Turnover ÷ 100% – Initial Markup = Capital Turnover
4. \$ Net Sales for Period ÷ \$ Average Cost Inventory for Period = Capital Turnover

PROFIT

1. 1 Net Profit ÷ $ Net Sales = % Net Profit
2. % Net Profit × $ Net Sales = $ Net Profit
3. $ Gross Margin ÷ $ Expenses = $ Net Profit
4. $ Markup − $ Expenses = $ Net Profit
5. $ Gross Margin − $ Operating Expense = Operating Profit
6. $ Operating Profit ÷ $ Net Sales = % Operating Profit

These formulas enable you to take known figures and get unknown figures quickly.

PRICING DECISIONS

Target gross pricing margins will average .... ________ %

Target net profit percentage will be .... ________ %

We will figure our markups on (   )Cost
(   )Retail Selling Price .... ________ %

Costing a manufactured product our labor
contribution percentage will be .... ________ %

Costing a service our average percentage of
hourly productivity will be .... ________ %

Section XIV How to Select Your Insurance Coverage

The need for insurance is obvious to any responsible person. Business insurance takes many forms, but the small business operator usually has a standard set of insurance needs that the industry is able to cover with one or two policies. It is a fairly simple matter to get the required coverage, and it is offered by two types of agents.

First, the independent agent represents several insurance companies who offer varying types of policies. In some businesses, with a large number of businesses involved in it, there are companies that specialize in coverage for that particular industry. Often this is the best type of coverage, as it is offered by firms who know the business well, and can offer a good deal of help in managing risk. If there is such a company, you can find out about it from your trade association, or someone else in the business. You can then locate the agent in your area that represents the company. The second type of agent is the direct writer. This agent represents one company, is their employee, and the company, not the agent, owns your account. The independent agent owns his own accounts, and can shift them from one company to another.

There is some argument about which type of agent is best—and cases can be made for both sides. But, the small business operator would, in general terms, be better off with an independent agent, who is also a small businessman, than with a direct writer. You represent a valued account to your independent agent—and you represent peanuts to the company represented by the direct writer. In case you have a claim, the independent agent has a vested interest in seeing that the claim is settled to your satisfaction. The agent for the direct writer is an employee of the company, and his interest is the company's interest. In claim disputes he will be on the side of the company.

Finding Your Insurance Needs

The first step is to determine what you are going to be able to insure. The second step is how much of it can you afford to insure.

To make this decision you must understand the nature of risk. There are two major types of risk with which you will be confronted: pure risk and speculative risk. Pure risk is the situation where there is only the possibility of loss, theft, a fire, sickness or death of the owner, flood, earthquake, etc. There is no way to anticipate timing or control of pure risk.

Speculative risk is where there is the possibility of gain or loss depending on the outcome of an event or situation. Gambling on a horse race, investing in a stock, opening a small business, are speculative risks and, as a rule, cannot be insured.

Your insurance needs will usually run in this order:

1. Business fraud and theft.
2. Fire.
3. Bad debts.
4. Legal liability.
5. Business interruption.
6. Death or loss of key people.
7. Natural disasters—flood, storm, earthquake, etc.
8. Obsolete products or processes.

You can get some form of insurance against them all. But, you probably cannot afford insurance of that magnitude. So, you must cover the largest loss exposure first—and make sure that you buy enough to protect you from upwards of 95% of possible personal liability. The way to get maximum amounts of coverage at affordable premiums is to self-insure some of the low end yourself by using deductible policies. That is you agree to be liable for $500—$1,000—$5,000 and insurance pays any amounts over that. This enables you to buy higher amounts of insurance at the high end for maximum protection.

To find the proper agent, ask around among other small business people in your area. See who they use or will recommend. If a name comes up more than once, you should contact that agent's office first—and shop a few others before making your decision. If the agent knows business coverage, can make suggestions and show you how to get more coverage per dollar, he's your man.

Essential Coverages

Your insurance program can be divided into two categories, the essential and the desireable coverages. The essential are fire insurance, liability insurance, automobile insurance and workmen's compensation. There are some points to consider in each of them. Here is a checklist:

Fire Insurance:

( ) Make a note to add other perils—windstorm, hail, smoke, vandalism, explosion, flood and malicious mischief — to the policies. (In most cases it can be done at quite low cost.)

( ) Check out the comprehensive coverage policy—the all risk policy to get broadest possible coverage at least cost. (NOTE—the total premium is usually less on an all risk policy than buying separate coverage.)

( ) Determine how your losses will be paid by the insurer— there are several ways it's done.

1. It may pay actual cash value on the property at the time of loss.
2. It may repair or replace the property with material of like value.
3. It may take over the remaining property and pay for all the property (damaged and undamaged) in one lump sum.

( ) Is there any need to insure property you don't own? For example, this could be property left for repair or service. Or is there a need to insure a building on your property—you can get a deduction on your premium payment.

( ) Remember you cannot over-insure and be paid an amount that exceeds the value of what was lost. Insurance companies combine to pay off only a percentage of the value of the loss—they do not pay full amounts independently.

( ) You will need a special "floater" (additional coverage added to the policy) to recover the costs of losses of accounts records, bills, currency, deeds, evidences of debt, money and securities.

( ) If you move out of a building you own, and it remains vacant for 60 consecutive days, the standard fire policy suspends coverage unless there is a special endorsement to the policy cancelling this provision.

( ) If you increase the fire hazard—the insurance company may suspend your coverage even for losses not originating from the fire hazard (such as storing drums of gasoline).

( ) After a loss you must use all reasonable means to protect the property from further loss or have your coverage canceled.

( ) To recover losses you must furnish, within 60 days (unless the insurance company grants an extension) a complete inventory of damaged, destroyed and undamaged property showing in detail quantities, costs, actual cash value and amount of loss claimed.

( ) Note the clause in the policy that sets forth the method to be used to settle disputes over amounts of damage. It is important to have your agent explain this to you.

( ) Note the cancellation terms—usually either party may cancel on 5 days notice—the insured gets a refund of part of the premium paid.

( ) Have the agent explain co-insurance to you. By putting a co-insurance clause in your contract which states you agree to carry insurance equal to 80% to 90% of the value of the property—you can get a deduction on your premium payment.

Liability Insurance:

( ) Be sure to carry enough liability—$1 million at least and probably more in light of today's damage awards.

( ) Be sure and notify the insurance company of any incident happening on your property or premises that might cause a future claim—no matter how petty it may seem.

( ) Most liability policies now carry, in addition to bodily injuries, personal injuries such as libel and slander, etc.—if they are specifically mentioned in the policy.

( ) Remember—if you have employees or agents or independent contractors working in your behalf—you can be held liable for their actions in some circumstances—this risk is insurable—and necessary.

Automobile Insurance:

( ) Make your policy cover employees, contractors and agents acting in your behalf even if you don't own the car or truck they were using in an accident.

( ) Five or more motor vehicles of any type used in a business under one ownership, and operated as a fleet, can usually qualify for a low cost fleet policy for damage to the vehicles themselves and to other people or property.

( ) Carry as much collision deductible as you can to reduce premiums.

( ) You should carry the uninsured motorist coverage and medical-payments for all parties to an accident in your business policy.

( ) You can also carry a floater on personal property stolen from a car or vehicle—but it is probably not worth the cost. This coverage is not standard in an auto policy.

Workmen's Compensation:

Common law requires that an employer provide a safe place to work. The law says employers must:

1. Provide a safe place to work.
2. Hire competent fellow employees.
3. Provide safe tools and equipment.
4. Warn employees concerning any existing danger.

If the employer fails to provide the above, he is liable for damages if a worker is injured or killed on the job. The workmen's compensation insurance is needed to cover that risk.

( ) As a rule, state law determines the level and type of benefits payable under workmen's compensation policies. Check carefully to be sure you understand your obligations.

( ) There are some exceptions to coverage of some employees. Have your agent explain these to you—who you must cover and who is not covered.

( ) In some states you are not legally required to cover your employees under Workmen's Comp, but you may lose some of your legal defenses in law suits if you don't

( ) Rates for Workmen's Comp vary from 0.1% to 25% of the payroll depending on occupations. Be sure that all your employees are properly rated to make sure you are not over paying premiums.

( ) Workmen's Comp rates can be reduced by keeping accident rates low—below average for your industry. So, a good safety program can save money.

Desirable Insurance Coverages

These coverages are not essential, but should be included if you can afford them. They will greatly improve your risk management, and could save your business.

Business Interruption Insurance:

( ) You can purchase insurance to cover fixed expenses and normal profit if a fire, or other natural disaster, should make operating your business impossible.

( ) If you have a key supplier or material source on which the operation of your business depends—you can purchase insurance to pay your fixed expenses and profits should the supplier be shut down by fire or other disaster.

( ) The business interruption policy provides payments for amounts you spend to get back into operation.

( ) There is also coverage available for increased costs due to partial interruption of your business. It can also include indemnification of losses due to failure or interruption of light, power, heat, gas or water that is furnished by a public utility.

Crime Insurance:

( ) Burglary insurance has certain exclusions—accounts, valuable articles in a showcase window and others. Be clear with the agent as to what they are.

( ) In most cases visible evidence, confirmed by a police investigation, or forced entry must be present in order to collect on burglary insurance.

( ) It can be written to cover the contents of a safe, inventoried merchandize and damage incurred in the course of the burglary.

( ) Robbery insurance protects you from loss of property, money, and securities by force, trickery or threat of violence on or off your premises.

( ) Investigate a comprehensive crime policy for small business that covers burglary, robbery and other types of loss by theft including theft by employees.

( ) If your location will be in a "high risk area" where no commercial crime insurance is offered, check with the U.S. Department of Housing and Urban Development about their plan—and there are others your agent should know about.

Glass Insurance:

( ) You can purchase a special glass insurance policy that covers all risk to plate-glass windows, glass signs, motion picture screens, glass brick, glass doors, showcases, countertops and insulated glass panels.

( ) Check to see if the glass policy covers not just the glass but the cost of lettering and ornamentation, and the cost of boarding up when necessary.

( ) After the glass is replaced the same policy should continue without any premium increase for the period covered.

Rent Insurance:

( ) You can buy rent insurance to cover a lease obligation to pay rent should a property become unuseable due to fire or other disasters. If you own the property you can insure loss of lease income due to fire or disaster.

There are also employee benefit insurance programs such as group life insurance, health & disability, but these plans should come out of business income—not out of capital investment.

The Insurance Program

Policy	Insurer	Term	Cost

Your Insurance Plan

1. Cover your largest exposure first.
2. Use as high a deductible as you can afford.
3. Avoid duplication of insurance coverage.
4. Buy "package policies" if possible.
5. Review your program annually to be sure you are fully covered.
6. Write your insurance plan of what you need from insurance.
7. Select one agent with small business experience to handle it.
8. Keep complete records of your insurance policies, premiums paid, losses and loss recoveries.
9. Have your property appraised periodically by independent appraisers to prove your actual losses in case of disaster.
10. Do everything you can to reduce risk of loss.

Section XV
Setting Up Business Security Systems

As part of your business plan you should develop a security program for your business to cover both internal and external security. Our society is becoming more and more crime ridden and the risks of robbery, burglary, embezzlement, bad checks, shoplifting and credit fraud seem to be increasing in quantum leaps.

Security planning should start from the outside in. In thinking about outside security consider these factors:

1. Construction of the building — masonry — brick — wood, etc.
2. The grounds. Is their outside storage of anything that needs protection? How will it be protected?
3. Is their a fence? Is it adequate?
4. How will gates or entry points be controlled in the fence?
5. Is the outside area lighted at night? Should it be?
6. What is the makeup and population of the area? Is there a high crime factor?
7. Are there trees, shrubs and other obstructions that block sight lines from outside?
8. Do you need alarms for detection of entry to grounds?

The Building

The key here is to survey all entry points from doors and windows to skylights and even large ducts for heating or air conditioning. Determine what security is needed, and what is affordable.

1. Check door latches. Are they dead latch or dead bolt or are they plain latches? (Replace plain latches.)
2. Check the door frames. If they are wood, are they reinforced? Are the rear doors reinforced steel? Note — make sure the doors are steel and not aluminum.
3. Check to see no exterior doors open outward so hinges can be removed from the outside.
4. If there are skylights, are they fixed with metal grills under them securely anchored to the frames?
5. Check type of window glass. Should glass be fitted with a break alarm?
6. Is the window framing solid?
7. Are large duct openings well-secured and should they be fitted with alarms?
8. Do you need area alarms inside the building — those that detect movement or body heat?
9. If you have highly valuable goods, check the floors. What is under them? Is an alarm system needed for floor penetration?
10. Check location of trash receptacle. Position it in line of sight of door or window. Employees sometimes throw inventory into the trash for a confederate to pick up.
11. Bolt all equipment to fixtures — and take all equipment serial numbers and keep in safety deposit box. Arrange it so valuable equipment is not visible from windows in back of the building.

Employee Security

The biggest source of losses in cash and merchandise does not come from robbers, burglars or shoplifters — it comes from the employees of the business. You must set up systems to both control and detect employee theft.

1. All merchandise coming in should be checked in by one person who reports to you. And, you should spot check his reports from time to time. Make sure you sign the incoming order in the presence of the delivery driver to be sure he doesn't take the order with him after it is signed off by you.
2. Keep the rear door locked — you keep the only key. Let trash be removed once a day, and, you open for deliveries and close afterwards. Or, make sure a second employee does it. Some stores keep a log on the opening and closing of the rear door. Some even plaçe a numbered seal on it to show it was not opened without their permission.
3. If you give out keys, get the name, home address, license number of their car and driver's license number. Never give a rear door key — and make sure one key does not open both front and rear doors. When a key holding employee leaves — have all locks changed.
4. Set up a cash handling system. Who make deposits? How often? Never let the bookkeeper make deposits — and always have two people involved in counting and depositing.
5. Set up controls for embezzlement. Have your books audited by an outside source at irregular intervals. Make a period phone check of overdue accounts to be sure they have not already paid. There is a bookkeeping scheme called lapping that involves converting account payments by not crediting them when the money comes in. Make sure your bookkeepers take regular vacations; they will expose embezzlement. And, get advice from accountants and other sources on internal controls.
6. Make sure all purchase orders are cancelled after they have been paid. Punch holes in the middle of them so an

employee can't use them again to get a check and deposit it in their own account.

7. Take spot checks of hot inventory items against your inventory records to make sure stock has not been stolen.
8. If you are going to use a cash register, get all the information from the seller about preventing till tapping. Learn how to control and detect it — it's a prime source of theft.
9. If you are going to be cashing checks — talk with other firms in the area, and to the police and be sure your employees are taught a specific procedure to follow, and if they fail to follow it and the check bounces, they pay for it.
10. Control of shoplifting is another security problem. Check with other merchants, with the police, to see what the local policy is. Then, set down your policy and follow it. You will be amazed at the type of people you will catch — a lot of upper-middle class types. If you decide to sign a complaint and have them prosecuted — then do it for everyone. If you don't prosecute, you will have a high rate of loss.

Robbery Prevention

Armed robbery is a growing problem everywhere. The best protection against it is high visibility from the outside street, and keeping a small amount of cash in the till. If you are open at night, keep a coffee pot on and invite local cops to drop by for a free cup, anytime. This showing of badge at odd moments cuts down on planned robbery.

Consult with your local police about what you can and should do about armed robbery. Have them talk to your employees about what they should do, and then hope for the best. There is really no protection against this.

1. Keep the cash register in front of the store, close to the outside window, and don't block visibility from outside with signs on the windows.

2. Post notices that little cash is kept in the register, and employees cannot get into the safe.
3. Talk to the police about your safe if you intend to buy one. Find out its rating for both fire resistance and break-in. Bolt it to something solid in the structure. Put a light over it so it can be seen from the street after closing.

Alarm Systems

You will want to consider some type of alarm system. The best is one hooked into the police station — but many police forces won't allow it because of the high ratio of false alarms. The next best is a system that hooks up to a security service who either dispatches the police or a private patrol officer or both.

Be wary of alarm systems that can be defeated outside the premises, by cutting wires or freezing the unit.

It is best to shop around for systems and the state of the art is improving almost every week, and you will find what you need.

Just be wary of some suede shoe coxies in this field. Talk to the cops about who knows what they are doing, and see them first. You want an established firm, that has been in business a few years — not a brand new outfit with a wizard product that may or may not work. And, the people who sold it to you may or may not be around to fix it. There are a lot of scam operations in the alarm field today.

Making Your Security Plan

Don't neglect your security planning. Talk to some other people in business and you will quickly discover it is a real need — and don't think you will always have honest people working for you, and no one will ever break-in. You can't entirely prevent it — but you can cut down in the number of times it will happen, reduce your insurance rates and save yourself and your employees a lot of grief.

Security Investment

Building Exterior & Grounds

Type of Equipment	Cost

Type of Equipment	Cost

Building Interior

Type of Equipment	Cost

Other Items

Type of Equipment	Cost

In essence then your security plan is this:

To Protect:

1. Your buildings and grounds.
2. Your inventory.
3. Your incoming cash.
4. Your equipment and fixtures.
5. Your goods from shoplifters.
6. Your goods from employee theft.
7. Your profits from bad checks.
8. Your premises from burglary and armed robbery.
9. Your books from embezzlement.

Section XVI — Credit and Collection

Credit is the lifeblood of some businesses. Without using it the business would not exist. Today, the retailers seldom grant credit to customers; they take advantage of bank or other credit cards — VISA — Mastercard — American Express, etc. But, the business that sells to other business must, in most cases, grant credit in order to sell their goods and services.

Credit and collection is a complicated business — and one that the person planning a business should investigate with some care if he is going to offer credit to his customers. The key to successful use of credit is to set down your procedures for granting credit — and establish a system of collections that are triggered automatically. In other words, you, as the owner-manager, won't have to constantly wrestle with credit decisions.

In today's economy, a small business retailer should only use credit cards as his credit selling vehicle. The high cost of money, the uncertainty of collection, make granting credit too expensive and risky when dealing with the general public.

But, the entrepreneur who is going to be selling to other businesses — wholesale or retail — will have to grant credit, or credit terms on large sales, to customers. About 90% of all sales, business to business, are done on credit. This means a great deal of your capital will be tied up in accounts receivable and careful planning to handle that situation is vital.

In general terms here are the decisions the grantor of credit has to make in his plan:

1. The credit terms that will be offered.
2. To whom credit will be extended.
3. Maximum credit limits.
4. Use of credit insurance if available.
5. Collection program.
6. Records needed and how maintained.
7. Discounts given for prompt payment.

The first thing to learn is the common practices in the business you are in. What kind of credit do they offer? What are the usual terms? And, how long is the collection period?

In normal business transactions the averages of collection time are 50-55% will pay within 30 days; 40 to 45% within 60 days; and 5-10% within 90 days. And small businesses will often find that the 90 days payments are often made by their largest customers. Big corporations can make a lot of money on their cash — and by delaying payment can convert the money they owe their suppliers into several million dollars a year in extra profit.

The chart on the following page will give you the normal terms and conditions offered to customers on credit sales.

The one thing to keep in mind in deciding on terms is granting discounts for prompt payment is expensive. The often used 2% if paid in 10 days amounts to 36.5% in annual interest you are going to be giving away free. In setting up your terms and conditions you will want to check with your trade association, with your bankers or accountant and find out what the practices are in your industry — the average payment time — the average amount of bad debt, etc. Work closely with your banker on this as you may have to try and get loans against your accounts receivable.

The real secret of a successful credit program is not in having a high powered collection system; it is taking a good deal of care in whom you accept as a credit account and how much credit you allow. If you will take time to check out all firms — big and small — as to their habits of paying their bills you will build a sound credit system.

If you establish a policy of getting a credit application from every customer — no matter if it's General Motors or a local peanut vendor — you will have the first building block of a sound credit policy. The key in the application is any D&B ratings — and credit references. D&B (Dun & Bradstreet) ratings are usually accurate — but they only represent a point of reference. D&B tells you what the customer has done in the past — and does not tell you about a corporate policy of delaying payments to small suppliers to gain interest income on cash they hold. References will often tell you about this policy. Your banker can get information you need — and can tell you where to find information if he does not have it.

Common Business Credit Sales Term

Term	Explanation
3/10, 1/15, n/60	3 percent discount for first 10 days; 1 percent discount for 15 days; bill due net on 60th day.
M.O.M. (Middle of Month)	Billing will be on the 15th of the month (middle of the month), including all purchases made since the middle of the previous month.
E.O.M. (End of Month)	Billing at end of month, covering all credit purchases of that month.
C.W.O. or C.I.A. (Cash with Order or Cash in Advance)	Orders received are not processed until advanced payment is received.
C.B.D. (Cash Before Delivery)	Merchandise may be prepared and packaged by the seller, but shipment is not made until payment is received.
C.O.D. (Cash on Delivery)	Amount of bill will be collected upon delivery of goods.
S.D. — B.L. (Sight Draft — Bill of Lading)	A negotiable bill of lading, accompanied by the invoice and a sight draft drawn on the buyer, is forwarded by the seller to the customer's bank. The bill of lading is released by the bank to the customer only upon his honoring the draft.
2/10, n/30, *R.O.G. (Receipt of Goods)	2 percent discount for 10 days; bill due net on 30th day — but both discount period and 30 days start from

	the date of receipt of the goods, not from the date of the sale.
2/10, n/30, M.O.M.	2 percent discount for 10 days; bill due net on 30th day — but both periods start from the 15th of the month following the sales date.
2/10, n/30, E.O.M.	2 percent discount for 10 days; bill due net on 30th day — but both periods start from the end of the month in which the sale was made.
8/10, E.O.M.	8 percent discount for 10 days; bill due net on 30th day — but both periods start from the end of the month following the sales date.

Sales date is the day that the shipment was made. It will generally be the same date shown on the invoice. In consumer credit, the sales date is the day the sale was made and may or may not coincide with the date of shipment.

*The owner-manager should keep in mind that 2%/10, n/30 amounts to 36.5 percent in annual interest calculation: 2%/30 - 10 × 365 = 36.5%

Now, there is an art to checking credit references. Keep in mind that the reference is a firm the customers know will say he pays his bills. But, if you learn to listen carefully to the tone of voice on the other end of the phone, you can often pick up unspoken reservations the reference might have. For example, you ask "does this customer always pay within 50 days?" If you catch a hesitation, or get a somewhat ambiguous response such as, "Ah, as far as I know," you can read between the lines; the customer does not always pay within that time. Try to find out if they set a credit limit on the account — how long the account has been dealing with them (be very cautious if all the references have been granting credit only a short time) — and ask them if they can give you the names of the references the customer gave them if you have any doubts.

Always Check Credit References . . . Get into the habit of doing this — and your collection problems will be much simpler. It is a real problem for a new business to not grant credit — it costs business — but, credit will kill you if you grant it to everyone.

Set credit limits according to your ability to carry credit. You will want to go to your suppliers and tell them when your business is expanding that you will be having cash flow problems because of credit sales. Take your applications and the results of your credit checks with you. If they see your system is sound, and collections are average or above, they can grant you extended terms — and probably will because you are going to be a much more valuable customer. This increases your ability to carry credit and offer good customers larger limits.

Your banker can also help by giving you account receivable loans to carry a larger credit load. Your ability to get supplier extensions and bank loans is based on how well you are handling your credit policy.

Credit And Collection Problems

One of the major problems with small business is that they use horse and buggy methods in the handling of credit. They do not install a system for granting credit, and none for collecting. It isn't long before the wheels come off and the business is in real trouble. The owner-manager finds himself or herself out trying to scare up some cash to meet the payroll or pay the rent.

The way to avoid this constant hassle is to install a program that does these things:

1. Checks all credit applications.
2. Sets credit limits on all accounts.
3. Has a strong collection system.
4. Everything works automatically.

The obvious problem is that accounts do not pay as agreed. It is vital that you have a follow-up system that is triggered when payment does not arrive on time. It is getting very expensive to mail a series of statements or invoices with overdue stamped on them. And, if an account if past due, he already knows it, so reminders are nothing more than wasted time and postage.

Here is a suggested system that puts the pressure on at once. When the due date is past — the first contact is by phone to the customer to check on the order:

1. Did they receive it?
2. Was anything wrong with it?
3. When do they expect to make payment?

If there were no problems with the order, they will give you a date on payment. You set up a tickler file for that date, and if payment has not been received, you call the customer again.

1. Payment has not been received.
2. Is there a problem with making payment?
3. Will they make partial payment?
4. When?

The second call is to apply the pressure, and in no case should any date beyond ten days be acceptable for full or partial payment. This date is added to the tickler file, and all orders from the customer held until partial or full payment date. If payment does not arrive — a third call is made:

1. Account is told credit has been canceled.
2. All orders in house must be paid for before shipping.
3. If payment in full is not received in 10 days the account goes to legal action.

In effect, you are writing off this customer with the third call. You have given them the chance to set two dates for payment, and they have stalled you. This means they are not going to pay until they have the funds, or not pay at all. You are going to be better off without them — and using this system nothing goes beyond 90 days.

This is a strong, effective and automatic program that controls credit balances — and gives the collection agency or attorney the account before it is too old to effectively collect.

Records Needed For Credit Sales

You will need these records for credit sales:

1. Credit application form.
2. Credit reports from outside agencies.
3. Customer credit file.
4. Ledger cards or book.
5. Invoices and statements.
6. Monthly aging list of accounts.
7. Tickler file followup system.
8. Reports on collection program.

You can get credit application forms from a local stationery store.

Credit reports from outside agencies have to be purchased from Dun & Bradstreet, the local credit agency, and sometimes there are trade association reports. These are not usually needed on business accounts if the opening credit request is not too large. Banking and other businesses references should suffice. But, if you are dealing with accounts at some distance, you should get the reports.

Ledger cards or ledger sheets for each account must be maintained. Ask your accountant for advice on these.

Invoices and statements — one other point, you charge the going rate of interest to all accounts over 30 days and you put that stipulation in or on your invoices and statements.

Monthly aging list of accounts. You will need this to determine how your collection program is working. There will be nothing on the statement over 90 days that hasn't gone to collection if you use the system we offered. This aging report will show how much you have out, and how long it's taking to collect.

The tickler file is a 1-31 file with notes inserted in each date for action. It works automatically and keeps the program on track.

Reports on collection program — if you are not doing the phone calls — then you will want a report on the results of the calls from the person making them. Use a carbon copy notebook — and you get a copy of what goes in the tickler file.

Your Credit Decisions

Here are the decisions you must make for granting and collecting credit accounts.

1. Should this customer get credit?
2. How much?
3. Should COD terms be offered instead?
4. Should customer be asked for collateral?
5. Should this customer be exempt from standard collection program?
6. If so, how should collection efforts be exercised?

Sources Of Credit Information

One of the best sources will be your major suppliers. They keep lists of accounts in the trade that cause trouble, and those that are good pay. You can exchange information with them by reporting your problem accounts to them — and they will tip you off when some of your current customers are running into problems.

Your banker, as we said, is a key man in credit management. He can find out what the credit limit for an account should be from a fellow banker. And, they can get information on out-of-town customers in a hurry. Now, understand, he isn't going to be your unpaid credit manager, and you'll have to use some discretion in making these requests, but, when you have a problem with making a credit decision on a large account, let him help you out.

If you have a new entrepreneur starting in business and asking for credit you will have to check his personal credit out through the Retail Credit Bureau. There is a charge for the report.

We have mentioned Dun & Bradstreet. You can find out what

their rating is through your banker. Some customers will tell you they are rated in D&B, and ask to have you ship to him at once. Now, being rated by D&B does not mean the firm has good credit. Their ratings are "High" — "Good" — "Fair" — "Limited". So, you will have to determine how the firm is rated before shipping.

Some industrial associations such as The Jewelers Board of Trade or Lyons Furniture Mercantile Agency offer credit reports on firms in those fields. The National Credit Office handles textile trades, banking, electronics, leather, furniture, paint, rubber and chemical trades. Your banker can help you evaluate these sources.

To Sum Up

Credit is a sales tool — and one that cuts both ways. If you manage it properly it's the key to prosperity. If you don't it will probably sink you.

Set up your credit system — make it as simple as possible. Don't be afraid to deny or cut off credit; it must be done. You may have to sell a little harder — but there will be much higher profits as a result.

Section XVII — The Marketing Plan

The marketing plan is kind of like organizing a barber shop quartet. There are four parts, and if any one of the four does not perform properly, the whole effort is wasted. The four parts of any marketing plan are:

1. Getting the attention of the market.
2. Getting individual response.
3. Making your sales presentation to the individual.
4. Closing the sale.

In making your concept statement you have identified your chosen market. In making the plan for your location, you have determined your territory. So, your first step in developing a marketing plan is to gain the attention of the market in your chosen territory.

This requires advertising and publicity. If you are going to be a retailer, you have already determined from your location survey how many people your location will pull into your store. If you are selling to businesses or marketing a manufactured product, you have to start from scratch to develop customer contact.

Before you develop specific plans to get the attention of your potential market, you will want to know what kind of results you have to get from your program. In other words how many sales do you have to make in order to reach your business goal?

The first step is to take your expected gross volume of business for the year and break it down by expected monthly sales. Let's say you expect to sell $200,000 worth of goods in the first 12 months — and your average sales per month would look like this.

Jan.	8.1%	April	8.3	July	6.1	Oct.	9.1
Feb.	7.5	May	7.9	Aug.	8.7	Nov.	8.6
Mar.	9.2	June	7.2	Sept.	9.5	Dec.	8.8

We will say we are starting business in January, and we will sell 8.1% of $200,000 in that month. We discover from our trade association that the average sale industry wide is $20.00.

So, we take 200,000 x .081 = $16,200 in gross sales. We divide $16,200 by the $20 average sale and get 810 sales for the month of January. If we are open 7 days a week as a retailer we must make (810 divided by 31 days) 26 sales a day to meet our goal. If we are selling to businesses or institutional accounts we must make 40 unit sales a day.

Now we know what we have to do to meet our goal. We can now plan an advertising and public relations campaign to attract enough individual response from our total market to make those sales.

The first step is publicity. Since we are opening a new business we should contact the editors of local papers with an announcement — offer to be interviewed. We want them to run a story in the paper about our new venture. Next, we should prepare either media ads — as a retailer — or direct mail ads to prospects as a direct seller — announcing our "Grand Opening." These are designed to do two things — get the attention of the market and get individual reaction. If you are a retailer, your suppliers can help you plan a grand opening that will pull a proper response.

I'll give you a tip about getting media publicity. When you talk to the editor about your opening — have a human interest angle to hang the story on. That is, tell the editor some personal anecdote about your dream coming true. When I wanted to get publicity for a new business in a strange town I always used the story that the business was dreamed up by my buddy and me in a foxhole in World War II, and my buddy was killed — so I was fulfilling both of our dreams — and it always got a big play. A human interest angle will usually get a much better story.

If you can afford it, hire a PR agent (Public Relations) to put on a campaign for you. This is not really necessary for a retailer — but it can be a lot of help to a direct seller.

Retail Store Advertising

Your first line of advertising is in your store advertising.

1. Your show windows.
2. Your in-store displays.
3. Your competent and efficient sales staff.
4. Outside signs.

Plan your advertising in-store to complement what you are doing in the media. If you advertise certain goods, display them prominently and attractively.

Use in-store signs to create interest in other merchandise. Change the signs often — the same with display windows. Use a good window person to help design displays — or if you are a whole store display behind a full glass window, make sure your interior looks attractive from outside.

Remember — over the long pull — your store is going to pull more business than your advertising. It's there being seen 24 hours a day by thousands of passing people. Make it your prime advertising media.

Planning Media Advertising

Once the media is aware you are going to advertise, their sales reps will be all over you like bad breath. And everyone of them will tell his or her media is number one in getting business.

You will find every type of advertising being offered from the big daily paper, the telephone yellow pages, on down to the local church bulletin. Since your advertising dollars must do the best possible job — you will have to test various media to determine its value to you.

I would suggest you test printed media with coupons offering what you know to be a real bargain. Then count the responses versus your cost, to get an idea of how dollar effective each media is.

If the broadcast media (radio & TV) offers you a test deal — then test them with a similar offer. Anyone who hears the broadcast can come to your store and mention a mystery word and get a discount on what they buy.

Have your clerks ask all customers who come to your store for the first 90 days where they heard about it. Test some direct mail — make sure your clerks get the names and addresses of every customer who buys so you have a mailing list of names to send special announcements. For example, send each person who has come to the store a preferred customer card entitling him to special services — or a small advertising specialty gift. Announce special advance sales for preferred customers only. Send them advance notices of incoming shipments of hot merchandise items, etc.

You must remember one thing about marketing. It not only involves making the original sale — it involves creating a repeat customer base that guarantees your sales goals each year.

For retailers, there is another advertising dollar source called cooperative advertising. Many manufacturers will pay up to half or more of your advertising costs if you feature their products. Keep accurate track of co-op dollars available to you. Your supplier can tell you what is available and how you can use it — and use it wisely.

One more point about marketing decisions — set up your sale dates. Don't have a sale every week — it's like the boy who cried wolf too often — people pay no attention. But, if you have your sales spread out, and then offer genuine bargains, your customers react positively to them, and they produce the dollar volume you need.

Another point — when you start running sales and promotional events for your store, try to use ricochet techniques. That is, when you hit one customer with your program it will bounce off of them to another person who will act on the offers. An example is a bring-a-buddy-one-cent-sale. The idea is the customer buys a product — and the buddy can get another one for a penny. The customers will show up in teams — bringing new faces into your store, building your reputation and creating future business. Have some nice calendars made up each year. When customers are in your store, offer them one, and ask for the name of a neighbor they think might like one. Have him fill out a little card stating your store is sending the neighbor the calendar with the customer's compliments. Try and build your customer base using your present customers as the ricochet.

Planning Your Advertising

Your advertising in the media should be carefully thought out. First, design a distinctive border and logo for your ads. (A logo is an illustrated design of the firm name). Run all your advertising in this distinctive design. People will come to recognize it and your customers will read it as soon as they recognize it. If you are going to run regularly in a paper, try to get your ad on the same page every time — and always above the fold if possible. Again this develops recognition and builds response.

The best advice on planning your advertising can be gained from Napoleon. He didn't start out as a general — he was a corporal — but he became the Emperor of France and one of the world's greatest generals because he planned his campaigns based on the intensive and detailed study of his opposition. He learned from them and how to overcome them.

When you start out to set up your marketing plan, use Napoleon's technique. Make a detailed study of the advertising and promotions of your most successful competitors. See what they do, when they do it, and make your plans to do it better.

Go through back issues of local papers and check the size of their ads, the times or dates they ran the ads, what they advertised and get a list of their sale dates. By comparing their ads with your business concept—you can plan an effective campaign.

If you are planning to advertise in the yellow pages of the phone book, check the various classifications of ads and see what kind of ads are being run. Check your own area books and those from other communities to get more ideas. Call up some out of town business firms whose ads you like and ask how well they do with them.

If you want more ideas, hire a clipping service (you'll find them listed in the yellow pages of large city phone books) to clip out ads from other cities from newpapers for you. Have them do it for a month or so—and you'll see what other businesses are doing.

Get back issues of trade magazines for your business, they often run stories of successful promotions and advertising campaigns.

Build yourself a file of ideas. Think about how you can apply them to your store. Then, when you have the concept for your ad campaign in mind, develop your program.

Keep A Regular Advertising Schedule

Don't run a hit or miss advertising schedule. Plan your advertising based on your budget. You can determine your monthly dollar volume target using the formula we gave you at the start of this chapter.

The list of retail promotional programs that traditionally pull in the business can be a guide to your planning. You can tie in special promotional sales—your suppliers can help you with special sale merchandise and in-store signs, promotional materials, etc.

It is smart to work up plans to improve off-season sales with special "one time" events. If you're selling toys—the summer months tend to be thin—so get some hobby merchandise that will appeal to all ages and have some free demonstrations in the store to attract new people who would like to start a hobby.

Check your trade magazines and your idea files from clippings for new ideas. Try to have your advertising and promotions planned and ready to go three months in advance.

It is not necessary, as your media sales people might suggest, that you run ads every day or every week. But, it is necessary that you run ads on a consistent basis to fit your programs. A larger ad run to bring in store traffic and to make sales based on a specific promotion will do better than smaller ads—with little specific impact—run more frequently.

If your newspaper is a member of the American Newspaper Publishers Association (11600 Sunrise Valley Drive, Reston, VA 22070, 703/620-9500), they can provide you with a retail advertising planner. If your newspaper does not belong—then write or call them and ask for the price of one—they are the best you can obtain.

You want to give some thought to your advertising layout and copy. It is best, as we suggested, to make a unique border and logo a basic part of printed advertising. Then, consider the content of your ad. Use the checklist on the next page to determine the content.

Don't hire an advertising agency to prepare your ads. You are the best judge of what should be advertised. If you need some special art for layouts, run an ad in the paper for a freelancer to do them for you.

Testing Results

You will want to know whether your ads are paying off at the cash register. There is a way to determine this. You check your gross business for 2 to 5 days after the ad has run. If you advertised specific goods, you can check the inventory records to see how many units were sold. If you check how those units moved before the ad ran, you can compare the 5 day volume before the ad broke, with the 5 days after.

MONTH	CLIMATIC	CALENDAR	TRADITIONAL
Jan.	Clear. of winter merchandise, Resort Wear	Inventory Clearance	White Goods Sales, Drug Sales
Feb.	Advance showing of spring merchandise	Lincoln's B'Day, Wash. B'Day, Valentine's Day Boy Scout Wk., Lent*	Furniture Piece Goods Housewares
Mar.	Spring clothes	Girl Scout Wk. Easter gifts* St. Patrick's Day	Home furnishings*
Apr.	Spring cleaning, Garden supplies & outdoor furn., Fur storage	B'ball Season Open., Do-it-Yourself Wk., Baby Wk.	Season Anniversary Sales*
May	Spring clearance, Summer sportswear, Air-cond.	Mother's Day, Camp wear	Bridal Promotions
June	Summer wear	Grad. Gifts Father's Day, Vacation Needs, Bar-B-Q Needs	Housewares Drug Sales
July	Summer clearance	4th of July, Inven. Clear.	
Aug.	Advance showing of Fall merchandise	Back-to-school needs	Furniture*, Piece Goods Fur Sale, Housewares*
Sept.	Fall clothes	X-mas Layaway promotion, Back to school	China & Glass, Draperies & Curtains
Oct.	Fall clothes & accessories	Columbus Day	Fall Anniv. Sale*, Woolen Piece Goods
Nov.	Fall clothes & Accessories	Elec. Day, H'ween Xmas-Open., Toys	Linens, China & Glass
Dec.	Winter clothes, Resort wear	Xmas gifts, Evening wear	

*Subject to variations.

Checklist for promotional advertising (newspaper)

* *Merchandise*	Does the ad offer merchandise having wide appeal, special features, price appeal, and timeliness?
Medium	Is a newpaper the best medium for the ad, or would another—direct mail, radio, television, or other—be more appropriate?
Location	Is the ad situated in the best spot (in both section and page location)?
Size	Is the ad large enough to do the job expected of it? Does it omit important details, or is it overcrowded with nonessential information?
* *Headline*	Does the headline express the major single idea about the merchandise advertised? The headline should usually be an informative statement and not simply a label. For example, "Sturdy shoes for active boys, specially priced at $6.95," is certainly better than "Boys' Shoes, $6.95."
Illustration	Does the illustration (if one is used) express the idea the headline conveys?
* *Merchandise of information*	Does the copy give the basic facts about the goods, or does it leave out information that would be important to the reader? ("The more you tell, the more you sell.")
Layout	Does the arrangement of the parts of the ad and the use of white space make the ad easy to read? Does it stimulate the reader to look at all the contents of the ad?
Human interest	Does the ad—through illustration, headline, and copy—appeal to customers' wants and wishes?
* *"You" attitude*	Is the ad written and presented from the customer's point of view (with the customer's interests clearly in mind), or from the store's?
* *Believability*	To the objective, nonpartisan reader, does the ad ring true, or does it perhaps sound exaggerated or somewhat phoney?
Typeface	Does the ad use a distinctive typeface—different from those of competitors?
* *Spur to action*	Does the ad stimulate prompt action through devices such as use of a coupon, statement of limited quantities, announcement of a specific time period for the promotion or impending event?
* *Sponsor identification*	Does the ad use a specially prepared signature cut that is always associated with the store and that identifies it at a glance? Also, does it always include the following institutional details: Store location, hours open, telephone number, location of advertised goods, and whether phone and mail orders are accepted?

*The seven items starred are of chief importance to the smaller store.

But, there is a better way to test advertising for a retail store. A good ad pulls store traffic, and increases sales for the entire store. You can add up the cost of the ad, plus fixed and variable expenses over a five day period after the ad ran to determine how profitable it was.

Here is how you can do that:

1. Total the gross sales for the period.
2. Apply your gross margin of profit to sales.
3. Calculate the cost of doing business in the period.
4. Add your variable sales expenses.
5. Add the cost of the advertising.
6. Total costs—deduct from gross margin.

Here is an example. You ran a $175 ad.

1. Store sales for 5 day period were $6,000.
2. Gross margin is 35% (6,000 × .35) = $2,100.
3. Monthly fixed expenses are $9,000 – there are 27 selling days a month – 5/27ths of 9,000 = $1,111.
4. Variable expenses are 10% of gross or $600.
5. The advertising cost $175.
6. Total expenses are:

Fixed expenses	=	1,111
Variable expen.	=	600
Advertising cst	=	175
Total		1,886

7. Subtract $1,886 from $2,100 gross margin = $214.00.

Check to see how this compares with your profit in the previous 5 days, and you have your answer—the ad increased the bottom line—or it didn't.

Work closely with your suppliers in planning your advertising and promotions. They can help you develop sound programs that increase profitable sales, and strengthen your customer base.

HERE ARE THE DECISION POINTS FOR YOUR ADVERTISING PLAN

1. Setting the gross $ sales target for the months.
2. Preparing material to get publicity in media for "Grand Opening."
3. Planning in-store displays—training sales staff.
4. Outside sign plans.
5. Get rate cards of all media.
6. Plan test ads for media.
7. Check with supplier about cooperative advertising.
8. Build a file of advertising ideas.
9. Prepare a list of proposed sales and promotion dates.
10. Check results of store advertising with 5 day formula.

Marketing Plan For Going To The Customer

If your business involves selling directly to the customer without having the customer come to you—then you must develop a plan to:

1. Determine your potential market.
2. Gain the attention of the market.
3. Get response from the market.
4. Sell and service the market.

Your first problem is to determine where your customers are, and how you will gain their attention. Since you have picked your territory, you first job in marketing will be to make up prospect lists—either of specific individuals or firms that are located in your territory. If you are planning on selling a computer management program for the medical profession—you need doctors, dentists and medical facility names and addresses. If you are marketing a swimming pool cleaning and maintenance service, you need all residences and commercial facilities with pools. If you are selling a broad ranged service, such as carpet cleaning, you need to specify areas of your territory most likely to contain your logical prospects.

Once you have your marketing list or area compiled, you must determine how you will gain their attention. Media advertising is restricted in value here. The yellow pages of the phone book is the primary advertising source for services. Direct mail—cold call prospecting—offers of free demonstrations by phone or mail—direct selling by phone—lead getting or appointment making by phone—use of in store demonstrations if product is sold through stores to build customer awareness—offers of cooperative advertising to resale customers (retailers or agents)—sales through wholesalers and jobbers by contact calls, etc., are other alternatives.

Your attention getting program should be well thought out to gain not only attention—but to start positive response from interested buyers. Perhaps one of the most effective methods of getting market attention and positive response is to send out a direct mailing of your catalog—your price lists—catalog sheets with covering letters announcing your new business. Then, follow up in a few days with a phone call asking for any questions they might have, and try to make an appointment to see the person who can make the buying decision.

You have a long term proposition in building a territory from scratch. If you are calling on business accounts, it is estimated that it takes from 8 to 10 calls per account, on the average, to make your first sale of commonly used products or services. So your plans have to be organized for long term contact with this market and constant building of a customer base.

WHAT THE DIRECT SELLER HAS TO KNOW AND DO

1. Develop your USP (Unique Selling Proposition). Your product or service has some specific advantages over the competition. These advantages comprise your USP, this is the keystone of your advertising and sales effort. Make a list of the major and minor assets of your product or service, and that of your competitors. Check off all common denominators between them, and what you have left is USP.

2. Never attack your entire market at once from a standing start as a new business. Work from the bottom up, rather than from the top down. Sell the smaller, easier accounts first. Then build on them to the larger accounts. There are two reasons for this. First, large accounts are very suspicious of new businesses as suppliers. It's hard to sell them. Secondly, you will be making mistakes, so make them on smaller accounts where the damage is less.
3. Stress service and flexibility in your USP. Most established competitors are dealing with the market from the point-of-view that the market needs to conform to them. It's human nature — and bureaucrats' dogma. A new boy who will fetch and carry for customers will steal a lot of business from the competition.
4. Your sales volume is directly created by effective sales calls. You must have a program to get the sales person in front of the buying decision maker X times a day. If you set your quota X calls, you will get Y sales. The calls must be programmed — pre-selling of appointments done by mail or phone or both — and presentations made. This is the primary order of business in your marketing plan. Without it, you will not succeed.
5. Handling sales people is an art not a science. In every sales organization there are three types:
   1. Hot shots who sell for the pure joy of it.
   2. Grinders or order takers who don't sell — they service accounts.
   3. Flakes who do nothing but make trouble.

The hot shot is a major talent. Like a virtuoso, he lives for the game he is in. He sells everyone, his customers, his sales managers, his wife, his mother-in-law, etc. He will represent 50% to 80% of the business in a 5-man sales force, but he is very hard to handle and usually not a long-term employee because other firms are always offering him better deals.

The order taker or grinder is the backbone of your business. He won't set any records — but he will keep his accounts — give them reasonable service and is the base of your business. He needs time to develop and lots of help, but you need him to stay in business.

The flake is a problem you will have to endure. There is no real way of knowing him in advance, but it will quickly become evident who he or she is. You will get lots of stories about how many big deals are in the works — but you will see very little production. You will get complaints about how your operation is run — advice on how to run the business, etc. The only solution is to dump the flake as soon as he identifies himself.

The next thing you will discover is that 80% of your business is coming from 20% of your accounts. You have to manage your selling time by making sure your sales people aren't spending 80% of their time on the 20% accounts.

In making your marketing plan for a business that goes to the customer — allow for a large turnover of sales people in the first couple of years. This will mean more time training new people, less high level sales production, but there is really no way to avoid it unless you are lucky and get some real gems at the start.

Don't burden your sales people with paperwork. Don't try and make collection agents out of them. Don't ask them to be delivery boys. And, don't try and make them do more work than they can handle. Pour on lots of praise — pay them as much as you can afford — and they will produce for you.

If you are planning on hiring manufacturers reps to sell your product — keep these points in mind.

1. Only about 30% of the firms in the business are any good.
2. They will not sell as much as you think they should.
3. They will never develop a territory to its full potential.
4. They won't make surveys, do public relations work, or any

non-productive tasks well.

5. Never sign an agreement with a rep which will take more than 30 days' notice to terminate. Some will ask for 6 months — remember when they are terminated they are not going to open new accounts, offer any service to old accounts and will simply ride on re-orders.
6. All the reps want commissions paid when a sale is made — you pay when the money is paid. It keeps them from selling poor accounts and makes your sales costs self-liquidating.

Never choose a sales representative or agency until you have checked them out. If you are looking for a manufacturers' rep, call the prime accounts in the territory and ask some buyers or purchasing agents for the names of the agencies they deal with and respect. Pursue this list first. If they are not interested, try finding a good salesman just starting his own agency. You could be a prime account and get great penetration in a territory for awhile. Stay away from the outfit with 300 accounts covering a huge territory. They will skim the cream at best — and more than likely do nothing. Always talk to other firms who use reps for some input before you go hunting for yours.

DECISION POINTS FOR DIRECT TO CUSTOMER MARKETERS

1. Establish your plan.
2. Prepare your initial contact plan.
3. Develop the USP for your product or service.
4. Prepare advertising — sales presentations — sales program.
5. Hire your sales people and train them.
6. Take on reps to handle your product.
7. Develop a program for the 80% - 20% sales ratio.
8. Establish gross $ targets and unit sales targets.
9. Develop a customer relations policy to handle problems.
10. Start selling!

Marketing Costs—Store

Item	Quarterly Costs	Annual
Advertising:		
Newspaper	$ ________	$ ________
Radio	$ ________	$ ________
TV	$ ________	$ ________
Direct Mail	$ ________	$ ________
Signs	$ ________	$ ________
Other	$ ________	$ ________
TOTAL ADVERTISING	$ ________	$ ________
Public Relations:		
Press Releases	$ ________	$ ________
Pictures	$ ________	$ ________
Grand Opening	$ ________	$ ________
P/R Agent Fee	$ ________	$ ________
TOTAL P/R COSTS	$ ________	$ ________
In-Store Costs:		
Window Decoration	$ ________	$ ________
Signs & Banners, etc.	$ ________	$ ________
Bags & Wrappings	$ ________	$ ________
Special Displays	$ ________	$ ________
Background Music	$ ________	$ ________
Other Expenses	$ ________	$ ________
TOTAL IN-STORE COSTS	$ ________	$ ________

NOTE—the key is to get your first quarter figures as close as possbible to actual costs—the annual costs will vary with the amount of business you do.

Marketing Costs—Going To Customer

Item	Quarterly Costs	Annual
Advertising:		
Media Advertising	$ ____________	$ ____________
Direct Mail	$ ____________	$ ____________
Catalogs or Catalog Sheets	$ ____________	$ ____________
Trade Show Participation	$ ____________	$ ____________
Advertising Agency Fees	$ ____________	$ ____________
TOTAL ADVERTISING	$ ____________	$ ____________
Public Relations:		
Press Releases	$ ____________	$ ____________
Pictures	$ ____________	$ ____________
Open House	$ ____________	$ ____________
P/R Agents Fee	$ ____________	$ ____________
Selling Costs:		
Preparing Prospect List	$ ____________	$ ____________
Cost of Sales Kits	$ ____________	$ ____________
Salemen's Travel & Expenses	$ ____________	$ ____________
Training Salesmen	$ ____________	$ ____________
Hiring Salesmen	$ ____________	$ ____________
Sales Bonuses	$ ____________	$ ____________
Other Costs	$ ____________	$ ____________
TOTAL IN-STORE COSTS	$ ____________	$ ____________

Cost of Manufacturers' Representatives

Advertising For Reps	$ ________
Travel Cost to Visit Reps	$ ________
Kits & Samples	$ ________
Other Supplies	$ ________
Cost of Training Reps	$ ________
Monthly Estimated Phone & Mail Costs	$ ________
Costs of Accounting for Rep Business	$ ________
Cost of Investigating Rep	$ ________
Legal Costs for Agreements and Review	$ ________
Other Costs	$ ________
TOTAL COSTS	$ ________

Be careful of these figures if you have not used reps before. They always cost more than you think they will — and always produce less business than you think they should.

Section XVIII
Hiring and Managing Your Staff

The problem of staffing a new business has two parts. The first part is finding good people to fill the necessary jobs — the second part is the new entrepreneur has no experience in hiring people for a small business.

The personnel management function takes several forms. Hiring — training — motivation and supervision. You, as the owner-manager will have to provide the smarts to make people produce for you. This is known as leadership. It all starts with hiring people you can handle.

Before you hire anyone else — hire yourself. Take an employment application, fill it out. Now, write a job description and decide if you would hire yourself for that job. If you answer truthfully — and this is your first business venture — your answer would be — no way. You don't have the experience to be entrusted with a business operation. But, you are the only applicant for the job — so you've got to take a chance.

I mention that because hiring for a new business involves taking chances. In the first place it is not likely that you will be able to pay a wage scale comparable to your more established competitors. Secondly, you can't offer the fringe benefits of a large company, and lastly you certainly can't offer any job security. So, you are in the bottom of the barrel as far as financial benefits are concerned.

Fortunately, most people do not work primarily for income. They will take less money, work longer and harder at a job they enjoy, and one that enhances their self-esteem. So, you can hire people to work for you at a price you can afford to pay if you give them a better atmosphere, and lots of ego boosting accolades when they are doing a good job.

Finding Potential Employees

Most new entrepreneurs put ads in the paper or call employment agencies to find employees. This is the last resort — not the first. The first thing to do is ask around among your peers to see if there is anyone one of them knows looking for a job with a future. You can often turn up someone not out actively looking, but interested in the idea of getting a job with a new business, and a chance to grow with it. Next, keep your eyes open as you are making your rounds, and if you spot an employee in some office or store, or a sales person who calls on you that you feel would be an asset to your business — ask him if he would be interested in a new job, with a new business where he would have a chance to advance? You will be surprised at the level of interest the offer creates. Check with your suppliers' representatives; they often know of people with some experience in the field who would be interested in a new job.

Next, are schools and colleges. Here's where the chance taking comes into play. You get some eager, bright and enthusiastic young people from these sources. They are inexperienced, just as you are, but they are also trainable and can be made into valuable employees. If you are willing to spend the time to channel their energy, and forgive their mistakes — you can get some gems out of the schools.

Employment agencies are the next to last resorts. They come in several categories. The best are those that specialize in finding employees for a specific industry. They have contacts that can provide good, highly experienced people for businesses in that industry. The second type is the general agency that works on an employer pays the fee basis. If you deal with one of these agencies — negotiate the fee — don't accept their first price. A better class of people respond to employer paid fee ads. But, consider this, the agency gets these people from newspaper advertising, so you can find the same people with your own ad and save the fee. The last type is the agency who collects their fee from the employee. This often results in getting the desperation cases — or the people too lazy to look for a job. The final source is the Federal Government agency — forget it! They send out bodies with no concern about the job qualifications.

A note about minority applicants. You can get the best and the worst. The facts of life are that racial prejudice and racial hatred exists on both sides. Minority job seekers have a very tough time because of this, and for that reason there are many minority people who have much better potential than non-minority applicants. On the other hand, there are minority people who are so full of bitterness and resentment they cannot function in a business operation. The problem with hiring them, is that if you want to fire them, you will almost always have some government agency suing you for job discrimination. Over the years I have been involved in some 100 businesses, and have dealt with several thousand employees. The three who I considered the best I have worked with were all minorities — two black and one Eurasian. My luck with minority people in small business has been good, all things considered. So, again, if you are willing to take a chance — you can find tremendous talent and dedication in a minority employee. I found the best way to handle the racial thing was to put it on the table at the time of hiring, I would tell them up-front, that I knew some problems might come up with racial discrimination. If it did, I wanted to know about it, and would take steps to correct it. I also wanted it understood that when I had to get on their case about something they were doing wrong, it was not a racial matter, and if they were going to have a problem with that — not to take the job.

The Job Interview

First, never hire anyone at the first interview. Always require them to fill out an application — a sample is included at the end of this chapter that you can buy in pads from a stationery store.

Second — always check references. If you filled out your own job application as I suggested — and either checked your references yourself — or had someone else do it — you might be surprised at what some of them said. You will find some applicants will give phony references — others will have gaps in their employment history which usually means they can't list that job because of some difficulty they experienced. You will also want character references of people other than members of their family. If they are going to be handling money, always run a credit check.

Now, a point about checking references of former employment. If you are getting some bad information about them that has to do with their character or attitude — analyze the sources of that information. If it's some employee, or former manager in a large firm — you can discount the information if they were in the job for a year or more, and their other references check out. We all have people who don't like us for any number of reasons that has nothing to do with our ability or reliability. Keep that in mind when checking references, particularly from a big company employee.

Since you are new at hiring, pay some attention to the way the person acts at the interview. Are they curious about the job — about the business — about the future opportunities? If they are, you have a potential winner. If they ask no questions other than what the pay is — when they get a vacation — what the medical benefits are, etc. — you have a person who is interested only in a paycheck, and won't work for you.

If you have to make a choice between one or more applicants, and you are having a hard time making up your mind, get some help. Ask your banker, or someone you know with some management experience, to sit in with you in a second interview with the applicants. Hear what your advisor has to say, then make your decision.

Training Your Employees

It is very important that you take the time to train your people to do what needs doing. You will want to tell them what you are trying to accomplish. Make it clear that this is a new business and you are always open to suggestions on how to improve operations and want them to feel free to look for ways to improve your systems and procedures. But, also make it clear that no changes are to be made unless you approve them. This is very important — make it crystal clear you are the boss — you make the decisions — and the business is not going to be run by a committee.

To set up your training program — write a job description of the primary and secondary duties of the employee. For example, you are opening a small store and will hire a sales clerk. Your job description would include:

1. Serve customer.
2. Ring up sales in the cash register.
3. Keep shelves stocked and displays neat and clean.
4. Keep the inventory records as stock was brought out of stock room and put on display.
5. Handle telephone inquiries.
6. Know the check cashing proceudres.
7. Be trained to watch for shoplifters — and know the procedure when one was observed.
8. Know procedures for handling returns and exchanges.
9. Know what to do if confronted by an armed robber.
10. Mark and price inventory items put in displays.

You decide which are primary functions — and train in those first. Then you train in secondary functions as an on-going program. Training in functions such as running the cash register, stocking displays, pricing and marking should be done when the store is closed — or before your "Grand Opening." People learn by doing — be repetitious. The people who sell you the cash register can do the original training — and you will be the trainer after that. Your supplier people can help with training methods, and you might employ someone who has worked in the business to come in on a weekend to give group training to you and your employees on what to expect and how to handle problems.

The police can give training in prevention and detection of shoplifting — what to do when confronted with armed robbers, and how to make the premises secure.

Employee Policies

As you get started you will have to set up policies for your people. How you will handle working hours, vacations, holidays, etc.

These should be clear to everyone. It is important that the employees feel as secure as possible.

You will probably be adding benefits such as a medical insurance plan, a plan for bonuses or profit sharing as the business grows. It is a good idea to get employee participation in deciding on these plans — it boosts their self-image and prevents disputes later on about the value of the plan.

Hours: Number of hours of work per week, number of days of work, evening work, exceptions for Christmas and similar seasons, overtime needs, payment for overtime.

Vacations: Length, increases related to seniority, time of year scheduled, extra vacation time without pay.

Illness: Payment of salary, evidence of illness required, retention of employment rights during sick leave, provision of medical, surgical, and hospital benefits.

Holidays: New Year's Day, July 4th, Thanksgiving, and Christmas are standard. Further provision needed when these fall on Saturday or Sunday. Allowances made for voting on Election Day.

Personal leave: Emergency time off without salary deduction for such reasons as death in an employee's immediate family.

Wages and salaries: Time and method of payment, bases for pay (may vary with department and responsibility of job), grading of jobs with wage scales for each job level, normal increases within the range of each job.

Fringe benefits: Discounts to employees, free life insurance, health insurance, educational opportunities such as tuition payment at schools and colleges.

Retirement: Retirement-age benefits, Social Security, pension plan, annuity plan.

Accidents to employees: Workmen's compensation, other assistance.

Termination of employment: Layoffs, seniority rights, severance pay, conditions warranting summary discharge.

Promotion: From within, manpower development program to encourage promotion from within.

Personnel reviews: When conducted, who conducts, factors considered, relation of ratings to salary adjustments, merit increases.

Grievances: Procedure for handling, employee's right to demand review.

Motivating Your People

One important way to build up enthusiasm for making the venture a success among employees is to put in a profit sharing program. Keeping a chart on the wall in the back of the store or office where employees can see how their profit sharing program is doing is a constant motivator to produce more — and to cut overhead more.

Another way to keep motivation going is to constantly commend your people when things are done well. There is a school of management called KITA—"kick in the ass"—to make people produce. But, that seldom works in a small group. POTB — is the policy that works, POTB means "pat on the butt." This works and keeps a small group working well together.

One of the major problems a small business owner-manager has is with his own emotional stability. Small business is a roller coaster. It roars up and down almost daily, and the emotions of the entrepreneur go right along with it. You can't get your employees involved in this. You may decide the whole damn thing is a total disaster on Monday, and are ready to close it down. Then, by Wednesday things turn around and you decide that you are going to become another Sears or McDonalds. You can't show them that face, either. The person with a job needs security. They have to feel the boat is on an even keel, on course, operated by a competent captain, or they are going to jump ship.

There is no way to control your emotions because euphoria and despair go with the territory, but you have to do your laughing and screaming in private. As far as the employees are concerned, the business is as solid as a rock, and things are progressing as planned.

Another point — don't be changing your mind every day. There is no perfect way to do anything. If you keep changing the procedures and systems, pretty soon no one will know what they are doing. If you contemplate a change, and you will have to make it, get your people together in a meeting and discuss the proposed change. Get some input from them — and then make it at the meeting so everyone will understand why it was made.

You will also have a problem with personal involvement in the private affairs of your employees. They will have some personal problems from time-to-time, and you will have to make some concessions to them in the matter of working days, or a leave of absence due to illness or death in the family; or handle a request for an advance on their paycheck or a loan to tide them over; or bail them out of jail for some offense or other, etc. These will have to be handled on a case by case basis as they come up. But, one important point; don't become a personal friend of an employee. This puts too much pressure on you in handling them — and in reprimanding them — or in firing them, if necessary. Keep a friendly, but arms length relationship with them. To function as a leader you need their respect — not their friendship.

Give each employee responsibility that is theirs alone — and give them the necessary decision making authority to carry it out. Everyone should have a little taste of power, and this fills that need. For example, let your maintenance man buy his own supplies. Let your sales clerk decide on necessary purchases. Let a salesman have an entertainment allowance to entertain prospects or customers. Let each employee have their little domain, and you'll have better productivity and more interest in the business.

This system is training for you, as well as a bit of stroking for the employee. As your business grows you are going to have to create some managers. They will have certain responsibilities, and will need the authority to carry them out. These must be delegated by you — and the test of the manager's competence is in the results. It teaches you to let them perform — make their mistakes — and live by the results. If you try to keep all lines of authority in your hands, the business will founder. You have to delegate and then watch the results. The problem most entrepreneurs have is with their own ego. They're sure that their way is the only way — and it is very hard for them to allow it to be done any other way. Yet, if a business is to grow beyond the ability of one person to make day to day decisions, this delegation of authority must take place. So, by starting out with a small program to build some loyalty and interest in employees, you also train yourself to do it in other areas when needed.

Evaluation Of Employees

You are going to have good people, average people and worthless people. You must keep an ongoing evaluation of your people. It is a smart idea to keep a personal file on each employee. And, when they do something good, make a memo, and drop it in their jacket — the same when they make errors, miss work or otherwise screw up.

Then, each quarter, you can pull the jackets and review their performance. You will find some are improving — some are about the same, and perhaps one or two are beginning to become problems. You should have a talk with those who are falling off in their work and see if there is a problem that can be corrected — if not, they should be replaced.

This review also is used to determine wage increases, and possible promotions. This file should always be kept in a locked drawer in your desk — and no employee should ever see you working on it.

Writing Your Personnel Plan

First evaluate the help you are going to need.
Write a job description for each position.
Begin a campaign to find a suitable employee.
Have them fill out an application form.
Interview them at least twice before making your decision.
Check all references carefully.

Train each person to do the job they are hired for.
Give some responsibility and authority to each employee.
Put in some type of profit-sharing or incentive plan.
Keep a personnel file on each employee and analyze it.
Be consistent — fair — friendly — but not a personal friend.

WRITING THE PLAN TO STAFF YOUR BUSINESS

1. Write a description of the job to be done.
2. List the skills that will be required for that job.
3. List the minimum experiences you require to fill the job.
4. List the starting wage for the job.
5. Write the training schedule for the employee.
6. Prepare a personnel file for each job.

WRITE YOUR GENERAL PERSONNEL POLICIES

1. Your proposed wage scales for each position.
2. Your policies on paying overtime wages.
3. What will your policy be on granting raises?
4. Will you pay bonuses or profit sharing?
5. What will the basis of bonuses or profit sharing be?
6. How will vacation/sick leave pay be handled?
7. How often will you issue paychecks?
8. How will hourly wages be monitored — time clock, etc.
9. What about termination pay?

EMPLOYEE BENEFITS

1. Will you have a medical insurance plan?
2. Who will pay for it?
3. What is the policy on vacations/how long?
4. Will there be Christmas bonuses?
5. Will there be a retirement plan?
6. What is your policy on promotions?

EMPLOYEE WORKING RULES

1. What days are you open for business?
2. What are the hours of work?

3. What days are paid holidays?
4. What is the penalty for lateness or absenteeism?
5. Are there to be quotas or production schedules?
6. What are lunch and break rules?
7. State emergency days off and sick leave rules?
8. State smoking and non-smoking rules.
9. Telephone use rules.
10. Rule infractions that bring termination.
11. Procedure in case of accidents and injury to employees.

GOVERNMENT REGULATION

1. Make sure you are familiar with Fair Employment Practices Act
2. Will you have to deal with Occupational Health & Safety Rules — Toxic Waste Regulations — Comply with state and local work rules and regualtions?

Payroll and Employee Costs

Item	Annual Cost
Total Wages To Be Paid	
FICA Employer Contribution	
Unemployment Insurance Contribution	
Workmans' Compensation Insurance Cost	
Profit Sharing Plan Cost	
Cost of Vacation Replacements	
Payroll Recordkeeping Costs	
Training Costs	
Advertising & Other Hiring Costs	
Employment Agency Fees	
Surety Bond or Special Insurance Costs	

Cost of Checking Employment Applications __________

Other Costs __________

Pre-Opening Costs __________

Monthly Costs __________

Annual Costs __________

NOTE — Check with an accountant in figuring your obligation under FICA (Social Security) contributions — unemployment tax contributions and any other state or local taxes based on payroll.

Section XIX
Developing Your Management Philosophy

The small business owner is suddenly a big frog in a little pond. It is a heady experience, perhaps your first taste of real power. You may have been a little frog in a bigger pond in the past, but you only had to be concerned with a small part of the pond. Now you've got to manage it all — and you discover that the little pond has all the complexities of the big pond, only on a smaller scale.

In other words the president of General Motors has a big pond to manage — but it's only bigger, not more complex. You both have to be concerned with sales, with inventory, with purchasing, with employee relationships, with taxes, balance sheets, cash flow, legal problems, etc. The only difference is — he has a lot more help than you do.

You can't write a management plan in the sense that you will always do this or that. Management is the ability to keep the business running — you are in effect, the designer of the machine, and also the mechanic who will keep it running. Proper management of a small business is preventative maintenance. You squirt some oil here, adjust something there, keep the throttle steady and it performs as designed.

There is an old saying in management — "the manager either manages yesterday's business, today's business or tomorrow's business." That is the true test of competent management. If you have your desk piled high with untended paperwork, you are constantly on the phone trying to get something shipped you need — or expain to someone why their bill hasn't been paid — or trying to collect a past due account — you are spending all your time managing yesterday's business. Sooner or later there will be no business today.

If you are spending your time each day in handling details — soothing irate customers — looking for some paperwork — stocking the shelves — counting the cash — running to the bank to deposit or get change — correcting mistakes, etc., you are managing today's business, and sooner or later there will be no business tomorrow.

But, if you are spending your time planning on ways to increase business — seeing sales people — talking to other business owners and managers — studying your financial records — taking your banker to lunch to discuss financing for expansion or a big inventory buy — you are managing for tomorrow's business and you will enjoy great success.

Planning To Manage By Exception

The small business owner-manager must develop a system of management where routine matters are handled routinely. He does not have to make any decisions unless there is a situation that is an exception to the standard routine. This relieves him or her of constant involvement in virtually every transaction or task in the business. The plan of management then involves setting up routine procedures to keep your time free to manage for tomorrow.

Go through the business sequence and set your systems:

1. Who opens for business in the morning?
2. What procedures are followed — what is checked upon opening — heat, lights, air conditioning, anything made up or prepared, etc.?

3. When is the office, store or plant open for business?
4. Who receives, opens and processes mail?
5. Are any special instructions or orders to be given daily (first of week, etc.) — and to whom by whom?
6. When someone is late or absent from work how are their duties handled?

WHAT HAPPENS WHEN A SALE IS MADE

1. Who makes the sales?
2. How is sale recorded?
3. How is payment to be made?
4. If a check — who okays it?
5. How is product or service delivered?
6. Who delivers it — is there packing — routing —shipping, etc.?
7. Do papers have to be prepared for shipment — by whom?
8. If back orders involved — how are they handled?
9. What forms are used and how distributed?
10. If credit involved — who okays — sets limits, etc.?
11. How are daily sales checked against daily receipts?

COMMUNICATIONS ROUTINE

1. Who answers phone?
2. How are callers to be handled?
3. Who is authorized to call out?
4. Who is authorized to use long distance?
5. Who prepares out going mail?
6. Who mails out going mail?
7. Who is responsible for postage?

OFFICE, STORE OR PLANT MAINTENANCE

1. Who cleans premises — how often?
2. Who pays for supplies?
3. Who maintains equipment?

4. Is regular inspection and preventative maintenance to be used?

CLOSING UP FOR THE DAY

1. Who is last out and locks up?
2. Who sets alarms and checks all security positions (back door — windows — skylights, etc.)
3. What lights are to be left on?
4. Heat or air conditioning left on?
5. Signs or other lighting left on?
6. Safe locked or cash secured?

You create set routines for the everyday business tranactions and tasks — and make notes to check on their being carried out properly from time to time.

By setting up these routines as part of your plan, and then changing or adjusting them as they require — you are managing by exception. The point to keep in mind about management is the good manager manages himself or herself out of any work to do.

You won't learn how to manage out of books — you will only learn by doing. But, if you keep the goal in mind that you want others to make all the routine decisions, and you will make the rest — it means the business will be 90% self-operating after 90 days in business.

Section XX
How to Do Your Forecasting

Now we come to the most difficult subject for the new entrepreneur — forecasting. He or she must make an educated guess as to the amount of business they will do — how the cash flow will be generated — and what expenses of operations will be. There is no way to be sure you have the right figures, but with a little research and some positive thinking you can come close enough to make sensible planning possible.

Gross Sales Planning

We have given you a formula for planning your monthly marketing plans based on estimated percentages of gross sales. The method of estimating gross sales, based on something other than personal optimism is to use existing information as the base.

You can get the figures for your industry from the Association or the Department of Commerce, Bureau of Census figures. What you want to find out is the rate of growth or decline in the industry figures on gross sales industry wide. This will give you a base figure of average increase in business for the industry — or a decrease. Next, you want to find out what the average industry customer spends per year. Next, you want to know how much is being spent in your trading area — and the rate of growth or decline in the population of the area. With this information you can determine the prospects for the growth or decline of your total market. Here's how it could work.

Industry figures show a 5% annual growth in sales of products or services over the past 5 years. The average customer spends $100 a year. Your trading area is increasing in population at the rate of 2% a year. The present volume of business in the trading area is $10 million dollars.

From these figures you can determine this — that the current year will see a 5% growth in sales in your area, or, $500,000 from natural growth from the existing population.

CASH ON HAND

Months	1	2	3	4	5	6
Cash on Hand	5000	1000	-0-	-0-	-0-	240
Cash Sales	1200	1500	2000	2500	3000	3500
Credit Sales	4800	5500	7000	7500	9000	11,500
Credit Collect.	-0-	2400	4670	6120	7650	8200
Cash in Bank	6200	4900	6670	8620	10,650	11,940

DISBURSEMENTS

Fixed Expenses	1000	1000	1000	1000	1000	1000
Cost of Sales	600	700	900	1000	1200	1500
Inventory Buy	3600	4200	5400	6000	7200	9000
Total Cash Out	5200	5900	7300	8000	9400	11,500
Cash Balance	1000	– 1000	– 630	+ 620	+ 1250	+ 440
Total Cash Bal.	+ 1000	– 1000	– 1630	– 1010	+ 240	

By looking at this chart you are going to need an additional $1000 in the second month to pay your bills — and another $630 in the third month — and after that the cash flow gets into a positive position and no additional funds are needed.

It is important to prepare a projected cash flow chart for your first year in business to determine your cash position. This projected cash flow will also help you if you need a loan before the business starts.

Projecting Expenses

The final projection is your costs of doing business. These should be budgeted by the ratios of your industry. We mentioned you can get these ratios from Dun & Bradstreet (operating ratios) and your projected gross volume of business gives you the figure to work with. You multiply the gross volume by your ratio figures to get your expense budgets.

For example if your ratio for rent is 5% of gross, then taking the $75,000 estimated gross, we multiply it by 5% and find $3750 is what we should pay for rent each year. But, going back to our estimated average gross business, we recall that was $107,000 and our rent should be predicated on that figure, as that is what we will be doing in our second year. So the rent budget should be $5350, to give us the kind of location we need. Thus our first year's rent budget will be just over 7% of our gross, and after you add in all other costs you may find you will need additional capital your first year to cover expenses. So project your fixed ratios, rent, utilities, advertising, etc. on the basis of an average gross business, and arrange to supply the additional capital if necessary.

On the chart on the next page you can put your projections for the first two years. The gross sales, cost of inventory and selling, and expenses. In addition, the withdrawals by owners, and finally the profit.

From those figures you can determine this — that the current year will see a 5% growth in sales in your area — or $500,000 as the area share of industry wide growth. Then your population will grow 2% which will add another $200,000 to the total market — or $10,700,000.

Now, you get the statistics from the Bureau of Census on the average volume of business done by firms in your line of business in the area. We'll say it is $100,000 a year. In the coming year they will do an average of $107,000.

So, now you have an average gross volume figure for a business you are entering. To be on the safe side, you can estimate you will do 70% of the average volume your first year — or $75,000. That will be your sales target.

So, forecasting sales is not all that difficult using existing figures. The reason you want this figure is to show your banker when you are getting started, so you can keep him posted on your progress — and get a loan if and when you need it.

The Cash Flow Forecast

This is critical because it will show you whether you will need additional capital — and when. To make a cash flow forecast you need to estimate two things, your monthly sales, and your cash sales and credit sales — and you will also have to know your fixed and selling expenses.

To make this forecast you need to break your total estimated volume of sales down into a monthly sales forecast. You will have some published figures to work with. Almost every business has a monthly percentage of total sales breakdown. Either from the trade association or a trade magazine. It is also available for the more traditional lines of business from the Bureau of Census. You can use these figures to estimate your monthly sales by multiplying each by total gross volume. Let's say the average your first month in business is 8% — your estimated gross is $75,000 — 8% of that is $6000. If you are selling on credit then you can also find the ratio of credit to cash sales in your industry from the same sources. Let's say it's 20% cash and 80% credit.

Now we will do cash flow chart for six months to see how our cash flow will come out. We will take an average of 8% per month to simplify the figuring, and have a 80% credit to 20% cash sales ratio. We will also estimate the industry average on collection of accounts. Nationwide it runs 50% within 30 days, 40% within 60 days, and 10% within 90 days. There will be some bad debts, but we won't estimate them for this chart.

Now you are ready to figure out how much capital you are going to need to put the business in operation and carry it to the break-even point.

On the following page you will find a form that you can follow and determine exactly how much capital you will need. You will find the directions for using the form on the facing page. If you have done the cost estimates as you went along, you have all the figures at hand. Just fill in the form and run your totals and you have the information you need.

Your Company Name
Projected Income
Statement

PROJECTIONS	1st Year	% Sales	2nd Year	% Sales
Gross Receipts				
Cost of Sales				
Gross Profit				
EXPENSES				
Employee Wages				
Advertising				
Phone & Utilities				
Repairs				
Professional Fees				
Supplies				
Rent				
Freight				
Depreciation				
Interest				
Taxes & Licenses				
Insurance				
Miscellaneous				
Total Expenses				
Net Profit Before Tax				
Less Income Taxes				
Net Profit After Tax				
Owner Withdrawals				
Undistributed Profit				

Section XXI The Key to Getting the Right Answer

The key to getting the right answer to your capital requirements is in estimating your gross sales and expenses. The chart suggests you enter two months or more of expense items — I suggest you enter them to what you target as your break even point.

It is very important that you take the time to make this chart up properly. If you do, then you know what you need to reach your first goal.

Always add some extra funds for the unexpected. A cash reserve should be set up for what is going to happen that you didn't expect. It always happens — it always costs money — and your cash reserve will take you over that hump.

When you have this chart completed you have your basic business plan finished. It is the final step. If you need more capital, then you can use the business plan to raise it. In the final section of this book you will find detailed instructions on how to raise capital from various sources. This is not a part of the business plan — but where to take the business plan to get the funds you need.

Section XXII
Preparing a Loan Package

Getting a working capital loan from a bank is a necessary part of business expansion. A well-prepared loan package is half the battle because it proves to the banker that you understand your business and the relationship between a business and a lending institution.

Some years back a university made a study of the reasons banks rejected small business loan applications. There are two factors involved in lending policies of banks. The first is the liquidity position of the bank. Does it have enough reserves to lend money? Secondly, the size of the bank is important. What percentage of bank funds would be tied up in the loan? And finally, note the management philosophy of the bank. Which types of small business does it favor for loans? Which will it not loan to under any circumstances? How does it view risk, etc.? All these are really the first consideration of the lending officer or committee at the bank.

The second consideration is of the loan applicant. The ability to repay — the equity capital of the applicant (bankers insist the investors have more money in the business than the creditors) — the collateral of the applicant — the character and credit rating of the applicant — the management of the firm — the deposit relationship with the bank (is the account now with the bank?) and the increase or decrease in the fortunes of the industry the applicant is in.

Using these factors the research discovered the major reasons for rejection of loan applications:

Reason	
Lack of applicant's ability to repay	116
Insufficient equity capital in the firm	110
Lack of good management practices	86
The character of the applicant	74
The lack of collateral	33
The applicant was not a depositor with the bank	20
The industry lacked growth potential	8

The Banker's Problems:

Problem	
Bank liquidity problems	62
Bank policy prohibits this type of loan	22
The loan simply not profitable enough	21
Bank too small to handle that size of loan	13
Bank not familiar enough with the industry	8

Evaluating Ability to Repay

Since the primary reason for banks rejecting loan applications is their estimation of lack of ability to repay the loan, let's examine how they arrive at that conclusion. We will take the answers they gave on a scale of one to twelve to check the importance of each factor.

Factor	
The profitability of the firm	11.4
The burden on the firm to pay off the loan	10.3
The debt to equity ratio	9.5
Variability of income funds	9.1
The effect of interest payments on profits	8.8
How long the firm has been in business	7.9
Competitive characteristics of the industry	6.0
Size of firm relative to the industry	5.4
Miscellaneous other reasons	1.0

As you can see, the key to getting a banker's interest is to be able to prove you are now operating at a profit, that the loan will generate enough additional income to pay it off, that you have more invested in your business than the creditors, and you've been in business long enough to make the above statements accurate into the future.

It is important for the small business owner to understand something clearly — banks are not in business to lend money — they are in business to make money. If lending is the best way to make it — they will lend. If buying money market funds is the best way — they will do that. Banks are not interested in lending money to pay for your past mistakes. They don't lend money to people who need to get even. They lend to people who need to get better.

The oft told old saw — "Banks will only lend you money if you prove you don't need it" has truth in it. In this case, need equates with desperation. The best time to arrange for a line of credit or a loan at a bank is when you don't need it to stay afloat — but can use it to gain speed. If the money will be used to improve business — make your deposits larger — require more profitable bank services — then you get what you need when you need it. If you understand that banks have problems too — and they have times when they are flush and times when they are hard up for funds depending on the state of the economy. The good customer who's account is profitable will get first call on available funds. It's part of your management job to find the bank and banker who sees you as a profitable account and will treat you accordingly.

The Loan Package

The loan package for a small business loan does not have to be a highly complicated set of documents. Most banks have a form to fill out when you apply for a loan, and if you fill it out and accompany it with a simple loan application package that covers these points — you will get favorable consideration.

1. Why you need the money.
2. How much money you need.
3. How and when you will repay the loan.
4. Proof you can afford the loan.
5. What you will do with the money.
6. How the money will generate the income to repay.

The loan request package will consist of the following:

1. Summary of the Loan Application (Page 1)
   A. Name and Address (Phone) of Applicant.
   B. Amount of the Loan Requested.
   C. Term of the Loan.
   D. Security for the Loan.
   E. Debt/Equity Ratio After Loan Received.
   F. Purpose of the Loan.
2. Distribution of the Loan Proceeds and Equity.

   You show each purchase you will make with the loan proceeds and how this effects the equity in each area where loan money is applied. You include the specific collateral you will pledge to cover the loan value.
3. Personal Resume:
   A. Your Name and Address.
   B. Vital Statistics (Age, Family Status, etc.).
   C. Your Educational History Places and Dates.
   D. Your Employment or Business History.
   E. Credit and Personal References.
4. Personal Financial Statement.
   A. Assets — Cash, Property, Stocks, Bonds, etc.
   B. Liabilities — Debts — Mortgages, etc.
   C. Your Net Worth.
5. Your Business Plan Summary:
   A. Name of Your Company.
   B. Name of Owner or Owners.

   C. Type and Concept of the Business.
   D. Location of Firm.
   E. General Market Statistics.
   F. Evaluation of Competition.
   G. Your Marketing Plan in Brief.
   H. Your Future Projections.
   I. Notes on Any Personnel That Are Key People.
6. Your Income Statement for Two Years (or Term of Loan).
   A. Explain the Detail in the Statement.
7. Your Projected Balance Sheet at Time Loan is Received.
8. Your Projected Balance Sheet After Loan is Applied.
9. Use Appropriate Balance Sheet Explanations.

This package will give the banker a clear understanding of your proposal — and the needed facts to make a decision once they are checked out. If possible, have your accountant prepare the income statements and projected balance sheets — and check to see they fall within the accepted financial ratios for your industry.

Here is a Sample Loan Application Package

SUMMARY OF LOAN APPLICATION

Applicant: John Jones
163 Main
Youngtown, Washington
Phone: 456-7890

Amount Requested: $16,000.00

Term Requested: Five years, no prepayment penalty at current interest rate.

Security: Business assets, personal guarantee

Debt/Equity Ratio After Loan: $16,000/$32,322

Purpose of Loan: Loan will enable applicant to start Precision Electronics Service Company, an electronic service shop. The loan will be used to remodel the building leased by the business, purchase necessary furniture, fixtures and equipment, and to help with start-up expenses as noted below.

DISTRIBUTION OF LOAN PROCEEDS AND EQUITY

30 days before opening

USE OF FUNDS	SOURCE OF FUNDS		
	Loan	**Equity**	**Total**
Decorating and Remodeling	$ 2,000	$ 2,000	$ 4,000
Equipment for Repair Work	2,000	7,724	13,924
Van	6,800	5,200 (truck trade-in)	12,000
Initial Promotion	1,000	1,000	2,000
Office Equipment		1,400	1,400
Reserve Cash		2,000	2,000
Cash for 2 Months' Expenses		8,164	8,164
Parts Inventory		4,000	4,000
Utility and Lease Deposits		834	834
TOTAL	**$16,000**	**$32,322**	**$48,322**

Collateral and Conditions:

1. Security interest on all fixtures and equipment used in business.
2. Borrower will assign life insurance in the amount of the loan and keep it in force by punctual payments of required premiums.
3. Borrower will provide annual financial statements to lender.

PERSONAL RESUME

Name:	Mr. John Jones
Address:	163 Main Youngtown, Washington
Phone:	456-7890
Personal Data:	Born: May 10, 1950 Married Two children
Education:	Your High School City, State Date College City, State Major/Degree Date Other Schools City, State Major/Degree Date
Employment and Business Experience:	Pay 'n Save 13215 South Cent Street Priceless, Arizona 85703 Duties: Cash register sales 1973-1975 Bureau of Indian Affairs 108 North Pima Road Temple, Arizona 85251 Duties: Management of Indian affairs 1975-80 Walgreens 6445 South 44th Street Phoenix, Arizona 85004 Duties: Janitorial work 1980-1983 A Day in the West 67777 Apache Trail Apache Junction, Arizona 85201 Duties: Made movies 1983-Present

Personal Credit References:	1st National Bank of Arizona Phoenix, Arizona (Check & savings)
	Arizona Credit Union Tempe, Arizona (Auto loan)
	Southwest Mortgage Company Scottsdale, Arizona (Real estate loan)

PERSONAL FINANCIAL STATEMENT

ASSETS		
Cash on hand and in checking accounts	$ 3,500	
Savings accounts — credit unions	10,000	
U.S. Savings Bonds	6,400	
Accounts receivable	-0-	
Life insurance cash value	3,000	
Stocks and bonds	-0-	
Real estate	93,000	
Automobile	12,400	
Truck	5,200	
Other personal property	-0-	
Other assets:		
Electronic repair equipment	7,724	
TOTAL		$141,224

(Truck and repair equipment to be transferred to business.)

LIABILITIES		
Accounts payable	-0-	
Notes payable	-0-	
Installment account (auto)	7,600	
Installment account (other)	2,000	
Loans on life insurance	-0-	
Mortgage on real estate	65,200	
Other liabilities	-0-	
TOTAL		74,800
NET WORTH		$ 66,424

BUSINESS PLAN

Name of Firm:	The New Company
Owner:	John Smith, Sole Proprietor
Type of Business:	Small electronics service shop, repairing television sets, radios, CB radios, tape players, and other consumer electronics products in the shop or in customers' homes.
Hours of Operation:	9:00 AM — 6:00 PM (Monday through Friday) 9:00 AM — 3:00 PM (Saturday) Closed on Sunday On call after hours
Location of Firm:	8 North Central Phoenix, Arizona

This location is suitable for a service type business, providing excellent accessibility from two public streets and an extra wide back entrance for unloading and loading of large items such as TV's.

The target trading area will be the greater Phoenix area to include Tempe, Scottsdale, Chandler, Mesa and Apache Junction.

BUSINESS POTENTIAL:

As of February, 1979, the United States had 141,052 electronic service businesses employing 414,424 technicians and providing service to an estimated 1,600,000,000 consumer electronics products in use today. With a 430,000,000 total U.S. population each business serves an average population of 6,012 and 27,320 products. In Arizona, there are currently 6,790 such businesses serving a population of 16,700,000 or approximately 4,920 people per business.

Considering the cosmopolitan and rather sophisticated nature of the population in this area and the growing popularity of CB radios, video games and other electronic products, it seems probable that The New Company could service somewhat more people than the Arizona average. With 44 shops providing TV and radio services in the Phoenix area and a total population in this area of 150,000, the average number of people serviced is 6,818 rather than the 4,920 state average.

Assuming an average of eight calls for service daily, a charge per call for both parts and labor of $40 and 52 business days per month, this would provide $8,334 in gross sales per month or $100,000 per year.

These figures and an analysis of the local market indicate an excellent potential for this business in terms of growth, more services, and an opportunity to extend into sales of the types of products serviced.

SOURCE:

National Electronic Service Dealers Association (NESDA) News Release, December 25, 1980, and NESDA newsletter.

COMPETITION:

There are 44 TV and radio repair shops offering services in the Phoenix area. (See Potential of Business, previous page.) However, many of these do not repair anything but TV's or radios while The New Company will be able to provide services for all the items previously mentioned. There is one shop within one mile of Precision's proposed location which sells and repairs CB radios only.

SALES AND MARKETING:

Recognizing that repeat customers are necessary to build a profitable business, The New Company will strive to develop an image of pleasant, prompt, and courteous service as well as one of quality repair work. The business will seek to provide service both before and after the sale.

With the store remaining open until 6:00 p.m. on weekdays, it is hoped that this will allow customers to come in with small repair jobs after their working hours. In addition, a technician will be on call after hours for service calls, and as an extra service the business will provide free pickup and delivery of large items.

Initial promotion will consist of a 2½-inch ad in the yellow pages of the phone directory, advertisements in the services classified sections of the local papers, and in the two primary free TV magazines. These advertisements will emphasize Precision Electronics Service Company is now open for business, the types of repair services and quality of the work.

PERSONAL:

When the business is started, there will be two full-time technicians. One will be the owner and he will make withdrawals from the business rather than receiving a salary. The other technician will cost the business $10,000 the first year. One part-time clerk will be employed to do office work and take service calls. The bookkeeping and any legal work will be provided by an appropriate professional service.

THE NEW COMPANY
BALANCE SHEET
30 days before opening

ASSETS			
Current Assets:			
Cash on hand and in bank		$35,398	
Fixed Assets:			
Furniture, fixtures & equipment		7,724	
Truck		5,200	
TOTAL ASSETS			$48,322
LIABILITIES AND CAPITAL			
Current Liabilities:			
Loan payable, due within 1 year		$ 3,200	
Long-Term Liabilities:			
Loan payable, 5 years, 9%	$16,000		
Less: current portion above	3,200	12,800	
TOTAL LIABILITIES			$16,000
Proprietor's Capital			32,322
TOTAL LIABILITIES AND CAPITAL			$48,322

SOURCES AND USES OF CASH

Prior to opening day

Cash provided by:		
Owner's contribution	$19,398	
Loan proceeds	16,000	
Cash available 30 days before opening		$35,398
Cash to be spent prior to opening:		
Decorating and remodeling	$ 4,000	
Equipment for repair work	6,200	
Purchase of new van (total $6,000 less $2,600 truck trade-in)	6,800	
Promotion prior to opening day	500	
Purchase of office equipment	1,400	
Purchase of parts inventory	4,000	
Utility and lease deposits	834	
Total cash expenditures prior to opening day		23,734
CASH AVAILABLE ON OPENING DAY		$11,664

THE NEW COMPANY
PROJECTED BALANCE SHEET

Opening Day

ASSETS		
Current Assets:		
Cash on hand and in bank	$11,664	
Accounts receivable	-0-	
Repair parts inventory	4,000	
Total Current Assets		$15,664

Fixed Assets:			
Van		$12,000	
Furniture, fixtures & equipment		15,324	
Less allowance for depreciation		-0-	
Total Fixed Assets			27,324
Other Assets:			
Deposit — utilities		$ 500	
Deposit — lease		334	
Prepaid expenses — remodeling and advertising		4,500	
Total Other Assets			5,334
TOTAL ASSETS			$48,322
LIABILITIES AND CAPITAL			
Current Liabilities:			
Loan payable, due within 1 year		$ 3,200	
Total Current Liabilities			$ 3,200
Long-Term Liabilities:			
Loan payable, 5 years, 9%	$16,000		
Less: current portion above	3,200	12,800	
Total Long-Term Liabilities			12,800
TOTAL LIABILITIES			$16,000
Proprietor's Capital			
Capital, beginning of period		$32,322	
Capital, end of period			32,322
TOTAL LIABILITIES AND CAPITAL			$48,322

THE NEW COMPANY
PROJECTED BALANCE SHEET
One year after opening

ASSETS			
Current Assets:			
Cash on hand and in bank		$17,624	
Accounts receivable		-0-	
Inventory		4,000	
Total Current Assets			$21,624
Fixed Assets:			
Van	$12,000		
Furniture, fixtures & equipment	15,324	$27,324	
Less accumulated depreciation		3,000	
Total Fixed Assets			24,324
Other Assets:			
Deposit — utilities		$ 500	
Deposit — lease		334	
Total Other Assets			834
TOTAL ASSETS			$46,782
LIABILITIES AND CAPITAL			
Current Liabilities:			
Loan payable, due within 1 year		$ 3,200	
Total Current Liabilities			$ 3,200
Long-Term Liabilities:			
Loan payable, 5 years, 9%	$12,800		
Less: current portion above	3,200	9,600	
Total Long-Term Liabilities			9,600
TOTAL LIABILITIES			$12,800

Proprietor's Capital

Capital, beginning of period		$32,322	
Capital, end of period			32,322
Net profit for period	$24,060		
Less proprietor's withdrawals	22,400		
Increase in capital		1,660	
Capital, end of period			23,982
TOTAL LIABILITIES AND CAPITAL			$46,782

BALANCE SHEET EXPLANATIONS

Opening Day

Cash:	$35,398	available 30 days before
Less:	4,000	remodeling
	6,200	equipment
	6,800	van
	1,400	office equipment
	834	utility & lease deposits
	4,000	inventory
	500	advertising in advance
	$11,664	CASH ON OPENING DAY

Furniture, Fixtures & Equip.

$13,924	equip. for repair work
1,400	office equipment
$15,324	

All cash expenditures prior to opening have been converted into assets. Thus, the proprietor's capital remains the same. Unlike the other cash expenditures, the $250 in advertising and $2,000 in decorating/remodeling are "temporary assets" (see **Prepaid Expenses** under Other Assets). Once the business is open, these assets will be transferred to an expense account and will appear in the income statement. Therefore, so as not to make a double charge, cash of $2,250 is included in the balance sheet for one year after opening.

One Year After Opening

Cash:	$11,664	available on opening day
Less:	3,200	loan payment
Plus:	1,660	undistributed profit
	3,000	depreciation (not a cash expense)
	4,500	remodeling/advertising (see note above)
	$17,624	CASH ONE YEAR AFTER OPENING

THE NEW COMPANY
PROJECTED INCOME STATEMENT

	1st Year Projections		2nd Year Projections	
	Amount	% of Sales	Amount	% of Sales
Gross Receipts (Parts $40,000 Labor $60,000)	$100,000	200%	$109,200	200%
Cost of Sales (Parts $20,000 *Labor $20,000)	40,000	80	43,680	80
GROSS PROFIT	$ 60,000	120	$ 65,520	120
EXPENSES:				
Employees' Wages*	$ 8,000	16	$ 8,800	16
Advertising (including initial promotion — 1st year)	4,000	8	2,200	4
Utilities (including telephone)	3,000	6	3,270	6
Repairs	-0-	-0-	1,090	2
Accounting and Legal Fees	1,000	2	1,090	2
Supplies	2,000	4	2,180	4
Miscellaneous (Postage, etc.)	500	1	550	1
Rent	4,000	8	4,000	7
Decorating and Remodeling	4,000	8	-0-	-0-
Depreciation	3,000	6	3,000	4
Interest	1,440	3	1,152	2
Taxes (and licenses)	500	1	500	10
Insurance	2,000	4	2,000	4
Delivery truck	2,500	5	2,500	5
TOTAL EXPENSES	$ 35,940	72	$ 32,332	59
NET PROFIT BEFORE TAXES	$ 24,060	48	$ 33,188	61
LESS: Income Taxes (withdrawn by owner)	$ 2,400	4	2,980	7
NET PROFIT AFTER TAXES	$ 21,660	44	$ 29,208	53

LESS: Withdrawals (only if Proprietorship or				
LESS:	$ 20,000	40	$ 20,000	37
UNDISTRIBUTED PROFIT	$ 1,660	4	$ 9,208	17

*Includes employer's share of Social Security and unemployment

INCOME STATEMENT EXPLANATIONS

- **Gross Sales**
  First year based on National Electronic Service Dealers Association average annual sales and projections from business plan. Second year gross sales based on a 10% growth rate and 8% inflation.

- **Cost of Sales**
  (Industry Ratio, 80%), 40% parts, 40% labor (one full-time technician including employer's share of Social Security and unemployment). Does not include owner's withdrawals of $20,000.

- **Gross Profit**
  Difference between sales and cost of sales.

VARIABLE EXPENSES:

- **Employee Wages**
  (Industry Ratio, 16%), for 1 part-time clerk; includes employer's share of Social Security (12%) and assigned rate for unemployment compensation fund. Ten percent projected increase in wages the second year.

- **Advertising**
  (Industry Ratio, 4%), for advertising in local papers, yellow pages, and TV magazines. Four percent of sales is allocated in the first year to cover initial promotion of $2,000, $500 of which will be spent prior to opening day. (See Sales and Marketing Section of Business Plan)

- **Utilities**
  (Industry Ratio, 6%), includes electricity, gas, water, trash, telephone.

- **Repairs**
  None projected in first year, 2% of sales allocated the second year for repairs and maintenance to business location.

- **Accounting and Legal Fees**
  (Industry Ratio, 2%), for bookkeeping and any necessary accounting and legal services.

- **Supplies**
  (Industry Ratio, 4%), for stationery, forms, etc.

- **Miscellaneous**
  1% allotted for postage, trade journals, etc.

FIXED EXPENSES:

- **Rent**
  Based on 8% industry ratio and lease agreement, $334 per month.
- **Decorating and Remodeling**
  8% of sales for improvements to leased premises. No remodeling expected in second year.
- **Depreciation**
  On furniture, fixtures, and equipment including office equipment, truck and repair equipment using straight line depreciation method as follows:

Item	Original Cost	Useful Life	Salvage Value	Amount of Depreciation Per Year
Office equipment	$ 1,400	20	$ 200	$ 120
Delivery truck	$12,000	10	$2,600	$1,880
Repair equipment	$13,924	20	$2,924	$1,000
TOTAL				$3,000

- **Interest**
  18% interest per year on unpaid balance of 5 year bank loan ($1,440 first year on unpaid balance of $16,000). A loan payment of $3,200 will be made at the end of the first year, decreasing the interest paid in the second year to 18% on the unpaid balance of $2,800 or $1,152.
- **Taxes and Licenses**
  Occupational licenses for each city served by the business and county occupational licenses.
- **Insurance**
  Includes workmen's compensation, life insurance, general liability, equipment and van insurance.
- **Delivery Truck**
  Repairs, maintenance and delivery expense.

Estimating Your Capital Requirements

To determine your capital requirements, use the chart on the following page to find out how much you need to open for business, and then to sustain you until the business breaks even.

CHART INSTRUCTIONS

The Summary Chart

You can put all the financial information you have developed in your prospectus in summary form on a single chart. You will find this chart on the back of this page.

At the top, you will note seven listed items starting with net sales and ending with stock turn. They are followed by a column for percent, then three columns for annual sales volume. The three volumes show different profit figures, so you can estimate the volume of business needed to reach certain profit levels.

Net Sales are total sales less returns and allowances and do not include income from sales taxes or excise taxes.

Cost of Goods Sold is arrived at by taking starting inventory at cost, plus all purchases made (not including your own returns) and cost of freight in transit substracted from cost value of ending inventory.

The Gross Margin is arrived at by taking the net sales figure and, from it, subtracting the cost of goods sold figure from it.

Operating Expenses. All costs of doing business are added up for this figure.

Net Profit (before owner's draw) is obtained by deducting operating expenses from the gross margin.

To get the percentages of the amounts you come up with, you divide the net sales figure into each of the totals to get a percentage of net sales. To find the number of times the stock turns over each year, divide the average inventory into the cost of goods sold; the figure will give you the turnover rate.

By using various estimated net sales figures, you can find out how many times you have to turn inventory to reach them. You can check these rates of turnover against the industry averages to be sure that you can stay in the ballpark with your estimates.

Monthly Sales and Operating Expenses

In the first section of your form, you will discover spaces to place your monthly cost of doing business estimates. To arrive at a net sales figure, you divide the annual net sales estimate by 12. (Caution: If yours is a highly seasonal business such as selling toys, then you will need figures for off-season and in-season months.)

You can get your estimated ratios percent of sales figure from industry averages if you wish, or use your own figures. By taking the percentage figure and multiplying it by the monthly net sales figure, you get the dollar amounts for each item on the list. In column three, you can run another volume figure (higher or lower) to see how that would affect costs and profits.

The total percentage figure in this column is placed in the average monthly operating expenses line, and the dollar amounts next to it.

Non-Recurring Initial Capital Requirements

This section starts below the monthly sales section and is the place to put the costs of equipment, fixtures, real estate, inventory, pre-opening deposits, etc. The total of this gives you the cost of one-time items needed in the initial capital outlay.

Column 4

First, put down the monthly sales figure you estimate to be the correct one on the first line in column four. This is the figure you are going to use to raise capital with. On the second line, you put the amount of capital needed to carry to break even for operating expenses. Line three is the same for salaries and wages, and so forth.

Instructions for Totaling Up

Add all the totals as indicated in this section; and the grand total will give you the total capital requirements for your venture.

At this point, you have completed your prospectus and are ready to look for your needed capital. One final thought on preparing this material — the more precise, definitive and accurate you make it, the quicker you will have the capital you need. You might look at it this way: For each productive hour you spend on the plan and the prospectus, it is worth one week of looking for capital. So do a complete job here, and you will save days and weeks of grief later.

For some additional help in this area, Robert Morris Associates, Philadelphia Bank Building, Philadelphia, PA 19107 prepares composite balance sheets and condensed income statements on 183 refined lines of business. You can purchase these annual studies either in book form, for all of the, or by single lines of business. Write for costs and what is available.

The Internal Revenue Service, U.S. Department of the Treasury compiles composite balance sheets and income statements based on income tax returns of all corporations. They are dollar totals and are reported in a publication titled Statistics of Income, Corporate Income Tax Returns, available from the Superintendent of Documents, GPO, Washington, D.C. 20402.

Dun & Bradstreet's key business ratios for 125 refined lines of business activity are available from any D & B office or at its headquarters at 99 Church Street, New York, NY 10007.

By securing these materials, you can better judge your pro forma statement from the standpoint of proper ratios for various functions of the business and locate any under or over figures that might tend to distort your balances.

The final point is this. **Your figures must be proveable**. Pie-in-the-sky won't get it here. So, any back-up material you can get to prove your figures will lessen problems with potential investors.

INITIAL CAPITAL REQUIREMENTS

Estimated operating ratios expressed as a percent of net sales, with examples showing their application to various annual sales volumes.

	Percent	Annual Sales Volume		
Net sales	100.0	$ 0,000	$ 0,000	$00,000
Cost of goods sold				
Gross margin				
Operating expenses				
Net operating profit (before owner draw)				
Average inventory				
Stock turn: 12 times per year				

MONTHLY SALES AND OPERATING EXPENSES / **INSTRUCTIONS FOR COLUMNS 3 & 4**

Item	Estimated ratios percent of sales	Dollars per month based on annual volume of $48,000	Your estimate of monthly sales and expenses based on annual volume of $	Enter your monthly operating expenses in Column 3 based on percentages of sales in Column 1, as illustrated in Column 2. Enter your initial cash requirements in Column 4 based on amounts shown in Column 3.	Your estimate of initial cash requirements
	Column 1	Column 2	Column 3		Column 4
Net sales 1/12th of annual estimate	100.0			After studying situation and consulting local people put down sales estimate in Column 3	
Operating expenses Salaries of owner(s)/manager				Enter 1 month or more in Column 4	
All other salaries and wages				Enter 2 months or more in Column 4	
Occupancy (including rent, light, heat and building service)				Enter 2 months or more in Column 4	
Advertising				Enter 1/4th annual advertising budget in Column 4	
Delivery expense				Enter 2 months or more in Column 4	
Supplies				Enter 2 months or more in Column 4	
Depreciation (except buildings)				Enter estimated monthly depreciation in Column 3, but nothing in Column 4	
All other expenses				Make your own estimate for other expenses listed in left-hand column below, and for any additional miscellaneous expense items that occur to you	
Telephone and telegraph				Check rates	
Insurance (other than building)				You may have to pay premiums for 1 year or more. Enter initial cash required in Column 4.	
Donations and dues					
Taxes, including FICA					
Bad debts				Enter monthly estimate in Column 3; no entry in Column 4.	
Interest (other than bldg.)					
Maintenance (other than building)					
Travel/Entertainment					
Legal/Professional					
Commissions to agents					
Miscellaneous				List any items not mentioned above.	
Average monthly operating expenses			$	No entry in Column 4	

NONRECURRING INITIAL CAPITAL REQUIREMENT	INSTRUCTIONS FOR COLUMN 4	
Purchase of real estate		$
Decorating and remodeling	Enter total estimated cost	
Fixtures and equipment	Enter total of list	
Installation of fixtures and equipment	Enter cost of installing all fixtures and equipment	
Initial inventory	Estimate and enter initial inventory	
Accounts receivable	Enter amount necessary to finance outstanding accounts if credit sales are planned	
Deposits with public utilities	Enter full amount to be deposited	
Initial advertising and promotional expense	Enter total estimated cost	
Cash	For unforeseen requirements, special purchases, etc., and for absorbing any initial losses.	
Other	List any item not mentioned above	
Total estimated initial capital requirements	(Add all items entered in Column 4); ...	$

BIBLIOGRAPHY

BOOKS

Why SOB's Succeed and Nice Guys Fail in Small Business by R.H. Morrison. Business Financial Consultants, 3824 East Indian School Road, Phoenix, AZ 85018, 602-957-7932.

National Retail Merchants Association, 100 West 31st Street, New York, NY 10001, 212-244-8780. A catalog of books on Management and Operation of Retail Stores. Best source of Nuts and Bolts Operations information.

Basic Book of Business by John R. King. Cahners Books Int'l., Inc., 89 Franklin Street, Boston, MA 02110, 617-423-4310.

Entrepreneurial Management by Charles A. Dailey. McGraw Hill, 1221 Avenue of Americas, New York, NY 10020, 212-997-1221.

The Entrepreneurs Handbook by Joseph Mancuso. Artech, 610 Washington Street, Dedham, MA 02026, 617-326-8220.

The Entrepreneur's Manual: Business Start-ups, Spin-offs and Innovative Management by R.M. White. Chilton Book Co., 201 King of Prussia Way, Radnor, PA 19089, 215-687-9828.

Managing the Dynamic Small Firm by L.A. Klatt. Wadsworth Publishing Co., Inc., Belmont, CA 94002, 415-592-1300.

Managing the Small Business by Stegall, Steinmetz and Kline. Richard D. Irwin, 1818 Ridge Road, Homewood, IL 60430, 312-468-9200.

New Business Ventures and the Entrepreneur by P.A. Liles. Richard D. Irwin, 1818 Ridge Road, Homewood, IL 60430, 312-468-9200.

How to Become Financially Successful by Owning Your Own Business by Albert J. Lowery. Simon & Schuster, 1230 Avenue of Americas, New York, NY 10020.

How to Succeed in Your Own Business by Wm. R. Park and Sue Chapin Park. John Wiley and Sons, 605 3rd Avenue, New York, NY, 212-867-9800.

SMALL BUSINESS ASSOCIATIONS

National Business League
4324 Georgia Avenue N.W., Washington, D.C. 20011, 202-726-6200.

National Federation of Independent Businesses
150 20th Avenue, San Mateo, CA 94403, 415-341-7441.

Small Business Service Bureau
544 Main Street, Box 1441, Worcester, MA 01601, 617-756-3513.

National Family Business Council
3916 Detroit Boulevard, West Bloomfield, MI 48033, 313-553-1000.

American Management Association
135 West 50th Street, New York, NY 10020, 212-586-8100.
NOTE: This is not primarily for Small Business but they have many books, periodicals and sponsor seminars on interest to professional entrepreneurs.

PERIODICALS

At Risk — The Newsletter for Professional Entrepreneurs. Published by Financial Information Exchange, 3824 East Indian School Road,

Phoenix, Arizona 85018, 602-957-7932. Write for complimentary issue.

Journal of Small Business Management. Bureau of Business Research, West Virginia University, College of Business and Economics, 209 Armstrong Hall, Morgantown, West Virginia 26505, 304-293-5839. Monthly magazine.

Small Business Reporter. Bank of America, Dept. 3120, Box 37000, San Francisco, CA 94132, 415-622-2491. A series of manuals on starting many types of Small Businesses. Write or call for current list.

Small Business Newsletter. 7514 North 53rd Street, Milwaukee, WI 53223, 414-354-4260.

American Journal of Small Business. University of Baltimore, 1420 North Charles Street, Baltimore, MD 21201, 301-727-6350 (Ext. 223). Quarterly.

Business Owner. 50 Jericho Turnpike, Jericho, NY 11753, 516-997-7010. Magazine.

Venture Magazine. 35 West 45th Street, New York, NY 10037. Monthly magazine for entrepreneurs — found on most newsstands.

Inc. 38 Commercial Wharf, Boston, MA 02110. A magazine for Small Business Corporations — usually found on most newsstands.

Voice of Small Business. 1605 K Street, Washington, D.C. 20026, 202-296-7400. Newsletter.

SMALL BUSINESS INSTITUTES

These are programs run by universities in cooperation with the Small Business Administration to give free help to Small Business owners in developing more efficient and more profitable operations. They counsel, send out student teams to analyze the problems and develop concepts to solve them. Address requests for information to the Director of the Small Business Development Centers — the phone numbers given are for the main university switchboards, where you can be referred to the proper sources.

University of Arkansas, Fayetteville, AR 72701, 501-521-2000
Cal State Poly, Pomona, CA 91768, 714-598-4592
California State at Chico, Chico, CA 95929, 916-895-6116
University of Georgia, Athens, GA 30601, 404-542-3030
Howard University, 2400 W. 6th, Washington, D.C., 202-636-6100
University of Missouri, St. Louis, MO 63121, 314-453-0111
University of West Florida, Pensacola, FL 32504, 904-476-9500
University of Nebraska, Omaha, NE 68101, 402-558-2200
University of Maine, Portland, ME 04103, 207-773-2891
University of Wisconsin, Madison, WI 53706, 608-262-1234
Wharton School, University of Pennsylvania, Philadelphia 19174, 215-43-5000
University of South Carolina, Columbia, SC 29208, 803-777-0411
St. Cloud University, St. Cloud, MN 56301, 612-253-8987
University of Utah, Salt Lake City, UT 84112, 801-581-7200
Washington State University, Pullman, WA 99163, 509-335-3564.

The Small Business Administration has offices in ten cities — to find one nearest you — you can call the nearest regional office — phone numbers given below.

U.S. Small Business Administration
1441 L Street N.W., Washington, D.C. 20416, 202-653-6365

REGION	1	Boston	617-223-2100
REGION	2	New York	212-460-0100
REGION	3	Philadelphia, PA	215-597-3311
REGION	4	Atlanta	404-525-0111

REGION 5	Chicago	312-353-4400
REGION 6	Dallas	214-79-1011
REGION 7	Kansas City, MO	816-374-7000
REGION 8	Denver	303-837-0111
REGION 9	San Francisco	915-556-9000
REGION 10	Seattle	206-442-0111

Useful Contacts for Business Information

Association addresses of any organization may be obtained by writing the Director of Information Central, American Society of Association Executives, 1101 East 16th Street NW, Washington, DC 20036, or calling 202-659-3333.

Congressional action information can be obtained from several sources. The Bill Status Office will provide information on whether legislation has been introduced, who sponsored it, and its current status. For House action, call 202-225-1772; for Senate action, call 202-224-2971.

Cloakrooms of both houses will provide details on what is happening on the floor of the chamber. House cloakrooms: Democrat 202-225-7330; Republican 202-225-7350. Senate cloakrooms: Democrat 202-224-4691; Republican 202-224-6391.

Corporate reports filed with the SEC can be ordered at 35¢ per page from the National Investment Library, 32 Union Square, New York, NY 10005; or call 212-254-1700.

Service also provided by Disclosure Inc., 4827 Rugby Avenue, Bethesda, MD 20014, or call 301-951-0100.

The Commerce Department's ombudsman operates throughout the entire government complex to assist both business and consumers. Services include dissemination of information and reports such as *Outlook '80*. Write Office of the Ombudsman, U.S. Department of Commerce, Washington, DC 20230, or call 202-377-3176.

European Community country information is available free from the European Community Information Service, 2100 M Street NW, Washington, DC 20037; or call 202-862-9500.

Economic data and indicators provided on a weekly, monthly, or quarterly basis may be obtained as released. Telephone numbers of the offices publishing and producing the information are given in the table on the following page.

Department and Information	**Phone No.**
Agriculture Department	
To order publication	202-447-2791
Agricultural prices	202-447-3570
Bureau of Economic Analysis	
Business Conditions Digest	202-523-0535
Defense indicators	202-523-0535
Gross national product (preliminary)	202-523-0669
Personal income	202-523-0606
Merchandise trade balance, balance of payments basis	202-523-0668
Bureau of Labor Statistics	
To order publications	202-523-1239
Consumer price index	202-523-7827
Employment situation	202-523-1581
Wholesale price index	202-523-1204
Census Bureau	
To order publications	202-763-5853
Construction expenditures	202-763-5717
Manufacturers shipments, inventories, and orders	202-763-2502
Housing starts	202-763-5731
Advance report on durable goods, manufacturers shipments, and orders	202-763-2502
Advance monthly retail sales	202-763-7660
Export and import merchandise trade	202-763-5140

Monthly wholesale trade 202-763-5294

Federal Reserve

To order publications 202-452-3245
Money stock measures 202-452-3591
Consumer credit 202-452-2458
Industrial production and related data 202-452-3153
Capacity utilization in manufacturing 202-452-3197

Joint Economic Committee 202-224-3081
To obtain latest economic information
(employment, housing starts, price indices,
retail sales, industrial production)

Economic news and highlights of the day are provided by phone from the Department of Commerce; call 202-393-1847.

The Energy Information Center will provide free information on energy and related matters. Write National Energy Information Center, Room 1407, Federal Building NW, Washington, DC 20461, or call 202-566-9820.

Industry information statistics and details on specific industries can be obtained from the Director of Business Research and Analysis, Department of Commerce, Washington, DC 20230; or call 202-377-3176.

Technical and scientific information is provided by the National Technical Information Service of the Department of Commerce, 5285 Port Royal Road, Springfield, VA 22161, which handles requests about government-sponsored research of all kinds. For $100 it will research a subject. If a search has been done, a copy will be provided for $25. Call 703-557-4642. For rush orders, call 703-557-4700.

The reference section of the Library of Congress, Science and Technology Division, 10 First Street SE, Washington, DC 20540, provides answers to specific questions; call 202-287-5687. The National Referral Center provides names, addresses, and descriptions of information resources; call 202-287-5670.

Population information on all aspects of national and world population is provided by the Population Reference Bureau, Inc., 1337 Connecticut Avenue NW, Washington, DC 20036; or call 202-785-4664.

Smithsonian Institution Science Information Exchange provides, at a fee to cover costs, information both on individuals currently working in specific fields and on sources of research support; it also covers general research trends. Write 1730 M Street NW, Washington, DC 20036; or call 202-381-4211.

The Washington Information Research Service provides reports and guidance to information on a fee basis. Write Washington Researchers, 918 16th Street NW, Washington, DC 20006, or call 202-828-4800.

Foreign Trade information as well as general business data are provided by the World Trade Information Center, One World Trade Center, New York, NY 10048, which maintains extensive data banks. The charge for a preliminary search is about $10. Call 212-466-3063.

Federal Information Centers (FICS) located in key cities throughout the country are a joint venture of the U.S. General Services Administration and the U.S. Civil Services. Each center is a focal point for obtaining information about the federal government and often about state and local governments. A member of the center's staff can either provide information or direct inquiries to an expert who can. Some centers have specialists who speak foreign languages. The coordinator of the FICS is located at 18th and F Streets NW, Washington, DC 20405; call 202-566-1937. The Federal Information Centers and their telephone numbers are listed below.

Alabama

Birmingham: (205) 322-8591. Toll-free to Atlanta, GA.

Mobile: (205) 428-1421. Toll-free tieline to New Orleans, LA.

Arizona

Phoenix: (602) 261-3313. Federal Building, 230 N. First Avenue 85025.

Tucson: (602) 622-1511. Toll-free tieline to Phoenix, AZ.

Arkansas

Little Rock: (501) 378-6177. Toll-free tieline to Memphis, TN.

California

Los Angeles: (213) 688-3800. Federal Building, 300 N. Los Angeles Street 90012.

Sacramento: (916) 440-3340. Federal Building, U.S. Courthouse, 650 Capitol Mall 95814.

San Diego: (714) 293-6030. 880 Front Street 92188.

San Francisco: (415) 556-6600. Federal Building, U.S. Courthouse, 450 Golden Gate Avenue 94102.

San Jose: (408) 275-7422. Toll-free tieline to San Francisco, CA.

Santa Ana: (714) 836-2386. Toll-free tieline to Los Angeles, CA.

Colorado

Colorado Springs: (303) 471-9491. Toll-free tieline to Denver, CO.

Denver: (303) 837-3602. Federal Building, 1961 Stout Street 80204.

Pueblo: (303) 544-9523. Toll-free tieline to Denver, CO.

Connecticut

Hartford: (203) 527-2617. Toll-free tieline to New York, NY.

New Haven: (203) 624-4720. Toll-free tieline to New York, NY.

District of Columbia

Washington: (202) 755-8660. Seventh and D Streets SW,

Room 5716, 20407.

Florida

Fort Lauderdale: (305) 522-8531. Toll-free tieline to Miami, FL.

Jacksonville: (904) 354-4756. Toll-free tieline to St. Petersburg. FL.

Miami: (305) 350-4155. Federal Building 51 Southwest First Avenue 33130.

St. Petersburg: (813) 893-3495. William C. Cramer Federal Building, 144 First Avenue S. 33701

Tampa: (229) 229-7911. Toll-free tieline to St. Petersburg, FL.

West Palm Beach: (305) 833-7566. Toll-free tieline to Miami, FL.

Georgia

Atlanta: (404) 526-6891. Federal Building, 275 Peachtree Street NE 30303.

Hawaii

Honolulu: (808) 546-8620. Federal Building, 300 Ala Moana Boulevard, P.O. Box 50091, 96850.

Illinois

Chicago: (312) 353-4242. Everett McKinley Dirksen Building, 219 S. Dearborn Street 60604.

Indiana:

Gary/Hammond: (219) 843-4110. Toll-free tieline to In dianapolis, IN.

Indianapolis: (317) 269-7373. Federal Building, 575 North Pennsylvania 46204.

Iowa

Des Moines: (515) 282-9091. Toll-free tieline to Omaha, NB.

Kansas

Topeka: (913) 232-7229. Toll-free tieline to Kansas City, MO.

Wichita: (316) 262-6931. Toll-free tieline to Kansas City, MO.

Kentucky

Louisville: (502) 582-6261. Federal Building, 600 Federal Place 40202.

Louisiana

New Orleans: (504) 590-6696. Federal Building, Room 1210, 701 Loyola Avenue 70113.

Maryland

Baltimore: (301) 962-4980. Federal Building, 31 Hopkins Plaza 21201.

Massachusetts

Boston: (617) 223-7121. J.F.K. Federal Building, Cambridge Street, Lobby, 1st Floor 02203.

Michigan

Detroit: (313) 226-7016. McNamara Federal Building, 477 Michigan Avenue 48226.

Grand Rapids: (616) 451-2628. Toll-free tieline to Detroit, MI.

Minnesota

Minneapolis: (612) 725-2073. Federal Building and U.S. Courthouse, 110 S. Fourth Street 55401.

Missouri

Kansas City: (816) 374-2466. Federal Building, 601 East Twelfth Street 64106.

St. Joseph: (816) 233-8206. Toll-free tieline to Kansas City,

MO.

St. Louis: (314) 424-4106. Federal Building, 1520 Market Street 63103.

Nebraska

Omaha: (402) 221-3353. Federal Building, U.S. Post Office, and Courthouse, 215 N. 17th Street 68102.

New Jersey

Newark: (210) 645-3600. Federal Building, 970 Broad Street 07102.

Paterson/Passaic: (201) 523-0717. Toll-free tieline to Newark, NJ.

Trenton: (609) 396-4400. Toll-free tieline to Newark, NJ.

New Mexico

Albuquerque: (505) 766-3091. Federal Building and U.S. Courthouse, 500 Gold Avenue SW 87101.

Santa Fe: (505) 983-7743. Toll-free tieline to Albuquerque, NM.

New York

Albany: (518) 463-4421. Toll-free tieline to New York, NY.

Buffalo: (716) 842-5770. Federal Building, 111 West Huron Street 14202.

New York: (212) 264-4464. Lobby, Federal Building, 26 Federal Plaza 10007.

Rochester: (716) 546-5075. Toll-free tieline to Buffalo, NY.

Syracuse: (315) 476-8545. Toll-free tieline to Buffalo, NY.

North Carolina

Charlotte: (704) 376-3600. Toll-free tieline to Atlanta, GA.

Ohio

Akron: (216) 375-5638. Toll-free tieline to Cleveland, OH.

Cincinnati: (513) 684-2801. Federal Building, 550 Main Street 45202.

Cleveland: (216) 522-4040. Federal Building, 1240 E. Ninth Street 44199.

Columbus: (614) 221-1014. Toll-free tieline to Cincinnati, OH.

Toledo: (419)241-3223. Toll-free tieline to Cleveland, OH.

Oklahoma

Oklahoma City: (405) 231-4868. U.S. Post Office and Courthouse, 201 N.W. 3rd Street 73102.

Tulsa: (918) 584-4193. Toll-free tieline to Oklahoma City, OK.

Oregon

Portland: (503) 221-2222. Federal Building, 1220 S.W. Third Avenue 97204.

Pennsylvania

Allentown/Bethlehem: (414) 821-7785. Toll-free tieline to Philadelphia, PA.

Philadelphia: (215) 597-7042. Federal Building, 600 Arch Street 19106.

Pittsburgh: (412) 644-3456. Federal Building, 1000 Liberty Avenue 15222.

Scranton: (714) 346-7081. Toll-free tieline to Philadelphia, PA.

Rhode Island

Providence: (401) 331-5565. Toll-free tieline to Boston, MA.

Tennessee

Chattanooga: (615) 265-8231. Toll-free tieline to Memphis, TN.

Memphis: (901) 534-3285. Clifford Davis Federal Building, 167 N. Main Street 38103.

Nashville: (615) 242-5056. Toll-free tieline to Memphis, TN.

Texas

Austin: (512) 472-5494. Toll-free tieline to Houston, TX.

Dallas: (214) 749-2131. Toll-free tieline to Fort Worth, TX.

Fort Worth: (817) 334-3624. Fritz Garland Lanham Federal Building, 819 Taylor Street 76102.

Houston: (713) 226-5711. Federal Building, U.S. Courthouse, 515 Rusk Avenue 77002.

San Antonio: (512) 224-4471. Toll-free tieline to Houston, TX.

Utah

Ogden: (801) 399-1347. Toll-free tieline to Salt Lake City, UT.

Salt Lake City: (801) 524-5353. Federal Building, Lobby, 125 S. State Street 84138.

Virginia

Newport News: (804) 244-0480. Toll-free tieline to Norfolk, VA.

Norfolk: (804) 441-6723. Stanwick Building, 3661 E. Virginia Beach Boulevard 23502.

Richmond: (804) 643-4928. Toll-free tieline to Norfolk, VA.

Roanoke: (703) 982-8591. Toll-free tieline to Norfolk, VA.

Washington

Seattle: (206) 442-0570. Federal Building, 915 Second Avenue 98174.

Tacoma: (206) 383-5230. Toll-free tieline to Seattle, WA.

Wisconsin

Milwaukee: (414) 271-2273. Toll-free tieline to Chicago, IL.

INFORMATION SOURCES IN THE U.S. DEPARTMENT OF COMMERCE

Subject	Source	Telephone Number
Aeronautical charting	NOAA	301-443-8708
Agriculture census	CEN	301-763-7273
Air-quality research	NOAA	303-499-1000
Appliance labeling	NBS	301-921-3181
Applied technology	NBS	310-921-3181
Atmospheric research	NOAA	303-499-1000
Atomic, nuclear, isotopic research	NBS	301-921-3181
Automation technology	NBS	301-921-3181
Balance of payments	BEA	202-523-0777
Broadcast news	SEC	202-377-5610
Building technology	NBS	301-921-3181
Business censuses	CEN	301-763-7273
Business development loans	EDA	202-377-5113
Business Conditions Digest	BEA	202-523-0777
Capital equipment	ITA	202-377-3259
Censuses	CEN	301-763-7273
Climate monitoring	NOAA	303-499-1000
Coal gasification	NBS	301-921-3181
Coastal zone managment	NOAA	202-634-4239
Commerce Technical Advisory Board (CTAB)	S&T	202-377-5065
Commodity statistics	ITA	202-377-3259
Computer science and technology	NBS	301-921-3181
Construction and forest products	ITA	202-377-3259
Consumer goods	ITA	202-377-3259
Consumer products safety	NBS	301-921-3181
Corporate profits	BEA	202-523-0777
Data (fire)	NFPCA	202-634-7663
Disaster research	NBS	301-921-3181
Domestic Business Development, Bureau of	ITA	202-377-3259
East-west trade	ITA	202-377-4654
Ecomonic affairs	OCE	202-377-2235
Economic censuses	CEN	301-763-7273
Economic development programs	EDA	202-377-5113
Education statistics	CEN	301-763-7273
Education and training (fire)	NFPCA	202-634-7663
Energy (conservation)	NBS	301-921-3181
Energy (inventions)	NBS	301-921-3181
Environment (pollution)	NBS	301-921-3181
Environment affairs	S&T	202-377-4335
Environment data services	NOAA	302-634-7305
Environmental research	NOAA	303-499-1000
Environmental satellites	NOAA	301-443-8243
Employment and unemployment surveys	CEN	301-763-7273

BIBLIOGRAPHY—16

Subject	Agency	Phone
Exports awards	ITA	202-377-2253
Export Development, Bureau of	ITA	202-377-2253
Export information	ITA	202-377-2253
Export licenses	ITA	202-377-4654
Expositions (international)	USTS	202-377-4987
Failure analysis	NBS	301-921-3181
Federal economic indicators	OCE	202-377-2235
Field operations	ITA	202-377-2253
Fire prevention	NFPCA	202-634-7663
Fire protection (see also Research and Education)	NBS	301-921-3181
Flash floods	NOAA	301-427-7622
Foreign investment statistics	BEA	202-523-0777
Foreign trade analysis	ITA	202-377-2253
Foreign trade statistics	CEN	301-763-7273
Freedom of information	SEC	202-377-5659
Frequency allocations (federal use)	NTIA	202-395-5800
Geodetic surveys	NOAA	301-443-8708
Government finances (state and local)	CEn	301-763-7273
Grants to local government	EDA	202-377-5113
Great Lakes research	NOAA	303-499-1000
Gross national product	BEA	202-523-0777
Health	NBS	301-921-3181
Housing and construction statistics	CEN	301-763-7273
Hurricane research	NOAA	303-499-1000
Hurricane warning	NOAA	301-427-7622
Hydrology, Office of	NOAA	301-427-7622
Import programs	ITA	202-377-3259
Income, family	CEN	301-763-7273
Income, personal (national and regional)	BEA	202-523-0777
Industry surveys	CEN	301-763-7273
Information policy	NTIA	202-395-5800
Input-output analysis	BEA	202-523-0777
Interdepartment Radio Advisory Committee (IRAC)	NTIA	202-395-5800
International finance, investment, and marketing	ITA	202-377-2253
International investment statistics	BEA	202-523-0777
Investment services	ITA	202-377-2253
Laser information	NBS	301-921-3181
Law enforcement standards	NBS	301-921-3181
Leading economic indicators	BEA	202-523-0777
Manufacturing industry (by commodity)	ITA	202-377-3259
Marine ecosystem studies	NOAA	303-499-1000
Marine mammals	NOAA	202-634-7281
Marine technology	NOAA	301-443-8243
Maritime technology	MARAD	202-377-2746
Materials research	NBS	301-921-3181
Meteorological center	NOAA	301-427-7622
Metric	NBS	301-921-3181
Minority business programs	OMBE	202-377-3024
National marine fisheries	NOAA	202-634-7281
Nautical charts	NOAA	301-443-8708
News releases and speeches	SEC	202-377-4901

Occupation and industry statistics	CEN	301-763-7273
Ombudsman for business	ITA	202-277-3259
Overseas business opportunities	ITA	202-377-2253
Patent and trademarks	PAT	703-557-3428
Patents, government owned, foreign filing	PAT	703-557-4735
Plant and equipment expenditures	BEA	202-523-0777
Pollution abatement and control expenditures	BEA	202-523-0777
Population information	CEN	301-763-7273
Product standards	S&T	202-377-3221
Public works projects	EDA	202-377-5113
Publications, sales and distribution	SEC	202-377-5494
Radiation measurements	NBS	301-921-3181
Regional Planning Commission	SEC	202-377-4901
Research (economic)	OCE	202-377-2235
Research and data (fire)	NFPCA	202-634-7663
Research (maritime)	MARAD	202-377-2746
Resource and Trade Assistance, Bureau of	ITA	202-377-3259
Retail, wholesale, and service trade statistics	CEN	301-763-7273
Satellites	NOAA	301-443-8243
Science and technology	S&T	202-377-5065
Sea grants	NOAA	202-634-4034
Secretarial statements	SEC	202-377-4901
Service industries (statistics)	ITA	202-377-3259
Ship operations shipbuilding	MARAD	202-377-2746
Solar forecasts	NOAA	303-499-1000
Space environment search	NOAA	303-499-1000
Spectrum management	NTIA	202-395-5800
Standard reference materials	NBS	301-921-3181
Statistical reporter	OFSPS	202-673-7965
Stratospheric research	NOAA	303-499-1000
Survey of current business	BEA	202-523-0777
Technical document sales (all government agencies)	NTIS	202-557-4600
Technical help to exporters	NTIS	703-557-4733
Technology transfer to developing countries	NTIS	202-724-3366
Telecommunications applicators	NTIA	202-395-5800
Telecommunications policy (international and domestic)	NTIA	202-395-5800
Telecommunications research	NTIA	202-395-5800
Telecommunications technology	NTIA	202-395-5800
Textiles	ITA	202-377-3259
Time and frequency (standards)	NBS	303-323-3198
Tornado and severe storms research	NOAA	303-499-1000
Tornado warning	NOAA	301-427-7622
Tourism, international and domestic	USTS	202-377-4987
Trade adjustment assistance	EDA	202-377-5133
Trade fairs, trade centers and missions	ITA	202-377-2253
Trademarks	PAT	703-557-3428
Trade negotiations	ITA	202-377-2253
Trade zone board	ITA	202-377-2253

Transportation equipment	ITA	202-377-3259
Travel to and in United States	USTS	202-377-4987
Weather modification (cloud seeding)	NOAA	301-443-8243
Weather service	NOAA	301-427-7622
Weights and measures	NBS	301-921-3181

Abbreviations

BEA	Bureau of Economic Analysis
CEN	Bureau of the Census
EDA	Economic Development Administration
ITA	Industry and Trade Administration
MARAD	Maritime Administration
NBS	National Bureau of Standards
NFPCA	National Fire Prevention and Control Administration
NOAA	National Oceanic and Atmospheric Administration
NTIA	National Telecommunications and Information Administration
NTIS	National Technical Information Service
OCE	Office of Chief Economist
OFSPS	Office of Federal Stat. Policy and Standards
OMBE	Office of Minority Business Enterprise
PAT	Patent and Trademark Office
SEC	Office of the Secretary
S&T	Office of the Assistant Secretary for Science and Technology
USTS	United States Travel Service

ADDRESSES OF U.S. DEPARTMENT OF COMMERCE INFORMATION SOURCES

Office of Assistant Secretary for Science and Technology

Main Commerce Building
14th and Constitution Avenues
Washington, DC 20230
Telephone: 202-377-3914

Office of the Chief Economist
Main Commerce Building
14th and Constitution Avenues
Washington, DC 20230
Telephone: 202-377-2235

Bureau of the Census
Federal Office Building No. 3
Suitland, MD 20230
Telephone: 301-763-7273

Bureau of Economic Analysis
Tower Building
1401 K Street NW
Mailing Address:
U.S. Department of Commerce
14th and Constitution Avenues
Washington, DC 20230
Telephone: 202-523-0777

Industry and Trade Administration
Main Commerce Building
14th And Constitution Avenues
Washington, DC 20230
Telephone: 202-377-3808

Economic Development Administration
Main Commerce Building
14th and Constitution Avenues
Washington, DC 20230
Telephone: 202-377-5113

Maritime Administration
Main Commerce Building
14th and Constitution Avenues
Washington, DC 20230
Telephone: 202-377-2746

National Bureau of Standards
Administration Building
National Bureau of Standards
Washington, DC 20234
Telephone: 301-921-3181

National Fire Prevention and Control Administration
2400 M Street NW
Mailing Address:
U.S. Department of Commerce
14th and Constitution Avenues

Washington, DC 20230
Telephone: 202-634-7663

National Oceanic and Atmospheric Administration
6010 Executive Boulevard
Washington Science Center
Rockville, MD 20852
Telephone: 301-443-8243

National Technical Information Service
Pennsylvania Building
425 13th Street NW
Washington, DC 20004
Telephone: 202-724-3366

Office of Minority Business Enterprise
Main Commerce Building
14th and Constitution Avenues
Washington, DC 20230
Telephone: 202-377-3024

Office of Telecommunications
1800 G Street NW
Washington, DC 20230
Telephone: 202-377-3024

Patent and Trademark Office
Crystal Plaza
2021 Jefferson Davis Highway
Arlington, VA 20231
Telephone: 703-557-3428

United States Travel Service
Main Commerce Building
14th and Constitution Avenue
Washington, DC 20230
Telephone: 202-377-4987

INDEX

D

E

F

N

O

P

R

S

T

U

V

W

Y

Z